International Folkloristics

International Folkloristics

*Classic Contributions
by the Founders of Folklore*

edited by
Alan Dundes

ROWMAN & LITTLEFIELD PUBLISHERS, INC.
Lanham • Boulder • New York • Oxford

ROWMAN & LITTLEFIELD PUBLISHERS, INC.

Published in the United States of America
by Rowman & Littlefield Publishers, Inc.
4720 Boston Way, Lanham, Maryland 20706
http://www.rowmanlittlefield.com

12 Hid's Copse Road
Cumnor Hill, Oxford OX2 9JJ, England

British Library Cataloguing in Publication Information Available

Library of Congress Cataloging-in-Publication Data

International folkloristics : classic contributions by the founders of
    folklore / edited by Alan Dundes.
        p.   cm.
    Includes bibliographical references and index.
    ISBN 0-8476-9514-X (cloth : alk. paper).—ISBN 0-8476-9515-8
(paper : alk. paper)
    1. Folklore.   I. Dundes, Alan.
GR71.I46   1999
398—dc21   99-29463
                                                       CIP

Printed in the United States of America

∞ ™ The paper used in this publication meets the minimum requirements of
American National Standard for Information Sciences—Permanence of Paper for
Printed Library Materials, ANSI Z39.48–1992.

Contents

Preface vii

Acknowledgments xi

1 Circular Concerning the Collecting of Folk Poetry 1
Jacob Grimm

2 Folk-Lore and the Origin of the Word 9
William Thoms

3 Request 15
Wilhelm Mannhardt

4 An Angel Flew Through the Room 25
Reinhold Köhler

5 The Study of Folk-Lore 31
Max Müller

6 The Method of Julius Krohn 37
Kaarle Krohn

7 The Message of the Folk-Lorist 47
W. B. Yeats

8 On the Need for a Bibliography of Folklore 55
Giuseppe Pitrè

9 A Dialogue in Gyergyó-Kilényfalva 63
Béla Bartók

10 In Search of Folktales and Songs 73
Boris and Yuri Sokolov

11 Epic Laws of Folk Narrative 83
Axel Olrik

12   The Rites of Passage   99
     Arnold van Gennep

13   The Principles of Sympathetic Magic   109
     James George Frazer

14   The Structure of Russian Fairy Tales   119
     Vladimir Propp

15   Observations on Folklore   131
     Antonio Gramsci

16   Geography and Folk-Tale Oicotypes   137
     Carl Wilhelm von Sydow

17   Irish Tales and Story-Tellers   153
     Séamus Ó Duilearga

18   Symbolism in Dreams   177
     Sigmund Freud

19   Wedding Ceremonies in European Folklore   197
     Géza Róheim

20   Strategy in Counting Out: An Ethnographic
     Folklore Field Study   231
     Kenneth S. Goldstein

Suggestions for Further Reading in the History of Folkloristics   245

Index   253

About the Editor   257

Preface

This book came into being for several reasons. First and foremost was to confirm the existence of international folkloristics as an independent, worldwide, world-class academic discipline. Second was to present a selective historical view of some of the theoretical highlights of the evolution of folkloristics, the study of folklore. And third was simply a pragmatic wish to facilitate the teaching of folkloristics. The letters and articles included in this volume are all writings I think serious students of folklore should read.

There has been much turbulent debate about the definition of folklore ever since the term was proposed in 1846. Some folklorists oppose its usage on nationalistic grounds, not wishing to employ an English word for "their" traditions. But even some English and American folklorists are not happy with the term and would like to do away with it and replace it with some other word. If one defines folkloristics as the study of folklore (as linguistics is the study of language), however, then it seems reasonable to retain "folklore" as the subject matter of folkloristics.

One way of defining folklore is to divide the word into its two constituent parts: "folk" and "lore." A "folk" is any group of people whatsoever who share at least one common linking factor. It does not matter what that linking factor is; it could be nationality, ethnicity, religion, occupation, kinship, or any similar factor. Folk is a flexible concept, and a folk can be as large as a nation and as small as a village or a family. Moreover, individuals can obviously belong to more than one folk group. A single person may know family folklore, ethnic folklore, occupational folklore, religious folklore, and national folklore.

"Lore" refers to several hundred forms or genres, any one of which could occupy the attention of a folklorist for a lifetime. Folklore genres include epic, myth, folktale, legend, folksong, proverb, riddle, folk dance, superstition, games, gestures, foodways, folk costume, and many, many more. Genres may range from the very complex—for example, a festival or holiday celebration—to the relatively simple, such as tonguetwisters and curses. All folklore, no matter what genre, will exhibit "multiple existence," mean-

vii

ing that an item will exist in more than one time and place; moreover, as a result of the transmission process from person to person, there will inevitably be variation. No two versions will be exactly the same. The presence of multiple existence and variation distinguishes folklore from so-called high culture and also from mass or popular culture. Great novels, symphonies, paintings do not change over time, and there is usually just one version of them. The same is true for motion pictures, television programs, comic books, and other types of popular culture. Moreover, the authorship of detective stories, science fiction, westerns, and romances is known, whereas the authorship of folklore is usually not known. Most folklore is transmitted orally or by example (e.g., gestures), but some folklore is written—for example, autograph book verse, epitaphs, latrinalia (bathroom wall writings), and photocopier or FAX folklore. These latter genres do manifest multiple existence and variation and therefore qualify as bona fide folklore.

Folklore as defined in the nineteenth century tended to be much more limited than the conception here. The folk were thought to be peasants, the illiterate in a literate society. Without literacy, the only forms of folklore were restricted to those that were orally transmitted. In Europe where the discipline of folkloristics began, the peasant was virtually the sole focus of folkloristics. The German term "*Volkskunde*" and the Scandinavian notion of "folk life" (rather than folklore) tended to refer to all aspects of peasant existence (or what anthropologists would call "ethnography"). *Volkskunde* or folk life was therefore essentially peasant ethnography. This meant that on the one hand the European concept of "folk" was rather narrow compared to the "any group whatsoever" definition, but at the same time the "lore" portion of the European concept was much broader than a specific set of genres inasmuch as it included everything a peasant did or thought.

It is necessary to know the older European concept of folk to understand the essays written by nineteenth- (and some twentieth-) century folklorists. Peasants were and are, of course, one type of folk, but the point is that they are not the only type of folk. There are many urban folk groups—for example, labor unions, civil rights groups, and professional athletes—with each of these groups sharing its own specific folk speech, folk beliefs, and other traditions. The shift from defining folk as peasant to folk as a variety of diverse groups, both rural and urban, is an important part of the evolution of international folkloristics. The recognition that although oral tradition is undoubtedly the most common means of transmitting folklore it is no longer considered a sine qua non as a criterion for defining folklore represents another critical change in the nature of folkloristic research.

Anyone who teaches folklore knows very well that no two folklorists would necessarily agree on exactly what required readings should be assigned. There are, as in any field of inquiry, legitimate differences of opinion as to what the "classics" are. Moreover, most college and university courses in folklore tend to be restricted either by national boundaries or intentional limitation of genre. Hence a course in, say, mythology or American folklore would be unlikely to insist that students enrolled read the majority of the essays in this book. On the other hand, it is my personal conviction that anyone interested in any aspect of folklore in whatever national context or whatever genre ought to be familiar with the contents of this book. There is an important intellectual heritage in folkloristics, and it deserves to be better known.

Clearly, then, there is bias in the selection of folklorists' contributions for this unusual anthology. Had it been conceived by some other folklorist, no doubt different essays might have been included and almost certainly some of those found in this volume would have been omitted. Not all of those whose writings were chosen qualify as full-fledged folklorists. Yeats was a poet, Freud was a psychoanalyst, Gramsci was a Marxist philosopher of political protest, but all of them nevertheless made significant contributions to folkloristics. To be sure, the majority of those selected were dedicated folklorists, including Jacob Grimm, Wilhelm Mannhardt, Reinhold Köhler, Giuseppe Pitrè, Kaarle Krohn, Axel Olrik, Arnold van Gennep, Vladimir Propp, and Carl Wilhelm von Sydow. The essays are presented more or less in chronological order to give some sense of the evolution of international folkloristics. Despite the diverse national origins of the contributors, the careful reader will discover that the majority of the folklorists knew one another and were familiar with their international colleagues' publications.

The array of nations from which the contributors come demonstrates that international folkloristics is truly a cooperative and collaborative enterprise. Nations represented include Denmark, England, France, Germany, Hungary, Ireland, Italy, Russia, Sweden, and the United States. The large number of European folklorists reflects the historical reality that folkloristics as a formal discipline had its origins in Europe. In future, perhaps theoretical advances will come from other parts of the globe, such as Africa, Asia, and Latin America. (For references to sources for the history of folklore research outside of Europe, see the Suggestions for Further Reading in the History of Folkloristics at the end of this volume.) But in terms of nineteenth- and twentieth-century scholarship, it is fair to say that folkloristics has been primarily a European field of study with folklorists outside of Europe using theories and methods developed by European folklorists. It is my sincere hope that the totality of the volume will provide unique access to some of the principal issues that have fascinated folklorists from the very outset of their discipline.

The matter of "access" calls to mind the importance of knowing languages for international folkloristics. A truly international folklorist must be able to read at least English, French, and German. Such a folklorist need not necessarily be able to write or speak these languages but must be able to read books and essays written in them. More than half of the letters and essays included in this volume were not originally written in English. (Five were translated from French and German especially for this volume.) This means that folklorists whose native language is other than English, French, or German must "double publish." That is why the many folklore theorists in Finland, Hungary, and elsewhere decided that if they wished to reach fellow folklorists outside of their own countries they had to publish their findings in one of the international languages. Accordingly, if one wishes to know what folklorists in Bulgaria or Japan think about a certain topic and one cannot take the time required to acquire a reading knowledge of Bulgarian or Japanese, one is likely to find that whatever relevant material exists outside of Bulgarian and Japanese is written in English, French, or German. Of course, the more languages one can read, the better. Dutch, Italian, Portuguese, Russian, and Spanish, to mention just a few, can be critical if one is interested in the folklore scholarship treating Indonesia, Ethiopia, Brazil, the Baltic countries, and Latin America.

My editorial role has consisted of far more than just selecting letters and essays. An extensive headnote introduces each selection, perhaps too extensive. The headnote is sometimes much longer than the item itself. One reason for this is that it may be difficult for folklore students to know much about the writers of the essays or to appreciate the context in which they were written. In theory, I suppose I might have simply summarized or paraphrased the essays themselves rather than presenting them. In a sense, however, I functioned as a fieldworker in the library. In this library fieldwork I sought out principal informants, all of them in this case deceased, but I wanted to preserve the informants' actual words, albeit often in translation. As a result, there are many voices in this volume. What they have in common is a great love of folklore and of the humanity that created the folklore in the first place. May they inspire many new generations of enthusiastic folklorists!

Acknowledgments

First, I am deeply indebted to Dean Birkenkamp, executive editor of Rowman & Littlefield, for his original inquiry that led to the planning of this volume. Second, I must express my gratitude to Jo Lynn Milardovich and her associates in the Interlibrary Borrowing department of Doe Library at the University of California, Berkeley, for their uncanny ability to locate fugitive and arcane sources for this and for my other research projects over the years. Several of the items in this volume would not have been included had I not had the benefit of their invaluable expertise and assistance. And third, I want to thank those publishers who were kind enough to grant permission to reprint the essays I selected.

Jacob Grimm's "Circular, Die Sammlung der Volkspoesie Betreffend," dated 1815, was reprinted in Grimm's *Kleinere Schriften,* Vol. 7 (Berlin: Ferd. Dümmler's Verlagsbuchhandlung, 1884), 593–595. It was first called to my attention in 1974 by Dr. Ruth-Inge Heinze who made an initial translation for me. The present translation from German to English was made by Johanna Micaela Jacobsen and Alan Dundes.

William Thoms's classic proposal of the term "Folk-Lore" first appeared in the *Athenaeum,* No. 982 (August 22, 1846):862–863. His note "Origin of the Word 'Folk-Lore' " was published in *Notes and Queries,* 4th Series, Vol. 10 (October 26, 1872):339–340.

Wilhelm Mannhardt's questionnaire was translated from the French "Demande," *Bulletin de la Société liègeoise de littérature wallonne* 7(2) (1864):10–17, and supplemented with a few details from the German "Bitte," which appeared in *Die Korndämonen* (Berlin: Ferd. Dümmler's Verlagsbuchhandlung, 1868), 44–48. The translation was made by Johanna Micaela Jacobsen and Alan Dundes.

Reinhold Köhler's "Ein Engel Flog Durchs Zimmer" first appeared in *Germania* 10 (1865):245–246. It was translated by Johanna Micaela Jacobsen and Alan Dundes.

Max Müller's "The Study of Folk-Lore" appeared in *The Academy* 21 (March 18, 1882):193.

Kaarle Krohn's "La méthode de M. Jules Krohn" was published in *Congrès International des Traditions Populaires* (Paris: Bibliothèque des Annales Économiques, 1891), 64–68. It was translated from French into English by Alan Dundes.

W. B. Yeats's "The Message of the Folk-Lorist" first appeared in *The Speaker* 8 (August 19, 1893):188–189.

Giuseppe Pitrè's "Sur La Necessité d'une Bibliographie des Traditions Populaires" was first published in *Congrès International des Traditions Populaires (10–12 Sept. 1900)* (Paris: Librairie Maisonneuve, 1902), 4–6. It was translated from French by Alan Dundes.

Béla Bartók's letter to Stefi Geyer of August 16, 1907, "A Dialogue in Gyergyó-Kilényfalva," was published in János Demény, ed., *Béla Bartók Letters* (New York: St. Martin's, 1971), 70–74.

Boris Sokolov and Yuri Sokolov, "In Search of Folktales and Songs," is reprinted from Felix J. Oinas and Stephen Soudakoff, eds., *The Study of Russian Folklore* (The Hague: Mouton, 1975), 13–22. It was translated from *Skazki i pesni Belozerskogo kraja* (Moscow: A. I. Snegirevoi, 1915), i–viii, by Stephen Soudakoff assisted by Professor Felix Oinas of Indiana University.

Axel Olrik's "Epic Laws of Folk Narrative" is reprinted from Alan Dundes, ed., *The Study of Folklore* (Englewood Cliffs: Prentice-Hall, 1965), 129–141. It appeared originally as "Epische Gesetze der Volksdictung," *Zeitschrift für Deutsches Altertum* 51 (1909):1–2, and was translated from German into English by Jeanne P. Steager.

Arnold van Gennep's "The Rites of Passage" is a brief excerpt from the English translation of his 1909 *Les Rites de Passage,* published in 1960 as *The Rites of Passage* (Chicago: University of Chicago Press, 1960), 10–13, plus his conclusions, 189–194. The translation from French into English was made by Monika B. Vizedom and Gabrielle L. Caffee.

James George Frazer's "The Principles of Sympathetic Magic" is reprinted from the third edition of *The Golden Bough: A Study in Magic and Religion,* Vol. 1 (London: Macmillan, 1913), 52–54.

Vladimir Propp's "The Structure of Russian Fairy Tales" is reprinted from the second English-language edition of his 1928 *Morfologija skazki.* It is the short second chapter of *Morphology of the Folktale,* 2d ed. (Austin: University of Texas Press, 1968), 19–24. The first edition, published in 1958, was translated by Laurence Scott, and the second edition was revised and edited by Louis A. Wagner.

Antonio Gramsci's "Observations on Folklore" is reprinted from Antonio Gramsci, *Prison Notebooks,* Vol. 1 (New York: Columbia University Press, 1992), 186–187, 487–488. It is paragraph or section number 89 and was probably written circa 1929. It was translated from Italian by Joseph A. Buttigieg and Antonio Callari.

Carl Wilhelm von Sydow's "Geography and Folk-Tale Oicotypes" is reprinted from C. W. v. Sydow, *Selected Papers on Folklore* (Copenhagen: Rosenkilde and Bagger, 1948), 44–59, 243–244. It was originally published in *Beáloideas* 7 (1932):346–355.

Séamus Ó Duilearga's "Irish Tales and Story-Tellers" is reprinted from Hugo Kuhn and Kurt Schier, eds., *Märchen, Mythos, Dichtung: Festschrift zum 90. Geburtstag Friedrich von der Leyens am 19. August 1963* (Munich: Verlag C. H. Beck, 1963), 63–82, with one small addition taken from the earlier, longer original version of the essay, "The Gaelic Story-Teller," *Proceedings of the British Academy* 31 (1945):177–221.

Sigmund Freud's "Symbolism in Dreams" is reprinted from Sigmund Freud, *A General Introduction to Psychoanalysis* (New York: Permabooks, 1953), 156–177. The translation from German to English was made by Joan Riviere.

Géza Róheim's "Wedding Ceremonies in European Folklore" is reprinted from *Samiksa* 8 (1954):137–173. The article was originally written in Hungarian, but Róheim himself rewrote it in English.

Kenneth S. Goldstein's "Strategy in Counting Out: An Ethnographic Folklore Field Study" is reprinted from Elliott M. Avedon and Brian Sutton-Smith, eds., *The Study of Games* (New York: John Wiley, 1971), 167–178.

1

Circular Concerning the Collecting of Folk Poetry

Jacob Grimm

There is no one specific point in time when it might be said that the discipline of folkloristics suddenly came into being. Presumably since time immemorial, some individuals have been endlessly fascinated by folksongs, folktales, children's games, and the like. In nearly every corner of the globe, one can find even to this day dedicated amateurs, antiquarians, and local historians who as a hobby and a matter of course faithfully record the folklore of their area. The scientific study of folklore from an international perspective, however, seems to have begun in the early nineteenth century in the context of romanticism, a penchant for historical reconstruction, and the emergence of nation-states.

In any event, there can be little doubt that one of the decisive factors that initiated international folkloristics was the prodigious scholarly effort of the brothers Grimm, Jacob (1785–1863) and Wilhelm (1786–1859). The publication of their famous *Kinder- und Hausmärchen,* the first volume in 1812 and the second in 1815, is a landmark in the development of folkloristics as it not only inspired collecting in other countries but has also been the point of departure for hundreds of monographs and articles. Indeed, the study of the Grimms' contributions to folklore constitutes a whole separate subfield of inquiry within folkloristics. For a tiny sample of that enormous literature, see Ludwig Denecke, *Jacob Grimm und sein Bruder Wilhelm* (Stuttgart: Metzler, 1971), Christa Kamenetsky, *The Brothers Grimm & Their Critics* (Athens: Ohio University Press, 1992), and the various publications issued by the Brüder Grimm-Museum in Cassel, Germany. There are also the Grimm brothers' autobiographical statements written in 1830; see Manfred Kluge, ed., *Die Brüder Grimm in ihren Selbstbiographien* (Munich: Wilhelm Heyne Verlag, 1985).

1

It is impossible even to summarize the full lives and many remarkable achievements of the Grimms. Born in Hanau in 1785, Jacob was followed by Wilhelm in 1786. Their father Philipp's premature death from pneumonia in 1796 placed heavy responsibilities on the young Grimms. Jacob in particular, as the oldest of six children, had to become a de facto head of household. Through the helpful intervention of an aunt, the brothers were permitted to attend a fine secondary school in Cassel. Each graduated at the head of his respective class in 1802 and 1803, then went to the University of Marburg to study law. At Marburg Jacob's scholarly demeanor attracted the notice of famed professor Friedrich Karl von Savigny (1779–1861), one of the founders of the field of historical jurisprudence. Savigny believed the traditional laws of a people reflected that people's *Volksgeist*, or national spirit, a view strikingly similar to that expressed by Johann Gottfried von Herder (1744–1803) who suggested that the soul of a people was articulated in that people's folksongs. (Herder, who coined the term "*Volkslied*" in 1773, published his pioneering anthology *Volkslieder. Stimme der Völker in Liedern* [Folksongs: The voice of the nations in songs] in 1778–1779.) Savigny was sufficiently impressed with young Jacob that he invited him to accompany him to Paris in 1805 as a research assistant to work at the Bibliothèque Nationale on a project on the history of law.

Jacob enjoyed his time in Paris, but he missed his brother Wilhelm. In a letter of July 12, 1805, he wrote Wilhelm urging that they never separate, and Wilhelm replied in agreement a month later. Even when Wilhelm married Dortchen Wild in 1825, Jacob did not move out of the Grimm household. He lived as a bachelor all his life, most of it in close proximity to his beloved brother. The early influence of Savigny eventually culminated in Jacob's publishing *German Legal Antiquities* (*Deutsche Rechtsaltertümer*) in 1828.

The Grimm brothers had very different personalities. Jacob was the scholar whereas Wilhelm was the poet, but they worked together well as a team.

Although the Grimms' most famous publication was unquestionably the *Kinder- und Hausmärchen,* they published many other important works— some jointly, some individually. Together they published a two-volume collection of German legends (*Deutsche Sagen*), the first volume in 1816 and the second in 1818. Jacob published a monumental study of German mythology (*Deutsche Mythologie*) in 1855.

In 1814 Wilhelm became an assistant librarian in Cassel, and Jacob, who had become a secretary to the Hessian legation, attended the Congress of Vienna. In 1816 Jacob was appointed a librarian in Cassel, and the brothers were reunited. They had hoped to remain permanently in Cassel as librarians, but in 1829 their application to be appointed first and second librarian was spurned; the Grimms therefore decided to accept an invitation from the

University of Göttingen. At Göttingen Jacob was appointed professor of philology and a librarian, and Wilhelm was also given a position in the library. The brothers remained at Göttingen until 1837 when a political upheaval erupted. A conservative king of Hanover sought to repeal the constitution and required that all members of the army and the civil service, as well as university employees—including professors—forswear their oath of allegiance to the constitution and swear a personal oath of allegiance to him instead. The Grimms were shocked at the idea of breaking a sacred oath and, with five others, protested as a matter of principle. The king, unimpressed, dismissed the "Göttingen Seven," ordering them to leave the country within three days or go to prison. Accompanied by sympathetic students, the Grimms departed and returned to Cassel.

The Grimms were scholars and were hardly political activists, but they were not afraid to make personal sacrifices for principles in which they believed strongly. Fortunately, their term of exile in Cassel did not last too long; in November 1840 both were offered professorships at the University of Berlin, where they moved in 1841.

The banishment from Göttingen in 1837 had served to facilitate a major project of the Grimms, one involving a monumental dictionary. The Grimms were interested as much in language as they were in folklore. One of their most ambitious projects was to compile a comprehensive dictionary of the German language. Jacob began thinking about this project in 1838, not long after the brothers had left Göttingen. As it turned out, the Grimms would work on this project for the rest of their lives. Even after Wilhelm died in 1859, a grieving Jacob continued until his own death in 1863. He died, in fact, while writing the entry for the word "*Frucht*" (fruit), and obviously many more words were yet to be covered. Indeed, the mammoth dictionary was not completed until 1960 when the last of the thirty-two volumes was finally published; see the *Deutsches Wörterbuch,* 32 vols. (Leipzig: S. Hirzel, 1854–1960).

The Grimms did not carry out fieldwork in the sense it is understood in modern times. Instead, storytellers (among their friends and neighbors) in Cassel came to their home where tales were told. One of these storytellers was Dortchen Wild, who became Wilhelm's wife. The informants were thus not illiterate peasants but reasonably well-educated members of the middle class.

One of the less-known writings of the Grimms is a short circular written and distributed by Jacob in 1815 when he was in Vienna. He evidently sent out 400 or so copies, eliciting 360 responses, in an attempt to found a folklore society whose members would be charged with collecting folklore where they lived. Of interest is Jacob Grimm's ability to explain succinctly exactly what folklore is and at the same time to give practical hints on the proper way to collect folklore. Also noteworthy is Jacob's awareness of negative attitudes toward folklore, attitudes that unfortunately continue unabated in the twenty-first century.

Some of the content of the circular strongly suggests that Jacob borrowed liberally from an earlier attempt to invite friends and acquaintances to join in a common endeavor to record folklore. This attempt took the form of a letter written on January 22, 1811, to Clemens Brentano (1778–1842) who had proposed to the Grimms that they assemble an anthology of old German traditions. In that communication, entitled *"Aufforderung an die gesammten Freunde deutscher Poesie und Geschichte erlassen"* [Appeal to all friends of German poetry and history], Jacob, with Wilhelm's concurrence, delineated ideal guidelines for collecting oral tradition. Made-up or embellished items were to be excluded. Proverbs, idiomatic expressions, legends, tales told to children were all to be taken down faithfully (*"buchstabentreu,"* that is, letter perfect or verbatim), with nothing left out and nothing added. Even what seemed to be nonsense should be recorded and not changed to try to make sense of it. For a full text of this 1811 letter, see Heinz Rolleke, *Die Märchen der Brüder Grimm: Eine Einführung* (Munich: Artemis Verlag, 1985), 63–69.

Although the Grimms called for the recording of unaltered texts, they did not always adhere to their own standards. Wilhelm, who more than Jacob was involved with the folktales, could not resist the temptation to combine elements from different versions of the same tale, thereby creating a synthetic, conflated text that had never been told in precisely that form by any informant. One has only to compare the "same" tale in different editions of the *Kinder- und Hausmärchen* to see how much they vary from edition to edition (see John Ellis, *One Fairy Story Too Many: The Brothers Grimm and Their Tales* (Chicago: University of Chicago Press, 1983).

An important discovery in 1920 has provided yet another means of assessing to some extent the degree of embellishment and censorial deletion in the Grimm folktale corpus. At the time the Grimms were amassing their folktales, they belonged to an intellectual circle that included Clemens Brentano and Achim von Arnim (1781–1831). The two edited a significant collection of folksongs entitled *Des Knaben Wunderhorn* [The boy's magic horn] in 1805, which included contributions—counting-out rhymes and folksongs—from the Grimms. Brentano encouraged the Grimms to collect folktales for a possible sequel volume. Jacob and Wilhelm sent approximately fifty tales to Brentano in 1810, but by that time the somewhat mercurial Brentano had cooled on the idea of the project. The Grimms in any case had been unhappy with what they felt was the excessive literary rewriting of the folksongs contained in *Des Knaben Wunderhorn,* so they decided to publish their folktales under their own names. Fortunately, Wilhelm, at Jacob's suggestion, had made a copy of the original manuscript submitted to Brentano, who claimed he had misplaced the manuscript and never returned it to the Grimms. The manuscript was eventually deposited in the Monastery of Oelenberg in Alsace, where it remained unnoticed until it was discovered in 1920. For an edition of the manuscript, see Heinz Rolleke, ed., *Die älteste Märchensammlung der Brüder Grimm* (Cologny-Geneva: Martin Bodmer Foundation, 1975).

Whereas some of the editorial revisions made by the Grimms were minor stylistic ones, others were not trivial. For example, in the Oelenberg 1810 manuscript version of "Hansel and Gretel," it is the mother who persuades her husband to send the children to the woods, but in the 1840 fourth edition of the tales the mother has been changed to a stepmother, presumably because the Grimms felt the "original" version did not reflect well on German motherhood.

In retrospect, it seems somewhat ironic that whereas the Grimms withdrew their folktale manuscript from Brentano because they objected to his policy of revamping the oral texts, they then proceeded over time to do just that. In fairness, it should be noted that virtually all nineteenth-century (and a good many twentieth-century) collections of folklore were duly adulterated and sanitized for literary and nationalistic ideological reasons. What is important for modern folklorists is thus not what the Grimms did but what they originally said they were going to do, and that is the context in which the following circular should be read. For discussion of this and other programs for folklore collection by Jacob Grimm, see Reinhold Steig, "Jacob Grimms Plan zu einem Altdeutschen Sammler," *Zeitschrift des Vereins für Volkskunde* 12 (1902), 129–138; Johannes Bolte, "Jacob Grimm als Volksliedsammler," *Jahrbuch für Volksliedforschung* 1 (1928), 157–159; and Kamenetsky, 159–162, 188–189. For an insightful discussion of the influence of the Grimm circular on the founder of Danish folkloristics, Svend Grundtvig (1824–1883) with respect to his conceptualization of the discipline, see Bengt Holbek, "Grimm and Grundtvig: A Footnote," in *Dona Folcloristica,* Leander Petzoldt and Stefaan Top, eds. (Frankfurt: Peter Lang, 1990), 69–76.

*   *   *

Dear Sir,

A society has been formed which will expand throughout all Germany and it has as its goal to salvage and collect all that there is in the way of song and legend from the common German country-people. Our fatherland still abounds everywhere with this treasure that our forefathers have transmitted to us. Despite all the ridicule and derision with which it has been treated, it has survived in secret, unconscious of its own beauty, and carrying its irrepressible essence alone within itself. Without researching it in detail, neither our poetry nor our history nor our language can be fully understood with respect to their ancient and true origins. With this in mind, we wish to diligently seek out and accurately record the following items:

1) Folksongs and rhymes which are sung at different seasonal events, at festivals, in spinning rooms, at dance halls, and accompanying various kinds of agricultural work in the fields. Above all, those songs and rhymes which contain epic content, that is, in which an action occurs, where possible with their words, manner and tunes.

2) Legends in prose, and especially as well the numerous nursery and children's tales of giants, dwarfs, monsters, bewitched and rescued princes and princesses, devils, treasures, and magical objects that grant wishes; also local legends which are told and known for their explanation of certain localities such as mountains, rivers, lakes, marshes, castle ruins, towers, rocks, and all monuments of remote antiquity. One should pay special attention to animal fables in which appear mostly the fox and the wolf, roosters, dogs, cats, frogs, mice, sparrows, etc.

3) Humorous trickster tales and jests; puppet-shows of olden days, with Hanswurst and the devil.

4) Festivals, customs, usages and games, ceremonies associated with birth, marriage, and burial, old folk laws, strange interest charges, taxes, land acquisition, border dispute adjudications, etc.

5) Superstitions about ghosts, specters, witches, good and evil omens, apparitions, and dreams.

6) Proverbs, striking idioms, similes, and word-combinations.

Above all, it is important that these items be recorded in the most exact and detailed fashion from the mouths of the informants, faithfully and truthfully, without any cosmetic touch-up or addition, and where feasible in and with their very own words. If the material could be obtained in its living local dialect, this would thereby double its value. On the other hand, incomplete fragments are not to be scorned. For it is the case that all variations, repetitions, and versions of one and the same legend could each become important. Because of the mistaken view that a given item has already been collected and written down, one should by no means be misled into refusing to record a narrative. For many a thing which appears to be modern is oftentimes only modernized, and underneath, it retains its basic identity.

A more thorough familiarity with the content of this folk poetry will gradually lead to a more enlightened judgment about its supposedly stupid, vulgar, and even tasteless characteristics. In general, however, we may state the following: That although there is almost no district which is completely devoid of folklore or stripped of it, nevertheless, it is provincial towns rather than big cities; and villages rather than provincial towns; and among the villages, the ones which are most of all quiet and impassable, located in the forests or in the mountains, it is these which are most endowed and blessed with folklore. Likewise, folklore tends to be more strongly retained by members of certain occupations such as shepherds, fishermen, and miners. And it is therefore preferable to question these individuals as well as old people, women and children whose memories of transmitted folklore are fresh.

In full confidence that you, my dear sir, will be persuaded by the usefulness and urgency of our cause which with the day-to-day ever more increasing devastating decline and disappearance of our folk customs can no longer be postponed without great harm, we hope you will offer our undertaking a helping hand and live in a place suitable for the purpose of exploring the region of _____, and for this reason you have been selected as a member of this society. The society wishes to collect data with silent diligence and to promote its work but does not want to hear about it or see its laudable goals proclaimed in the daily newspapers. Rather the society is of the opinion that it should be founded discreetly, avoiding any undue publicity, and happily taking root in the pure joy of doing what is good. In this connection, no member is obliged to submit his contribution within a certain time. Rather each person does whatever he can when, where and how he chooses. He who lacks sufficient spare time at home may perhaps find an occasion to collect when traveling.

Finally, in order to ensure the orderly preservation of the material received, you are asked to report each item on a separate piece of paper, indicating the place, community, and date it was collected, along with a notation next to your name, if need be, of that of the narrator.

In the name and by the authority of the society

P.S. We ask you expressly not to fail to search in archives and monasteries of your region for old-German books and manuscripts, and to notify us through the undersigned of their existence.

2

Folk-Lore and the Origin of the Word

William Thoms

Every discipline needs a name, and the study of folklore is no exception. The term "folklore" (originally hyphenated) was first proposed by William Thoms (1803–1885) using the nom de plume Ambrose Merton in his letter to the *Athenaeum* dated August 12, 1846, and published on August 22 of that year. Just one year later Thoms acknowledged his neologism in the first of a series of notes on "The Folk-Lore of Shakespeare" in the *Athenaeum* on September 4, 1847. In a footnote, written ostensibly to explain the term "Folk-Lore," Thoms could not forbear a bit of bragging: "We may be permitted to express some satisfaction at the universal adoption of this name— invented by our correspondent Ambrose Merton. In less than twelve months it has almost attained to the dignity of a 'household word.' "

As so often happens with any creation that becomes traditional, the original author may be forgotten. This is why Thoms found it necessary to answer inquiries as to the authorship of the term in his communication "Origin of the Word 'Folk-Lore,' " which appeared more than twenty-five years later in *Notes and Queries*, a periodical he had founded in 1849. The fact that Thoms was both the founder of *Notes and Queries* and the first to suggest the term "folklore" might explain why in 1859 he published a collection of some of the many items of folklore that had appeared in *Notes and Queries*, entitled logically enough *Choice Notes from "Notes and Queries": Folk Lore.*

Although Thoms specifically denied that his term was in any way derived from a German word, his unabashed admiration for the work of Jacob Grimm and the fact that the term *"Volkskunde"* was apparently coined in 1782 strongly suggest that Thoms was, consciously or unconsciously, influenced by the earlier German word. In any case, his insistence that the word "folklore" had an English origin is itself noteworthy as it reflects the nationalistic sentiment so often associated with folklore studies. Indeed, the supposed initial impetus for Thoms to suggest the term "folklore" came from a wish to substitute "a good Saxon compound" for the more Latinate "Popular Antiquities."

The nationalistic propensities of folklorists have tended to impede the general acceptance of the term "folklore," as folklorists prefer to use a term in their respective languages rather than adopt a "foreign" English word for the subject matter. So the Germans prefer *Volkskunde*, the French *Traditions populaires*, the Irish *Béaloideas*, and so on. With the increasing prominence of English as the preferred language of scientific discourse, however, "folklore" has gradually become the term of choice. One difficulty remaining is that the word is used to refer both to the subject matter or data and to the formal study of that material. For this reason serious scholars are increasingly inclined to reserve "folklore" for the data and to employ "folkloristics" for the study of that data. On December 7, 1889, for example, American folklorist Charles G. Leland (1824–1903), in a greeting to the newly formed Hungarian folklore society, spoke of "Die Folkloristik" as one of the most profound developments in history. See his "Aus dem Begrüssungsschrieben an die Gesellschaft," *Ethnologische Mitteilungen aus Ungarn* 2(1) (1890–1892), 2–3; see also Eugen Kagarow, "Folkloristik und Volkskunde," *Mitteilungen der Schlesischen Gesellschaft für Volkskunde* 30 (1929), 70–77.

Thoms cannot be considered a major theoretician in folkloristics, but his creation of the term "folklore" has secured for him an honored place in the history of the discipline. He was apparently well aware of his claim to fame. He once gave a picture of himself to fellow folklorist George Laurence Gomme (1853–1916), on the back of which was inscribed the following immodest quatrain, one he also apparently sometimes wrote on the back of his visiting cards:

> If you would fain know more
> Of him whose photo here is
> He coined the word *folk-lore*
> and started *Notes and Queries*.

For further discussion of Thoms's contributions to folkloristics, see Duncan Emrich, " 'Folklore': William John Thoms," *California Folklore Quarterly* 5 (1946), 355–374; Richard M. Dorson, *The British Folklorists: A History* (Chicago: University of Chicago Press, 1968), 75–90; W. F. H. Nicolaisen, "A Gleaner's Vision," *Folklore* 106 (1995), 71–76; Gillian Bennett, "The Thomsian Heritage in the Folklore Society (London)," *Journal of Folklore Research* 33 (1996), 212–220; and R. Troy Boyer, "The Forsaken Founder, William John Thoms: From Antiquities to Folklore," *The Folklore Historian* 14 (1997), 55–61. For representative discussions of the history of the term "folklore," see Raffaele Corso, "Folklore. Dall'etimologia alla definizione," *Revista di antropologia* 24 (1921), 1–23; Fritz Willy Schulze, *Folklore, Zur Ableitung der Vorgeschichte einer Wissenschaftsbezeichnung* (Halle: Max Niemeyer Verlag, 1949); Elisée Legros, *Sur les noms et les tendances du folklore* (Liège: Editions du Musée Wallon, 1962); and Giovanni B. Bronzini, "Nascita e significato del termine 'Folk-Lore,' " in his *Folk-Lore e Cultura Tradizionale* (Bari: Adriatica Editrice, 1972), 7–45. For documentation of the early date for *Volkskunde,* see Uli Kutter, "Volks-Kunde—Ein Beleg von 1782," *Zeitschrift für Volkskunde* 74 (1978), 161–166.

In addition to the original letter proposing the new term, *Athenaeum* editor Charles Wentworth Dilke's published addendum-response to the proposal, with its markedly restrained enthusiasm and its seemingly snide rebuke to Thoms for not using his "real name," has also been included, along with Thoms's 1872 note in *Notes and Queries* proudly recounting his accomplishment.

*   *   *

FOLK-LORE.

August 12.

Your pages have so often given evidence of the interest which you take in what we in England designate as Popular Antiquities, or Popular Literature (though by-the-bye it is more a Lore than a Literature, and would be most aptly described by a good Saxon compound, Folk-Lore—*the Lore of the People*)—that I am not without hopes of enlisting your aid in garnering the few ears which are remaining, scattered over that field from which our forefathers might have gathered a goodly crop.

No one who has made the manners, customs, observances, superstitions, ballads, proverbs, &c., of the olden time his study, but must have arrived at two conclusions:—the first, how much that is curious and interesting in these matters is now entirely lost—the second, how much may yet be rescued by timely exertion. What Hone endeavoured to do in his 'Every-Day Book,' &c., the *Athenæum*, by its wider circulation, may accomplish ten times more effectually—gather together the infinite number of minute facts, illustrative of the subject I have mentioned, which are scattered over the memories of its thousands of readers, and preserve them in its pages, until some James Grimm shall arise who shall do for the Mythology of the British Islands the good service which that profound antiquary and philologist has accomplished for the Mythology of Germany. The present century has scarcely produced a more remarkable book, imperfect as its learned author confesses it to be, than the second edition of the '*Deutsche Mythologie:*' and, what is it?—a mass of minute facts, many of which, when separately considered, appear trifling and insignificant,—but, when taken in connexion with the system into which his master-mind has woven them, assume a value that he who first recorded them never dreamed of attributing to them.

How many such facts would one word from you evoke, from the north and from the south—from John o'Groat's to the Land's End! How many readers would be glad to show their gratitude for the novelties which you, from week to week, communicate to them, by forwarding to you some record of old Time—some recollection of a now neglected custom—some fading legend, local tradition, or fragmentary ballad!

Nor would such communications be of service to the English antiquary alone. The connexion between the FOLK-LORE of England (remember I claim the honour of introducing the epithet Folk-Lore, as Disraeli does of introducing Father-Land, into the literature of this country) and that of Germany is so intimate that such communications will probably serve to enrich some future edition of Grimm's Mythology.

Let me give you an instance of this connexion.—In one of the chapters of Grimm, he treats very fully of the parts which the Cuckoo plays in Popular Mythology—of the prophetic character with which it has been invested by the voice of the people; and gives many instances of the practice of deriving predictions from the number of times which its song is heard. He also records a popular notion, "that the Cuckoo never sings till he has thrice eaten his fill of cherries." Now, I have lately been informed of a custom which formerly obtained among children in Yorkshire, that illustrates the fact of a connexion between the Cuckoo and the Cherry,—and that, too, in their prophetic attributes. A friend has communicated to me that children in Yorkshire were formerly (and may be still) accustomed to sing round a cherry-tree the following invocation:—

> Cuckoo, Cherry-tree,
> Come down and tell me
> How many years I have to live.

Each child then shook the tree,—and the number of cherries which fell betokened the years of its future life.

The Nursery Rhyme which I have quoted, is, I am aware, well known. But the manner in which it was applied is not recorded by Hone, Brand, or Ellis:—and is one of those facts, which, trifling in themselves, become of importance when they form links in a great chain—one of those facts which a word from the *Athenaeum* would gather in abundance for the use of future inquirers into that interesting branch of literary antiquities,—our Folk-Lore.

AMBROSE MERTON.

P.S.—It is only honest that I should tell you I have long been contemplating a work upon our *'Folk-Lore'* (under *that title,* mind Messrs. A, B, and

C,—so do not try to forestall me);—and I am personally interested in the success of the experiment which I have, in this letter, albeit imperfectly, urged you to undertake.

*   *   *

We have taken some time to weigh the suggestion of our correspondent—desirous to satisfy ourselves that any good of the kind which he proposes could be effected in such space as we are able to spare from the many other demands upon our columns; and having before our eyes the fear of that shower of trivial communication which a notice in conformity with his suggestion is too likely to bring. We have finally decided that, if our antiquarian correspondents be earnest and well-informed, and subject their communications to the condition of having something worthy to communicate, we may—now that the several antiquarian societies have brought their meetings, for the season, to a close—at once add to the amusement of a large body of our readers and be the means of effecting some valuable salvage for the future historian of old customs and feelings, within a compass that shall make no unreasonable encroachment upon our columns. With these views, however, we must announce to our future contributors under the above head, that their communications will be subjected to a careful sifting—both as regards value, authenticity, and novelty; and that they will save both themselves and us much unnecessary trouble if they will refrain from offering any facts or speculations which do not at once *need* recording and deserve it. Brevity will be always a recommendation—where there are others; and great length in any article will, of necessity, exclude it, even where its merits would recommend. The cases will be very rare in which an article should exceed a couple of our columns,—and the exception can be only when the article itself will bear dividing without injury. But notices much shorter will always be more welcome;—and, in fact, extent will be, on all occasions, an important element in our estimate of the admissibility of a communication. We will hint, also, to our correspondents, that we should, in each case, prefer receiving (though we do not make it absolute as a rule,) the confidential communication of the writer's real name and address.

ORIGIN OF THE WORD "FOLK-LORE."
(4th S. x. 206, 319.)

I am greatly indebted to W. E. A. A. for giving me an opportunity of putting on record in "N. & Q." how I was led to the coinage of this now universally recognized word. For I may say, as Coriolanus said of the fluttering of the Volscians, "Alone I did it."

Popular antiquities and superstition, and the relation of national legends and traditions to one another, had long been a subject of great interest to me—an interest greatly fostered by the perusal of Grimm's *Deutsche My-thologie*. Some time after the appearance of the second edition of that masterly work, I began to put in order the notes which I had been collecting for years, with a view to their publication; and feeling sure that the Iron Horse then beginning to ride roughshod over every part of the country would soon trample under foot and exterminate all traces of our old beliefs, legends, &c., I besought *The Athenæum* to lend its powerful influence towards their collection and preservation.

My kind friend, Mr. Dilke, most readily fell into my views. The subject was "tapped" (as Horace Walpole would say) in that journal on the 22nd August, 1846, in a paper written by myself under the pseudonym of AMBROSE MERTON, and headed FOLK-LORE.

In the opening of that appeal, I described the subject as "what we in England designate as popular antiquities, or popular literature (though, by-the-bye, it is more a Lore than a Literature, and would be most aptly described by a good Saxon compound, FOLK-LORE—the Lore of the People)."

When seeking to prove that the object I had in view would not be of service to English antiquaries only, I added:—

"The connexion between the FOLK-LORE of England (mind, I claim the honour of introducing the epithet FOLK-LORE, as Disraeli did of introducing FATHER-LAND, into the literature of this country) and that of Germany is so intimate that such communications will probably serve to enrich some future edition of Grimm's *Mythology*."

And my communication closed with the following postscript, in which, with a precaution which was subsequently justified, I reiterated my claim:—

"It is only honest that I should tell you that I have long been contemplating a work upon our *Folk-Lore* (under that title, mind, Messrs. A, B, and C, so do not try to forestall me), and I am personally interested in the success of the experiment, which I have in this letter, albeit imperfectly, urged you to undertake."

The word took its place, for it supplied a want; and when Dean Trench's *English Past and Present* appeared (1855), I was pleased to find one so qualified to judge of the value of the word speaking of it as follows:—

"The most successful of these compounded words *(borrowed recently from the German)* is 'Folk-lore,' and the substitution of this for the long and latinized 'Popular Superstitions' must be deemed, I think, an unquestionable gain."

The impression that the word was borrowed from the German is a very natural one. But should the Archbishop of Dublin ever see this note, I am sure that accomplished scholar will in future editions of his book do justice to the English origin of the word Folk-lore.

WILLIAM J. THOMS.

3

Request

Wilhelm Mannhardt

One of the great figures of nineteenth-century folkloristics was Wilhelm Mannhardt (1831–1880). His research on European agricultural rituals and his account of what he believed were vegetative spirits provided much of the inspiration for James George Frazer (1854–1941), who acknowledged Mannhardt in his 1890 preface to the first edition of his celebrated *Golden Bough:*

> I have made great use of the works of the late W. Mannhardt, without which, indeed, my book could scarcely have been written. . . . Mannhardt set himself systematically to collect, compare, and explain the living superstitions of the peasantry. Of this wide field the special department which he marked out for himself was the religion of the woodman and the farmer, in other words, the superstitious beliefs and rites connected with trees and cultivated plants. By oral enquiry, and by printed questions scattered broadcast over Europe, as well as by ransacking the literature of folk-lore, he collected a mass of evidence, part of which he published in a series of admirable works.

French folklorist Henri Gaidoz (1842–1932), in a review of Mannhardt's works, said they surely justified the placement of his name among the great mythologists of the century and that above all he deserved credit for reinvigorating the theory of myth through the investigation of living contemporary folk traditions, a technique that validated the worth of the collecting efforts of modern-day folklorists. Gaidoz also gave Mannhardt credit for having collected superstitions from French soldiers who had been captured in the Franco-Prussian War (1870–1871) and housed in Germany. Because these prisoners of war came from every province and from many walks of life, the published collection represented an interesting sampling of French superstitions in general. See "M. Mannhardt et ses Travaux," *Mélusine* 1 (1878), 578–582.

Twentieth-century folklore theorist Carl Wilhelm von Sydow (1878–1952) was no less lavish in his praise of Mannhardt. In an article that originally appeared in the English journal *Folklore* in 1934, von Sydow, despite criticizing Mannhardt's theories, began by stating, "Few investigators have had such a decisive significance for the study of mythology and folk tradition as Wilhelm Mannhardt. He was the first to realize the importance of a systematic collection of folk tradition parish by parish, village by village, and he was the first to start magnificent collection work by sending out thousands of copies of printed questionnaires in Germany, Scandinavia, and other countries."

Mannhardt's importance for the development of international folkloristics rests primarily on his designing a questionnaire concerned with agricultural customs—especially those concerning the disposition of the "last sheaf" gathered by harvesters—and sending around 150,000 copies (at his own expense) to correspondents in Germany, Scandinavia, Lithuania, Poland, Switzerland, Holland, Austria-Hungary, Italy, and France. In spite of a relatively low return rate—he received only slightly more than 2,100 responses—the data elicited provided an empirical basis for some of his later publications: *Die Korndämonen* (Berlin, 1868), *Der Baumkultus der Germanen* (Berlin, 1875), *Wald- und Feldkulte* (Berlin, 1877), and his posthumously published *Mythologische Forschungen* (Strassburg, 1884).

Mannhardt was a comparativist, and in a letter to the great Italian folklorist Giuseppe Pitrè (1841–1916) in December 1876 he indicated his goal:

> I have become ever more convinced that for an understanding and explanation of folk tradition, collection cannot be restricted to a single country but rather it is only with a complete overview of the nature of the tradition in all of Europe that one can succeed in finding answers to a series of the most important questions. Taking the popular tradition of northern Europe as a reference point, I have attempted to illuminate a number of striking similarities between the ideas and customs of the ancient world and those of the peoples of northern Europe. . . . As you can see from my writings central to my endeavor is a comprehensive collection and explanation of mythical agricultural customs.

(For the letter, see Giuseppe Bonomo, "Lettere di Usener, Mannhardt e Krohn a Giuseppe Pitrè," *Annali des Museo Pitrè* 5–7 (1954–1956), 1–11, reprinted in Bonomo, *Studi Demologici* (Palermo: Flaccovio, 1970), 253–266.) Mannhardt had hoped to complete a mammoth project entitled *Monumenta mythica Germaniae,* which was to include mythological songs as well as customs and superstitions, but he did not live to finish it.

The high quality of the data elicited by Mannhardt is attested by the fact that one hundred years later it still served as the basis for research. See Ingeborg Weber-Kellermann, *Erntebrauch in der Ländlichen Arbeitswelt des 19. Jahrhunderts auf Grund der Mannhardtbefragung in Deutschland von 1865* (Marburg: N. G. Elwert Verlag, 1965); see also the same author's "Betrachtungen zu Wilhelm Mannhardts Umfrage von 1865 über Arbeitsgerät und bäuerliche Arbeit," *Zeitschrift für Agrargeschichte und Agrarsoziologie* 14 (1966), 45–53, and "Der Geist des Flachses. Versuch einer strukturalistischen Analyse aus dem Mannhardtmaterial von 1865," *In Memoriam António Jorge Dias,* Vol. 2 (Lisbon: Instituto de Alta Cultura, 1974), 423–441.

Mannhardt was not the first individual to utilize a questionnaire to collect folklore. In 1805 the Academie Celtique was formed in Paris, in part as a French nationalistic effort to counter hegemonic claims of classical Greek and Roman origins. As a means of eliciting supposedly authentic "Celtic" survivals, a folkloristic questionnaire was designed containing fifty-one questions written principally by Jacques-Antoine Dulaure (1755–1835), author of the classic study of phallic cults, *Des Divinités Génératrices,* which also appeared in 1805. Inasmuch as Jacob Grimm was in Paris that same year, it is possible that the founding of the Academie Celtique and its questionnaire might have inspired his attempt to initiate a comparable effort with his 1815 "Circular." This is the opinion of Gaidoz, who pointed out that on June 9, 1811, Grimm was elected a corresponding member of the Academie. For a discussion of this, as well as a consideration of the importance of the Academie Celtique for the development of folkloristics in general, see Henri Gaidoz, "De l'influence de l'Académie celtique sur les études de folklore," *Recueil de Mémoires du Centenaire de la Société des Antiquaires de France, 1804–1904* (Paris: C. Klincksieck, 1904), 135–143. See also Harry Senn, "Folklore Beginnings in France: The Academie Celtique: 1804–1813," *Journal of the Folklore Institute* 18 (1981), 23–33; and Mona Ozouf, "L'invention de l'ethnographie française: Le questionnaire de l'Académie celtique," *Annales économies sociétés civilisations* 36 (1981), 210–230. For a convenient text of that questionnaire, see Nicole Belmont, ed., *Aux sources de l'ethnologie française: L'académie celtique* (Paris: Editions du C.T.H.S., 1995), 23–37. For a substantial inventory of folklore questionnaire scholarship, see Eleanor Fein Reishtein, "Bibliography on Questionnaires as a Folklife Fieldwork Technique," *Keystone Folklore Quarterly* 13 (1968), 45–69, 121–166, 219–232. For a text of a fascinating seventeenth-century questionnaire, namely the Memorial issued by King Gustavus Adolphus of Sweden on May 20, 1630, which specifically charged antiquarians and historians to collect among other things "tales and poems about dragons, dwarfs, and giants" as well as "different cures" and "signs for forecasting the weather," see Dan Ben-Amos, "Foreword," *Nordic Folklore,* edited by Reimund Kvideland and Henning K. Sehmsdorf (Bloomington: Indiana University Press, 1989), viii–ix. This pioneering proclamation was evidently drafted by the king's mentor and advisor Johannes Bureus (1568–1652). For further details, see Hans Hildebrand, *Minne af riksantikvarien Johannes Bureus* (Stockholm: P. A. Norstedt, 1910).

Mannhardt deserves to be remembered for more than his questionnaire. For instance, he was one of the editors of the first major folklore periodical, *Zeitschrift für deutsche Mythologie und Sittenkunde* (1853–1859). It was founded by Johann Wilhelm Wolf (1817–1855), but Mannhardt edited it after Wolf's death. (For details about Wolf, who appears to have published the very first folklore journal, *Grootmoederken,* in 1842, renamed *Wodana* in 1843, see Marc Moonen, *Johann-Wilhelm Wolf: De Grondlegger der Volkskunde in Vlaanderen* (Brussels: De Burcht, 1944); for a commemorative centennial appreciation of Wolf's Flemish periodical, see A. Schmidt, "Het eerste Vlaamsch Volkskundig Tijdschrift 1842–3," *Volkskunde* 45 (1943), 190–201. Despite the title, the *Zeitschrift für deutsche Mythologie und Sittenkunde* was decidedly comparative in scope and did include non-German materials.

For further consideration of Mannhardt's contributions to folkloristics, see Arno Schmidt, *Wilhelm Mannhardts Lebenswerk* (Danzig, 1932); and Richard Beitl, "Wilhelm Mannhardt und der Atlas der deutschen Volkskunde," *Zeitschrift für Volkskunde* 54 (1933), 70–84; for his influence on Norwegian folklore scholarship, see Nils Lid, "Wilhelm Mannhardt og hans nyskaping av den folkloristiske metoden," *Syn og Segn* 31 (1925), 314–329, and his *Wilhelm Mannhardt og hans samling av norske folkeminne* (Oslo: Norsk folkeminnelag, 1931); for Swedish scholarship, see Richard Broberg, "Ett nyupptäckt svar fran Varmland pa Wilhelm Mannhardts fragelista," *Arv* 17 (1961), 99–139, and Nils-Arvid Bringeus, "Debatten om Wilhelm Mannhardts fruktbarhetsteorier," *Rig* 74 (1991), 7–24; for the Swiss response to the questionnaire, see Eva M. Düblin-Honegger, "Schweizerische Antworten auf Wilhelm Mannhardts Fragebogen," *Schweizerisches Archiv für Volkskunde* 67 (1971), 324–352; for the results of the questionnaire in the former Austro-Hungarian empire, see Olaf Bockhorn, " 'Vor dem Binden bringen die Schnitter dem Gutsherrn eine Erntekrone . . .' Die Mannhardt-Umfrage auf Gutshöfen im Gebiet der österreichisch-ungarischen Monarchie," in *Gutshofknechte und Saisonarbeit im Pannonischen Raum* (Vienna: Gesellschaft für pannonische Forschung, 1990), 53–64. For Frazer's tribute, see Volume 1 of *The Golden Bough,* 3d edition (London: Macmillan, 1913), xii–xiii; von Sydow's 1934 article in *Folklore,* "The Mannhardtian Theories about the Last Sheaf and the Fertility Demons from a Modern Critical Point of View," was reprinted in his *Selected Papers on Folklore* (Copenhagen: Rosenkilde and Bagger, 1948), 89–105.

Mannhardt's questionnaire exists in slightly different forms in different languages. The version presented here is one that appeared in a Belgian periodical, *Bulletin de la Société liégeoise de littérature wallonne* 7 (2) (1864):10–17, but it has been supplemented with a few details from the version in Mannhardt's *Die Korndämonen* (Berlin: Ferd. Dummler's Verlagsbuchhandlung, 1868), 44–48.

*   *   *

Science is the business of humanity. Elevated well above all the petty restrictions of nationality, its results profit all civilized peoples and it is science which forms an impartial fraternity, even among those who are separated by language and politics.

It is in this sense that the undersigned dares to ask French-speaking peoples if they would be willing to participate with a lively and fraternal interest in an international project designed to answer important questions which have been endorsed by such distinguished scholars as Burnouf, Ad. Pictet, A. Maury, M. Bréal, etc.

Influenced by Jacob and Wilhelm Grimm, Fr. Bopp, A. Weber, H. Steinthal, closely associated with Adalbert Kuhn, the undersigned has as the principal aim of his life to dedicate himself to the research and explication of folk life in Europe. He has been occupied for several years with the publication of works on comparative Germanic mythology. The principal sources of this research often come from things which are not easily perceived and which are misunderstood. These are traditions, folktales, customs, beliefs of peasants in which the expert discovers the distinct vestiges of the most ancient beliefs of humanity from which careful research can produce the most precious and trustworthy findings with respect to the primitive history of the Indo-European race, the ancient mythology of the Slavs, the Germans, the Celts, and of Christian archaeology.

It is the last moment to gather these valuable scientific materials; they are disappearing every day in the face of increasing civilization, and it is only our generation which will still be able to save for our posterity the last remnants of the customs of our ancestors before they disappear completely. Nevertheless, in order to put this study on solid ground, it is necessary to follow traditions from country to country in nearly all of Europe. It is necessary to determine to what extent each tradition has spread, what was its primitive form, and from where did it originate: in a word, we must obtain an abundance of facts concerning popular usages.

It is with great personal sacrifices that the undersigned has begun to collect in this manner the agricultural customs according to a historical and philological method. The Academies of Sciences of Berlin and of Vienna as well as the Association of Historical and Archaeological Societies of Germany and the Germanic Section of the Philological Congress at Heidelberg have carefully examined the design of the enterprise and have wished the undersigned great success. More than four thousand scientific contributions have already been sent to me and these materials, when compared one with another, have already thrown an astonishing light on the beginning of the ancient cult of Ceres. So the inhabitants of France and French-speaking Switzerland also have the duty to save the forgotten heritage of their ancestors be they Romans, Franks, Celts or Burgundians, a heritage contained in folk traditions, and to prepare a scientific explanation of them by comparing them with the traditions of neighboring peoples. I address, therefore, a request, as urgently as possible, to all the members of antiquarian societies, to college students, and to all the friends of people who have the opportunity of witnessing agricultural customs to be kind enough to respond, in the interest of science, to the following questions and to send their responses to the place where they received this questionnaire.

1. Are there still in your country any particular customs associated with tilling the land, sowing seed, the manner of fertilizing the fields with dung, the harvesting of hay, corn, hemp, flax, and wine, or potatoes? Are there any special customs connected with the threshing of grain, the scutching of flax and hemp? You are sincerely asked to communicate all that you can learn about such matters.

2. What procedures are followed during sowing time? At harvest time? Is the grain mowed down with a scythe or cut with a sickle? Is it bundled immediately into sheaves or put first into piles? Does the practice vary with different kinds of grain? Have you observed that the wind must touch the peasant's sickle?

3. Are they always the same persons who cut the grain and bind the sheaves? Men? Women? Foreigners? Laborers?

4. Are there ancient customs associated with sowing-time? Does one, for example, on Palm-Sunday or Easter place holy crosses or maple branches in a field of grain or flax in order to protect them from lightning and from hailstorms? Is it believed that certain days (such as Monday, Wednesday, Maundy Thursday) are propitious or unpropitious for sowing certain types of grain? Has one observed planting in accordance with the phases of the moon or with other phenomena? Has it been noticed that the seedbag be spun by the hands of a seven-year-old child? Do processions with Saints' images take place around the recently sown fields? Is the first plow sprinkled with water? Is there something particular which is mixed in with the first seed? Is it ever said that the person who sows will die if he forgets to sow even one single solitary field? Are there specific symbolic practices carried out with flax so as to make it grow higher?

5. Are there superstitious measures to protect grain-fields from caterpillars, beetles, mice, and moles?

6. Are there particular rituals regarding the cutting of the first ears of corn, as, for example, to put the first two handfuls in the form of a cross, or to have a child under seven years of age cut the first stalks? Does one abandon the first sheaf to the mice in the barn? Are there any other special ceremonies?

7. After the harvesters have completed the harvest but before they have bundled the sheaves, do they bring to the owner a crown or a bouquet of ears of corn? What form do they take? And what do the workers say or sing?

8. You are urgently requested to pay particular attention to the following questions: Are there special ancient customs concerning the cutting of the last stalks of the field, the binding of the last sheaf, and the threshing of the last bundle? In many places in north and south Germany, the last sheaf is shaped in the form of an animal or it is decorated with a wooden image of such and such an animal. The animal varies with different districts: it can be a pig, a wolf, a billy goat, a rooster, a rabbit, or a cow. Similarly, the last sheaf may be given a name, as, for example, Roggensau (rye-sow), Halmbock (straw-goat), and the same for the wolf, the rooster, the rabbit, etc. Sometimes a live toad is enclosed in the last bundle of flax. In other countries (in Scotland, England, Germany, and in the Slavic countries) the last sheaf is formed into a doll in the shape of a human figure (sometimes a man, sometimes a woman). It is sometimes clothed, but it is often adorned only with flowers and ribbons and with arms, legs, and sexual parts roughly indicated. This doll has the following names in English: harvest lady, maiden, corndolly, corn baby; in German: Kornmutter [corn mother], grosse Mutter [big mother], Weizenbraut [wheat-bride], Haferbraut [oat-bride], der Alte [the old man], die Alte [the old woman], die alte Hure [the old whore], das Kornmännchen [the little corn man]; in Danish: Bygkjaelling, Fok, Fukke, den Gamle; in Wendish: Pucél; in Polish: Baba, Stary, Benkart (illegitimate child), Gel, Pepek (navel). The person who cuts the last stalk or binds the last sheaf is obliged to make the corn doll. One calls out to this person, "There is a billy goat, rooster, etc. sitting in the sheaf," "You have the old man and must keep him." The doll is placed high atop the grain wagon and carried to the barn where it is repeatedly doused with water. Also at threshing time, the last bundle is frequently made into such a doll, and the person who is the last to thresh grain must throw the doll on the threshing-floor of a neighbor who has not yet finished his threshing. This same person is enclosed in a sheaf and carted through the village. Then follows a banquet which the doll also attends, but in the form of a cake on the table. In other areas, the last sheaf is called: Lucky corn, Stem, Mother-sheaf, Rattlebird, etc.

Are such customs still practiced in your area, even if only in part? What name is given to the last sheaf? What is it that is called out to the person who ties it and who cuts the last stalks? Is a doll made after each harvest, be it rye, barley, wheat, peas, oats, potatoes, etc. Is a stone bound into the last sheaf? We would be very happy to receive a little drawing of the corn doll. What is done with the harvest doll in the courtyard of the farm?

9. Sometimes the last or the first sheaf (or flax bundle) is left in the field, as they say, for Wôd [Wotan], the terrifying maidens [Valkyrie], dwarfs, monks and mendicants. It is sprinkled here and there with wine or beer. Also a portion of grain or a corner of the field left unmowed is said to be for the poor. Are some such customs common in your area? If so, please report them in detail.

10. In some localities, the harvest workers have the right to cut cabbage heads in the garden of the farmer who refuses to give them a feast after they have brought in the last wagon-load of grain. There are also certain customs observed involving the tipping over of the last wagon-load of grain. Do you know of these customs in your area?

11. Here and there, immediately after the harvest, a bouquet of burdock, gooseberries and currants is made and put into a tub full of water and then covered with nettles, whereupon those present vie with one another to pick out the fruit. Do you also have this custom? What are the exact details? Are rhymes recited in conjunction with it? What are they?

12. Is the harvest doll made from the last sheaf presented to the proprietor by itself or is a crown of corn also presented? What are the details of this ceremony? What are the songs, the formulas used by harvestworkers in presenting the doll or the crown to the proprietor and his family members? Are there traditional dances and other particulars? Be so good as to give the text in the language or the dialect of the people.

13. In what manner are the harvest festival and the banquet celebrated in the courtyard? Does this festival still have special names? What foods and beverages are offered to the harvest-workers? When does the festival take place? Is it celebrated at the same time as the village festival?

14. In what manner and at what time is a harvest festival celebrated at the church? Are there still other religious festivals connected with agriculture?

15. Are there other religious ceremonies connected with sowing or harvesting, for example, sowing in the name of the Trinity, praying in a group in the field at harvest time, placing several ears of corn with

some money on the altar at the first communion following the harvest? According to folk belief, what saints exercise the greatest influence on agriculture and what is it that is recounted about them?

16. By what words does one greet one another at harvest time?

17. Are fires of joy lighted after the harvest?

18. Are there superstitious beliefs connected with the harvest and especially associated with the last sheaf, for example, placing at Christmas or in the spring several grains of this sheaf in the cattle's manger so as to make them prosper? Or is it believed that the person who ties the last sheaf will either marry or die in the course of the following year? Are there legends concerned with sowing, with harvesting, and with the sown field?

19. Are there any particular expressions among the folk referring to the wind blowing through the grain fields such as "The boar walks in the field"; "The wolves are chasing themselves in the corn"; etc.

20. Are there particular expressions designed to prevent little children from straying into the grain fields, for example, "The grain mother (in Polish: Babajedza, Zitnamatka; in Wendish: Serpashija) sits in the corn and squeezes the children against her iron bosom"; "The wolf is in the field"? Please report these items exactly as they are expressed in the language or dialect of the people.

21. Do the people still recount anything about the Corn Mother or a fairy, or a woman or a man who appears in the field? Does anyone tell anything about a ghostly woman who walks across the field at noon? What is said about her? Are legends told about crying nurslings found in the field? Does anyone tell of saints, fairies, heroes who by traversing the fields make them fertile?

22. In your area, are there traditions of winged dragons (in Wendish: zitni-zmié), dwarfs, goblins, elves, and witches which steal corn from the fields of the peasants and carry it through the air to other people? Is there among the people a belief in a demonic being or magician, armed at the feet with little sickles, who walks through the just-ripened corn and cuts off the ears in order to take half the crop for himself?

23. As for weather, do people know superstitions which are related to the growth of the corn, for example, "There will be an abundant crop if, in the month of May, a crow can already hide itself in a sown field"?

24. Are there still superstitious people who never pick the last fruit from trees and who leave a handful of flour in the flour-bin?

25. Are there still other folk names for ergot (secale cornutum) such as Corn mother, Rye mother, Wolf, Rabbitbread?

26. Are there still dialect terms for animals referring to grains, for example, the mole-cricket (Gryllus grillotalpa):Corn wolf; the little night-owl (strix aluco):oat-goat; and the snipe (scolopax gallinago):oat-goat?

27. Are there superstitious beliefs related to sowing and harvesting associated with Mardi Gras, Maundy Thursday, Easter, Pentecost, Saint John the Baptist, and particularly Christmas, for example, "One must count the stars on Christmas Eve in order to know how many piles of sheaves one will gather" or is there a custom of rolling around the same day in nonthreshed peas or walking about in the winter corn to influence the crop of the following year? Are there figures covered with straw going around at Christmas, Shrove-Tuesday, etc. called "Pea-Bear," "Oat-Goat," etc.? What do people say about these figures?

28. Are there particular expressions for winds and cloud formations, for example, "Tail of the pig" for whirlwind; "Beef, sheep" for clouds? Does one throw flour out of the window when the wind blows or when it hails? Do superstitious people still try in times of drought to attract rain by spraying water on individuals covered with leaves?

29. Is there a custom of tying up the proprietor with corn straw when he visits the harvest field for the first time? and is this same practice followed with strangers who come to visit the field? What words are used on this occasion? Or is there some other means of obtaining money from visitors?

30. Is there, during or after harvest, the custom of beating or decapitating roosters?

31. Is it the custom in your area on the occasion of a wedding to present an ear of corn to the bride or similarly to put several grains in her shoes?

32. At threshing, did one tease a novice by sending him to search, for example, for a "sack of wind"?

33. Please indicate past customs and also those which one still finds today.

34. Please indicate the names of the places, the districts, the counties, the provinces where one finds the customs reported.

Address: Danzig (Prussia) 5, Newmarket

Wilhelm Mannhardt
Doctor of Philosophy
Private Docent of the University of Berlin

4

An Angel Flew Through the Room

Reinhold Köhler

If one were asked to indicate the single most important characteristic of practitioners of international folkloristics, it would be their unswerving commitment to a comparative perspective. Unlike folklorists who are content to restrict themselves to local, regional, or even national traditions, the internationally minded scholar is ever seeking to relate such traditions to a wider context. Whether the goal is to identify similarities or to distinguish differences across cultures, the quest to find cognates—that is, genetically-historically related versions of a given item—is the hallmark of the truly international folklorist.

One of the unsung heroes of international folkloristics is Reinhold Köhler (1830–1892) who tends to be relegated to an occasional footnote in the history of folklore scholarship. He was a librarian and a very erudite one at that. His entire career was spent at the Ducal Library in Weimar. But as has been said, although he never left the confines of Germany, he traveled the world in thought and on paper. A walking encyclopedia, Köhler was one of only a handful of international comparativists who in a time well before the advent of tale type indexes, motif indexes, and computers had the extraordinary ability to cite numerous parallels for diverse items of folklore.

So great was his expertise that other scholars frequently called on him to write the annotations for their collections of folktales. He wrote comprehensive comparative notes for collections of Estonian, French, Icelandic, Sicilian, and Venetian folktales, among others. When two folktales collected by Andrew Lang (1844–1912), not known for his fieldwork, were published in the *Revue Celtique* in 1878, the tales—"Rashin Coatie" (Aarne-Thompson tale type 510, Cinderella) and "Nicht, Nought, Nothing" (Aarne-Thompson tale type 313, The Girl as Helper in the Hero's Flight)—were accompanied by ample lists of parallels provided by Köhler. Similarly, when Hermann Grimm (1828–1901), the son of Wilhelm Grimm, collected three folktales in Rome in February 1863 from a seventeen-year-old male artist's model who was from an area near Naples, it was Köhler who published them with notes several years later. Grimm had originally sent the tales to Jacob, but his uncle died in September 1863. See "Italienische Volksmärchen," *Jahrbuch für romanische und englische Literatur* 8 (1867), 241–270. Köhler's interest in folklore was by no means limited to folktales. His dozens of articles and notes, appearing in a wide variety of periodicals, ranged from ballads and customs to legends and proverbs. One need only consult the three volumes of his *Kleinere Schriften* (1898–1900), which gathered together many of his writings, to appreciate the enormous breadth of his knowledge. The first volume contains around forty reviews and notes on folktales; the second volume consists of seventy-six on medieval narratives; and the third volume includes eighty-four notes and reviews, fifty-four of which were devoted to folksongs, superstitions, proverbs, riddles, and folk speech. These three volumes do not include six essays found in an earlier publication, *Aufsatze über Märchen und Volkslieder* (Berlin: Weidmann, 1894). One important essay in the 1894 compilation is "Über die europäischen Volksmärchen," originally published in the *Weimarische Beiträge zur Literatur und Kunst* in 1865 (pp. 181–203).

Köhler's unusual erudition did not pass unnoticed in Europe. The eminent French scholar Gaston Paris (1839–1903), for instance, in his review of Köhler's *Kleinere Schriften* which appeared in the *Journal des Savants* in May 1901, commented on the fact that the many individuals who directed inquiries to the "Sage de Weimar" inevitably received both accurate and abundant references. In an earlier review of A. Schiefner's *Awarische Texte*—one of the many folktale collections annotated by Köhler—in the *Revue Critique d'Histoire et de Littérature* on July 4, 1874, Paris had given Köhler even more praise. After observing that Köhler, the "savant bibliothecaire de Weimar," had become a quasi-official commentator on all folktale collections, Paris asked Köhler to undertake a "general bibliography of folktales." He did not demand a theory of origins, meaning, or diffusion but insisted that before any of these issues could be studied the basic materials had to be duly assembled. And if this could be accomplished, the study of folktales would emerge from its embryonic stage and become a respectable discipline. Köhler was the right person for this task because, as Paris put it, he knew just about all one could know about the relations and variations of the folktales of all peoples of the world. For details about Paris, see Harry A. Senn, "Gaston Paris as Folklorist (1867–1895): The Rise and Decline of French Folklore Studies," *Journal of the Folklore Institute* 12 (1975), 47–56. For his writings on folklore, see the 100 entries in the listing of his nearly 1,200 publications in Joseph Bédier and Mario Roques, *Bibliographie des Travaux de Gaston Paris* (New York: Burt Franklin, 1969), 131–146.

Although Köhler was not particularly enamored of the term "folklore," he nonetheless wrote the entry for it in the 1887 *Supplement* to the thirteenth edition of the prestigious *Brockhaus' Conversations-Lexikon*. In that entry Köhler remarked on the possible confusion between the sense of folklore as "folk knowledge," meaning what the folk know, and of folklore as knowledge about the folk. He defined the meaning of folklore in the scientific world as encompassing all folk traditions, especially legends and folktales, songs and rhymes, proverbs, riddles, folk beliefs and superstitions, customs, and practices. He also indicated that the derivative term "Folkloristik" (or folkloristics) had gradually become internationally accepted. See "Folk-Lore or Folklore," *Brockhaus' Conversations-Lexikon, Supplementband* (Leipzig: Brockhaus, 1887), 335–336.

One reason for the declining appreciation of Köhler lies in the fact that comparative notes are almost always rendered somewhat obsolete by the subsequent publication of new texts, as well as more comprehensive listings of parallels by later scholars. In the case of the Grimm tales, for instance, the Grimm brothers themselves published the first set of comparative notes in a third volume of the second edition of the *Kinder- und Hausmärchen;* the second edition was published in 1819, with the volume containing the notes appearing in 1822. Köhler added many more parallels to the Grimm tales, and they were eventually incorporated in Johannes Bolte and Georg Polivka's massive five-volume work, *Anmerkungen zu den Kinder- und Hausmärchen* (Leipzig: Dieterichsche Verlagsbuchhandlung, 1913–1932), which continues to be the principal resource for anyone interested in locating parallels to any folktale in the Grimm corpus.

A brief sample of Köhler's technique of citing parallels is illustrated in his note "Ein Engel Flog durchs Zimmer," which appeared in *Germania* 10 (1865):245–246, around the time Mannhardt was sending out his questionnaire. The expression also exists in English. Martha Warren Beckwith collected folklore from forty-five Vassar College students in the 1920s, and one of the items she reported under "Miscellaneous" reads as follows: "A pause in conversation, in company, that occurs twenty minutes before or after the hour, means that an angel is passing" ("Signs and Superstitions Collected from American College Girls," *Journal of American Folklore* 36 [1923], 9). The tradition exists in California at the end of the twentieth century, although not always with the "twenty minutes" feature. Immediately following a sudden and awkward prolonged pause in a conversation, someone will say "an angel is passing through," presumably in part to break the pall of the embarrassing silence. There is also a French cognate: *"un ange passe."*

Surely the most detailed documentation of the tradition, however, is that provided by the results of a questionnaire distributed in Germany in 1935 as part of an ambitious attempt to compile the *Atlas der deutschen Volkskunde.* (For a useful introduction to the international effort to systematically demonstrate the geographical distribution of folklore data through the

cartographic method, see Robert Wildhaber, "Folk Atlas Mapping," in
Richard M. Dorson, ed., *Folklore and Folklife* [Chicago: University of Chicago Press, 1972], 479–486.) The results of the German questionnaire are
ably surveyed in Gerda Grober-Glück, *Motive und Motivationen in Redens-
arten und Meinungen: Aberglaube, Volks-Charakterologie, Umgangsfor-
meln, Berufsspott in Verbreitung und Lebensformen*, 2 vols. (Marburg:
N. G. Elwert, 1974). The discussion of "Ein Engel geht (fliegt) durchs Zimmer" is found as part of a more general treatment of "Plötzliche Gesprächs-
tille" [Sudden conversation silences] in Volume 1, pp. 251–273. For the
angel formula, see pp. 264–265, and for an idea of the formula's distribution in Germany, see map 27 in Volume 2.

Since Köhler's 1865 note, the expression has been mentioned by proverb
scholars. Archer Taylor lists it under "Conventional Phrases" in *The Proverb* (Cambridge: Harvard University Press, 1931), 129–130, and Matti
Kuusi discusses parallels in his pioneering worldwide study of expressions
uttered when the sun shines while it is raining, *Regen bei Sonnenschein: Zur
Weltgeschichte einer Redensart* (Helsinki: Academia Scientiarum Fennica,
1957), 389. It is also listed in K. Beth's entry on "Engel" in the monumental
ten-volume *Handwörterbuch des deutschen Aberglaubens* (Berlin: Walter
de Gruyter, 1927–1942), one of the most impressive compendiums of discussions of superstitions and customs ever assembled.

But technically speaking, the item is neither proverb nor superstition. It is
what folklorists call a "dite," a term proposed originally by C. W. von
Sydow (cf. Laurits Bødker, *Folk Literature [Germanic]* [Copenhagen: Rosenkilde and Bagger, 1965], 70). Unlike proverbs, which pass judgment or
recommend a course of action, a dite simply describes or responds to one
specific situation. Many dites refer to meteorological phenomena, for example, "The devil is beating his wife" for the co-occurrence of rain and sun-
shine (cf. Kuusi's work cited above). Thunder is described as "God moving
his furniture" or "potato wagons rolling across the sky." It is not uncom-
mon for dites to refer to angels. So thunder can also be described as "angels
rolling stones downhill," when it snows "the angels are having a pillow
fight," and rain is "angels crying." Some dites are more earthy, such as a
Greek expression explaining rain as "God urinating." This dite apparently
goes back to classical times, as a character in Aristophanes's *The Clouds*
(423 B.C.) speaks of rain as caused by Zeus urinating through a sieve. See
Walter Woodburn Hyde, *Greek Religion and Its Survivals* (New York: Coo-
per Square Publishers, 1963), 225, n.16. Not all dites, however, refer to
weather conditions.

The dite discussed by Köhler may be alluding to the "angel of death" who
is thought to come to collect the souls of those about to die. Implicit in any
case is the equation of death and silence. The "dead" are silent as opposed
to the "living," who can speak. In this context, one would speak to ensure

that all those present remain living. Presumably, the angel has passed through (the room) without stopping to seize an unwary soul. But whatever this bit of folk angelology may mean, anyone who researches it will have to begin with Köhler's original brief note on the subject.

*   *   *

AN ANGEL FLEW THROUGH THE ROOM

Do older sources exist for this well-known expression? It is missing in the Grimm *Dictionary* and therefore its editors did not give any examples of it and as a result forgot to touch upon it at all. That this expression was known to the Grimm brothers would have been likely even if Jacob Grimm had not mentioned it elsewhere. In his essay on the Finnish epic (Höfer's *Zeitschrift für die Wissenschaft der Sprache* 1 [1845], 55), he had occasion to observe, "If among a group of people there is suddenly a silence, it is said that an angel has passed through, or an angel flew through, its sublime appearance silencing worldly noise. The Greeks used to say 'Hermes Epei-selte.' "* Also Sanders is aware of only two sources written in our century to bring to our attention.**

From the works of Fernan Caballero, I see that this expression is also common in Spain. In that authoress's *Cuentos y Poesias populares anda-luces* (p. 41 of the Leipzig edition), we read, "We know that when a gathering of various people becomes silent, it is not because 'the car goes across the sand' as the cultured people say, but it is because an angel has passed over them, infusing the air with the silence of respect to their souls by the movement of its wings, without their being able to define the cause of their comprehension." And in the novel, *La familia de Alvareda* (Madrid, 1856), p. 49: "It is said that when everyone becomes silent at the same time that an angel has flown over us, and the air from its wings has infused us with the respect of silence." And in the novel *Un verano en Bornos* (Madrid, 1858), p. 131, "It is the case, according to the poetic religious beliefs of the people, that an angel flying past over us, causing a silence by the wind produced by its wings, is an incontrovertible sign of respect."

*Franz Passow has already noticed this Greek expression in his Greek dictionary, observing: It is indeed our "An angel flew through the room".
**Mörike's *Maler Nolten* (Stuttgart, 1832), p. 244: Is it not a polite proverb when one puts a stop to a prolonged silence following pleasant conversation by saying, "an angel is going through the living-room." Immermann's *Münchausen* (Düsseldorf, 1838) vol. 1, p. 71, "The myth says, in such times, an angel flies through the room, but judging by the length of such pauses, some angels whose feathers have become out of practice must linger to take flying lessons."

Weimar, February, 1865   Reinhold Köhler

5

The Study of Folk-Lore

Max Müller

Friedrich Max Müller (1823–1900) was primarily a Sanskritist, a philologist, and a student of comparative religion, but he also had a long-standing research interest in comparative mythology and folklore. This interest was initially reflected in his essay "Comparative Mythology," which appeared in 1856, and culminated in his two-volume *Contributions to the Science of Mythology* (1897). Müller reviewed a number of books, one of which was W. K. Kelly's *Curiosities of Indo-European Tradition and Folk-Lore* (1863). In that 1863 review, entitled "Folk-Lore," Müller began by saying, "As the science of language has supplied a new basis for the science of mythology, the science of mythology bids fair, in its turn, to open the way to a new and scientific study of the folk-lore of the Aryan nations." (The review was reprinted in Volume 2, *Essays on Mythology, Traditions, and Customs,* of Müller's five-volume *Chips from a German Workshop* [New York: Scribner, 1871], 195–205.)

As it happens, Müller's idea that myths were in part the result of the "disease of language" and in part primitive man's attempt to describe the rising and setting of the sun ("solar mythology") has not withstood the test of time. In the twentieth century his theories are often cited as examples of obsolete, discarded approaches to mythology. For folkloristic considerations of Müller's theories, see Richard M. Dorson, "The Eclipse of Solar Mythology," *Journal of American Folklore* 68 (1955), 393–416; Giuseppe Cocchiara's chapter "In the 'Workshop' of Max Müller," in his *History of Folklore in Europe* (Philadelphia: Institute for the Study of Human Issues, 1971), 277–295; Nicole Belmont, *Paroles Paiennes: Mythe et Folklore* (Paris: Editions Imago, 1986), 93–120; Robert Jerome Smith "The Creditable Max Müller," in F. Allan Hanson, ed., *Studies in Symbolism and Cultural Communication,* University of Kansas Publications in Anthropology 14 (Lawrence: 1982), 90–104; and Michael P. Carroll, "Some Third

Thoughts on Max Müller and Solar Mythology," *Archives Européennes de Sociologie* 26 (1985), 263–281.

Although Müller might have been considered a leading Indologist of the nineteenth century, he never once set foot in India. Some Indian scholars continue to value his achievements—for example, Nirad C. Chaudhuri, *Scholar Extraordinary: The Life of Professor the Rt. Hon. Friedrich Max Müller* (New York: Oxford University Press, 1974)—whereas others have been highly critical of him. For example, Brahm Datt Bharti, *"Max Müller: A Lifelong Masquerade* (New Delhi: Erabooks, 1992) accuses Müller of having had a secret proselytizing agenda—namely, the desire to convert Hindus to Christianity—and he presents some damaging evidence in Müller's own words in support of his claim. See also Jackie Assayag, *Orientalism and Anthropology: From Max Müller to Louis Dumont* (Pondicherry: Institut française de Pondichery, 1997).

Regardless of Müller's reputation in the twentieth century, there can be no question of his stature in his own time. A. A. Macdonell, in his obituary of Müller in *Man* (1 [1901]:18–23), called him "a personality that exercised a wider influence in the world of learning than perhaps any other scholar of the 19th century." This may explain why Giuseppe Pitrè, cofounder of *Archivio per lo Studio delle Tradizioni popolari* (1882–1906), invited Müller to write a dedicatory preface for the first issue of this important folklore periodical. Müller accepted the invitation, and his letter appeared in Volume 1 (1882):5–8. The letter, originally written in English, was published shortly thereafter in *The Academy* (21 [1882]:193–194). What is particularly striking is the letter's praiseworthy concern for accuracy and authenticity in collecting and reporting folklore. This is all the more remarkable inasmuch as Müller was strictly a library or armchair folklorist and was by no means a folklore collector. Still, he well understood the importance of eliciting multiple versions and of not tampering with the oral texts. His own theoretical interests are also expressed in his desire to know whether stories are "a natural product of the human mind," how they may have diffused, and whether their origin can be discovered in "the mythopoetic stratum of human language and human thought."

*   *   *

THE STUDY OF FOLK-LORE.

We have received the first number of a quarterly Sicilian Review for folklore, entitled *Archivio per lo Studio delle Tradizioni popolari,* and which is published at Palermo under the joint editorship of Signor G. Pitrè and Signor Salomone Marino. Both these gentlemen have long been known as diligent workers in the field of folk-lore, and they have been fortunate in securing the support of some of the most eminent scholars in Europe. This opening number contains contributions of great interest by Reinhold, Köhler, Consiglieri Pedroso, Finamore, de Puymaigre, Gianandrea, Carolina Coronedi, Berti, Costa, Ferraro, and the two editors. The Review is prefaced by a letter from Prof. Max Müller addressed to the editor, Dr. Giuseppe Pitrè, and published by him in Italian, of which we are enabled to give the original in English.

"Oxford: October 19, 1881.

"My dear Sir—

"You ask me to send you a Preface to a journal which you intend to publish, with some friends of yours, and which is to form an archive for popular traditions in Europe. I confess I feel some difficulty in complying with your request. The study of the popular traditions of Europe and of the whole world has made such gigantic strides during the last twenty years that I have only been able, not possessing myself a pair of those famous 'Meilenstiefel,' to watch it from a very respectful distance. Years ago, when that study was, if not despised, at least ignored, I spoke out as strongly as I could against its detractors. Now that I begin to feel old and tired, I find the trees which I helped to plant growing into such forests that often I feel tempted to cry out, 'Enough! enough!'

"And really there is a danger in all scientific pursuits of doing too much, of gathering too much material, more, I mean, than we can classify and survey, or of losing ourselves in minute distinctions—too minute for any practical purposes.

"And this applies with especial force to the subject which we both have at heart, and in which you have proved yourself a real master—I mean the collection of popular stories. That there should be a recognised journal in which the best students of folk-lore should publish their best treasures is most desirable, particularly if that journal stands under the censorship of such scholars as you and some of your *collaborateurs* have shown themselves to be. But let the gate to your journal be a strait gate.

"To collect popular stories is either a most difficult or a most easy task. Everybody who finds nothing better to do thinks he is able at least to write down the stories which his nurse has told him. But this, you know, is a great mistake. First of all, not every story that an old woman may tell deserves to be written down and printed. There is a peculiar earthy flavour about the genuine home-grown, or, if I may say so, autochthonic *Märchen*—something like the flavour of the dark-red wild strawberry—which we must learn to appreciate before we can tell whether a story is old or new, genuine or made-up; whether it comes, in fact, from the forest or from the hothouse. This is a matter of taste; but, as tasters of wine or tea will tell you, even taste can be acquired.

"Secondly, the same story should, whenever that is possible, be collected from different sources and in different localities, and the elements that are common to all versions should be carefully distinguished from those that are peculiar to one or more only.

"Thirdly, each collector should acquaint himself with the results already obtained in the classification of stories, in order to see and to say at once to what cluster each new story belongs. Hahn's classification of ancient myths, imperfect as it is, may give you an example of what ought to be done in order to arrive at a classification of modern myths. Here your archives might render very great service.

"Fourthly, wherever it is possible the story ought to be given in the *ipsissima verba* of the story-teller. This will be a safeguard against that dishonesty in the collection of stories from which we have suffered so much. It is quite true that a collector who trims and embellishes a story ought to be whipped; while a man who invents a story and publishes it as genuine ought to be shot. But, until such a Draconic law is carried into effect, your insisting on having in all cases the *ipsissima verba* will be a great protection against swindlers. Besides, it will have the advantage of making your journal not only an archive for stories, but also a treasury for the students of dialects. The study of dialects, I feel certain, is full of promise; and I still hold as strongly as ever that, in order to know what language is, we must study it in its dialects, which alone represent the real natural life of language. Only here again moderation is essential, as also is the practice of that art which is the secret of all true art and of all true knowledge—viz., *the art of distinguishing what is really important from what is unimportant.* Without that art, collectors of dialects and collectors of stories may fill whole libraries with their volumes; but real knowledge—the knowledge that gives us clear ideas, and strengthens and sharpens the mind for new work—will be impeded rather than advanced.

"The really essential points on which a scientific study of popular stories can, and ought to, throw light are not many. What we want to know is:

"(1) Whether these stories exist in many places, and are, therefore, a natural product of the human mind in its growth from savagery to culture.

"(2) Whether we can trace their history from modern to ancient times, and follow up their migrations from East to West.

"(3) Whether we can understand their origin or *raison d'être* by discovering their first formation in the mythopoetic stratum of human language and human thought.

"These are the three momentous questions; everything else is curious only, unless it serves directly or indirectly to throw light on them. To be able to suppress what is merely curious in order to make room for what is really important seems to me the test of the true scholar in every field of research. To do this requires great self-denial on the part of a student, and even greater firmness on the part of an editor of such a journal as you contemplate.

"As I take a warm interest in the success of your *Archivio,* I thought I might venture to address these warnings to you, though they are meant much less for you than for some of your *collaborateurs,* to whom you might yourself perhaps hesitate to address them. From what I know of your own writings, I believe I have only been expressing your own convictions, and I therefore look forward with high expectations to the appearance of the first number of your *Archivio per lo Studio delle Tradizioni popolari* in January next.

"Believe me to be, with sincere regard and all good wishes,

"Yours truly,
"F. Max Müller."

6

The Method of Julius Krohn

Kaarle Krohn

If one were to select the one country in the world where international folkloristics has flourished the most, that country would undoubtedly be Finland. Other countries have produced major folklorists who have contributed greatly to the development of the discipline, but nowhere has a nationally recognized series of academic folklorists equaled those of Finland.

The modern history of Finnish folkloristics begins with a young doctor named Elias Lönnrot (1802–1884) who in spring 1828 journeyed on foot to the eastern border of Finland to collect folksongs. The year before, Lönnrot had written his undergraduate thesis on Väinämöinen, an important figure in Finnish mythology. In 1831 Lönnrot and his friends formed the Finnish Literary Society, which is still in existence and whose massive building in Helsinki houses the extensive Finnish folklore archives.

After earning his medical degree, Lönnrot became a physician in Kajaani in northern Finland, which permitted him to continue his folklore fieldwork in nearby Karelia. More and more, he thought about arranging the different songs and placing them in some kind of logical narrative order. This resulted in the 1835 publication of an epic entitled *Runokokous Väinämöisestä*, normally referred to as the first edition of the *Kalevala*. The epic contained thirty-two poems totaling 5,052 lines. The *Kalevala* became an immediate success, touching as it did a nerve of national pride. It was known as the Finnish national epic, and the Finns felt it put them on the same footing as those who had produced the *Iliad*, the *Odyssey*, and the like. Lönnrot and his colleagues continued their collecting activities, and in 1849 a new edition of the *Kalevala* was published, consisting of around fifty poems and 22,795 lines. Despite the fact that neither the 1835 nor the 1849 version of the *Kalevala* had been elicited in toto from a single informant, Lönnrot's epic was deemed authentic in some sense. He honestly felt he had reconstructed a work of folk art he had found existing only in fragmentary form.

The *Kalevala* has fascinated Finnish folklorists ever since it was first published. One of these folklorists was Julius Leopold Krohn (1835–1888), who was born in Viborg the year of the *Kalevala*'s first appearance. Krohn had German parents—hence the non-Finnish surname—but he was an ardent Fennophile who studied the Finnish language, literature, and folklore. With this combination of interests, it is not surprising that he chose to consider the *Kalevala*. He was particularly concerned with the possible origins of the epic, specifically whether it had diffused from west to east or from east to west. Julius Krohn developed a methodology to answer these questions that involved elaborate comparisons of all available versions of each "rune," or poem, in the *Kalevala*. The idea was that the further variants were from the point of origin of the original "archetype," the more they differed, and the more widely diffused a feature or trait was, the older it was assumed to be. This portion of the theory is referred to in archaeology as the "age-area" hypothesis. By employing this comparative technique, Krohn believed it was possible to reconstruct the original form of each poem in the *Kalevala* and hence ultimately the entire *Kalevala*. Unfortunately, Julius Krohn drowned in a boating accident in Viborg Bay on August 28, 1888, before he could complete his investigation of the *Kalevala*.

The methodology proposed by Julius Krohn was adopted by his son Kaarle Krohn (1863–1933), who became not only Finland's leading folklorist but one of the founders of international folkloristics. At age eighteen he made his first collecting trip, which was to the same place in Karelia where Lönnrot had recorded many of his *Kalevala* songs. The next year (1882) Krohn, with the help of a scholarship from the Finnish Literary Society, visited Kajaani (where Lönnrot had practiced medicine) and recorded nearly 500 folktales. Krohn made many other field trips from 1883 to 1887, collecting around 18,000 items of folklore, half of them folktales.

Kaarle Krohn's interest in folktales made that genre an obvious choice for the subject of his doctorate, which he earned in 1888, the year his father died. In his dissertation on animal tales, *Bär (Wolf) und Fuchs. Eine nordische Tiermärchenkette,* Krohn applied to folktales the methodology his father had used with the *Kalevala*. Also in 1888 Krohn was appointed docent of Finnish and comparative folklore, the first official academic position in folklore at the University of Helsinki. Ten years later, in 1898, he was named extraordinary personal professor of Finnish and comparative folklore. Only in 1908 was the professorship in folklore regularized.

Krohn's devotion to his father, Julius, was exceptional. Not only did he complete many of his father's unfinished works in progress but he wrote treatises on some of the same subjects, including the *Kalevala*. (Almost all Finnish folklorists ever since have managed to write something about the *Kalevala!*) In 1889 the first international folklore congress was held in Paris, and Krohn's paper "La méthode de M. Jules Krohn" was presented there.

The essay marks the first formal introduction of the Finnish, or "Historic-Geographic," method to the world of international folkloristics.

It is worth noting the evolution of Krohn's choices of the title of the method. In 1889 Krohn called it "the method of Monsieur Jules Krohn," that is, the method of his late father. On January 31, 1909, when Krohn assumed the permanent chair of folklore established at the University of Helsinki in 1908, his inaugural lecture was "Suomalaisesta kansanrunou-dentutkimuksen metodista" [On the Finnish method in folklore research]. The address was published in German in 1910 as "Über die finnische folk-loristische Methode" in *Finnisch-Ugrische Forschungen,* a journal Krohn founded. Thus the method of his father had become the Finnish method.

Krohn continued to perfect the method, and in 1924 he gave a series of invited lectures at the Norwegian Instituttet for Sammenlignende Kultur-forskning in Oslo, published in 1926 under the title *Die folkloristische Ar-beitsmethode, begründet von Julius Krohn und weitergeführt von nor-dischen Forschern.* The method of his father was no longer the Finnish method but had become the "folkloristic method." Further, it was not *a* folkloristic method but *the* folkloristic method. Still, Krohn did insist on having his father's name listed in the full title of his last systematic descrip-tion of the methodology, and, in fact, the first chapter is devoted exclusively to the career and achievements of Julius Krohn.

It is not easy to summarize the Finnish method. Anyone interested is ad-vised to read Krohn's final version, translated into English as *Folklore Meth-odology* (Austin: University of Texas Press, 1971), or to consult any of the numerous historic-geographic studies that have been carried out, usually as doctoral dissertations. First, one assembles as many versions as possible of the item being investigated, including both literary and oral versions (e.g., unpublished versions in folklore archives). This can be an arduous labor, as it will almost certainly entail translating hundreds of versions of the item into the researcher's native language. Each version is given an identifying alphabetical prefix indicating first the general language family to which it belongs and second the specific language. Thus a tale designated CI 1 would refer to the first Celtic and Irish text; CI 2 would be the second text. GD would be Germanic and Danish, and so on. The tale, ballad, or game is then divided into its constituent "traits." Traits can be the actors, the place where the action occurs, the nature of a donor figure, and the like. All variations of each trait are noted and given a separate designation, such as A1, A2, A3. Then all texts are rewritten in terms of their trait characteristics, for exam-ple, A1, B4, C3, D7, and so on. This facilitates the comparison of as many as a thousand versions of a given folktale, ballad, game, or similar item. Without such a system of shorthand coding, it would be virtually impossible to compare hundreds of versions of a tale or ballad type.

Clusters of versions may be ascertained on the basis of a similar, if not identical, configuration of traits. Such clusters may constitute definite subtypes of the original tale or ballad type. Each trait is evaluated separately to determine its hypothetical original form. Criteria used to determine the possible "urform" are historic and geographic, hence the label "historic-geographic" for the methodology. Historic refers to the oldest dated printed texts, perhaps in a literary work; geographic refers to the spread of the trait (often indicated by using a map). Again, the more widespread the trait, the older it is assumed to be. After the urform or archetype of each trait has been determined using both historic and geographic criteria, the series of archetypal traits should, in theory, yield the original form of the tale. It may even be possible to show how different subtypes evolved from the presumed archetype of the tale and perhaps also to trace the paths of diffusion of the tale and its subtypes.

A number of key assumptions are involved in the Finnish method. In reconstructing the supposed original form of a folktale, Krohn assumed that all versions of that tale type were cognate—that is, genetically related—and that they were all derived from one parent archetype. Polygenesis, or independent invention, was possible, according to Krohn, only if one were investigating a single, relatively simple motif—for example, star-crossed lovers jumping off a cliff to avoid being separated by unwelcome arranged marriages by their respective parents. Clusters of two or more motifs occurring in sequence were thought to be the results of monogenesis and diffusion, not polygenesis.

The method has many serious problems. One is limited by the data base. The subsequent discovery of an older literary version with traits different from the presumed archetypal ones may cast doubt on conclusions. The manuscript and printed record go back only so far. Folklore can clearly be much older than the first recorded instance of it in print. There is also the difficulty of contamination from printed sources. Many informants may have learned their versions of an item from a standard collection, for example, the Grimm canon; consequently, statistics of frequency of occurrence of a trait may be a product of the influence of print. Greater collecting activity has occurred in some countries such as Finland and Ireland, so the numbers of texts available may again distort the statistical occurrences of particular traits.

A more fundamental difficulty is one of logistics. Very few libraries contain a sufficient sampling of folklore collections worldwide to permit ambitious comparative studies. It may take several years to complete a full-fledged historic-geographic study (to locate all extant texts, translate them, carry out the trait breakdown of every text, and determine subtypes, the archetype, and possible paths of diffusion), and few students of folklore are willing or able to commit that much time and energy to a project of this scope.

For more details about Lönnrot, see Martti Haavio, "Elias Lönnrot (1802–1884)," *Arv* 25–27 (1969–1971), 1–10. For the Finnish folklore archives, see Jouko Hautala, "The Folklore Archives of the Finnish Literature Society," *Studia Fennica* 7(2) (1957), 3–36. According to 1967 figures, these archives contain 52,400 charms, 96,300 folktales, 103,000 legends, 117,300 riddles, 129,000 rhymed folksongs, 187,000 games, 336,900 popular beliefs and magic practices, and 776,500 proverbs and proverbial phrases. See Gun Herranen and Lassi Saressalo, eds., *A Guide to Nordic Tradition Archives* (Turku: Nordic Institute of Folklore, 1978), 32–42. For the *Kalevala,* see John I. Kolehmainen, *Epic of the North: The Story of Finland's Kalevala* (New York Mills, Minnesota: Northwestern Publishing Company, 1973), and Juha Y. Pentikäinen, *Kalevala Mythology* (Bloomington: Indiana University Press, 1989).

For more information about Kaarle Krohn, see Uno Harva, *Dem Andenken Kaarle Krohns,* FF Communications No. 112 (Helsinki: Academia Scientiarum Fennica, 1934), and especially *Studia Fennica* 11 (1964), which includes essays on his life, his career as a folklorist, and his impact as a teacher. The volume also contains "Kaarle Krohn Bibliography" by Rauni Puranen (3–33). See also Juha Pentikäinen, "Julius and Kaarle Krohn," *Arv* 25–27 (1969–1971), 11–33. For insights into the remarkable history of folklore research in Finland, see Jouko Hautala, *Finnish Folklore Research 1828–1918* (Helsinki: Societas Scientiarum Fennica, 1968), and William A. Wilson, *Folklore and Nationalism in Modern Finland* (Bloomington: Indiana University Press, 1976).

For representative discussions of the Finnish method, see Archer Taylor, "Precursors of the Finnish Method of Folk-Lore Study," *Modern Philology* 25 (1928), 481–491; Walter Anderson, "Geographische-historische Methode," in Lutz Mackensen, ed., *Handwörterbuch des deutschen Märchens,* Vol. 2 (Berlin and Leipzig: Walter de Gruyter, 1934–1940), 508–522; Heda Jason, "The Russian Criticism of the 'Finnish School' in Folktale Scholarship," *Norveg* 14 (1970), 285–294; Bruce A. Rosenberg and John B. Smith, "The Computer and the Finnish Historical-Geographical Method," *Journal of American Folklore* 87 (1974), 149–154; William A. Wilson, "The Evolutionary Premise in Folklore Theory and the 'Finnish Method,' " *Western Folklore* 35 (1976), 241–249; Bertalan Korompay, *Zur finnischen Methode: Gedanken eines Zeitgenossen* (Helsinki: 1978); Christine Goldberg, "The Historic-Geographic Method: Past and Future," *Journal of Folklore Research* 21 (1984), 1–18; and Lutz Röhrich, "Geographisch-historische Methode," in *Enzyklopädie des Märchens,* Band 5 (1987), 1012–1030. For an idea of folklore research in Finland after Krohn, when the emphasis was no longer on origins but rather on function and structure, see Outi Lehtipuro, "Trends in Finnish Folkloristics," *Studia Fennica* 18 (1974), 7–36, and Lauri Honko, "Finnland," in *Enzyklopädie des Märchens,* Band 4 (1984), 1157–1179.

*   *   *

The major work of my late father is a comparative study of the *Kalevala* songs, a study which makes up the first part of his history of Finnish literature. Translated extracts have appeared in the well-known journals of Steinthal and Veckenstedt. A full translation will appear next year.

The studies of the *Kalevala* are of interest internationally because of the connections which are found between the epic Finnish songs on the one hand and the old songs of the Scandinavians, Russians, Lithuanians, on the other.

Of even more general interest is perhaps the method of my late father that I have followed in the interpretation of Finnish folktales compared with similar traditions in every country of the world.

You know that the brothers Grimm considered folktales as the last residue of old myths, that Benfey derived them from literary sources, that Lang searched in them for the remains of the ancient ideas and customs of savages.

But why not accord the folktale the right to form an independent object of scientific study? The mythological interpolations that are found in names such as Frau Holle in the Grimm tales are only chance accidents in the tale and express only a national characteristic. On the other hand, the international character of the folktale consists not only in a common general idea, but in the complication and in the denouement of the action of the entire plot.

An international science of folktale can only be born if the fundamental plot is stripped of every superfluous detail. With such an immense quantity of data, we will nearly drown if we do not have the shortest possible synopses which contain just the principal elements of the action.

But the action of a folktale, as we have found, is often complicated. It is necessary to divide it first of all into simple incidents consisting of a single complication and a single denouement of the action. Each incident is then examined separately.

In order to find the primitive form of an incident, it is first necessary to assemble all the variants, that is to say, all the incidents which present both the same complication and the same denouement. Incidents where the complication alone or the denouement alone are the same might, by chance, be parallel because of the homogeneity of human thought. But a double chance is not likely in the immense world of ideas.

For example, if we find in the Roman de Renard and in an ancient Greek proverb, a peasant who curses lazy cattle by saying to them, "May the bear eat you!" it is always possible that the French and the Greeks have by chance imagined independently something which is very natural. But if we find in the Roman de Renard and in modern folktales of the Greeks, the Russians, the Lithuanians, the Germans, the Scandinavians, the Finns, not only the bear who comes in effect to eat the cursed cattle (simple consequence of the curse), but also the fox "prince hunter!" who makes noise to frighten the credulous bear, and then a man who leads the dogs to the place of the chickens promised to the fox, etc. then it is nearly impossible to pretend that the French, the Greeks, the Russians, the Lithuanians, the Germans, the Scandinavians, the Finns have by chance (by means of the homogeneity of human thought) imagined the same thing so complicated.

The error of Benfey has been to attach the most importance to the first literary redactions of a tale and to accord only a secondary value to more recent folktales collected from people. It is nevertheless evident that the variants collected in our century, thanks to the fidelity of the conservative memory of people, often show forms much older than the most ancient purely literary versions of the same tale.

In the north of Europe, for example, folk variants are conserved in a form more ancient than the legend of Polyphemus or the fables of Renard in Ysengrinus and in the Roman de Renard. Thus, in the comparative study of folktales, all the variants, both literary and folk, must be consulted.

Nevertheless, they cannot be compared in no particular order. Two variants separated one from the other by time or distance may be too removed to show how the action developed without recourse to intermediary forms. It is thus necessary to arrange them in a historical order as much as the ancient literary sources permit; in addition, it is necessary to arrange in a geographical order all the variants recently collected from oral tradition. For the common origin of peoples has little to do with connections of tales whereas geographical proximity and reciprocal relations have much more relevance in spite of the great difference in languages. Folktales have no connection with language, but with culture, that is to say, with civilization.

In order to make a proper comparison in geographic order, it is necessary to have variants from each country, from each province, even from each community.

But it suffices to establish in a single country the direction and the paths of diffusion, as, for example, in Finland where one finds combinations of western and eastern forms of the same tale without there having been a point of transition. In this way, one can already make precise judgments about the diffusion of tales in other countries.

In addition, as the primitive form of an isolated incident is in no place ever preserved in an entirely pure state, a second analysis becomes necessary. One must analyze the actions of the principal elements: actors, objects, means, deeds, etc. and one must follow each element in geographic order in every series of variants in order to find the primitive or ur-form. One needs to observe not only the numbers of variants which are often misleading, but also the paths of diffusion and finally to note those which are the most natural (the idea of naiveté of Keller). It is only by ascertaining the primitive form of each isolated element of action that one can discover the original form of an incident.

And only when this is found is one able to come to a conclusion as to the place of origin, the nationality, the epoch of that origin, the primitive encounters with other incidents, and the general idea which serves as its basis.

It is then, gentlemen, that one will see how much of the mythological imagination is really found in folktales. If, for example, the castle of gold in the tales of northern Europe which is suspended from the sky by chains of gold and which is found behind two seas in the middle of the third exists in the primitive form of the tale, it is the sun which rises from the sea and which sets there. Then, gentlemen, one will see how the savage imagination and savage customs are found in effect in our folktales. For it seems to me that it is there. But I believe that we will find something more; we will find several traits of the history of civilization.

It is a strange thing that all the weapons and tools of the devil, are either of stone or rather gold, that is to say of bronze until man came to know the use of iron. I have been told a Finnish folktale in which a man explains to the devil that iron is much stronger than stone! Is this not the prehistoric struggle between the iron age and the stone or bronze age? The same antagonism is zoomorphized in the folktales of the credulous bear and the clever fox which are of folk origin, European origin, of northern origin.

But the discovery of the primitive form, the place of origin, the nationality, etc., the origin of folktales in general, is not all, nor is it the most interesting thing that the geographic comparative study of folktales offers. That which is perhaps even more important is the study of the changes that the original form has undergone in its peregrinations. You know that all the changes to do with language rest on physiological and absolute grammatical laws, or ought to be explained by analogy. In the same way, all the changes in the variegated texture of folktales are governed by fixed laws of thought and fantasy.

Among the limited number of laws, one can cite:
The forgetting of a detail; the adoption of an unknown theme; the generalization of specific description; the confusion of characters or actions; multiplication, especially with the numbers 3, 5, and 7; polyzooism, where several animals figure in place of one, anthropomorphism and zoomorphism, or the author himself fills the role of the hero, etc.

There is also the tendency to add to an incident interpolated episodes, to embellish it with an introduction, to end it gracefully with a final refrain, and in general expand as much as possible the thread of the story. It is this tendency toward expansion which combines several incidents into a single folktale. For the fantasy found among the people of today creates little that is new; rather it borrows nearly all the additions from materials already in existence, in combining a fragment of an incident or an entire incident to another fragment or to another whole incident. This joining together, naturally, is not without influence on the portions so united which are subjected to the majority of the most dramatic changes in order to produce a harmonious whole.

One must therefore attribute a large portion of the changes and alterations of an incident to the influence of another incident with which it has been combined.

This kind of change corresponds in language with the changes in phonemes caused by their proximity to other phonemes.

Finally, one must cite also changes by analogy, corresponding to changes *"ex analogia"* in language, or an incident ruled by a group of incidents.

The importance of the study of folktales is also great, if not greater than for the history of civilization as for the psychology of peoples. For it shows us the paths by which the tales are passed from one people to another verbally, not only by literature, but also from mouth to mouth.

We find in them certain proofs of the intellectual influence of one people upon another. For it is always worth recalling that folktales march in step, not with languages, but with civilization.

And just as little of our culture is derived from a single nation, from a single race, so, similarly, few folktales come from the creative genius of a single people, be they Indian or Eygptian; they are, rather, common property, achieved by a joint effort of the entire world, more or less civilized, and are thus a part of international science.

7

The Message of the Folk-Lorist

W. B. Yeats

One of the perpetually pressing problems in folkloristics concerns the proper way to present field data. From the social scientific perspective, there is no question that the ipsissima verba of informants should be reported as accurately as is humanly possible, whether taken down in some kind of shorthand or faithfully transcribed in tedious detail from recordings. Without such verbatim transcriptions, folklore cannot really serve as authentic data for the serious study of values and worldview. From a more literary viewpoint, however, folklore often appears to represent inspirational raw data that seems to require some reworking and fine-tuning to satisfy the aesthetic taste and artistic sensibilities of the nonscholarly public.

Professional folklorists have no objection to the creative use of folklore by artists, composers, and writers. Quite the contrary: the artistic utilization of folklore attests to its power and beauty. Moreover, even if folklorists did object, there would be no conceivable way they could stop anyone from recasting a folk melody, a legend, or a traditional image into a sonata, a novel, or a painting. But folklorists do object when authentic folklore, collected from bona fide informants, is altered (under the guise of "improving" it) and bowdlerized (ostensibly to protect an unwary prospective audience from being "shocked") and this ersatz fabrication is presented to the public as genuine folklore. This is what folklorists term "fakelore," not folklore. (The term "fakelore" was coined by American folklorist Richard M. Dorson (1916–1981) in 1950; see his *American Folklore and the Historian* (Chicago: University of Chicago Press, 1971), 3–14.

One of the first attempts to wrestle with this problem was made by William Butler Yeats (1865–1939), a man of letters and arguably one of the greatest poets of the twentieth century but not a scholar. In 1923 he was awarded the coveted Nobel Prize in literature. But he had a lifelong love of Irish folklore that not only proved to be a critical influence on his poems and plays but that he also enjoyed and studied for its own sake. When Yeats was asked in 1887 to compile a book of Irish folktales, he did do some fieldwork, spending summer 1887 in Sligo collecting oral traditions, but he devoted more time to reading published collections. His knowledge of spoken Gaelic was slight, and he tended to rely almost completely on English translations of Irish data. In his books *Fairy and Folk Tales of the Irish Peasantry* (1888) and the shorter sequel, *Irish Fairy Tales* (1892), Yeats borrowed freely from previously published works of others.

One source Yeats found disappointing was the organ of the English Folklore Society, the *Folk Lore Journal*. In a letter to Douglas Hyde (1860–1949) on July 11, 1888, asking for help in locating suitable sources for his forthcoming anthology of folktales, Yeats said, "*The Folk Lore Journal* . . . turns out useless, for scientific people cannot tell stories." Yeats said much the same thing in print. In a letter to the editor of *The Academy,* dated October 2, 1890, and published in the October 11 issue, Yeats expanded on his remark to Hyde and at the same time praised Hyde, whom he had known since college and very much admired:

I deeply regret when I find that some folk-lorist is merely scientific, and lacks the needful subtle imaginative sympathy to tell his stories well. There are innumerable little turns of expression and quaint phrases that in the mouth of a peasant give half the meaning, and often the whole charm. The man of science is too often a person who has exchanged his soul for a formula; and when he captures a folk-tale, nothing remains with him for all his trouble but a wretched lifeless thing with the down rubbed off and a pin thrust through its once all-living body. I object to the "honest folk-lorist," not because his versions are accurate, but because they are inaccurate, or rather incomplete. What lover of Celtic lore has not been filled with a sacred rage when he came upon some exquisite story, dear to him from childhood, written out in newspaper English and called science? To me, the ideal folklorist is Mr. Douglas Hyde. A tale told by him is quite as accurate as any "scientific" person's rendering; but in dialect and so forth he is careful to give us the most quaint, or poetical, or humorous version he has heard. I am inclined to think also that some concentration and elaboration of dialect is justified, if only it does not touch the fundamentals of the story. It is but a fair equivalent for the gesture and voice of the peasant tale-teller. Mr. Hyde has, I believe, done this in his marvelous Teig O'Kane, with the result that we have a story more full of the characteristics of true Irish folk-lore than all the pages given to Ireland from time to time in the *Folk-lore Journal.*

Yeats was right to praise Hyde. His book *Beside the Fire: A Collection of Irish Gaelic Folk Stories* (London: David Nutt, 1890) is a superb set of texts reported in both Gaelic and English translation. Hyde founded the Gaelic League in 1893 and later became the first president of the modern Irish republic (1937–1945). This is perhaps the only instance of a folklorist becoming the president of a country, and accordingly it is a stunning illustration of the connection between folklore and nationalism. In a letter to Katharine Tynan in September 1888, Yeats wrote, "Hyde is the best of all the Irish folklorists—His style is perfect—so sincere and simple—so little literary." Yeats repeated the sentiment to Hyde himself in a letter of August 23, 1889: "For I firmly believe . . . that you are the one great Folklorist Ireland has produced."

In fact, Yeats was not altogether happy that Hyde had forsaken folklore for politics. In his *Autobiography* Yeats, after remarking that Hyde had created "a great popular movement, far more important in its practical results than any movement I could have made," commented, "I mourn for the 'greatest folkloreist who ever lived.' " See *The Autobiography of William Butler Yeats* (New York: Collier Books, 1965), 147; for details of Hyde's career in politics, see Janet Egleson Dunleavy and Gareth W. Dunleavy, *Douglas Hyde: A Maker of Modern Ireland* (Berkeley: University of California Press, 1991).

Yeats's admiration for Hyde notwithstanding, generally speaking Yeats much preferred folklore to folklorists. His respect for folklore is revealed in his disparagement of writers who chose to ignore the folklore around them. Yeats took the occasion of reviewing a book entitled *The Ghost World* (1893), written by a minor English folklorist, the Reverend T. F. Thiselton Dyer (1848–1928), to articulate his strong opinions on folklore and folklorists. (The same author compiled *English Folk-Lore* (1878), *Folk-Lore of Shakespeare* (1883), and *Folk-Lore of Women* (1905), among other works.) This review essay, entitled "The Message of the Folk-Lorist," was published in *The Speaker* on August 19, 1893. A number of Yeats's most eloquent and rhapsodic comments on folklore and folklorists appeared in his reviews of books. Many are contained in his *Writings on Irish Folklore, Legend, and Myth,* edited by Robert Welch (London: Penguin, 1993).

In view of Yeats's undisguised dislike of "scientific" folklorists, it is somewhat ironic that folklorist Edward Clodd (1840–1930) invited him to provide commentary on several Irish superstitions contained in a note by Bryan J. Jones, "Traditions and Superstitions Collected at Kilcurry, County Louth, Ireland," published in *Folklore* 10 (1899), 119–122. Yeats's brief commentary on ten of the eleven superstitions presented served as an addendum to the note. See *Folklore* 10 (1899), 122–123. (For more details on Yeats's relationship to Clodd, see Genevieve Brennan, "Yeats, Clodd, *Scatalogic Rites* and the Clonmel Witch Burning," *Yeats Annual* 4 [1986], 207–215.)

Considerable scholarship is devoted to Yeats's involvement with folklore. See, for example, his son Michael Yeats's "W. B. Yeats and Irish Folk Song," *Southern Folklore Quarterly* 31 (1966), 153–178; Birgit Bramsback, "William Butler Yeats and Folklore Material," *Béaloideas* 39–41 (1971–1973),

56–68; Neil R. Grobman, "In Search of a Mythology: William Butler Yeats and Folklore," *New York Folklore Quarterly* 30 (1974), 117–136; and Mary Helen Thuente, "W. B. Yeats and Nineteenth-Century Folklore," *Journal of Irish Literature* 6 (1977), 64–79, and especially her book *W. B. Yeats and Irish Folklore* (Dublin: Gill and Macmillan, 1980). See also Steven D. Putzel, "Towards an Aesthetic of Folklore and Mythology: W. B. Yeats, 1888–1895," *Southern Folklore Quarterly* 44 (1980), 105–130; and Warwick Gould, "Frazer, Yeats, and the Reconsecration of Folklore," in Robert Fraser, ed., *Sir James Frazer and the Literary Imagination* (New York: St. Martin's, 1990), 121–153.

For the record, it should probably be mentioned that some "scientific" folklorists have been highly critical of Yeats on the grounds that he played fast and loose with his sources—sources which were not always properly acknowledged. See Russell K. Alspach, "The Use by Yeats and Other Irish Writers of the Folklore of Patrick Kennedy," *Journal of American Folklore* 59 (1946), 404–412; John V. Kelleher, "Yeats' Use of Irish Materials," *Tri-Quarterly* 4 (1965), 115–125; Sheila O'Sullivan, "W. B. Yeats's Use of Irish Oral and Literary Tradition," *Béaloideas* 39–41 (1971–1973), 266–279; Kevin Danaher, "Folk Tradition and Literature," *The Journal of Irish Literature* 1(2) (1972), 63–76; and F. Kinahan, "Armchair Folklore: Yeats and the Textual Sources of *Fairy and Folk Tales of the Irish Peasantry*," *Proceedings of the Royal Irish Academy* 83c (1983), 255–267. Sometimes the judgments are harsh, damning with only the faintest praise. Kelleher claims that although one of Yeats's notes "is mainly a frustrating mishmash of misremembered misquotation of bad nineteenth century pseudo-learning, at the very bottom there is a stratum of genuine folk-belief." Folklorist Danaher is less forgiving: "W. B. Yeats, it is to be feared, often blunders. He himself dabbled in folk lore, but he all too often brings into his poems, and even into his prose, an air of mystical moonshine which is very far from the clear black and white of folk tradition. . . . Indeed, it is hard to find anything Irish in Mr. Yeats, or anything of the ordinary people with whom, indeed, he had sympathy, but whom he never understood."

*   *   *

THE MESSAGE OF THE FOLK-LORIST.

In one of his unpublished watercolour illustrations to Young's "Night Thoughts," William Blake has drawn a numberless host of spirits and fairies affirming the existence of God. Out of every flower and every grass-blade comes a little creature lifting its right hand above its head. It is possible that the books of folk-lore, coming in these later days from almost every country in the world, are bringing the fairies and the spirits to our study tables that we may witness a like affirmation, and see innumerable hands lifted testifying to the ancient supremacy of imagination. Imagination is God in the world of art, and may well desire to have us come to an issue with the atheists who would make us "realists," "naturalists," or the like.

Folk-lore is at once the Bible, the Thirty-nine Articles, and the Book of Common Prayer, and well-nigh all the great poets have lived by its light. Homer, Æschylus, Sophocles, Shakespeare, and even Dante, Goethe, and Keats, were little more than folk-lorists with musical tongues. The root-stories of the Greek poets are told to-day at the cabin fires of Donegal; the Slavonian peasants tell their children now, as they did a thousand years before Shakespeare was born, of the spirit prisoned in the cloven pine; the Swedes had need neither of Dante nor Spenser to tell them of the living trees that cry or bleed if you break off a bough; and through all the long backward and abysm of time, Faust, under many names, has signed the infernal compact, and girls at St. Agnes' Eve have waited for visions of their lovers to come to them "upon the honeyed middle of the night." It is only in these latter decades that we have refused to learn of the poor and the simple, and turned atheists in our pride. The folk-lore of Greece and Rome lasted us a long time; but having ceased to be a living tradition, it became both worn out and unmanageable, like an old servant. We can now no more get interest in the gods of Olympus than we can in the stories told by the showman of a travelling waxwork company. For lack of those great typical personages who flung the thunderbolts or had serpents in their hair, we have betaken ourselves in a hurry to the poetry of cigarettes and black coffee, of absinthe, and the skirt dance, or are trying to persuade the lecture and the scientific book to look, at least to the eye, like the old poems and dramas and stories that were in the ages of faith long ago. But the countless little hands are lifted and the affirmation has begun.

There is no passion, no vague desire, no tender longing that cannot find fit type or symbol in the legends of the peasantry or in the traditions of the scolds and the gleemen. And these traditions are now being gathered up or translated by a whole army of writers. The most recent of books upon the subject—"The Ghost World" (War & Downey)—is neither a translation nor a collection of tales gathered among the people by its author, but one of those classifications and reviews of already collected facts of which we stand in great need. Its author, Mr. T. F. Thiselton Dyer, treats as exhaustively as his four hundred odd pages permit him with the beliefs about ghosts held in every part of the world. The outside of the book is far from comely to look at, and the inside is that mixture of ancient beauty and modern commonplace one has got used to in books by scientific folk-lorists. Mr. Dyer collects numbers of the most entirely lovely and sacred, or tragic and terrible, beliefs in the world, and sets them side by side, transfixed with diverse irrelevancies—in much the same fashion that boys stick moths and butterflies side by side upon a door, with long pins in their bodies. At other times he irritates by being hopelessly inadequate, as when he follows a story of priceless beauty with the remark that "these folk-tales are interesting as embodying the superstitions of the people among whom they are current." But then no one expects the scientific folk-lorist to have a tongue of music, and this one gives us a great deal less of himself than the bulk of his tribe, and has the good taste to gird at no man—not even the poor spiritualist.

He deals in thirty-one chapters with such subjects as "The Soul's Exit," "The Temporary Exit of the Soul," "The Nature of the Soul," "Why Ghosts Wander," "Phantom Birds," "Animal Ghosts," "Phantom Music," and the like. The pages upon the state of the soul after death are particularly interesting and have as much of the heart's blood of poetry as had ever Dis or Hades. Jacob Boehme held that every man was represented by a symbolic beast or bird, and that these beasts and birds varied with the characters of men, and in the folk-lore of almost every country, the ghosts revisit the earth as horses or butterflies, as doves or ravens, or in some other representative shape. Sometimes only voices are heard. The Zulu sorcerer, Mr. Dyer says, "hears the spirits, who speak by whistlings, speaking to him," while the Algonquin Indians of North America "could hear the shadow souls of the dead chirp like crickets." In Denmark, he adds, the night ravens are held to be exorcised evil spirits who are for ever flying towards the East, for if they can reach the Holy Sepulchre they will be at rest; and "In the Saemund Edda it is said that in the nether world singed souls fly about like swarms of flies." He might have quoted here the account in the old Irish romance called "The Voyage of Maclunds" of this great saint who dwelt upon the wooded island among the flocks of holy birds who were the souls of his relations, awaiting the blare of the last trumpet. Folk-lore makes the souls of the blessed take upon themselves every evening the shape of white birds, and whether it put them into such charming shape or not, is ever anxious to keep us from troubling their happiness with our grief. Mr. Dyer tells, for instance, the story of a girl who heard a voice speaking from the grass-plot of her lover, and saying, "Every time a tear falls from thine eyes, my shroud is full of blood. Every time thy heart is gay, my shroud is full of rose leaves."

All these stories are such as to unite man more closely to the woods and hills and waters about him, and to the birds and animals that live in them, and to give him types and symbols for those feelings and passions which find no adequate expression in common life. Could there be any expression of Nature-worship more tender and lovely than that tale of the Indians who lived once by the river Pascajoula, which Mr. Dyer tells in his chapter on "Phantom Music"? Strange musical sounds were said to come out of the river at one place, and close to this place the Indians had set up an idol representing the water spirit who made the music. Every night they gathered about the image and played to it sweet tunes upon many stringed instruments, for they held it to love all music. One day a priest came and tried to convert them from the worship of this spirit, and might have succeeded; but one night the water was convulsed, and the convulsion drew the whole tribe to the edge of the river to hear music more lovely than the spirit ever sang before. They listened until one plunged into the river in his ecstasy and sank for ever, and then men, women and children—the whole tribe—plunged after him, and left a world that had begun to turn from the ancient ways.

The greatest poets of every nation have drawn from stories like this, symbols and events to express the most lyrical, the most subjective moods. In modern days there has been one great poet who tried to express such moods without adequate knowledge of folk-lore. Most of us feel, I think, no matter how greatly we admire him, that there is something of over-much cloud and rainbow in the poetry of Shelley, and is not this simply because he lacked the true symbols and types and stories to express his intense subjective inspiration? Could he have been as full of folk-lore as was Shakespeare, or even Keats, he might have delivered his message and yet kept as close to our hearthstone as did the one in "The Tempest" and "Midsummer Night's Dream," or as did the others in "The Eve of St. Agnes;" but as it is, there is a world of difference between Puck and Peasblossom and the lady who waited for "The honeyed middle of the night" upon the one hand and the spirits of the hour and the evil voices of Prometheus upon the other. Shakespeare and Keats had the folk-lore of their own day, while Shelley had but mythology; and a mythology which has been passing for long through literary minds without any new influx from living tradition loses all the incalculable instructive and convincing quality of the popular traditions. No conscious invention can take the place of tradition, for he who would write a folk tale, and thereby bring a new life into literature, must have the fatigue of the spade in his hands and the stupors of the fields in his heart. Let us listen humbly to the old people telling their stories, and perhaps God will send the primitive excellent imagination into the midst of us again. Why should we be either "naturalists" or "realists?" Are not those little right hands lifted everywhere in affirmation?

W. B. YEATS.

8

On the Need for a Bibliography of Folklore

Giuseppe Pitrè

In almost every country of the world are dedicated individuals—some amateur, some professional—who have devoted their lives to the collection and study of folklore. The vast majority report their findings exclusively in their native languages, and if those languages are not ones customarily used in international scholarship (e.g., English, French, German), the remarkable efforts of these indefatigable researchers tend to be little known outside the confines of their home area.

There are dozens of such folklore collectors. Oskar Kolberg (1814–1890) published thirty-three volumes of folklore beginning in 1857. Each volume treats a different geographic region of Poland. The entire set of volumes contains more than 10,000 folk melodies, for example. He also collected approximately 13,000 proverbs. Kolberg left materials that have been published posthumously; as a result, his collected works run to around eighty-six volumes. But unless one reads Polish, Kolberg's materials are not easily accessible.

Another example is Pastor Jakob Hurt of Estonia (1839–1907), who organized over 1,000 assistants to help him but was himself an avid collector. In 1903 an old female singer, Miko-Ode, sang an amazing 20,720 lines of song for him. Hurt's Estonian materials include around 25,000 tales, 75,000 riddles, 110,000 proverbs, and 70,000 folksongs (with 15,000 melodies). (See W. F. Kirby, "On the Progress of Folk-Lore Collections in Esthonia, with Special Reference to the Work of Pastor Jakob Hurt," in *The International Folk-Lore Congress 1891* (London: David Nutt, 1892), 427–429; Kaarle Krohn, "Jakob Hurt (1839–1907)," *Anzeiger der Finnisch-Ugrischen Forschungen* 7 (1907), 72–76; Oskar Th. Kallas, "Estonian Folklore," *Folklore* 34 (1923), 101–116; and Oskar Loorits, "Estonian Folklore of Today," *Acta Ethnologica* 1 (1936), 34–52.) These data are in Estonian.

Another example is provided by Kunio Yanagita (1875–1962), the founder of folkloristics in Japan. His major works have been published in a set of thirty–six volumes, but except for a very occasional essay that was translated into German, such as "Die japanische Volkskunde. Ihre Vorgeschichte, Entwicklung und gegenwärtige Lage" (*Folklore Studies* 3 [1944]:1–76), Yanagita's materials remain closed to anyone unable to read Japanese. (See Ronald A. Morse, *Yanagita Kunio and the Folklore Movement* (New York: Garland, 1990).

Sometimes the accessibility issue is exacerbated by the fact that the materials are reported (as they should be!) in dialect. This is the case with one of the greatest folklore collectors ever, E. Tang Kristensen (1843–1929). In his home area of Jutland in Denmark, he collected abundant examples of virtually every genre of folklore. He provided informant data, including pictures, and without modern recording technology he managed through a self-devised system of shorthand to take down texts verbatim.

Kristensen's published works come to seventy-nine volumes. This corpus includes a thirteen-volume work, *Jydske Folkeminder* [Jutland folklore] (1871–1897), consisting of four books of ballads, four books of folktales, and five volumes of beliefs and legends. Between 1891 and 1894 Kristensen published six volumes of *Gamle folks fortaellinger om det jyske almueliv* [Old people's reports on Jutland folklife], followed by six supplementary volumes (1900–1905)—amounting to around 2,700 pages of detailed descriptions of Jutland peasant daily life. Between 1892 and 1901 he published seven volumes of *Danske Sagn* [Danish legends]. A supplementary series of six more legend collections was begun in 1928 but was not completed until 1939, ten years after his death. These thirteen volumes contain approximately 22,000 legends, the bulk of which were collected by Kristensen. This work alone would have constituted a major achievement, but it does not do justice to Kristensen's incredible productivity. Other books include *Danske ordsprog og mundheld* [Danish proverbs and idioms] (1890), 658pp.; *Danske Bornerim, Remser og Lege* [Danish children's rhymes, jingles, and plays] (1896), 752pp.; and *Danske Folkegaader* [Danish folk riddles] (1913), 320pp. This brief summary does not mention his hundreds of articles or his four-volume autobiography, *Minder og Oplevelser* [Memoirs and experiences] (1923–1928).

Kristensen's folktales provided the data base for Bengt Holbek's magnum opus, *Interpretation of Fairy Tales: Danish Folklore in a European Perspective*, FF Communications No. 239 (Helsinki: Academia Scientiarum Fennica, 1987), and his legends did likewise for Timothy R. Tangherlini's *Interpreting Legend: Danish Storytellers and Their Repertoires* (New York: Garland, 1994). Both Holbek and Tangherlini had to decipher Kristensen's idiosyncratic shorthand and deal with Jutland dialect. For more about Kristensen, see W. A. Craigie, "Evald Tang Kristensen, A Danish Folklorist,"

Folklore 9 (1898), 194–224; Bengt Holbek and Thorkild Knudsen, "Evald Tang Kristensen (1843–1929)," *Arv* 25–26 (1969–1970), 257; and Joan Rockwell, *Evald Tang Kristensen: A Lifelong Adventure in Folklore* (Aalborg: Aalborg University Press, 1982).

One might think no folklore collector could possibly match Kristensen's record of accomplishment, but Giuseppe Pitrè (1841–1916) carried out a program of collecting folklore in his native Sicily similar to that Kristensen employed in Jutland. Unlike Kristensen, however, Pitrè made a point of becoming an international folklorist. For this reason, he deserves an honored place in the history of international folkloristics.

Born into a fisherman's family in the Santa Lucia quarter of Palermo on December 22, 1841, Pitrè was only six when his father, Salvatore, died in New Orleans of yellow fever. At age nineteen he enrolled in the Faculty of Medicine and Surgery at the University of Palermo, graduating five years later in 1865. His practice really began with a cholera epidemic in 1868, but by that time he had already become heavily involved in collecting Sicilian folklore. All his life he felt divided between his chosen profession of medicine and his passion, the folklore of Sicily. In a letter dated February 3, 1874, Pitrè spoke of this conflict: "My nature and inclination drive me towards the study of dialect, but the necessity of earning a living constrains me to the sickbed in the midst of all the misery and grief of languishing humanity. Every evil results in some good, and it is thus that I have been able to collect, to resuscitate in myself those traditions which are such a great part of my poor studies. *Io vivo del popolo e col popolo* [I live among and with the people]." The fact that Pitrè was a doctor and that he practiced medicine in the poorer quarters of his native Palermo proved helpful to his folklore research. His patients trusted him and had reason to be grateful to him and thus were willing to share their traditions with him.

It is not easy to summarize Pitrè's remarkable accomplishments. He founded and coedited a major folklore journal, the *Archivio per lo studio delle tradizioni popolari*, which ran to twenty-four volumes (1882–1906), and he edited sixteen volumes of the *Curiosità popolari tradizionali* (1885–1899), but these activities reflected more his involvement in library scholarship than his work as a field collector. Pitrè's own extraordinary collections of Sicilian folklore appeared in his twenty-five-volume *Biblioteca delle tradizioni popolari siciliana* (1872–1913). The volumes cover almost every conceivable aspect of Sicilian folklore and include faithfully recorded data accompanied by comparative notes and often a monographic introductory essay. The titles of the *Biblioteca* volumes reveal the breadth of Pitrè's folklore collection:

Vols. 1–2	Sicilian folksongs
Vol. 3	Studies on folk poetry

Vols. 4–7   Folktales
Vols. 8–11   Proverbs
Vol. 12   Spectacles and Sicilian folk festivals
Vol. 13   Children's games
Vols. 14–17   Customs, beliefs, and superstitions
Vol. 18   Legends
Vol. 19   Folk medicine
Vol. 20   Riddles, tonguetwisters
Vol. 21   Patron saints' festivals
Vol. 22   Studies on legends
Vol. 23   Proverbs, mottoes, and oaths
Vol. 24   Posters, satirical songs, and customs
Vol. 25   The family, home, and life of Sicilian folk

The richness of Pitrè's data must be sampled to be believed. For example, his volume on children's games includes descriptions of more than 300 games, with Sicilian and Italian variants for each. He was also interested in material folklore, as a catalog of a museum exhibit he organized attests; see his *Catalogo Illustrato della Mostra Etnografica Siciliana* (Palermo: Stabilimento Tipografico Virzi, 1892, reprinted 1993). As a collector-editor Pitrè was adamant that none of the folklore he recorded be altered. Indeed, he criticized colleagues who could not resist the temptation to "improve" upon oral tradition.

Pitrè very much appreciated his informants, especially those whose love of folklore rivaled his own. His portrait of one of his principal informants, an illiterate seamstress named Agatuzza Messia who once worked in the Pitrè household as a maid-servant, may serve as an illustration. (This portrait is found in the introduction to the fourth volume of his *Biblioteca*, pp. xviii–xix.)

Anything but pretty, she has a facile tongue, a way with words, an engaging manner of narrating which makes one marvel at her extraordinary memory and here natural talent. Now in her seventies, Messia is a mother, grandmother, and great-grandmother. As a young girl, she heard tales told by her grandmother who had learned them from her mother who in turn had learned an infinite number of little stories and tales from one of her grandfathers. She had a good memory and never forgot them. There are women who have heard hundreds of stories but who can't remember a single one; and there are others who can remember them but who don't have the gift of storytelling. Among her friends of the Borgo district or, as the people say, quarter of Palermo, she enjoys a reputation as an exceptional storyteller—the more you heard her, the more you wanted to hear her. . . .

Messia cannot read but she knows so many things that no one else does and she recounts them so beautifully that it is a pleasure to listen to her. This is one of her characteristics that I would like to call to the attention of my readers. If the story is set on board a ship about to set sail, she, without seeming to notice or thinking about it, speaks using nautical phrases and vocabulary that only sailors or those who have to do with seafaring folk would know. And if the heroine of the tale arrives, poor and forlorn, at the house of a baker, looking for lodging, the language of Messia is so authentic with respect to that trade that you would think that she herself was doing the work, and baking the bread, even though in Palermo this job . . . is done exclusively by professional bakers. No need to mention domestic service, for this is where Messia is in her element; she is a woman, who like all her neighbors has brought up her own children and the children of her children "to serve the home and the Lord" as they say.

Messia witnessed my birth and has held me in her arms: that is the reason why I was able to gather from her lips the many beautiful traditions that bear her name. She repeated to the young man the tales she had told him as a little boy thirty years before. Nor had her narration lost a bit of its old forthrightness, ease, and elegance. He who reads them will find only cold, bare words, but Messia's narratives consist of much more than her choice of vocabulary; it includes the restless movements of her eyes, the waving of her arms, the movement of the entire body which rises, turns around the room, bends, lifts, making the voice weary, now excited, now frightened, now sweet, now stridulant, as she portrays the voices of the characters and their actions. Messia's ability to mimic is a special feature of her storytelling; without it, the narrative would lose half of its force and effect. Fortunately, her language remains as it is, full of natural inspiration and images drawn from all sorts of outside sources. In this way, abstract things become concrete, the invisible is given form, and things which had never before had life—or if they did, it was only a long time ago—come alive and speak.

An additional facet of Pitrè's contribution to international folkloristics is his appreciation of the critical importance of bibliography. After twelve years of work, Pitrè published his *Bibliografia delle Tradizioni Popolari d'Italia* in 1894, possibly the first major book-length bibliography of folklore published in any country. Its 608 pages list approximately 6,680 entries that cover the study of folklore in Italy up to the early 1890s. Pitrè continued to keep track of items after 1894 and planned to issue a supplement. Unfortunately, this did not occur in his lifetime, and the impact of two world wars delayed the publication of the supplement for nearly a century. The two-volume supplement was finally published as *Tradizioni Popolari d'Italia Bibliografia* (Palermo: Edikronos, 1985, 1987) and its 849 pages include 10,103 entries. Thanks to Pitrè's exemplary efforts and several subsequent works, e.g., Paolo Toschi, *Bibliografia delle tradizioni popolari d'Italia dal 1916 al 1940* (Florence: Barbera, 1946), and Alessandro Falassi, *Italian Folklore: An Annotated Bibliography* (New York: Garland, 1985), folklorists have ready access to the bulk of Italian folklore scholarship.

One indication of Pitrè's understanding of the vital importance of bibliography for international folkloristics is revealed in a letter he wrote on September 5, 1900, six years after his _Bibliografia_ had been published. The occasion was an international folklore congress held in Paris in mid-September 1900. (This was the fourth such congress; the first was also held in Paris in 1889, the second was held in London in 1891, and the third convened in Chicago in 1893.) Pitrè did not attend, but he sent a letter to French folklorist Paul Sébillot (1846–1918), the principal organizer of the congress, and asked him to communicate its contents to the congress participants. The letter, "Sur La Necessité d'une Bibliographie des Traditions Populaires," was published in the proceedings of the congress in 1902 (it also appeared in the _Archivio per lo Studio delle Tradizioni Popolari_ in 1901).

Pitrè's plea for an international cooperative effort to produce an international folklore bibliography did not go unheeded. After several sporadic, abortive attempts (e.g., annual lists of folklore journal contents such as three volumes of the _Volkskundliche Zeitschriftenschau,_ published as supplements to the _Hessische Blätter für Volkskunde,_ Vols. 3–5 [1903–1905], and two fascicles of a Flemish periodical, _Biekorf,_ Vols. 20 [1909] and 21 [1910], entitled _Volkskundige Boekenschouw,_ or _Bibliographia "Folklorica"_), Swiss folklorist Eduard Hoffmann-Krayer (1864–1936) began the _Internationale Volkskundliche Bibliographie_ in 1917, which remains the major annual worldwide listing of folklore books and articles, thereby fulfilling Pitrè's hopes.

Hoffmann-Krayer, one of the founders of Swiss folkloristics, is perhaps best known for his pithy dictum "Die Volksseele produziert nicht, sie reproduziert," which appeared in his "Naturgesetz im Volksleben?" _Hessische Blätter für Volkskunde_ 2 [1903]: 57–67. This idea that "the folk doesn't produce but only reproduces" contends that items of folklore are always created by individuals, not by a collective entity. Once created, these creations are re-created as an inevitable result of the transmission process as the item moves from person to person. Hoffmann-Krayer thereby anticipated American folklorist Phillips Barry's similar notion; see "Communal Re-Creation," _Bulletin of the Folk-Song Society of the Northeast_ 5 (1933), 4–6. For an appreciation of Hoffmann-Krayer, see Hermann Bausinger, "Eduard Hoffmann-Krayer—Leistung und Wirkung," _Zeitschrift für Deutsche Philologie_ 85 (1966):431–447, and Regina Bendix, _In Search of Authenticity: The Formation of Folklore Studies_ (Madison: University of Wisconsin Press, 1997), 103–118. For an account giving the history of the _Internationale Volkskundliche Bibliographie,_ see Rolf Wilhelm Brednich, "The International Folklore Bibliography," _International Folklore Review_ 1 (1981), 17–21.

It took some time for Pitrè's countrymen to recognize his many accomplishments. In fact, it was not until 1911 that Pitrè was given a professorship at the University of Palermo, where he taught until 1915. The chair was technically in "demopsicologia" (demopsychology), a would-be alternative to folklore, but Pitrè's inaugural lecture upon assuming the chair was entitled "Che Cos'e il Folklore?" [What is folklore?]. For references to this and other writings of Pitrè, see Giuseppe d'Anna, *Bibliografia degli Scritti di Giuseppe Pitrè* (Rome: Bulzoni Editore, 1993), which includes 473 annotated entries plus more than 800 book reviews written by Pitrè. For representative appreciations of Pitrè, see Giuseppe Cocchiara, *Giuseppe Pitrè e le Tradizioni Popolari* (Palermo: F. Ciuni, 1941); Giuseppe Bonomo, *Pitrè la Sicilia e i siciliani* (Palermo: Sellerio, 1989); and especially the proceedings of a conference held in 1966, fifty years after Pitrè's death, *Pitrè e Salomone Marino* (Palermo: S. F. Flaccovio, 1968).

Pitrè's international outlook is also attested to by his correspondence with folklorists in other countries. For a sample of six of the forty-nine cards and letters he wrote to Reinhold Köhler, see Rudolf Schenda, "Sizilianische Fiabe in Weimar, Deutsche Märchen in Palermo: Anmerkungen zu sechs Briefen von Giuseppe Pitrè an Reinhold Köhler," *Lares* 59 (1993), 679–698. He was also in contact with Machado y Alvarez (1846–1893), the founder of Spanish folkloristics; see Jole Trupia Scavone, "Lettere di Antonio Machado y Alvarez a Pitrè," *Lares* 45 (1979), 183–226. For evidence of Pitrè's continuing importance to the study of traditional Sicilian culture, see Aurelio Rigoli, "La recherche ethnoanthropologique en Sicile contemporaine et la 'Bibliotheque des traditions populaires' de Giuseppe Pitrè," *Ethnologia Europaea* 13 (1982–1983), 28–36, and a more critical view in Nancy Triolo, "Mediterranean Exotica and the Mafia 'Other' or Problems of Representation in Pitrè's Texts," *Cultural Anthropology* 8 (1993), 303–316.

*   *   *

To: Monsieur Paul Sébillot, Secretary General of the International Congress of Folklore

As an Italian folklorist moved by an untiring love of the work of science, I take part in spirit in the Folklore Congress which is about to take place in Paris. I take I take part there in my name as author of works on demopsychology; I take part as editor of the *Archivio per lo studio per le tradizioni popolari* which is the oldest of the journals of traditions and customs. Not being able to come in person to Paris, I ask you, my dear Monsieur Sébillot, to represent our *Archivio* which you can do with great authority.

I have no doubt that the important questions listed in the program will be studied and discussed, and I am certain that the Congress will afford more than enough time to demonstrate the variety of our subject matter and the competence of the theoretical framework which recommend our new and still young science. The younger scholars will learn to appreciate just how important is this new branch of science which occupies a place between ethnography and linguistics, and which provides a powerful aid to anthropology, sociology, and history. Those who are further along in their careers will be happy to see their Herculean labors appreciated and commented upon, works which still today have been considered as matters of little importance and regarded almost as ravings and delusions.

But after an affirmation so new, I do not wish to fail to speak of something already old and therefore I would like to draw the attention of the Congress to the need of a bibliography of folklore of various nations. At the time of the Chicago Congress, I had written a letter to the late Fletcher S. Bassett to insist on the need of an international effort which would inventory the publications of France, England, Germany, Russia, etc. You see that my proposal is not new and you, my very distinguished friend, you have given a fine example in publishing several fragments of this kind of thing for France, work which one would like to see completed and published in its entirety; for England, there has been a beginning by Monsieur Gomme in *Folk-Lore;* Italy has the good fortune to have a more complete work, but it awaits those of its sister nations.

Would you, my eminent friend, with the authority you have devoted to your numerous works, announce this proposal to the Paris Congress, and affirm the urgency of having a bibliography of folk traditions and usages. We need to know what has been done in order to know what remains to be done, and also to avoid the useless repetitions of work already done and so that we don't disseminate "old news". Definitive results of our science can be attained only with the knowledge of similar traditions and customs among diverse peoples, and without a bibliography, no one would be able to effectively undertake this work.

Please present to the Congress my best wishes and the felicitations of your very devoted friend.

Palermo, 5 September 1900

G. Pitrè

9

A Dialogue in Gyergyó-Kilényfalva

Béla Bartók

Not every folklorist is a generalist. In fact, most folklorists tend to specialize either in the folklore of a particular group, for example, Gypsy folklore, or in a particular genre, for example, folksong or proverb. Consider, for instance, the case of Francisco Rodriguez Marin (1855–1943), a prolific Spanish scholar. Although he did write on sixteenth-century children's games and Spanish folksongs, his real love was the proverb. Taking a 1627 collection of Castilian proverbs by Gonzalo Correas (1571–1631) as a point of departure, he began noting proverbs that were not included in this compendium.

This project seems harmless enough, but it evidently became virtually an obsessive passion. In 1926 Rodriguez Marin published *Más de 21,000 refranes castellanos, no contenidos en la copiosa colección del maestro Gonzalo Correas, allególos de la tradicion oral y de sus lecturas durante más de medio siglo (1871–1926).* As the subtitle of this 519-page book indicates, Rodriguez Marin "collected" proverbs from both oral tradition and printed sources. One would think 21,000 proverbs was a substantial collection, but it was just the beginning. In 1930 Rodriguez Marin issued *12,600 refranes más no contenidos en la colección del maestro Gonzalo Correas ni en "Más de 21,000 refranes castellanos";* this 314-page sequel was in turn followed in 1934 by a 198-page book whose title begins *Los 6,666 refranes de mi ultima rebusca, que con "Más de 21,000" y "12,600 refranes más" suman largamente 40,000 refranes castellanos no contenidos . . .* But this indefatigable paroemologist was not content to rest on his laurels. In 1941 he published a 315-page book entitled *Todavia 10,700 refranes más, no registrados por el maestro Correas, ni en mis colecciónes.* So it was that one single individual scholar collected more than 50,000 Spanish proverbs.

Another classic example of a folklore collector who concentrated on one particular genre is Krišjānis Barons (1835–1923), who devoted many years to the collection and publication of a special form of Latvian folksong called "daina." (Dainas had been much appreciated by Johann Gottfried Herder, who had spent five years in Riga and included twelve specimens in his 1778 *Volkslieder.*) The first volume of Barons's monumental six-volume collection, *Latvjuj dainas,* was published in 1894; the remaining five volumes were published from 1906 to 1915. These six volumes constituted 6,256 pages and contained 217,996 folksongs (including both songs and variants). Few folksong collectors in the world can match Barons's extraordinary achievement in recording Latvian dainas. For appreciations of Barons, see Ojars Kratins, "An Unsung Hero: Krišjānis Barons and his Lifework in Latvian Folk Songs," *Western Folklore* 20 (1961), 239–255; Gunars Priede, "The Father of Dainas," *Soviet Literature,* 1985 (no. 10), 154–159; Saulcerite Viece, *Krišjānis Barons: The Man and His Work* (Moscow: Raduga Publishers, 1985); and Janis Arveds Trapans, "Krišjānis Barons: His Life and Times," in Vaira Vikis-Freibergs, ed., *Linguistics and Poetics of Latvian Folk Songs: Essays in Honour of the Sesquicentennial of the Birth of Kr. Barons* (Kingston: McGill-Queen's University Press, 1989), 14–32. See also Rolfs Ekmanis, "Folklore in Soviet Occupied Latvia," *The Baltic Review* 17 (1959), 18–28.

Despite his prodigious efforts, Barons remains largely unknown outside of Latvia. This is not the case with another famous collector of folksongs, Béla Bartók (1881–1945) of Hungary. Born in a small town in Transylvania, which later became part of Romania, Bartók started taking piano lessons from his mother at age six. When he was eight, his father died. At age nine he began composing for the piano. In 1893 he and his mother moved to Pozsony (now known as Bratislava). This early exposure to Romanian and Slovakian cultures may help to explain why Bartók collected their folk music in addition to Hungarian material. In 1899 Bartók moved to Budapest to study music. It was then that his triple career began: as concert pianist, composer, and folk music scholar.

Piqued by what he felt was the public's unwarranted denigration of Hungarian folksongs, Bartók set out in 1905 to collect and analyze what he called Hungarian peasant music. It should be kept in mind that Hungarians generally felt oppressed by German culture in the Austro-Hungarian empire. The search for Hungarian folksongs represented an effective protest against that oppression. In a letter to Irmy Jurkovics in August 1905, Bartók remarked, "For we're in a surprisingly favourable position, compared with other nations, in regard to our folk-music. From what I know of the folk-music of other nations, ours is vastly superior to theirs as regards force of expression and variety." (See also Judit Frigyesi, "Béla Bartók and the Concept of Nation and Volk in Modern Hungary," *Musical Quarterly* 78 [1994], 255–287.)

In a 1933 lecture, Bartók reminisced about how he happened to become a specialist in folksong. The critical moment of inspiration came during summer 1904, the year following his graduation from the Academy of Music. At a villa in northern Hungary, where he was spending his days composing, he overheard a nursemaid singing an unusual song she had learned from her grandmother. In Bartók's words, "Making use of a chance opportunity that presented itself, I listened by way of experiment to a Székeley village girl, Lidi Dosá, and wrote down some 5–6 songs as she sang them, all entirely unknown melodies which were completely different from the known urban Hungarian popular song types. This first experiment pointed the way to unlimited possibilities: I decided I would follow this path, after suitable preparation." (See Tibor Tallián, *Béla Bartók: The Man and His Work* [Budapest: Corvina, 1981], 49.)

Bartók was later joined in his efforts to document this music by fellow Hungarian Zoltán Kodály (1882–1967), who like Bartók was both composer and scholar. In speaking of Bartók, Kodály observed: "At the beginning of his career he would not even have dreamt that he would ever become a folklorist." (See "Bartók the Folklorist," in *The Selected Writings of Zoltán Kodály* [London: Boosey & Hawkes, 1974], 102–108.) In 1907 Bartók accepted a post teaching piano at the Academy of Music in Budapest. By 1912, however, he had become somewhat disenchanted with the music establishment in Budapest and began to devote himself more and more to the study of folk music. In 1913 he collected Arabic folk music during an abbreviated two-week stay in Biskra in northeastern Algeria. Bartók explained part of the reason for his successful collecting efforts there in a letter to Ion Bîrlea in October of that year: "The sheiks were most obliging; they simply ordered people to come in and sing."

By the end of 1934, Bartók had resigned his professorship at the Academy of Music to work full-time on folk music research. He became a working member of the Hungarian Academy of Science, which commissioned him and Kodály to prepare their Hungarian folk music material for publication. In 1937 Bartók was invited by the Turkish government to lecture on folk music in Ankara, and he carried out fieldwork while he was in Turkey. By 1940 the outbreak of World War II forced Bartók to reluctantly leave his beloved homeland for sanctuary in the United States. In New York City, Columbia University awarded him an honorary doctorate that year and also appointed him an associate in music to transcribe the Serbo-Croatian folk music that had been recorded by Milman Parry (1902–1935) in the latter's pathbreaking fieldwork from 1933 to 1935.

In a brief 1942 essay, "The Parry Collection of Yugoslav Folk Music," Bartók called the Parry recordings "a most important collection of folk music, unique of its kind" and he thanked both Columbia and Harvard Universities for the privilege of transcribing and studying them. Milman Parry, a young classical philologist at Harvard, wanted to prove that Homer's *Iliad* and *Odyssey* had been composed orally. To do so he undertook fieldwork in Yugoslavia, where a living oral epic tradition could still be found. Yugoslavia also had the advantage of being adjacent to Greece, where the Homeric poems had been created.

After a brief summer of exploratory fieldwork, Parry returned to the field in June 1934, accompanied by his student Albert Lord (1912–1991), to carry out sixteen months of intensive research. Though re-eliciting the "same" epic from both the same and different informants, Parry and Lord concluded that epics were not memorized verbatim but rather that only the general plot outline was retained. As epic singers chanted various episodes, structural slots in the story line were filled by dipping into a repertoire of fixed formulas. This theory of epic composition is known as the "oral formulaic theory."

Parry died tragically in a firearms accident in December 1935, several short months after the fieldwork had ended in September of that year. Lord was left to complete Parry's mission, and he did so in his book *The Singer of Tales* (Cambridge: Harvard University Press, 1960). The music recorded by Parry and Lord was in effect only a by-product of the fieldwork, but thanks in part to the timing of Bartók's exile it received expert treatment at his hands. For an account of oral formulaic theory, see John Miles Foley, *The Theory of Oral Composition: History and Methodology* (Bloomington: Indiana University Press, 1988), and for a sample of the voluminous scholarship that theory has generated, see Foley, *Oral-Formulaic Theory and Research: An Introduction and Annotated Bibliography* (New York: Garland, 1985). For Bartók's tribute to the collection, see Benjamin Suchoff, ed., *Béla Bartók Essays* (New York: St. Martin's, 1976), 148–151. For the results of Bartók's Columbia University research, see his jointly authored (with Albert B. Lord) *Serbo-Croatian Folk Songs* (New York: Columbia University Press, 1951), which was later incorporated into the four-volume *Yugoslav Folk Music* (Albany: State University of New York Press, 1978). This work includes 3,449 transcribed melodies.

Bartók wrote many technical articles on folk music and ethnomusicology. For example, he modified a folksong classification system first developed by Finnish musicologist Ilmari Krohn (1867–1960), the brother of Kaarle Krohn. But Bartók was both an artist and a scientist. Romanian folklorist Constantin Brailoiu commented on this rare combination in his obituary of Bartók. (See "Béla Bartók folkloriste," *Schweizerische Musikzeitung* 88 [1948], 92–94). Bartók had firsthand knowledge of many musical traditions—including those of Hungary, Romania, Bulgaria, and Turkey—and he was also acquainted with Serbian and Slovakian folk music. Bartók distinguished his broad interest in folk music from the more narrow concerns of his friend and colleague Kodály. In an April 1926 interview he remarked, "Unlike Zoltán Kodály, however, I am interested not only in Hungarian folk songs but in the peasant music of all nationalities. Before the war I was in Biskra, among the Arabs. . . . You might say that I have been occupied with the folk music of almost every people." (See "A Conversation with Béla Bartók," in Peter Laki, ed., *Bartók and His World* [Princeton: Princeton University Press, 1995], 235–239.)

Because Bartók was both a major composer and a leading folk music scholar, he was especially interested in the relationship between so-called art music and folk music. He once noted that he was sometimes torn between preserving the original folk music intact and taking poetic license to compose an artistic work. As a folklorist he felt a twinge of disloyalty and remorse if he altered folk material, but as a composer he felt obliged to take what he deemed aesthetically appropriate liberties with folk material. Even the task of presenting authentic rural Hungarian folksongs to a sophisticated urban audience in Budapest posed a problem. In 1906 Kodály and Bartók articulated the issue with a striking metaphor: "To bring folksongs into the town one must dress them; but town clothes are too tight and do not fit. They must be cut so that the folksongs are allowed to breathe." (See Colin Mason, "Bartók and Folksong," *Music Review* 11 [1950], 292–392.)

Bartók also wrote several fascinating accounts of his fieldwork experiences, such as those in Turkey, but perhaps the most unusual was contained in a letter he wrote to Stefi Geyer (1888–1956) on August 16, 1907, still fairly early in his folk music–collecting career. The letter was intended as a parody of his first Transylvanian field trip.

In summer 1907 Bartók had fallen in love with Geyer, a beautiful, talented nineteen-year-old violinist to whom he wrote several long letters. Unfortunately, she did not feel the same way about him, even though he wrote a two-movement violin concerto for her (which was not performed until 1958 after both had died). Although she moved to Switzerland in 1920, where she lived with her husband, composer Walter Schulthess, for the rest of her life, she and Bartók remained friends. Evidently, she and her husband assisted the Bartóks in fleeing Hungary. Bartók reported that she even helped them pack on the eve of their departure in mid-October 1940 for their long journey from Budapest into exile in the United States.

In the August 1907 letter to Geyer, Bartók wrote a dialogue that was purportedly a conversation between a folklore collector and a prospective informant. The collector's frustration at the informant's failure to sing secular folksongs, offering instead either commercial popular songs or standard religious hymns, will be all too familiar to any folklorist who has spent time in the field. It is tempting to see in this literary duet-vignette a reflection of Bartók's personal plight of unrequited love: a male collector's request to a female informant is made to no avail.

Bartók also spoke about the difficulties in convincing reluctant rural peasant women to sing for "upper-class" collectors from the city in an interview conducted in 1925; see Dezso Kosztolányi, "Béla Bartók: An Interview," in Laki, *Bartók and His World*, 228–234. For his more conventional accounts of folklore fieldwork, see Bartók, "Collecting Folksongs in Anatolia," *Hungarian Quarterly* 3 (1937), 337–346. For facsimile reproductions of twenty-seven letters written by Bartók to Stefi Geyer, see *Béla Bartók. Briefe an Stefi Geyer, 1907–1908*, edited by Paul Sacher (Basel: Privatdruck, 1979). For some of his essays on folk music and ethnomusicology, see Suchoff, *Béla Bartók Essays*, and Suchoff, ed., *Béla Bartók Studies in Ethnomusicology* (Lincoln: University of Nebraska Press, 1997).

Bartók's contributions to folk music scholarship are far too numerous to enumerate. Samples include: "Die Volksmusik der Araber von Biskra und Umgebung," *Zeitschrift für Musikwissenschaft* 2 (1920), 489–522; *Turkish Folk Music from Asia Minor* (Princeton: Princeton University Press, 1976); and *Hungarian Folk Music* (London: Oxford University Press, 1931). His substantial collections also include a multivolume set of Slovak folksongs—the first volume of *Slovenske ludove piesne* (Bratislava: 1959) contains 752 pages—and the five-volume *Rumanian Folk Music* (The Hague: Martinus Nijhoff, 1967–1975), whose more than 3,000 pages include instrumental melodies, vocal melodies, texts, Christmas carols, and folk music from Maramures. For the enormous scholarship devoted to Bartók, see Elliott Antokoletz, *Béla Bartók: A Guide to Research,* 2d ed. (New York: Garland, 1997), which lists both his writings on folk music (pp. 165–180) and studies of the influence of folk music on his compositions (pp. 317–336).

*   *   *

TO STEFI GEYER

August 16th, 1907

A dialogue in Gyergyó-Kilényfalva.

The traveller: (entering) God bless you!
The peasant woman: Jesus keep you!
T: Is your husband at home?
W: He's not at home; he's taken the waggon to bring hay from the field.
T: And how are you faring, I wonder?
W: Oh, we get along somehow, though we have our troubles, too: We have work, and plenty of it.
T: Well, well, you can cope with it somehow.
W: And what does the gentleman want? (To her little girl) Bring a chair

for the gentleman!—Here's a chair, sit ye down. (To her daughter) Get the pigs in!

T: Now look here. I've come to ask you for something which, I think, you've never been asked for before.

W: ?

T: I've heard from your neighbour that you know all kinds of ancient folk-songs which you learnt from the old folks when you were a girl.

W: Me?! old songs?! You shouldn't poke fun at me, Sir. Old songs! Ha, ha!

T: Believe me, I'm not poking fun at you! I mean what I say! That's why I've made this long, long journey all the way from Budapest, specially to look for these very old songs which no one remembers except here!

W: And what are you gong to do with those songs? Do you want to print them?

T: No indeed! What we want is to preserve the songs by writing them down. For if we don't write them down, then in years to come no one will know the songs that are being sung here now. You see, even now, the young people sing quite different songs; they don't care for the old ones and don't even learn them; and yet they are much prettier than the new ones, aren't they?! In 50 years no one will have heard of them if we don't write them down now.

W: Really? (Pause) Hmmm. Hahaha. No, I just can't believe it.

T: (Desperate) But look here, mother, at this little book. Do you see, I have written them all down. (He whistles a song) That was sung by the wife of Andrew Gegő (he whistles another), and Bálint Kosza's wife sang that one. Now! you know them, too, don't you?

W: Eh! my singing-days are past. What would an old woman be doing to sing such secular songs! I only know sacred songs now.

T: Come, you're not as old as all that. And the others, Stephen Csata's wife and Ignatius Hunyadi's wife, both told me that you know a great many.

W: Eh! my voice is not what it was . . .

T: (Chimes in) You don't need a strong voice; if you hum it faintly, that will be all right.

W: Why don't you ask the young men and girls, they know plenty of songs.

T: No! they only know new songs; and I don't need those because I've already got them all. In these parts there are such sad songs like this (whistling):

You know it? What are the words?

W: Long ago I heard that song, but I did not learn the words.

T: Don't you know any others like it?

W: I could think of one or two; but they don't come into one's mind very readily. When I want them, I can't remember a single one. Aye! There was a time when I knew a great many. But hard work is the devil, it takes the joy out of singing. When I was a girl . . .

T: Yes, yes. Now just think back a little, perhaps you will remember some old song.

W: (To her son) Come here! Take that to István Ábrán's wife; she is helping Felix György's wife. (She thinks for a long time) . . . One has just come into my mind.

T: (Brightening) Let's hear it, let's hear it!

W: But what shall I do? Just say the words?

T: No! Sing the tune, as it used to be sung.

W: (Breaks into a song) (Sings to the end)

['I go around this wood . . .']
Aye! that is a very old song.

T: I know, I know, it's very nice. But don't you know anything older? Just think a little.

W: Older than that? (She thinks . . . then suddenly to her daughters) For the love of God! Why did you let out the geese? This morning, when I closed the door, I said not to let them out only at midday! (She thinks a painful pause . . .) Now another has come into my mind.

T: ?

W: ['I was born in a rose bush . . . ']

T: (Interrupts) That's no good . . . It is not even old, and it's sung by the gentry.

W: No, no! We often used to sing it in the village. (To her children) Now you think, too, and maybe you'll remember something.

T: We don't want those that the children know. They are new songs. Only the very, very old ones!

W: Where did you say you came from, sir?
T: I've already told you, from Pest.
W: God help ye! Are you married?
T: No, I'm not.
W: Then you're only a youth.
T: Just so! But think a bit more. Don't you know 'The thief of the large mountain', 'Kata Kádár's song' or 'Where are you going to, you 3 orphans?'
W: (With devastating determination) No!!
T: Never heard them?
W: (In the same tone) No!! But I'll sing the gentleman another.
T: Let's hear it.
W: The song of Mary Magdalen . . .
T: I don't think that will do. It's a sacred song! (Privately cursing all the sacred songs in the world.)
W: Have you got this one:

Ké - ped - del   al - szom el,   ké - ped - del   éb - re -

['I sleep and wake with your image . . . ']
T: (Bluntly) Yes, I have! (Clenching his teeth but preserving his friend-liest tones) Now try some real, village song that no one in Hungary knows.
W: Well, is this one good? It's very old.

Ke - rek   ez   a   zsem   -   le

['This roll is round . . . ']
T: They know that one, too, in Hungary. I've already got it.
W: But this one, the gentleman won't have put this one down yet . . . .

Ezt   a   ke - rek   er -

['I go around . . . ']
T: But you began with that! I don't want it. (Giving up at last, he puts his book and pen back into his pocket.)
W: I know a lot of holy songs. The song of Mary Magdalen . . . .
T: (Defiantly silent.)
W: The gentleman has never heard anything more beautiful.

T: Do you know anyone who remembers the very, very old songs? Is your mother at home?

W: She's out working . . . . If the gentleman were to come to our pig-killing feasts *(radina)* or listen when we are all working together *(kaláka),* then he would hear plenty of songs. Oh, how we sing then!

T: Splendid! But it's now that I need a song. Is there anyone who would know such a singer?

W: Gyurka Sándor's wife lives round the corner of the street; she knows *so many,* she couldn't recite them all if you stayed all day.

T: Will she be at home now?

W: Oh, yes, she will be working at her loom. And her grandmother helps with the weaving, and she knows lots of old songs.

T: Then I will go to her.

W: Yes, the gentleman should go there. She knows a great deal, especially when she has had a drink or two.

T: How do I find her? This way?

W: No, not that way, keep on down the road. It's quicker.

T: Thank you, thank you. God bless you!

W: May God keep you!

T: (Departs downcast.)

And so *da capo al fine* from morning to night, Monday to Sunday (day after day)! I can't bear it any longer. Impossible!

Endurance, perseverance, patience . . . to hell with you all . . . I'm going home.

I can't do with this farce for more than 6 weeks at a stretch. Even in my dreams I hear: 'Jesus keep you . . . Is she at home? . . . She's gone mowing . . . holy songs . . . Round is the forest . . . it doesn't fit in my pocket.'

Terrible! Good-bye to you, high plateau of Gyergyó, I shall not see you again till Easter.

I shan't wear high boots nor see preserves till Christmas.

Your Gyergyószentmiklós card reached me at Tekerőpatak. On the way back I will look at the Szentdomokos post-office in case your letter has arrived.

Many greetings—still from Gyergyó.

BÉLA BARTÓK

10

In Search of Folktales and Songs

Boris and Yuri Sokolov

To fully understand the development of international folkloristics, one should realize that in the nineteenth century and for a good part of the twentieth century the folk were thought to be limited to one segment of the population of any nation. Essentially, the folk were defined as peasants. In terms of a binary oppositional paradigm, the folk were contrasted with civilized individuals (from whose ranks most folklorists came); the folk were rural as opposed to urban, uneducated as opposed to educated, illiterate as opposed to literate. With this bias educated, literate, urban folklorists sought to elicit folklore from uneducated, illiterate, rural folk. When such folklorists departed from their home cities to go into the countryside in search of folklore, they often encountered suspicion and outright hostility from their prospective informants.

Not all folklorists reported problems in establishing the rapport so crucial for the collection of folklore. Bartók was a notable exception. Another, more detailed account is provided by twin brothers Boris Sokolov (1889–1930) and Yuri Sokolov (1889–1941), sons of a literature professor at Moscow University who both studied with Russian folklorist V. F. Miller (1848–1913) and became professional folklorists themselves. At this point in the history of folkloristics, folklore collecting no longer consisted of occasional haphazard local efforts by amateurs. Instead, expeditions were planned, and folklorists carried out fieldwork in areas distant from their homes.

In 1908 and 1909 the Sokolov brothers visited the Belozersk region of Novgorod Province. They had hoped to find vestiges of the Russian *byliny* tradition (*bylina* is the term for epic), and they did find some fragments, but they discovered that a more active tradition involved ordinary folktales and songs. They reported the results of their fieldwork in *Skazki i pesni Belozerskogo kraja* [Folktales and songs of the Belozersk region] (Moscow: 1915).

In their introduction to that important collection of Russian folklore, the Sokolovs present fascinating anecdotes of their experiences in the field.

Although technology has changed greatly since the days of the Sokolovs' fieldwork, the basic issues entailed in establishing collector–informant rapport remain essentially the same. Informants fear the collector is intending to make fun of them by collecting their traditions or that the collector will become wealthy by publishing the informants' folktales and folksongs. (The truth is that it is often difficult to find publishing outlets for folklore texts, and in the vast majority of cases such texts are published in subsidized academic monograph series that sell a limited number of copies to libraries and to a few interested private scholars. No royalties are paid to author-collectors for such publications.)

The reader should keep in mind that the Sokolovs' field expedition took place not long after the Russo-Japanese war (1904–1905) in which Russia suffered several embarrassing defeats, including the disastrous naval battle of Tsushima in May 1905 in which virtually the entire Russian fleet was sunk. These military defeats, in turn, helped precipitate the anti-Tsarist revolution of 1905, a precursor of the Russian Revolution of 1917. These events unquestionably adversely affected the Sokolovs' attempts to carry out their fieldwork.

The Sokolovs are probably best known for their textbook *Russkij fol'klor* (Moscow: 1938), which was translated into English in 1950. Although it was a joint enterprise, Boris died well before its completion, and Yuri was left to finish the book. Despite its obvious Marxist bias, for example, "folklore has been, and continues to be, a reflection and a weapon of class conflict" (p. 15), *Russian Folklore* remains a valuable source for the non-Russian to gain some insight into the development of folkloristics in the former Soviet Union. For other introductions to Russian folklore scholarship, see M. Azadovski, "The Science of Folklore in the USSR," VOKS 4 (1933), 39–60; Margaret Schlauch, "Folklore in the Soviet Union," *Science and Society* 8 (1944), 205–222; M. K. Azadovskii, *Istoriia russkoi fol'kloristiki*, 2 vols. (Moscow: Uchpedgiz, 1958); Felix J. Oinas and Stephen Soudakoff, eds., *The Study of Russian Folklore* (The Hague: Mouton, 1975); Felix J. Oinas, "Folklore Activities and Scholarship in Russia" in his *Essays on Russian Folklore and Mythology* (Columbus, Ohio: Slavica, 1984), 131–159; and Dana Prescott Howell, *The Development of Soviet Folkloristics* (New York: Garland, 1992). For Yuri Sokolov's discussion of *byliny,* see his "À la recherche des bylines," *Revue des études slaves* 12 (1932), 202–215.

*   *   *

Why would anyone go to a remote village on account of the village itself and not on "official business"? It is easy to understand why the arrival of unknown people would cause the Belozersk peasants so much anxiety and puzzlement. And what's more, from where? From Moscow! Looking for songs! "They haven't come for nothin' ", is the first thought that occurs to the peasant.

Actually, the position of the ethnographer is far from advantageous. Being interested in the life of the peasants, their mode of living and religious beliefs, he must live close to the people, become deeply involved with them and enter their society. In such troubled times as those (1908–09), fear and mistrust of the stranger became an obstacle blocking our way. How could one work as successfully as one would wish under these circumstances?

We arrive in a village and ask, "Can we stay somewhere around here?" "Well, whose people are you?" is the first question asked of us, which, in the course of our travels, we have had to answer a thousand times. "From far away, ma, from Moscow." "From Moscow?!" repeats some peasant woman distrustfully and somewhat surprised. "And what for?" We explain as best we know how, as simply and as clearly as we can.

We see that they don't understand half of it. "You mean to write books and then sell them? And will they give you a lot for it?" "No, we won't get anything; we came because we're interested." "For nothing?" "Yes." "So you say, you're looking for songs. What kind of songs do we have? Are you short of songs of your own in Moscow? Our songs aren't any good. Everyone knows—they're just village songs. We're back-country people!"

"It's yours that we need, the village ones; we know our own." "These people from Moscow!?" reflects an old woman, "I am just a stupid peasant woman; whatever they lie to me about, I'm glad to believe it all!" "Well then auntie, can we stay with you?" "You want to be put up? Why not? Sure you can! I'll go and ask the master."

By this time, nearly half of the people in the village have already gathered around the carriage. They are whispering and looking us over from head to foot and it starts again: "Whose people are you?" and so on. "They haven't come for any good", we hear a voice expressing anxiety; mistrust is written on all of their faces.

At last shelter is found. We drag our things into the hut, unpack, and let the driver go. During this time, the doors are opening constantly and the front hall and hut itself are crammed full of people. Everyone wants to have a look.

"Hey you, look, look; look what the two people from Moscow have brought!" says one of the peasants, indicating the phonograph we had brought: "What is it?" "Well, you'll see. It's a phonograph. It records and sings songs." "You mean that machine?" "Hasn't anyone ever seen one?" "Well, where would we see it?" In some places we find a few people who have had occasion to hear a gramophone in the town tavern. Such people

sometimes gave us quite a bit of help by dispelling their fellow villagers' fear
of the mysterious machine.

But there is no time to rest from the trip. Besides, a large crowd of people
has gathered, and on our part, we want to find out as soon as possible
whether we will find any interesting material at this location, and we want
to pave the way for the recording. But that often happened to be far from
easy. We begin by asking about storytellers. "Sure there have been storytellers, how could there not be?" "Are there any now?" "Sure there are. Look,
go see Petr Vasil'ev, he'll know." "Of course, he knows. He knows a lot",
assures a neighbor. "Sometimes you sit around all night and he talks you to
death."

We make our way to Petr Vasil'ev's. "Hey, what are they talking about, I
don't know nothin'." "Well, how come you don't know? After all, everyone
here points you out. Don't you really know anything yourself, not a single
tale, not one song?" "I've heard some all right, but I'm not too smart.
There's little they won't lie about, I've heard a lot." "Well, how about telling it to us? Not now, but maybe later?" "Oh no! My memory's gone
weak—I don't remember nothin'." You begin to suggest, you name tales
and songs; it turns out that he knows a lot. But how do you approach him?
It is obvious right away that the man is afraid. Sometimes you don't accomplish anything.

One rarely succeeds in attaining any kind of significant results on the first
day. The whole day is spent by the peasants and us in getting acquainted
with each other. By that time, the entire village has called at the hut, the old
as well as the young. Each one has seen us and given his own interpretation.
"Listen", one peasant turns to us, "nothin' will happen to us, will it?" "But
why should it?" we ask in amazement. "Well, because of the songs!" "Oh,
come on! You should be ashamed even to think of it. We have come because
we collect old songs and tales. It's an innocent matter. Would you get into
trouble for that?" "Well, they say out there that you were sent for a purpose: to find out where people sing about the tsar and to put those people
in jail." "Who told you that?" "Oh, in the village. They don't sing about
the tsar at our place—but if you want to, go to district X. There will be
something for you to do over there!" You begin again to convince and dissuade. Nevertheless, half of the peasants still have their doubts.

In some villages, thanks to idle gossips, the rumor that it was "secret police" traveling around would become so entrenched that it cost us great efforts to dissuade the villagers. It seems that even then a few would still
doubt the true aims of our journey. Others, however, would try to dissuade
their overly skeptical neighbors. "Secret police! Well, would the secret police travel around so openly? They would dress in our clothes and come like
a peasant or a beggar." "And why are you sticking up for them so? Are you
one of them yourself?" you would hear in reply.

However, we were not always taken for secret police. We were just as often assigned to the opposite camp: that is, to "insurgents", politikers", "politicians", "strikers", "students", and so on. But even in these cases, we didn't have an easy time of it. "They'll burn our village!" "Why would they burn our village? What could they take from us?" "They'll just burn it down and then they will organize a mutiny among us", spoke those who were especially troubled. But in that situation, the majority had another fear: that they might get into trouble for dealing with us and concealing us. "You have to be pretty careful with these politikers, you'll do a lot of sitting in jail because of them."

No matter where you turned, you ran against a stone wall. It was equally bad all over. Under the influence of such reasoning, no one began by believing the actual purpose of our visit. "Would they come from Moscow just for songs and tales, to waste money? We're not big enough fools to believe them!" That was what the thoughts of the majority boiled down to. Therefore, when one supposition or another did not prove to be correct, they would invent a third one. "They are Japanese spies! They're traveling with a map (we actually did have a district map with us). They'll draw plans of the area", a former soldier expresses his opinion. Finally in one village a friendly peasant approached us and said: "Here they think you've come to return serfdom." "How so?" "You give all of your attention to the old things, to old men and women. You ask about the old songs and ways, and so they say that the gentlemen want to return old times." You'd think that it could go no further than that!

However, it did go further. In one district which lay on the return road of our second trip, we came upon a large village. We were fairly tired and had already stopped recording. While waiting for horses at the *Zemstvo* station, we went to buy some embroidery and local products that were of interest to us. We got acquainted with the peasants and were bargaining with a peasant woman for a towel. She was glad for the chance to sell, but was afraid she could get into trouble for it! She expressed her fears to us right away: "What about it? It's not a sin to sell? Nothing will happen to me, will it? If I was selling something stolen, but this is mine!" At last she made up her mind and sold it. But soon the matter got almost completely out of hand. We paid for one purchased item with seven silver ten-copeck pieces. The woman gave the money to her husband. He weighed the coins for a long time in his palm, threw them on the table but still was not convinced. He placed one of them between his teeth and bit it with all his might. The ten-copeck piece bent a little. That was enough. "Counterfeiters!" he began to shout and rushed through the village. He ran up to us and began to curse us, and the people gathered around. There was a terrible uproar! We reassured the peasants, but they wouldn't listen.

Counterfeiters, and that was it! Fortunately, it was the local peasant coachman who had given us the unfortunate ten-copeck pieces in change.

We asked him to persuade the aroused crowd. He went out to the people and began to scold and shout. After much effort he convinced them, "The coins are good, you gave them to me yourselves. Why do you curse these people for nothing?" And we got into similar situations every time we came to a new place.

When you've lived long enough in one place, the people get used to you. They see that you are no different from other people, and then work gets underway. But, until then, one has to exert much effort and lose much time all for nothing. It is also no use to place great hopes on the village "intelligentsia" or on the authorities who have been asked in a document "to render their enlightened cooperation".

Of course, there were people who now and then gave us valuable aid, and we thank them for that; but the majority at best were indifferent, or else showed us not so much cooperation as opposition. This was particularly felt when you moved further away from the district town. Here, almost the only representative of the "intelligentsia" was the priest, and now and then there happened to be a doctor's aid. Of the "authorities", you had the village policeman. The teachers, who could truly help in our work, were usually gone in the summertime.

The local "authority" gave us curious "cooperation". One of us had to set out for a village which interested us and which lay at some distance in a forest. We had collected a whole series of interesting information about it beforehand. Here is his story:

I come in—they meet me with the greatest of mistrust, very unfriendly. At first I thought I had gone so far out of my way for nothing—I wouldn't accomplish anything anyway.

But little by little, things took a turn for the better. Some daredevils showed up—they began "to tell tales", and we sat around till morning. The same thing happened the next day. We had been working since morning. The hut was full of people, everyone took a personal interest. Only a few continued to look askance and to stop the others. We were sitting and writing down a tale. Laughter was heard all over the hut; the storyteller was filled with enthusiasm and didn't even notice me, so that I could barely get it all down in writing. When things were going full swing, the constable suddenly came in.

The peasants grew quiet, the storyteller stopped talking for a while, but then continued. The constable began to listen himself. The tale was recorded and read back. I was about to record another one, but at that moment one of the peasants tugged at my sleeve and asked me to his place "to have some tea". I began by refusing. "No, let's go. The samovar is hot." There was nothing I could do, so I went. The peasant also invited the constable. We went into the hut, into a separate room, and the host discreetly closed the door after us.

"Do you travel around just for this?" the constable began the questioning. "Yes", I said. "Please be so good as to show me your documents. Please excuse this, but I am a subordinate; they'll make me account for this." I took out all the papers I could from my pocket, even our letter of authorization; everything that I had with me. The constable evidently was not convinced. "You know they require this of us, we're just little people", he said, nevertheless copying every line letter for letter.

At every incomprehensible word he encountered, which for him were quite a few, he asked to be given a written explanation. I had to write out what these expressions meant—dialectology, ethnography, archaeology, and others. After diligently copying all the papers and explanations of the strange words, he still was not satisfied. "Will you be going right back?" he asked me. "No, I think I'll be here for a while longer." "Well, I'll wait for you." After drinking the "politic" tea, I went again to the hut intending to continue the recording. I could hear them shouting and cursing. It turned out that the village elder and the foreman were ordering everyone out into the fields right away, to go divide the work in the meadows. "Well, what's with you?" the peasants said to him. "Why did you suddenly take this into your head? We'll get it done. There's no sense going out just before night time." "You've been told, haven't you! You've found yourself quite a pastime telling tales! We're up to our neck in work, but all of you guys have dragged yourselves into a house to listen to tales!" The peasants scratched the backs of their heads, the village elder threatened them, and they went away. I saw that there was no one left in the hut. And I had nothing left but to set out on the return trip with a police escort. It then turned out that the foreman had sent for the constable in the morning, and together they had made a plan to drive out the "politiker".

We have said that the first day one gets to a village almost nothing gets done. One must limit oneself to inquiries and to getting acquainted.

At last the phonograph is wound up. Lately, it has become customary to take along a phonograph on an ethnographic expedition. It is indeed very useful and lets one record the melody along with the contents of the song, something that a non-musical collector was not able to do before. The phonograph is also important for recording samples of local speech which, in spite of all existing diacritics, cannot be transcribed with total accuracy. Finally, the phonograph renders an important service in a practical sense. It attracts and interests the people and in this way permits the collector to achieve great results. But, on the other hand, it sometimes adds a new log to the fire: it confuses and frightens.

"Oh, who is sitting in there?" they ask us. We explain the structure of the phonograph as best we can. "No, someone is sitting in there and singing songs." "It's the devil", says a peasant woman, and having realized the truth, recoils from the phonograph. Other collectors, who have been to the north, also have had to take into consideration the people's conviction that the phonograph is a devil. And the devil's name carries over from the phonograph to the collector himself. That is what happened before us to the song collector E. È. Lineva, who, we are told, was suspected of being "antichrist".

In a neighboring parish it was two antichrists who were destined to appear at the same time. "What kind of antichrists are they!" a few tried to disagree. "After all, we do know the woman they're staying with, she's a pious and devout woman." "That's the whole point", was the answer, "antichrists approach that kind first of all. It's that kind they want to catch in a net. It wouldn't take them long to corrupt us weak ones. They'd trap us right away." Finally, in a completely different locale, one peasant listened and listened to the phonograph, took a look at us, and couldn't stand it. He expressed his doubts out loud, "As for you yourselves, are you human?"

The inhabitant of the northern village tries with great effort to comprehend the mechanism of the phonograph which is puzzling to him, and attributes to the machine all the characteristics of man or, in any case, of a living being. As a child instinctively tries to get to the horn when they wind up the gramophone, so he, this grown child, looks attentively into the megaphone for a long time. And for a long time, he cannot reconcile himself to the fact that this is only a mechanism. Therefore, when the winding runs down, the peasant sympathizes quite sincerely, "See, the old man is tired. His throat has gone dry." Often you won't detect here even a bit of irony,—the peasant is absolutely serious in his sympathy. When you record a song on the phonograph and play it back right away, along with amazement and laughter there is even more confusion: "Look, it's teasing you. What a devil! It has even taken over your voice." But the furor is even greater when a singer happens to stop during the song to take a breath, to cough or sometimes to say quite unconsciously, "Oh, I made a mistake" or "That's all". And when the phonograph reproduces all of this with absolute exactitude, there are cries, noise and laughter. Some laugh and roar so hard that they can't stay on their feet. On the other hand, others become completely convinced of the "devil's witchcraft". "Look, the devil is laughing at us. Lord save us! It's a sin, such a sin."

We often recorded on the phonograph a few stanzas of a song, which nevertheless would be enough to determine the tune. But we would copy down the words completely. When the phonograph played back the excerpt recorded by us and the song would break off, they would ask us: "Why didn't it sing the whole thing?" "Well you see, it performs just what you sang to it." "But you wrote down the whole song, didn't you?" "That was me, not the phonograph." "Well, teach it all the words."

Persuading people to sing for the phonograph is even more difficult than getting them simply to say something. In addition to every excuse, such as "It makes me awful 'shamed", or "Oh, I don't know how", there was again, first and foremost, the fear that the singer would be taken to Moscow or that one would get mixed up with the devil. We remember the time when a certain girl singer found courage in spite of everything, made a "what will be will be" sign, and was just about to start singing, when her mother ran up to her, grabbed her and dragged her away from the phonograph. "Oh, you fool, you fool! Don't we have enough grief and misfortune? What have you dreamed up now? Do you want to go to prison or something?"

Of course, we sometimes managed to achieve the desired result more quickly. We would find bold individuals who inspired others by their example. Recordings which were made earlier in other villages by people known to the crowd particularly helped our task.

"Goodness gracious! That's really Vasilij Suslov. That's how it is! Even the voice is his!" the listeners would say. Something already familiar to them aroused their interest. "We don't do it that way." "And how do you do it?" And, from that point on we would begin to get closer to the task at hand.

The wailings and laments were very close to old women's hearts, especially if they were composed by a person known to them. The reasons for her grief would be known, and so the wailing acquired real meaning. It often happened that the old women would be so moved that they would start wailing right there in the hut. All we had to do was provide the beginning, and the job would take care of itself. Little by little they would get used to the Moscow people, although perhaps their doubts were not completely dispelled. In a few places they took a long time to get used to us. But on the other hand, it sometimes happened that we would be lucky: we would quickly become friends and many of the peasants themselves would try to help in any way possible with whatever they could.

Some tried to remember what would be of interest to us; others sought out storytellers or asked about them. Among these persons we remember with particular gratitude the Šarašov family in the Belozersk district and the Eršov family in the Kirillov district.

We usually did our recording in the middle of a hut full of people. In a village, everyone in the community is in plain view. A good storyteller is quick to collect a sizable audience around him.

We came across remarkable storytellers, who told tales with enthusiasm and feeling, particularly when they were in good form. The people sitting in the hut all enter into the very essence of the story and with great attentiveness follow the development of the tale, now and then crying out at exciting places: "Isn't he something!" "Oh, the scoundrel!" or, in funny places, everyone would give the storyteller friendly support with roars of laughter.

In such circumstances the work went along with great success. The storyteller would get worked up, the words would flow spontaneously and on all sides you would find those who would want to tell "such an interesting little incident that, the way Uncle Sozon told it, all the folk lay flat on their backs".

But we have stayed in the same place for some time now and we must go on. The questions will come again, "Whose people are you?" "Well, what for?" The "secret police", "politikers", "antichrists", and the like, will come on stage once again. Again it will be the interrogations and persuasions. . . . Some people, in order to convince themselves that we were actually telling the truth, would make up their own kind of "trials". "Well, if you are from Moscow", said one old woman with provocation in her voice, "now I was in Moscow, when I went on a pilgrimage to Kiev. At the entrance to Moscow stands a post and on the post stands a big woman, some kind of witch. She's holding reins in her hands and driving horses. In her other hand is a bread roll. That's her riding to Kiev, to Bald Mountain, and so she's having a bite to eat. Did you see it?" One had to figure out right away that the talk was about the Triumphal Gates on Tverskaja Street. Otherwise, the crafty old woman's suspicions would have been strengthened. The witch with the bread roll in her hand was one of the clear impressions preserved in the memory of the pilgrim who had been to the capital. Incidentally, we will remark that notions about Moscow among the people who had never been there were extremely vague. The capital city was imagined simply as a big village. On several occasions we were asked: "Is the slack period over?" or, "What about your vegetable gardens in Moscow? They must be really big." It is under such conditions that a contemporary collector of folklore has to work.

The peasant, who has been under guardianship for centuries and who sees no end to his state, cannot look at a stranger calmly and fearlessly. Everyone looks like an enemy to him, regardless of the shape they take: be it the police watching him, or a squire come back to reestablish serfdom, or agitators, association with whom leads to trouble. The motivations for a trip with ethnographic goals are incomprehensible to him. To a peasant they seem so trivial that, at best, he suspects a squire's whim to be their real hidden purpose. And so, one frequently has to listen to complaints about one's lot: "O lord, Lord! People like us have nothing to eat, and here they come from Moscow looking for songs." And you feel that you cannot say much against this. The peasant is right in his own way.

But in spite of everything, we recall our trips to the Belozersk region with a feeling of deep gratitude to the local population. The close, at times cordial, relationships with the hard-working villagers gave us much vigor and vitality, and brought much warmth and light into our hearts. The original sense of insult and annoyance at the suspicion and distrust with which the remote village greeted us, gradually was erased and was finally replaced by a deep appreciation for the kindness and welcome with which the hearts of the simple people are so richly endowed.

11

Epic Laws of Folk Narrative

Axel Olrik

By the beginning of the twentieth century, it had become patently clear that folkloristics was of necessity an international discipline. Inasmuch as the data of folklore crossed national boundaries, the study of those data had to perforce be equally free of purely nationalistic biases. It was also obvious that as an academic discipline folkloristics had to go beyond the mere collection of data. It was time to search for patterns and for possible general principles governing the generation, dissemination, function, structure, and meaning of folklore.

One of the key figures in the establishment of folkloristics as an international academic discipline was Danish folklorist Axel Olrik (1864–1917). In 1897 he was appointed lecturer in Scandinavian folklore at the University of Copenhagen and was promoted to professor in that subject in 1913. His contributions to international folkloristics include organizational leadership and a pioneering effort to delineate "laws" of folk narrative. Olrik's organizational skills were in play at both national and international levels. In Denmark in 1904 he co-founded the journal *Danske Studier,* which proved to be an important forum for discussions of Danish folklore. That same year a new society of Nordic folklorists, the Nordiske Folkemindeforskere, was founded in Copenhagen. This society turned out to be the forerunner of an international society formed in 1907, a society that has had a prominent role in the growth of folkloristics as a field of study. In that year Olrik invited Kaarle Krohn (1863–1933) of Finland and Carl Wilhelm von Sydow (1878–1951) of Sweden to come to Copenhagen to found a forum for all the folklorists of the world. Although Olrik acted as host, he later indicated that the original impetus for the meeting came from Krohn. In any event, that meeting resulted in the formation of the FF organization. The initials "FF" were chosen because they functioned equally well in a variety of languages, for example, Folklore Fellows, Fédération des Folkloristes, Folkloristischer Forscherbund, Foreningen af Folkemindeforskere.

The distinguished German folklorist Johannes Bolte (1858–1937) was also brought into the group early on. Bolte was an extraordinarily erudite folklorist and a prolific one too. His publications, including monographs, articles, notes, and book reviews, number 1,400. He wrote on almost all folklore genres. Among his major achievements are his historical overview of children's games, "Zeugnisse zur Geschichte unserer Kinderspiele," *Zeitschrift für Volkskunde* 19 (1909), 381–414, and above all his compilation (with Georg Polívka) of the five comprehensive volumes of comparative notes to the Grimm tales, *Anmerkungen zu den Kinder- und Hausmärchen der Brüder Grimm* (Leipzig: Dieterich'sche Verlagsbuchhandlung, 1913–1932). Bolte was the primary force in this vast project with Polívka's role limited to citing the Slavic sources. For appreciations of Bolte, see Fritz Boehm, "Johannes Bolte: Sein Leben und sein volkskundliches Werk," *Zeitschrift für Volkskunde* 46 (1936–1937), 1–15, and Walter Anderson, *Johannes Bolte: Ein Nachruf*, FF Communications 124 (Helsinki: Academia Scientiarum Fennica, 1939). For a listing of 1,298 of Bolte's publications, see Boehm, "Bolte-Bibliographie," *Zeitschrift für Volkskunde* 42 (1932), 1–68. For an additional 102 entries, see Boehm, "Nachträge zur Bolte-Bibliographie," *Zeitschrift für Volkskunde* 46 (1936–1937), 219–223.

The organization began publishing its FF Communications monograph series in 1910 under the editorship of Kaarle Krohn. Olrik authored FF Communications No. 1, which gave a brief listing of the contents of the Dansk Folkemindesamling (DFS), the National Collection of Folklore, located in Copenhagen. FFC No. 2 was written by Olrik's student Astrid Lunding, and it gave the classificatory breakdown of the folktales in the DFS. FFC No. 3 was the epoch-making *Verzeichnis der Märchentypen* by Finnish folklorist Antti Aarne (1867–1925)—the very first tale type index, later revised by American folklorist Stith Thompson (1885–1976) in 1928 and again in 1961. FFC No. 4 was the first report of the activity of the FF group, and it was written by Kaarle Krohn. Krohn had published an account of the formation of the Folklore Fellows three years earlier in Danish ("Första Meddelande Från Förbundet F.F.," *Danske Studier* 4 [1907]:221–224), and Olrik gave an account in English two years later ("The 'Folklore Fellows': Their Organisation and Objects," *Folklore* 23 [1912]:111–114).

The FF Communications, the most prestigious folklore monograph series, has been published in Finland from the beginning. With its several hundred volumes, it continues to be the primary outlet for scholarly studies of folklore. Thus that meeting in Copenhagen Olrik hosted in 1907 turned out to be a very fruitful one. For a useful discussion of the first twenty-one numbers of the FF Communications, see the survey essay by T. F. Crane (1844–1927), the first major American international folklorist, in *Romanic Review* 7 (1916):110–125.

Olrik's principal contribution to folkloristics, however, lies perhaps in his articulation of possible "laws" of oral tradition. Olrik had originally studied folklore with Svend Grundtvig (1824–1883), the founder of Danish folkloristics whose monumental twelve-volume compilation of Danish ballads, *Danmarks gamle Folkeviser,* Vols. 1–12 (Copenhagen: 1976), had been the explicit model for Francis James Child's (1825–1896) canonical five-volume edition of some 305 *English and Scottish Ballads* (Boston: Houghton Mifflin, 1882–1898). (For more about Grundtvig and Child, see the chapters devoted to them in Sigurd Bernhard Hustvedt, *Ballad Books and Ballad Men* [Cambridge: Harvard University Press, 1930], 175–204 and 205–229, as well as their correspondence, 241–300.) Olrik's inspiration for his "epic laws," however, came from Norwegian folklorist Moltke Moe (1859–1913) whom he had met in February 1892. After defending his doctoral dissertation in May of that year, Olrik went to Oslo (then known as Christiana) to study with Moe for a semester.

Moe was the son of Jörgen Moe (1813–1882), who with Peter Christen Asbjörnsen (1812–1885) had published *Norske Folkeeventr* in a series of pamphlets beginning in 1841. This major collection of Norwegian folktales became almost as popular as the Grimm canon, especially in its 1858 English translation, *Popular Tales from the Norse.* In 1885 a chair in Norwegian dialect and folklore research was established at the University of Oslo. According to Olrik, the original chair was intended to be a professorship restricted to vernacular language or dialect, but when Moltke Moe was offered it he agreed to accept the position only if "Norse traditions" was added to the title. This condition was met, and Moe was officially offered the position in January 1886, thereby becoming the very first university professor of folklore.

Moe was not a prolific writer, but he did propose the concept of "Episk love," or epic laws, in 1889. His articles on the subject eventually appeared posthumously in the journal *Edda* (see "De episke grundlove," *Edda* 2 [1914], 1–16, 233–249; 4 [1915], 85–126; 7 [1917], 72–88). Moe's notion of epic laws, however, differed greatly from Olrik's. Moe tried to formulate principles concerned with how traditions develop or evolve; in contrast, Olrik sought to identify the formal features or characteristics of traditions. To put it another way, Moe's epic laws were diachronic whereas Olrik's were synchronic. In any event, it is Olrik's delineation of epic laws that enjoys the status of a classic in international folkloristics.

Olrik had evidently completed a draft of his consideration of epic laws as early as 1906, but it was not until 1908 that he published "Episke love I folkddigtningen" (*Danske Studier* 5:69–89) and "Folkedigtningens episke love" (*Nordisk tidskrift för Vetenskap, Konst och Industri,* 547–554). It was likely the publication in German of "Epische Gesetze der Volksdichtung" in 1909 (*Zeitschrift für Deutsches Alterthum* 51:1–12) that brought Olrik's insights to the attention of the scholarly world. Olrik later included his delineation of epic laws as a chapter in his *Nogle Grundsaetninger for Sagnforskning* (Copenhagen: 1921), a general treatise that has been translated into English as *Principles for Oral Narrative Research* (Bloomington: Indiana University Press, 1992). But the basic definitions of Olrik's epic laws did not change radically from the earlier essays.

One of Olrik's apparent goals was to determine whether there were characteristics of what he called "Sage," an inclusive term by which he meant myth, folktale, legend, and folksong that could help to distinguish folklore from written literature. He suggested that as a given oral narrative enters the written domain, it tends to lose its distinctive character as reflected in various epic laws. Regardless of whether this is so and also of whether Olrik's laws apply to the folklore of non-European cultures, there can be no question that his effort to articulate laws or principles of folk narrative constitutes a landmark in international folkloristics.

For more information about the history of Olrik's discovery of epic laws, see Danish folklorist Hans Ellekilde's (1891–1966) remarks on "The Origin of the Work" in *Principles for Oral Narrative Research*, 138–140. See also the entry on "Episk lov" in Laurits Bødker, *Folk Literature (Germanic)* (Copenhagen: Rosenkilde and Bagger, 1965), 84–85. For further discussion of Moltke Moe, see Axel Olrik's moving personal reminiscence of his teacher, *Personal Impressions of Moltke Moe*, FF Communications No. 17 (Hamina: 1915). See also Helmut de Boor, "Moltke Moes Wirken für Volkskunde und Volkstum," *Mitteilungen der Schlesischen Gesellschaft für Volkskunde* 30 (1929), 78–90; Knut Liestøl, *Moltke Moe* (Oslo: Aschehoug, 1949); Dag Strömbäck, "Moltke Moe (1859–1913)," *Arv* 25–26 (1969–1970), 339–351; and Jorunn Fløstra, *Moltke Moe som folklorist* (Oslo: Norsk Folkeminnelag, 1995). For appreciations of Olrik, see Kaarle Krohn, "Axel Olrik," FF Communications No. 29 (Hamina: 1919), and Bengt Holbek, "Axel Olrik (1864–1917)," *Arv* 25–26 (1969–1970), 259–296, as well as his "Introduction" to *Principles for Oral Narrative Research*, xv–xxviii. For discussions of the epic laws, see Janne Vibaek, "La Costruzione del Racconto: Le Leggi Epiche," *Uomo & Cultura* 6(11–12) (1973), 197–232; Bengt Holbek, "Epische Gesetze," *Enzyklopädie des Märchens* 4 (Berlin: Walter de Gruyter, 1982), 59–69; and Brynjulf Alver, "The Epic Laws of Folk Narrative," in Michael Chesnutt, ed., *Telling Reality: Folklore Studies in Memory of Bengt Holbek* (Copenhagen: Nordic Institute of Folklore, 1993), 195–204.

For criticism, see Bruce A. Rosenberg, "Olrik's Laws: A Judicial Review," *Folklore Forum* 11 (1978), 152–162, the gist of which was reprised in Rosenberg's *Folklore and Literature: Rival Siblings* (Knoxville: University of Tennessee Press, 1991), 15–21. For a consideration of the utilization of Olrik's epic laws in biblical scholarship (to disentangle oral from written tradition), see Patricia G. Kirkpatrick, *The Old Testament and Folklore Study*

(Sheffield: Sheffield Academic Press, 1988), 55–64. For attempts to apply epic laws to Eskimo and Filipino folklore, see Erik Holtved, "De eskimoiske sagns opbygning, belyst ved Axel Olriks episke love," *Danske Studier* 40 (1943), 20–61, and Evelyn H. Nunes, "Some Epic Laws of the Labaw Donggon: A Study in Structure," *Unitas* 45(4) (1972), 39–52.

*   *   *

The most recent advances in folklore research have been based mainly on a variety of highly specialized studies. I certainly hope that the number of such specialized studies will increase, but at the same time, it seems to me that we must also pay attention to more general questions. A method of folklore research, a biology of the *Sage,* is what we need.

I have been concerned with such questions for some time now, and I have found capable collaborators in seminars at the University of Copenhagen. I shall not present all of my endeavors in this field at this time; however, a sample of the biological elements might be appropriate.[1]

Anyone who is familiar with folk narrative has observed when he reads the folklore of a faraway people that he feels a sense of recognition even if this folk and its world of traditional narrative were hitherto completely unknown to him.

Two factors are often cited to explain this recognition: (1) the common intellectual character of primitive man, and (2) the primitive mythology and concept of nature which corresponds to this character. But the matter is not so easily settled. For what touches us the most is not the familiar conception of the entire world of narrative so much as the recognition of certain characteristic details. Why, for example, is the youngest brother the luckiest? Why does the creation of the world or of man occur in exactly three stages among various peoples of the Old and New World?

Let us attempt to put together these pervading similarities so that we get not merely a biology of *Märchen,* or just a taxonomy of myth, but rather a systematic science of a more comprehensive category: the *Sage.* This category would include myths, songs, heroic sagas, and local legends. The common rules for the composition of all these *Sage* forms we can then call the *epic laws of folk narrative.* These laws apply to all European folklore and to

---

1. This essay, in somewhat shorter form, was given as an address to the Historians' Congress in Berlin, in August 1908. I have expressed the same views although with other illustrative examples in *Danske Studier* (1908), pp. 69–68. As an earlier study, a chapter in Gudmund Schütte's book *Oldsagn om Godtjod* (Copenhagen, 1907), pp. 94–117, must be mentioned. From Schütte, I have borrowed the terms *"Toppgewichts"* and *"Achtergewichts ("forvaegt"* and *"bagvaegt")*; see my review, "Episke Love I Gote-Aettens Oldsagn" in *Danske Studier* (1907), pp. 193–201. Recently Astrid Lund has treated the scope of the epic laws in American Indian materials ("Indiansk sagndigtning og de episke love," *Danske Studier* [1908], pp. 175–88). I am indebted to Astrid Lund for *Märchen* materials for the "Law of Closing."

some extent even beyond that. Against the background of the overwhelming uniformity of these laws, national characteristics seem to be only dialect peculiarities. Even the traditional categories of folk narrative are all governed by these general principles of *Sage* construction. We call these principles "laws" because they limit the freedom of composition of oral literature in a much different and more rigid way than in our written literature.

I shall mention first the law which is certainly best known to you. The *Sage* does not begin with sudden action and does not end abruptly. This is the *Law of Opening (das Gesetz des Einganges)* and the *Law of Closing (das Gesetz des Abschlusses)*. The *Sage* begins by moving from calm to excitement, and after the concluding event, in which a principal character frequently has a catastrophe, the *Sage* ends by moving from excitement to calm. For example, the epos cannot end with the last breath of Roland. Before ending, it needs to relax the clenched fist of the sword-hand; it needs the burial of the hero, the revenge, the death through grief of the beloved, and the execution of the traitor. A longer narrative needs many such restpoints; a shorter narrative needs only one. Hundreds of folksongs end, not with the death of the lovers, but with the interweaving of the branches of the two roses which grow up out of their graves.[2] In thousands of legends, one finds the revenge of the dead or the punishment of the villain appended to the principal action. Often the ending takes the form of a locally established continuation of the plot: the ghost in the ruined castle, the description of the tumulus, the perennial return of the victim, or the like. The constant reappearance of this element of terminal calm shows that it is based, not just on a manifestation of the inclination of an individual narrator, but on the formal constraint of an epic law.

A colleague in a Copenhagen seminar who wanted to know whether there were any exceptions to this law read through a multitude of Danish *Märchen* all of which ended with the release from an enchantment. Here, more than anywhere else, one would expect to find an abrupt ending; but the *Märchen* never ends with the statement "she was set free." Sometimes, right after the sudden disenchantment, the tale continues with a new, loosely attached episode. Most frequently following the catastrophe or climax, one finds the release of a minor character or the suggestion of future events. And if there are no other possibilities for continuation, then the storyteller always adds a long jesting closing formula in order to quiet the mood. He hangs a fig leaf on the *Märchen*, as it were, in order to cover its nakedness. Thus, the Law of Closing invariably holds for the various forms of *Sage*.

Yet I should not say that there are no exceptions in the world of folk narrative. In Spanish ballads one may encounter the phenomenon of a sudden

---

2. This is Motif E631.0.1, Twining branches grow from graves of lovers.—ED. NOTE.

beginning or sudden end. For example, the captive sits and awaits his death but—in the last line of the song—the king's daughter, his liberator, opens the door. The frequency of such a phenomenon, however, within this essentially literary domain is sufficient to show that here one has a new type of poetic effect which is lacking in true folk poetry, but which is well known in modern literature.

Another important principle of *Sage* composition is the *Law of Repetition (das Gesetz der Wiederholung)*. In literature, there are many means of producing emphasis, means other than repetition. For example, the dimensions and significance of something can be depicted by the degree and detail of the description of that particular object or event. In contrast, folk narrative lacks this full-bodied detail, for the most part, and its spare descriptions are all too brief to serve as an effective means of emphasis. For our traditional oral narrative, there is but one alternative: repetition. A youth goes into the giant's field three days in succession and each day he kills a giant. A hero tries three times to ride up the glass mountain. Three would-be lovers are magically rendered immobile in one night by a maiden.[3] Every time that a striking scene occurs in a narrative, and continuity permits, the scene is repeated. This is necessary not only to build tension, but to fill out the body of the narrative. There is intensifying repetition and simple repetition, but the important point is that without repetition, the *Sage* cannot attain its fullest form.

The repetition is almost always tied to the number three. But the number three is also a law in and of itself. That three appears in *Märchen* and myths and even in simple local legends with incredible frequency, you all know; but perhaps it has not been made sufficiently clear to you though that in hundreds of thousands of folk traditions, three is the highest number with which one deals. Seven and twelve and sometimes other numbers occur of course, but they express only a totally abstract quantity. Three is the maximum number of men and objects which occur in traditional narrative. Nothing distinguishes the great bulk of folk narrative from modern literature and from reality as much as does the number three. Such a ruthlessly rigid structuring of life stand apart from all else. When a folklorist comes upon a three, he thinks, as does the Swiss who catches the sight of his Alps again, "Now I am home!"

However, the entire world of folk narrative does not obey the *Law of Three (das Gesetz der Dreizahl)*.[4] In the Indic stories, especially the literary

---

3. Motif H331.1.1, Suitor contest: riding up glass mountain, appears in Tale Type 530, The Princess on the Glass Mountain; Motif D2006.1.1, Forgotten fiancée reawakens husband's memory by detaining lovers through magic, appears in Tale Type 313, The Girl as Helper in the Hero's Flight.—ED. NOTE.

4. Olrik was not the first to note the frequent occurrence of threefold repetition. Earlier studies include H. Usener, "Dreiheit," *Rheinisches Museum für Philologie*,

tales, the *Law of Four (des Gesetz der Vierzahl)* often replaces it. This is connected with the religious conceptions of the Indian people. In India, there are also collections of traditional oral tales in which the number three is completely avoided in an attempt to reflect the authentic fullness of life. Here the investigator can see that the three was once present, but that it has been eliminated by the narrator. The number three has been tenaciously retained though, in the great mass of popular tradition—Greek, Celtic, Germanic—in *Märchen*, myth, ritual, and legend, in all that has the appearance of the primitive. The Law of Three extends like a broad swath cut through the world of folk tradition, through the centuries and millennia of human culture. The Semitic, and even more, the Aryan culture, is subject to this dominant force. The beginnings of its rule are, in spite of all the recent excavations and discoveries, lost in the obscurity of prehistory. We can, however, observe the end of its rule where three gradually succumbs to intellectual demands for greater realism.

In Homer, it has lost its power over the characters and it is limited to such minor details as the number of times an action is performed. Hector, followed by Achilles, runs three times around Troy. It is also found in weakened form in our Danish folksongs. In the heroic songs of the elder Edda,[5] the number three is in a way restricted, but it does play a large role in the mythological songs. The Icelandic family sagas go even one step further, and seem quite modern because of their lack of threes. Only one isolated saga from an outlying region of Iceland (Isfirding's *Hawardssaga*) follows the ancient practice. Everywhere in classical antiquity, and especially in the European Middle Ages, one sees how narrative slowly detaches itself from the

---

Vol. 58 (1903), 1–47, 161–208, 321–62; Raimund Müller, "Die zahl 3 in sage, dichtung und kunst," in *XXX Jahresbericht der K.K. Staats-Oberrealschule in Teschen am Schlusse des Schuljahres 1902–1903* (Teschen, Ger., 1903), pp. 1–23. (It is customary in Europe for scholars to write articles in secondary school graduation programs. Many of these, like the Müller study, are very valuable. Unfortunately, they are often hard to find even in the best libraries.) Some of the scholarship concerning the number three since Olrik's paper includes Alfred Lehmann, *Dreiheit und dreifache Wiederholung im Deutschen Volksmärchen* (Leipzig, 1914); Eugene Tavenner, "Three as a Magic Number in Latin Literature," *Transactions of the American Philological Association*, Vol. 47 (1916), 117–43; Emory B. Lease, "The Number Three, Mysterious, Mystic, Magic," *Classical Philology*, Vol. 14 (1919), 56–73; Fritz Göbel, *Formen und formeln der epischen dreiheit in der Griechischen dichtung* (Stuttgart, 1935); and W. Deonna, "Trois, superlatif absolu," *L'antiquité Classique*, Vol. 23 (1954), 403–28. This partial list shows one problem folklorists often encounter in the course of their research: Important studies of folklore are published in non-folklore journals, and the problem is finding these scattered studies.—ED. NOTE.

5. The "elder Edda" is the Poetic Edda. The "younger Edda," written several centuries later in the thirteenth century by Snorri Sturluson, is usually called the Prose Edda.—ED. NOTE.

number three, with a certain inconstancy according to whether one strives for a realistic representation or a fantastic coloring. But the end result is always the loss of the number three.

In true folk narrative, or more precisely, within the realm of narrative which has traditionally been under the influence of the number three, the Law of Three continues its indomitable rule. About 150 to 200 versions of the *Märchen* about the lucky ring lie before us.[6] Without exception, three magic gifts appear therein. Only in one literary version, the Fortunatus tale, are there two.[7] Thus the Law of Three reigns supreme in the purely oral versions.

I shall now turn to other numbers. Two is the maximum number of characters who appear at one time. Three people appearing at the same time, each with his own individual identity and role to play, would be a violation of tradition. The *Law of Two to a Scene (das Gesetz der scenischen Zweiheit)* is a strict one. The description of Siegfried's battle with the dragon can serve as an example. Throughout, only two people appear on the stage at one time: Siegfried and Regin, Siegfried and his mother, Siegfried and Odin, Siegfried and Fafnir, Siegfried and the bird, Siegfried and Grani. The Law of Two to a Scene is so rigid that the bird can speak to Siegfried only after Regin has gone to sleep (and this is entirely superfluous in terms of the epic itself).

For the same reason, the princesses of folktales can attend the battle with the dragon only as mute onlookers. The interaction of three or more characters, which is so popular in literary drama, is not allowed in folk narrative.

The Law of Two to a Scene is correlative to the important *Law of Contrast (das Gesetz des Gegensatzes)*. The *Sage* is always polarized.[8] A strong Thor requires a wise Odin or a cunning Loki next to him; a rich Peter Krämer, a poor Paul Schmied; near a grieving woman sits a joyful or comforting one. This very basic opposition is a major rule of epic composition: young and old, large and small, man and monster, good and evil.

The Law of Contrast works from the protagonist of the *Sage* out to the other individuals, whose characteristics and actions are determined by the requirement that they be antithetical to those of the protagonist. An appro-

---

6. This is Tale Type 566, The Three Magic Objects and the Wonderful Fruits (Fortunatus).—Ed. Note.

7. See Aarne's valuable *Vergleichende Märchenuntersuchungen* (Helsinki, 1907), p. 131. [The correct reference would appear to be Aarne's *Vergleichende Märchenforschungen*, Mémoires de la Société Finno-Ougrienne, Vol. 25 (Helsinki, 1908), pp. 85–97.—Ed. Note.]

8. Olrik has anticipated Claude Lévi-Strauss's structural analysis of myth insofar as Lévi-Strauss sees myth as a logical model in which polarities are mediated. See Claude Lévi-Strauss, "The Structural Study of Myth," *Journal of American Folklore*, Vol. 68 (1955), 428–44.—Ed. Note.

priate example is the Danish King Rolf who is so celebrated in our heroic sagas because of his generosity. He thus requires a stingy opponent. However, in this example, the identity of the opponent changes. Now it is a Skoldung: Rörik; now it is a Swede: Adisl.[9] But even if only one such contrasting person is found, this is sufficient to satisfy the demands of narrative composition.

Some types of plot action correspond exactly to the Law of Contrast. (1) The hero meets his death through the murderous act of a villain (Roland, Rustem, Rolf Kraki, Siegfried);[10] (2) the great king has an insignificant and short-reigning successor (Hjarward after Rolf, Hjarni after Frodi, "Shorthair" after Conchobar).[11]

Further, we might observe that whenever two people appear in the same role, both are depicted as being small and weak. In this type of close association, two people can evade the Law of Contrast and become subjugated instead to the *Law of Twins (das Gesetz der Zwillinge)*. The word "twins" must be taken here in the broad sense. It can mean real twins—a sibling pair—or simply two people who appear together in the same role. The persecuted children of Greek and Roman kings are real twins and we might mention Romulus and Remus as the most famous example.[12] Even more common in northern Europe are the king's two children who are pursued or murdered,[13] as in the *Märchen* of Hansel and Gretel.[14] However the law

---

9. Most of the individual characters and sagas from Danish and Icelandic tradition used by Olrik as illustrative examples in this essay are discussed in his *The Heroic Legends of Denmark* (New York, 1919) to which the interested student may refer.—ED. NOTE.

10. These heroes appear in the *Chanson de Roland*, the *Shahnamah* of Firdausi, *Hrólfssaga Kraka*, and *Volsunga Saga*, respectively.—ED. NOTE.

11. Hjarward and Rolf appear in *Hrólfssaga Kraka*; the account of Hjarni and Frodi may be found in Saxo Grammaticus, Book VI, article 172 of the *Gesta Danorum*; Conchobar and Shorthair are part of the Cuchulain cycle of Celtic tradition.—ED. NOTE.

12. Other examples include Amphion and Zethos in Thebes, Pelias and Neleus in Mycenae, Leukastos and Parrhasios in Arcadia (Hahn, *Sagwissenschaftliche Studien*, p. 340: 'Arische Aussetzungs- und Rückkehr-Formel').

13. Hroar and Helgi *(Hrólfssaga)*, Hrêdric and Hrêthmund *(Beowulf)*, Erp and Eitil *(Atlamál)*, Signy's two children *(Volsunga Saga)*, Hadding and Guthorm (Saxo I), Regner and Thorald (Saxo II), Roe and Scatus (Saco II). In terms of the action, the second of the two brothers is most frequently quite unimportant; he is strictly a silent person. "The two Haddings perform together a valiant deed since they are twins and the youngest" *(Hervarar Saga)*. For two as the number of insignificant or indifferent things, see the examples from R. M. Meyer, *Die Altgermanische Poesie*, pp. 74f. In a broader sense, the "twin-structuring" is the preference of folk narrative for a pair of brothers as personages of secondary rank. Gunnar and Hogni, but not Sigurd; the two Saxon warriors and the two sons of Frowin against Uffi; Svipdag and Geigad against Starkad. (One exceptional example is Hamdir and Sörli as either historical survivals or perhaps as secondary characters in relation to Svanhild and Jormunrek.)

14. This is Tale Type 327A, Hansel and Gretel.—ED. NOTE.

applies even further. Beings of subordinate rank appear in duplicate: two Dioscuri[15] are messengers of Zeus; two ravens or two Valkyries, messengers of Odin. If, however, the twins are elevated to major roles, then they will be subordinated to the Law of Contrast and, accordingly, will be pitted against one another. This may be illustrated by the myths of the Dioscuri. One is bright and one is gloomy; one immortal and the other mortal. They fight over the same woman and eventually kill each other.[16]

Leaving the subject of numbers, I shall mention briefly another law: The *Importance of Initial and Final Position.* Whenever a series of persons or things occurs, then the principal one will come first. Coming last, though, will be the person for whom the particular narrative arouses sympathy. We may designate these relationships with nautical expressions, "the Weight of the Bow" *(das Toppgewicht)* and "the Weight of the Stern" *(das Achtergewicht).* The center of gravity of the narrative always lies in the *Achtergewicht.* Now that this theorem has been stated, it appears to be self-evident. You all know how much the last attempt of the younger brother in *Märchen* signifies.[17] *Achtergewicht* combined with the Law of Three is the principal characteristic of folk narrative—it is an epic law. Note that when we find ourselves in a religious context, then *Toppgewicht* rules; then is Odin greater than his two attendants. However, when these figures appear in folk narratives, then they are governed by *Achtergewicht;* then Odin no longer acts as the principal member of the triad. Instead the principal member is—as the last of the three gods—Loki.[18]

Thus I have discussed the more obvious formulas of folk narrative. Still the question is open as to whether one should attempt to reduce all of the remaining essential structure of the tales to set formulas.

I shall mention only in passing the general principle that each attribute of a person and thing must be expressed in actions—otherwise it is nothing.[19]

---

15. The Dioscuri are Kastor and Polydeukes in Greek mythology, Castor and Pollux in Roman mythology.—ED. NOTE.

16. This event does not occur in all accounts. See H. J. Rose, *A Handbook of Greek Mythology* (London, 1958), pp. 230–31.—ED. NOTE.

17. See Motif H1242, Youngest brother alone succeeds on quest, and L10, Victorious youngest son.—ED. NOTE.

18. This is also the case in the myths of Idunn, of Andvari, and in the Faroese *Lokkatáttur.* In the *Voluspa,* however, the divine function present at the creation of man consists of: Odin, Villi, Vé; Hár, Jafnhár, Thrithi, with the last two in each instance being only associates or reflections of the first. [For a recent study of Loki, see folklorist Anna Birgitta Rooth's *Loki in Scandinavian Mythology* (Lund, 1961) and also John Lindow, *Scandinavian Mythology: An Annotated Bibliography* (New York, 1988)—ED. NOTE]

19. I shall present only a single example here. If one were to begin "There was once a young motherless girl who was unhappy but beautiful and kind...," it would be entirely too complicated a thought for a *Märchen.* It is much better when these ideas are expressed in action and when these actions are all connected: (1) the step-daughter is sent out to the heath to gather heather and is given only ash-cakes as

Modern literature—I use this term in its broadest sense—loves to entangle the various threads of the plot amongst each other. In contrast, folk narrative holds the individual strand fast; folk narrative is always *single-stranded (einsträngig)*. It does not go back in order to fill in missing details. If such previous background information is necessary, then it will be given in dialogue. In the city, the hero of the tale hears of the man-eating dragon who has caused misery throughout the land. Siegfried hears the story of the Rhinegold from Regin. When one finds such phrases as "now the two stories proceed along together" in the Icelandic sagas, then one no longer has folk narrative; one has sophisticated literature.

With its single thread, folk narrative does not know the perspective of painting; it knows only the progressive series of bas-reliefs. Its composition is like that of sculpture and architecture; hence the strict subordination to number and other requirements of symmetry.

How strictly the *patterning (die Schematisierung)* is followed must be astonishing to a person who is not familiar with folk narrative. Two people and situations of the same sort are not as different as possible, but as similar as possible. Three days in succession the youth goes to an unfamiliar field. Each day he encounters a giant, carries on the same conversation with each one, and kills each one in the same manner.

This rigid stylizing of life has its own peculiar aesthetic value. Everything superfluous is suppressed and only the essential stands out salient and striking.

The *Sage* invariably rises to peaks in the form of one or more major *tableaux scenes (Hauptsituationen plastischer Art)*. In these scenes, the actors draw near to each other: the hero and his horse; the hero and the monster; Thor pulls the World Serpent up to the edge of the boat; the valiant warriors die so near to their king that even in death they protect him; Siegmund carries his dead son himself.

These sculptured situations are based more on fantasy than on reality: the hero's sword is scorched by the dragon's breath; the maiden, standing on the back of a bull or a snake, surveys the scene; from her own breasts the banished queen squeezes milk into the beaks of a swan and a crane.

---

provisions; (2) she speaks kindly to the little red-capped man who peeks out from the knoll of heather and she gives him some of her ash-cakes; (3) the little man presents her with gifts; pearls fall from her hair when she combs it and gold pieces from her mouth when she opens it. (E. T. Kristensen, *Jyske Folkeminder*, Vol. 5, No. 15.) Thus, her unhappiness, her kindness, and her beauty are conveyed as three phases of the plot. [Olrik cites this version of Tale Type 480, The Spinning-Women by the Spring, from one of the many collections of E. T. Kristensen, who was one of most active collectors of folklore of all time. For an account of the unbelievable industry of Kristensen, see W. A. Craigie, "Evald Tang Kristensen, A Danish Folklorist," *Folklore*, Vol. 9 (1898), 194–224.—ED. NOTE]

One notices how the tableaux scenes frequently convey not a sense of the ephemeral but rather a certain quality of persistence through time: Samson among the columns in the hall of the Philistines; Thor with the World Serpent transfixed on a fishhook; Vidarr confronting the vengeance of the Fenris Wolf;[20] Perseus holding out the head of Medusa. These lingering actions—which also play a large role in sculpture—possess the singular power of being able to etch themselves in one's memory.[21]

The *Sage* has its *logic (Logik)*. The themes which are presented must exert an influence upon the plot, and moreover, an influence in proportion to their extent and weight in the narrative. This logic of the *Sage* is not always commensurable with that of the natural world. The tendency toward animism and even more toward miracle and magic constitutes its fundamental law. It is important to realize that above all else, plausibility is always based upon the force of the internal validity of the plot. Plausibility is very rarely measured in terms of external reality.

Unity of plot (die Einheit der Handlung) is standard for the *Sage*. One sees this best when one compares the true *Sage* with literary works. The presence of loose organization and uncertain action in the plot structure is the surest mark of cultivation. For particular cases, however, there are various degrees of unity: in *Märchen,* songs, and local legends, it is strong; in myths and heroic sagas, it is less strong but still obvious.

It thus appears that the actual *epic unity (epische Einheit)* is such that each narrative element works within it so as to create an event, the possibility of which the listener had seen right from the beginning and which he had never lost sight of. As soon as an unborn child is promised to a monster, then everything hinges on the question of how he can escape the monster's power.[22]

On the other hand, there is also an *ideal epic unity (eine ideale Einheit der Handlung):* several narrative elements are grouped together in order to best illuminate the relationships of the characters. The king's son is liberated through the cleverness of the monster's daughter, but—and this is the next element—he forgets her and must be won by her once more.[23]

The greatest law of folk tradition is *Concentration on a Leading Character (Konzentration um eine Hauptperson)*. When historical events occur in the *Sage,* concentration is the first consideration.

---

20. Vidarr, son of Odin, killed the World Serpent after it had killed Odin. This episode is found in the description of Ragnarök (the destruction of the world) in the Völuspá of the Poetic Edda. For further discussion, see Axel Olrik, *Ragnarök: die Sagen vom Weltuntergang* (Berlin, 1922).—Ed. Note

21. For a discussion of this point based upon some experimental evidence, see Walter Anderson, *Ein Volkskundliches Experiment,* Folklore Fellows Communications No. 141 (Helsinki, 1951), pp. 42–43.—Ed. Note

22. This is Motif S211, Child sold (promised) to devil (ogre.)—Ed. Note

23. This is Tale Type 313, The Girl as Helper in the Hero's Flight.—Ed. Note

The fates of leading characters sometimes form a loose agglomeration of adventures as in the case of the tales of "Strong John" or "The Youth Who Wanted to Learn What Fear Is."[24] Only the formal single-strandedness and a certain regard for the character hold the pieces together. In general, however, protagonist and plot belong together. Hamlet with his folly and his father-revenge is—in spite of his verbosity—an example of the total concentration on a leading character. It is only his later adventures which fall outside the province of folk tradition and take on the character of a novel.

It is very interesting to see how folk narrative proceeds when the *Sage* recognizes two heroes. One is always the formal protagonist. The *Sage* begins with his story and from all outward appearances he is the principal character. The king's son, not the monster's daughter, is the formal protagonist of the folktale about the forgotten fiancée. Siegfried, not Brynhild, is the most important person in the *Volsunga Saga*. When a man and woman appear together, the man is the most important character. Nevertheless, the actual interest frequently lies with the woman. It is the forgotten fiancée and not the king's son for whom we have greater sympathy; Brynhild has moved the poets of the Edda songs more profoundly than Siegfried has; Aslaug outshines her husband, the Viking king Ragnar.[25] Folk narrative finds even within its constraints of form the ways to freer and more artistic development.

In summary, we find that folk narrative is formally regulated to a far greater degree than one would think. Its formal rules we may call the epic laws. The principal ones which I have discussed here include the Law of Opening and Closing *(das Gesetz des Einganges und des Abschlusses)*, the Law of Repetition *(das Gesetz der Wiederholung)*, the Law of Three *(das Gesetz der Dreizahl)*, the Law of Two to a Scene *(das Gesetz der scenischen Zweiheit)*, the Law of Contrast *(das Gesetz des Gegensatzes)*, the Law of Twins *(das Gesetz der Zwillinge)*, the Importance of Final Position *(das Achtergewicht)*, the Law of the Single Strand *(die Einsträngigkeit)*, the Law of Patterning *(die Schematisierung)*, the Use of Tableaux Scenes *(die Plastik)*, the Logic of the *Sage (die Logik der Sage)*, the Unity of Plot *(die Einheit der Handlung)* (both actual and ideal unity), and the Concentration on a Leading Character *(die Konzentration um die Hauptperson)* (just as much on the actual character who finally has our sympathies as in certain cases on the character who is the object of formal concentration).

What the limits are of these laws, further empirical research must show. I have not concerned myself with problems such as "Gothic-Germanic" or "Aryan"; as "mythical" or "ritual."

I find myself outside the circle of thought of not a few of my colleagues. They will, for example, view these things as religious history. If I speak of

---

24. These are Tale Types 650A and 326 respectively.—ED. NOTE

25. For an English translation of the saga of Ragnar Lodbrok, see Margaret Schlauch, *The Saga of the Volsungs*, 2nd ed. (New York, 1949), pp. 183–256.—ED. NOTE

the Law of Twins, then they think "myth of the Dioscuri"; if the Law of Three appears, then they think "ritual triad." But why should I seek the explanation in religion? My Law of Twins is applicable not only to the god-like Dioscuri but also to Odin's Valkyries, who are not the objects of ritual worship. It is a principle common to all narrative tradition that only two people appear together; it applies to Agamemnon's heralds as it does to the maidens of our folksongs. Life itself must be sufficient to create these types.

And so also with the Law of Three. It certainly appears in folk narrative as the number of divine forces in such a manner that all which is great exists in threes. It is unnecessary to trace these back to a religious origin because the organization of nature itself brings it forward: animals, birds, fish; earth, sky, sea; earth, heaven, hell—they are all divided into three. And if nothing constrains it, then three appears as the highest number of persons and things. It is a question whether or not religious as well as epic triads depend upon an ancient folk psychology.[26]

Here are new problems to resolve: to pursue each epic law in its full range over all humanity, and by so doing, to explain the significance of these compositional formulas for the development of man.

However, we do not want to only wander far afield in the search for the solution of the greatest and most perplexing problems. We should also apply the epic laws to the materials nearest at hand. From these stable features, we can determine the characteristics of particular peoples, their special types of composition and cultural themes. Our work on individual traditions can properly begin only when we can measure them along these sharp lines. And this is perhaps the best thing about our theories: they compel us to make empirical observations of things.

---

26. By arguing that three is in the nature of nature rather than in the nature of culture, Olrik is unable to see that the folk or native category of trebling and tripartition has infiltrated most of our so-called objective analytic schemes. Nature does not come in threes; we in Western civilization *see* nature in threes. (American Indians, in contrast, see nature in fours.)

Not all peoples divide the continuums of time and space into threes: past, present, future; length, width, depth. Nor do they eat three meals a day using three basic implements. Nor do they have three names. Neither do they have three levels of education (primary, secondary, and higher) with three advanced degrees: B.A., M.A., and Ph.D. Not all languages distinguish three persons: first, second, and third; and three degrees of comparison: good, better, best.

The analytic schemes of science as well as art are under the influence of the Law of Three. Is there really an outer, inner, and middle ear? Are there really three developmental stages: larva, pupa, and adult? Are there really three states of matter: solid, liquid, and gas (= land, sea, and air)? Are immunization shots or pill dosages really more effective when given in series of three?

The science of folklore is no exception. One finds three types of prose narrative: myth, folktale, and legend. Aarne's tale type system divides folktales into animal tales, ordinary tales *(Märchen),* and jests.—ED. NOTE

12

The Rites of Passage

Arnold van Gennep

If ever an international hall of fame for folklorists is established, Arnold van Gennep (1873–1957) will be one of the first to be nominated for membership. Born in Ludwigsburg in the kingdom of Würtemberg, a former independent state in Germany, van Gennep moved to Lyons at age six with his mother who was of Dutch descent. Van Gennep's parents were not married, so he took his mother's maiden name, retaining it even after she married Lyons surgeon Paul Raugé (Personal communication from Professor Rodney Needham, Oxford University). Van Gennep was educated in France, developing an early interest in numismatics and languages. A true polyglot, he claimed in 1951 that he had a working knowledge of some eighteen languages, not to mention dialects.

More or less blacklisted by sociologist Émile Durkheim and his followers, van Gennep was never able to obtain an academic position in his adopted home country. His only university experience was a brief stint occupying a chair of ethnography at the University of Neuchâtel in Switzerland from 1912 to 1915. But because of letters he wrote to a Toulouse newspaper suggesting that Swiss neutrality during World War I might have been compromised by Swiss Germanophiles, the Swiss government expelled him, and he lost his only academic post. Van Gennep was forced thereafter to eke out a living through lecturing, translating, and free-lance writing. After an extensive and exhausting trip to the United States and Canada in 1922, where he gave eighty-six lectures on French folksong and folk arts and crafts, he gave up his work and took his family to the south of France where he raised chickens. After six months he recovered, and having had enough of the chicken business he returned to his life of translating, writing features for the *Mercure de France,* and, above all, carrying out the folklore research to which he was so committed.

Despite van Gennep's singular lack of success in the academy, he achieved a great deal in the area of folklore research. Some of his important publications include the five-volume *Religions, moeurs et légendes* (1908–1914), *Les Rites de Passage* (1909), *La Formation des légendes* (1922), *Le Folklore* (1924), and his nine-volume *Manuel de folklore français contemporain* (1938–1958). His articles on folklore theory and method include "De la méthode à suivre dans l'étude des rites et des mythes," *Revue de l'Université de Bruxelles* 16 (1910–1911), 505–523, and "Contribution à la méthodologie du Folklore," *Lares* 5 (1934), 20–34. His survey essays include "Le Folklore en France depuis la Guerre," *La Grande Revue* 36 (1932), 543–565, and "Le Folklore en France," *Revue de Paris* 46(13) (1939), 195–216. He also wrote a delightful set of parodies of various sorts of academics (including a folklorist obsessed with researching the evil eye) entitled *Les Demi-Savants* (1911) and translated as *The Semi-Scholars* (London: Routledge, 1967).

Van Gennep had a habit of undertaking very ambitious projects, perhaps too ambitious, and he did not always complete them. For example, van Gennep was much interested in "property marks and trademarks," and he published a questionnaire on the subject for France, Switzerland, Italy, and Spain in 1901 in the *Revue des traditions populaires*. In that same journal in 1904 he announced a forthcoming book on the subject, but it never appeared. In 1922 he published *Traité comparatif des nationalités;* it was intended to be the first of a three-volume work, but the second and third volumes were never completed. Even his monumental *Manuel* suffered from the same sort of problem. Volumes 3 and 4 were published first, in 1937 and 1938, before the first of the seven parts of Volume 1 appeared in 1943. Volume 2, which was supposed to treat movable and fixed feasts, among other subjects, was never published. It must be said, however, that van Gennep's *Manuel* remains the principal source for the study of French folklore. Volumes 3 and 4, for example, contain an extraordinary bibliography of some 6,510 annotated entries that begins with a section called "Folklore International."

Van Gennep definitely preferred the term "folklore" to French terms. He understood that folklore was "living" rather than wrongly considered solely to be "dead" survivals from the past, and he advocated the establishment of the study of folklore as a separate and independent discipline.

Although van Gennep said in his preface to Volume 3 of the *Manuel* that "folklore is not a library science; it is both a field and laboratory science, laboratory in the sense that all of France constitutes a laboratory or just one of its parts, whether large or small, province, region, or even a tiny village," he himself was primarily a library folklorist. Although he did carry out several months of fieldwork in Algeria and collected folklore in France, he tended to rely heavily on the questionnaire approach. His early books, *Tabou et totémisme à Madagascar* (1904) and *Mythes et légendes d'Australie* (1906), were based strictly on library research. The work for which he is most famous is an analytic one that utilizes the fieldwork of others, *The Rites of Passage*. It is probably fair to say that no example of folkloristic analysis has had more impact on the scholarly world than this classic study. The title, in fact, has entered the general lexicon of many languages and disciplines and is used as often by literary critics as by psychologists and sociologists.

Before van Gennep's study, folklorists tended to consider different rituals separately. Accordingly, one might compile a set of birth rituals, another might investigate marriage rituals, and a third might explore death rituals. What van Gennep discovered is that virtually all rituals share the same tripartite sequential structure: separation, transition, and incorporation. The argument anticipates structuralism by several decades. Those interested in the argument are urged to read van Gennep's book in its entirety rather than just the brief excerpt presented here. In the book he demonstrates the validity of his scheme with references to many rituals and ceremonies around the world. Even the common experience of leaving a country by air, landing at an intermediate airport (and being confined in the designated "transit" lounge before finally arriving at one's destination), and being admitted into that country by passing through passport or customs control illustrates the soundness of van Gennep's brilliant analytic framework (cf. Julian Pitt-Rivers, "Un Rite de Passage de Société Moderne: Le Voyage Aérien," in Pierre Centlivres and Jacques Hainard, eds., *Les Rites de Passage Aujourd'hui: Actes du Colloque de Neuchâtel, 1981* [Lausanne: Editions L'Age d'Homme, 1986], 115–130).

For more detail about van Gennep, see H. A. Senn, "Arnold van Gennep: Structuralist and Apologist for the Study of Folklore in France," *Folklore* 85 (1974), 229–243; Nicole Belmont, *Arnold van Gennep: The Creator of French Ethnography* (Chicago: University of Chicago Press, 1979); and Rosemary Lévy Zumwalt, *The Enigma of Arnold van Gennep (1873–1957): Master of French Folklore and Hermit of Bourg-la-Reine*, FF Communications No. 241 (Helsinki: Academia Scientiarum Fennica, 1988). For a list of his writings, see his daughter Ketty van Gennep's *Bibliographie des oeuvres d'Arnold van Gennep* (Paris: A. & J. Picard, 1964). Her introduction to the bibliography (pp. 3–12) contains valuable details on van Gennep's life. For a selection of posthumously published articles by van Gennep and annotated by Nicole Belmont, see *Textes inédits sur le folklore français contemporain* (Paris: Maisonneuve, 1975).

For representative examples of the continuing interest in van Gennep's rites of passage, see Géza Róheim, "Transition Rites," *Psychoanalytic Quarterly* 11 (1942), 336–374; Max Gluckman, "Les Rites de Passage," in Max Gluckman, ed., *Essays on the Ritual of Social Relations* (Manchester: Manchester University Press, 1962), 1–52; Victor W. Turner, "Betwixt and Between: The Liminal Period in *Rites de Passage*," *Proceedings of the 1964 Annual Spring Meeting of the American Ethnological Society* (Seattle: American Ethnological Society, 1964), 4–20; W. S. F. Pickering, "The Persistence of Rites of Passage: Towards an Explanation," *British Journal of*

Sociology 25 (1974) 63–78; Monika Vizedom (who translated *Rites of Passage* from French into English), *Rites and Relationships: Rites of Passage and Contemporary Anthropology* (Beverly Hills: Sage Publications, 1976); Terence S. Turner, "Transformation, Hierarchy and Transcendence: A Reformulation of Van Gennep's Model of the Structure of *Rites de Passage*," in Sally F. Moore and Barbara G. Myerhoff, eds., *Secular Ritual* (Assen: Van Gorcum, 1977), 53–70; Miklós Tomka, "Les rites de passage dans les pays socialistes de l'Europe de l'Est," *Social Compass* 29 (1982), 135–152; Barbara Myerhoff, "Rites of Passage: Process and Paradox," in Victor Turner, ed., *Celebration: Studies in Festivity and Ritual* (Washington: Smithsonian Institution Press, 1982), 109–135; Nicole Belmont, "La Notion du Rite de Passage," in Centlivres and Hainard, eds., *Les Rites de Passage Aujourd'-hui*, 9–19; and Pertti J. Anttonen, "The Rites of Passage Revisited: A New Look at Van Gennep's Theory of the Ritual Process and Its Application in the Study of Finnish-Karelian Wedding Rituals," *Temenos* 28 (1992), 15–52.

*   *   *

I have tried to assemble here all the ceremonial patterns which accompany a passage from one situation to another or from one cosmic or social world to another. Because of the importance of these transitions, I think it legitimate to single out *rites of passage* as a special category, which under further analysis may be subdivided into *rites of separation, transition rites,* and *rites of incorporation.* These three subcategories are not developed to the same extent by all peoples or in every ceremonial pattern. Rites of separation are prominent in funeral ceremonies, rites of incorporation at marriages. Transition rites may play an important part, for instance, in pregnancy, betrothal, and initiation; or they may be reduced to a minimum in adoption, in the delivery of a second child, in remarriage, or in the passage from second to the third age group. Thus, although a complete scheme of rites of passage theoretically includes preliminal rites (rites of separation), liminal rites (rites of transition), and postliminal rites (rites of incorporation), in specific instances these three types are not always equally important or equally elaborated.

Furthermore, in certain ceremonial patterns where the transitional period is sufficiently elaborated to constitute an independent state, the arrangement is reduplicated. A betrothal forms a liminal period between adolescence and marriage, but the passage from adolescence to betrothal itself involves a special series of rites of separation, a transition, and an incorporation into the betrothed condition; and the passage from the transitional period, which is betrothal, to marriage itself, is made through a series of rites of separation from the former, followed by rites consisting of transition, and rites of incorporation into marriage. The pattern of ceremonies comprising rites of pregnancy, delivery, and birth is equally involved. I am trying to group all these rites as clearly as possible, but since I am dealing with activities I do not expect to achieve as rigid a classification as the botanists have, for example.

It is by no means my contention that all rites of birth, initiation, marriage, and the like, are only rites of passage. For, in addition to their over-all goal—to insure a change of condition or a passage from one magico-religious or secular group to another—all these ceremonies have their individual purposes. Marriage ceremonies include fertility rites; birth ceremonies include protection and divination rites; funerals, defensive rites; initiations, propitiatory rites; ordinations, rites of attachment to the deity. All these rites, which have specific effective aims, occur in juxtaposition and combination with rites of passage—and are sometimes so intimately intertwined with them that it is impossible to distinguish whether a particular ritual is, for example, one of protection or of separation. This problem arises in relation to various forms of so-called purification ceremonies, which may simply lift a taboo and therefore remove the contaminating quality, or which may be clearly active rites, imparting the quality of purity.

In connection with this problem, I should like to consider briefly the pivoting of the sacred.[1] Characteristically, the presence of the sacred (and the performance of appropriate rites) is variable. Sacredness as an attribute is not absolute; it is brought into play by the nature of particular situations. A man at home, in his tribe, lives in the secular realm; he moves into the realm of the sacred when he goes on a journey and finds himself a foreigner near a camp of strangers. A Brahman belongs to the sacred world by birth; but within that world there is a hierarchy of Brahman families some of whom are sacred in relation to others. Every woman, though congenitally impure, is sacred to all adult men; if she is pregnant, she also becomes sacred to all other women of the tribe except her close relatives; and these other women constitute in relation to her a profane world, which at that moment includes all children and adult men. Upon performing so-called purification rites, a woman who has just given birth re-enters society, but she takes her place only in appropriate segments of it—such as her sex and her family—and she remains sacred in relation to the initiated men and to the magico-religious ceremonies. Thus the "magic circles" pivot, shifting as a person moves from one place in society to another. The categories and concepts which embody

---

1. This pivoting was already well understood by Smith (see *The Religion of the Semites*, pp. 427–28 and discussion of "taboo", pp. 152–53, 451–54, etc.). Compare the passage from sacred to profane, and vice versa, among the Tarahumare and the Huichol of Mexico as described by Karl Sofus Lumholtz, *Unknown Mexico: A Record of Five Years' Exploration among the Tribes of Western Sierra Madre* (London: C. Scribner's Sons, 1903), *passim*.

them operate in such a way that whoever passes through the various positions of a lifetime one day sees the sacred where before he has seen the profane, or vice versa. Such changes of condition do not occur without disturbing the life of society and the individual, and it is the function of rites of passage to reduce their harmful effects. That such changes are regarded as real and important is demonstrated by the recurrence of rites, in important ceremonies among widely differing peoples, enacting death in one condition and resurrection in another. These rites are rites of passage in their most dramatic form.

*   *   *

CONCLUSIONS

Our brief examination of the ceremonies through which an individual passes on all the most important occasions of his life has now been completed. It is but a rough sketch of an immense picture, whose every detail merits careful study.

We have seen that an individual is placed in various sections of society, synchronically and in succession; in order to pass from one category to another and to join individuals in other sections, he must submit, from the day of his birth to that of his death, to ceremonies whose forms often vary but whose function is similar. Sometimes the individual stands alone and apart from all groups; sometimes, as a member of one particular group, he is separated from the members of others. Two primary divisions are characteristic of all societies irrespective of time and place: the sexual separation between men and women, and the magico-religious separation between the profane and the sacred. However, some special groups—such as religious associations, totem clans, phratries, castes, and professional classes—appear in only a few societies. Within each society there is also the age group, the family, and the restricted politico-administrative and territorial unit (band, village, town). In addition to this complex world of the living, there is the world preceding life and the one which follows death.

These are the constants of social life, to which have been added particular and temporary events such as pregnancy, illnesses, dangers, journeys, etc. And always the same purpose has resulted in the same form of activity. For groups, as well as for individuals, life itself means to separate and to be reunited, to change form and condition, to die and to be reborn. It is to act and to cease, to wait and rest, and then to begin acting again, but in a different way. And there are always new thresholds to cross: the thresholds of summer and winter, of a season or a year, of a month or a night; the thresholds of birth, adolescence, maturity, and old age; the threshold of death and that of the afterlife—for those who believe in it.

I am certainly not the first to have been struck by the resemblances among various components of the ceremonies discussed here. Similarities have been noted between entire rites, as well as among minor details. Thus, for example, Hartland[2] observed the resemblances between certain initiation rites and some rites of marriage; Frazer[3] perceived those between certain puberty rites and funerals; Ciszewski,[4] those among certain rites of baptism, friendship, adoption, and marriage. Diels[5] followed by Dieterich[6] and Hertz,[7] pointed out similarities among certain ceremonies of birth, marriage, and funerals, and Hertz added to the list rites for the opening of a new house (but did not present evidence) and rites of sacrifice. Goblet d'Alviella[8] pointed out the resemblance between baptism and initiation; Webster,[9] that between initiation into secret societies and the ordination of a shaman.

Hertz[10] was interested in the order of funeral rites and alluded to what he called the "transitory stage"—the period that lasts from marriage to the birth of the first child and that corresponds to the "transitory stage" of the dead in Indonesia (especially in Borneo). But except for him, all these scholars, including Crawley,[11] saw only resemblances in particulars. For instance, the communal meal (Smith's "communion sacrifice"), union through blood, and a number of other ties of incorporation furnished the subject matter for several interesting chapters by Hartland. Certain rites of separation, like temporary seclusion and dietary and sexual taboos, Frazer and Crawley found recurring in a great many sets of ceremonies. Diels, Dieterich, and, in general, all those who have been concerned with classical religions have demonstrated the importance in these religions of the so-called rites of purification (anointing, lustration, etc.). It was inevitable that marked resemblances would appear when a specific rite, such as the exchange of blood, was isolated for analysis in a monograph and when contexts were superimposed.

A host of ethnographers and folklorists have demonstrated that among the majority of peoples, and in all sorts of ceremonies, identical rites are

---

2. Hartland, *The Legend of Perseus*, II, 335–99.

3. Frazer, *The Golden Bough*, pp. 204–7, 209, 210 ff., 418, etc.

4. Ciszewski, *Künstliche Verwandschaft bei den Südslaven*, pp. 1–4, 31, 36, 53, 54, 107–11, 114, etc.

5. Hermann Diels, *Sibyllinische Blätter*, p. 48.

6. Dieterich, *Mutter Erde*, pp. 56–57.

7. Hertz, "La représentation collective de la mort," pp. 104, 117, 126–27.

8. Goblet d'Alviella, "De quelques problèmes relatifs aux mystères d'Éleusis," p. 340.

9. Webster, *Primitive Secret Societies*, p. 176.

10. Hertz, "La représentation collective de la mort," p. 130, n. 5.

11. Crawley (*The Mystic Rose*) points out the precise similarities in the rites of marriage and funerals (p. 369) and rites of marriage and initiation (p. 326); on the last point, see also Reinach, *Cultes, mythes, et religions*, I, 309.

performed for identical purposes. In this way, and thanks first to Bastian, then to Tylor, and later to Andree, a great many unilateral theories were destroyed. Today their orientation is of interest because, in the long run, it will make possible the delineation of cultural sequences and the stages of civilization.

The purpose of this [essay] is altogether different. Our interest lies not in the particular rites but in their essential significance and their relative positions within ceremonial wholes—that is, their order. For this reason, some rather lengthy descriptions have been included in order to demonstrate how rites of preliminary or permanent separation, transition, and incorporation are placed in relation to one another for a specific purpose. Their positions may vary, depending on whether the occasion is birth or death, initiation or marriage, but the differences lie only in matters of detail. The underlying arrangement is always the same. Beneath a multiplicity of forms, either consciously expressed or merely implied, a typical pattern always recurs: *the pattern of the rites of passage.*

The second fact to be pointed out—whose generality no one seems to have noticed previously—is the existence of transitional periods which sometimes acquire a certain autonomy. Examples of these are seen in the novitiate and the betrothal. It is this concept of transition that provides an orientation for understanding the intricacies and the order of rites preliminary to marriage.

Third, it seems important to me that the passage from one social position to another is identified with a *territorial passage,* such as the entrance into a village or a house, the movement from one room to another, or the crossing of streets and squares. This identification explains why the passage from one group to another is so often ritually expressed by passage under a portal,[12] or by an "opening of the doors." These phrases and events are seldom meant as "symbols"; for the semicivilized the passage is actually a territorial passage. In fact, the spatial separation of distinct groups is an aspect of social organization. The children live with the women up to a certain age; boys and girls live separated from married people, sometimes in a special house or section or in a special kraal; at marriage one of the two spouses, if not both, changes residence; warriors do not keep company with blacksmiths, and sometimes each professional class has its assigned place of residence.[13] In the Middle Ages the Jews were isolated in their ghettos, just as the Christians of the first centuries lived in remote sections. The territorial separation

---

12. Trumbull has even noted (*The Threshold Covenant,* pp. 252–57)—among the Chinese, the Greeks, the Hebrews, and others—an identification of the woman and the door.

13. [The reader will note that all these instances are not equally applicable to all societies.]

between clans may also be very definite,[14] and each Australian band camps in a specific place when on the march.[15] In short, a change of social categories involves a change of residence, and this fact is expressed by the rites of passage in their various forms.

As I have said several times, I do not maintain that all rites of birth, initiation, etc., are rites of passage only, or that all peoples have developed characteristic rites of passage for birth, initiation, and so forth. Funeral ceremonies in particular, since they depend on local beliefs concerning man's fate after death, may consist primarily of defensive procedures against the soul of the deceased and rules of prophylaxis against the contagion of death; in that case they present only a few aspects of the typical pattern. Nevertheless, it is always wise to be careful about such conclusions; the pattern may not appear in a summary description of the funeral ceremonies of a particular people, although it is clearly evident in a more detailed account. Similarly, among some peoples who do not consider the woman impure during her pregnancy and who allow anyone to be present at delivery, childbirth is only an ordinary act, painful but normal. But in that case the pattern will be transposed to the rites of childhood, or it may be included in the rites of betrothal and marriage.

The units of ceremonial life among certain peoples sometimes differ from those which are prevalent in our own and most other societies and those around which the chapters of this book have been organized. It has been pointed out, for example, that among the Todas there is a single set of ceremonies extending from the parents' adolescence to the birth of the first child and that it would be arbitrary to divide this set into ceremonies preliminary to puberty, pertaining to puberty, to marriage, to pregnancy, to delivery, to birth, and to childhood. This amalgamation recurs among many other groups, but in the last analysis this effort at synthesis is not affected by it. Although the pattern of the rites of passage occurs in a different form in these instances, it is present nonetheless, and it is clearly elaborated.

Another general observation seems pertinent. The preceding analysis has shown variations in the internal division of societies, the relation of the diverse sections to one another, and the breadth of the barriers between them, which range from a simple imaginary line to a vast neutral region. Thus it would be possible to draw a diagram for each people in which the peaks of a zigzag line would represent recognized stages and the valleys the intervening periods. The apexes would sometimes be sharp peaks and sometimes flat-

---

14. See the separation of the clans in the Pueblo villages as described, among others, by Cosmos Mindeleff, *Localization of Tusayan Clans* (Nineteenth Annual Report of the Bureau of American Ethnology [1897–98], Part II [Washington, D.C.: Government Printing Office, 1900]), pp. 635–53.

15. See, among others, Howitt, *The Native Tribes of South East Australia,* pp. 773–77 (on camping rules).

tened lines of varying length. For example, among certain peoples there are practically no betrothal rites except a meal shared at the moment of the preliminary agreement; the marriage ceremonies begin immediately afterward. Among others, on the contrary, there is a whole series of stages from the time of the betrothal (at an early age) until the newly married couple's return to ordinary life, and each of these stages possesses a certain degree of autonomy.

Whatever the intricacies of the pattern, the order from birth until death must often consist of successive stages best represented in rectilinear form. Among certain peoples like the Lushae, however, it is circular, so that all individuals go through the same endless series of rites of passage from life to death and from death to life. This extreme cyclical form of the pattern has acquired in Buddhism an ethical and philosophical significance, and for Nietszche, in his theory of the eternal return, a psychological significance.

Finally, the series of human transitions has, among some peoples, been linked to the celestial passages, the revolutions of the planets, and the phases of the moon. It is indeed a cosmic conception that relates the stages of human existence to those of plant and animal life and, by a sort of pre-scientific divination, joins them to the great rhythms of the universe.

13

The Principles of Sympathetic Magic

James George Frazer

One of the giants in the history of folkloristics, James George Frazer (1854–1941), was born in Glasgow, Scotland, on New Year's Day. After graduating from the University of Glasgow in 1874, where he studied classics, Frazer moved to Trinity College at Cambridge University where he spent the rest of his life, mostly in the library. He subscribed to the governing intellectual evolutionary paradigm of the nineteenth century—namely, the idea that man had evolved through a succession of unilinear stages from initial savagery to civilization by way of barbarism.

An armchair anthropologist and folklorist, Frazer never ventured far from the sanctuary of his study. An avid reader, he read ethnographic reports from all over the world, extrapolating bits and pieces from here and there in support of his various comparative undertakings. Perhaps the most famous Frazerian apocryphal chestnut, apparently first reported by Ruth Benedict in her presidential address to the American Anthropological Association in December 1947, confirms his distance from the field. Supposedly, American psychologist William James once asked Frazer about the natives he had known. Frazer's succinct and pointed response: "But heaven forbid!" (See Ruth Benedict, "Anthropology and the Humanities," *American Anthropologist* 50 [1948], 585–593.) Even if this conversation never occurred, the traditionality of this bit of Frazer folklore attests to the perception of him as an isolated inhabitant of the ivory tower—aloof, somewhat supercilious, and unreservedly far removed from the field and from contact with living informants.

The nearest Frazer ever came to doing fieldwork was his observation of an Easter celebration on April 13, 1890, in Athens during a three-month visit to Greece, as well as his report of May Day activities elsewhere in Greece; see "Easter in Greece" and "May Day in Greece," *Folklore* 1 (1890), 275–276, 518–520. Frazer's interest in these two topics is also reflected in his brief notes on them in Spain, also based on a trip; see "A Spanish Easter Custom," *The Folklore Journal* 6 (1888), 210, and "Spanish Folklore," *The Folklore Journal* 7 (1889), 174–175. His Scottish fieldwork is equally scant, consisting of a few brief reports of superstitions communicated to him by Isabella Ross, a family servant (see "Sutherlandshire Folk-Lore," *The Folklore Journal* 7 [1889], 53–54, and "Highland Superstitions in Inverness-shire," *Folklore* 1 [1890], 276), as well as burial customs from his mother and harvest customs from his sister (see "Death and Burial Customs, Scotland," *The Folklore Journal* 3 [1885], 281–282, and "Notes on Harvest Customs," *The Folklore Journal* 7 [1889], 47–53). This last article was unquestionably inspired by Mannhardt's investigations of agricultural customs—Mannhardt is cited by name—as was Frazer's most detailed bit of field research "Folk-Lore at Balquhidder," *The Folklore Journal* 6 (1888), 268–271, an excellent ethnographic account of last-sheaf rituals that begins, "The following scraps of folk-lore at Balquhidder were collected by me, from personal observation and inquiry at Balquhidder, Perthshire, in September 1888." But these few sporadic fieldwork efforts pale in comparison with Frazer's incredible library research.

Because Frazer believed all peoples on the earth had passed through identical stages from savagery to civilization, he employed a form of the comparative method to ascertain the origins of folklore which he regarded as survivals from the savagery period. To illuminate folklore (which was essentially limited to the traditions of peasants living in a state of barbarism or the vestiges thereof retained among civilized peoples), it was necessary to compare folklore items with what Frazer assumed were the fuller, more complete and "original" forms still to be found among contemporary "savages." With this premise and its assumption of universalism, Frazer felt perfectly justified in taking data out of particular cultural contexts to be cited in his vast compendiums of "parallels" to particular myths and customs. A fine example of his technique is his compilation of *Myths of the Origin of Fire* (London: Macmillan, 1930), which includes texts from all over the world drawn from extremely arcane and fugitive printed sources.

One problem that inevitably arose from consideration of the whole world as a potential source of parallels was that the task of accumulating additional data was endless. This is perhaps why Frazer's research projects kept expanding to inordinately swollen proportions. Thus an original encyclopedia article on totemism in 1885 turned into an 87-page book two years later and by 1910 became the four-volume 2,000-page *Totemism and Exogamy*. Similarly, a *festschrift* essay for E. B. Tylor, "Folk-Lore in the Old Testament," in *Anthropological Essays presented to Edward Burnett Tylor* (Oxford: 1907), 101–174, developed into the three-volume *Folklore in the Old Testament* in 1918. But the most incredible example of all is Frazer's magnum opus, *The Golden Bough*.

In 1885 Frazer wrote a three-page essay, "Taboo," for the *Encyclopaedia Britannica*. By 1890 this essay had become the first edition of *The Golden Bough*, consisting of two volumes. Ten years later the second edition, now three volumes, was published. Frazer continued to ransack ethnographies and missionary reports for further parallels. Finally, in 1913 the third edition appeared in twelve volumes. Even then Frazer was not finished. In 1936 a single volume entitled *Aftermath: A Supplement to "The Golden Bough"* was published, bringing the total number of volumes to thirteen.

The alleged impetus for this colossal work was a passage in Virgil's *Aeneid* in which a priest in a sacred Arician grove of Diana located on the shore of Lake Nemi participated in a peculiar succession ritual. It was this one single ritual or custom that supposedly intrigued Frazer. Here is how Frazer described the scene at Nemi as he imagined it in the first chapter of the first volume of *The Golden Bough*:

> Down to the decline of Rome a custom was observed there which seems to transport us at once from civilisation to savagery. In the sacred grove there grew a certain tree round which at any time of the day, and probably far into the night, a grim figure might be seen to prowl. In his hand he carried a drawn sword, and he kept peering warily about him as if at every instant he expected to be set upon by an enemy. He was a priest and murderer; and the man for whom he looked was sooner or later to murder him and hold the priesthood in his stead. Such was the rule of the sanctuary. A candidate for the priesthood could only succeed to office by slaying the priest, and having slain him, he retained office till he was himself slain by a stronger or a craftier.

The only significant detail omitted in this account is that the would-be successor was obliged first to pluck the "golden bough" from the tree guarded by the incumbent before slaying him. Inasmuch as it took thirteen bulky volumes to explicate this passage, one could perhaps call *The Golden Bough* the longest footnote in the history of scholarship!

But to be fair to Frazer, he honestly believed his version of the comparative method might be of benefit to mankind. In his preface to the second edition, Frazer said,

> But the comparative study of the beliefs and institutions of mankind is fitted to be much more than a means of satisfying an enlightened curiosity and of furnishing materials for the researches of the learned. Well handled, it may become a powerful instrument to expedite progress if it lays bare certain weak spots in the foundations on which modern society is built—if it shows that much which we are wont to regard as solid rests on the sands of superstition rather than on the rock of nature.

On the other hand, Frazer had no illusions about the ultimate probable fate of his own theoretical biases. Again calling upon an image involving sand, he had this to say in the preface to Part 7, *Balder the Beautiful,* Volume 1, the tenth volume of *The Golden Bough:*

> In this as in other branches of study it is the fate of theories to be washed away like children's castles of sand by the rising tide of knowledge, and I am not so presumptuous as to expect or desire for mine an exemption from the common lot. I hold them all very lightly and have used them chiefly as convenient pegs on which to hang my collections of facts. For I believe that, while theories are transitory, a record of facts has a permanent value, and that as a chronicle of ancient customs and beliefs my book may retain its utility when my theories are as obsolete as the customs and beliefs themselves deserve to be.

Frazer repeated his self-deprecatory assessment of his theoretical stance in 1936 in the preface to the *Aftermath* supplement: "Now as always, I hold all my theories very lightly, and am ever ready to modify or abandon them in the light of new evidence. If my writings should survive the writer, they will do so, I believe less for the sake of the theories which they propound than for the sake of the facts which they record."

One cannot help wondering if Frazer's seeming lack of total commitment to his theories is merely a pose of false modesty. It was certainly a consistent letimotif. Just six years after the publication of the first edition of *The Golden Bough,* Frazer confessed publicly that even he found his theory of the sacred tree ritual at Nemi to be "far-fetched." This admission was voiced in a letter to folklorist Edward Clodd (1840–1930), then president of the English Folklore Society, but it was actually intended as a response to a letter written by novelist and poet Thomas Hardy (1840–1928). Clodd read both letters at a meeting of the English Folklore Society on Tuesday, November 17, 1896. The letters are of interest not only because of Hardy's accurate account of an evil-eye episode that Frazer fails to recognize as such but also for Frazer's expression of gratitude for any bit of data that might possibly lend support to his "far-fetched" theory.

*   *   *

TUESDAY, NOVEMBER 17th, 1896.
The PRESIDENT (Mr. Edward Clodd) in the Chair.

Minutes of Meeting.

The President also read the following letters from Mr. Thomas Hardy and Mr. J. G. Frazer:—

MAX GATE, DORCHESTER.
October 30, 1896.

MY DEAR CLODD,

Here is a bit of folklore that I have just been reminded of.

If you plant a tree or trees, and you are very anxious that they should thrive, you must not go and look at them, or look out of the window at them "on an empty stomach." There is a blasting influence in your eye then which will make them pine away. And the story is that a man, puzzled by this withering of his newly-planted choice trees, went to a white witch to enquire who was the evil-worker. The white witch, after ascertaining the facts, told him it was *himself.*

You will be able to classify this, no doubt, and say exactly where it belongs in the evolutionary chain of folklore. . . .

Yours sincerely,
THOMAS HARDY.

The President having communicated the substance of this letter to Mr. Frazer, and suggested that the explanation lay in the *hungry* man looking on the trees, which thereby became sympathetically starved, and so died, Mr. Frazer replied:—

TRINITY COLLEGE, CAMBRIDGE.
November 1st, 1896.

DEAR MR. CLODD,

The superstition you mention was unknown to me, but your explanation of it seems highly probable.

As explained by you, the superstition is a very interesting example of the supposed sympathetic connection between a man and a tree. As you say, it bears very closely on my explanation of the connection between the priest of Diana at Aricia and the sacred tree, he having to be always in the prime of health and vigour in order that the tree might be so too. I am pleased to find my theory (which I confess often seems to me far-fetched, so remote is it from our nineteenth century educated ways of thought) confirmed by evidence so near home. It is one more indication of the persistence of the most primitive modes of thought beneath the surface of our civilisation. Thank you for bringing it to my notice. . . .

Yours very truly,
JAMES G. FRAZER.

*   *   *

The letters were published in *Folklore* 8 (1897), 11–12. (For discussion of Hardy's frequent use of folklore in his writing, see Ruth Firor, *Folkways in Thomas Hardy* [Philadelphia: University of Pennsylvania Press, 1931] and other references in Florence E. Baer, *Folklore and Literature of the British Isles: An Annotated Bibliography* [New York: Garland, 1986]. For an entrée into the considerable scholarship devoted to the evil eye, see Alan Dundes, ed., *The Evil Eye: A Casebook* [Madison: University of Wisconsin Press, 1992].)

An inordinate amount of scholarship has been devoted to Frazer, more perhaps than to any other folklore pioneer. Some of the evaluation has been laudatory, but much has been critical. If one were to summarize or synthesize a portion of the criticism, one could note the following.

Frazer's "pillaging" of ethnographic sources from all over the world is parallel to the situation of the colonialist British Empire, which exploited materials from subject peoples throughout the nineteenth and early twentieth centuries. His choice of a passage from Virgil to begin his voyage of exploration in *The Golden Bough* might well reflect his basic orientation as a classicist, but the particular passage chosen may have symbolic significance. Breaking the golden bough allowed Aeneas to enter the underworld (see Mary Beard, "Frazer, Leach, and Virgil: The Popularity (and Unpopularity) of *The Golden Bough*," *Comparative Studies in Society and History* 34 [1992], 203–224). Frazer used the passage as a metaphorical excuse to enter the "underworld" of what he deemed "savagery."

From a Freudian perspective, just as savagery supposedly underlay civilization, so the instinctual forces of the id underlie the social conscience of superego. Although Frazer did not much like Freud's approach, his own reveling in savage rites has been compared with Freud's plumbing the depths of id impulses (see John B. Vickery, "*The Golden Bough*: Impact and Archetype," *Virginia Quarterly Review* 39 [1963], 37–57). But a critical difference is that whereas Frazer thought it was good that savage custom and belief were dying out and giving way to (British) civilization, Freud felt the suppression of the id by the civilizing superego was not a good thing.

What, then, can be salvaged from Frazer's weighty tomes of data gathered from all over the world? Unfortunately, not very much. His unilinear evolutionary framework has long been discarded as he predicted, but sad to say even the data he presented cannot really be relied upon. Frazer was a gifted literary stylist, as the earlier passages attest, and he invariably rewrote the ethnographic material he cited. This made it much more presentable to a large and enthusiastic literary readership, but it effectively destroyed its value as an accurate source of folklore for analytic purposes. One is therefore well-advised to check and verify Frazer's original sources before trusting anything he cites in *The Golden Bough*.

Perhaps the one theoretical nugget that can still be mined from the Frazer treasure trove is his incisive analytic breakdown of what he called the principles of sympathetic magic. The two principles of (1) Homeopathic and (2) Contact or Contagious magic seem to have cross-cultural validity. With Homeopathic magic, we have "like produces like," such that one can enact through mimetic imitation the desired event or outcome. Thus one can perform a hunting dance to ensure a successful hunt or pour out a container of water to cause rain to fall. With Contact or Contagious magic, one can carry out an action on an element that was once touched by or connected to the designated target of a magical act. So if someone gains possession of a potential victim's clothing, hair, fingernail cuttings, or any type of bodily emission (saliva, urine, feces), one can inflict harm on the victim by injuring the material once physically attached to the victim.

As Frazer observed, both principles may be involved in one and the same custom. For example, in the common technique of burning an enemy or a rival in effigy, one would have an instance of Homeopathic magic. Sticking a pin in the wax image of an opponent (to cause discomfort in the area stuck by the pin) would be another illustration of what is termed *"envôutement."* If, say, the image were constructed out of the opponent's hair or discarded shirt, however, the principle of Contagious magic would be entailed as well.

The two principles may be perceived as analogous to metaphor (Homeopathic) and simile (Contact). In both tropes comparisons are involved, but only with similes is the comparison linked ("in contact"), usually by the word "like." Actually, most literary tropes have analogs in magical practice. Thus metonymy would be equivalent to "pars pro toto" in magic where one can affect the totality of an object or a victim by attacking just one part of that object or victim.

The power of Frazer's analysis can be easily demonstrated by showing that otherwise enigmatic and puzzling traditions can be greatly illuminated. For instance, Mannhardt mentioned a custom whereby the last sheaf of the harvest was wrapped around a stone. With the help of Frazer's two principles, we can understand the likely underlying rationale. The stone is an emblem of heaviness, and the custom is intended to ensure that next year's harvest is a "heavy," not a "light," one. Because the sheaf is wrapped around the stone, it is touching the stone. Thus both Homeopathic and Contagious magic are involved. Or take the Jewish superstition that claims it is very bad luck to repair a garment while that garment is being worn by an individual. Once one realizes that the only time a garment is sewn on a person is when a body is being prepared for burial, one can understand the custom. In other words, repairing a garment—for example, by sewing on a button—is enacting a funeral ritual, which is essentially treating a living person as a prospective corpse. In such instances the person wearing the garment being repaired must chew on bread or thread to counteract the potential danger.

For details of Frazer's career, see the superb intellectual biography by Robert Ackerman, *J. G. Frazer: His Life and Work* (Cambridge: Cambridge University Press, 1987). See also Robert Fraser, *The Making of the Golden Bough: The Origins and Growth of an Argument* (New York: St. Martin's, 1990). For a brief poignant, sad portrait of Frazer at the end of his life, seemingly tyrannized by his well-intentioned but totally controlling wife,

Lady Frazer, see P. W. Filby, "Life under the Golden Bough," *Gazette of the Grolier Club*, No. 13 (June 1970), 31–38. For a list of Frazer's writings, see Theodore Besterman, *A Bibliography of Sir James George Frazer* (London: Macmillan, 1934), supplemented by additions in Ackerman (1987), 309–310. For a sample of the voluminous scholarship devoted to Frazer, much of which is concerned with his influence on modern literature, see John B. Vickery, *The Literary Impact of "The Golden Bough"* (Princeton: Princeton University Press, 1973), and Robert Fraser, ed., *Sir James Frazer and the Literary Imagination: Essays in Affinity and Influence* (New York: St. Martin's, 1991); for a sampling of anthropological assessments both positive and negative, see Edmund Leach, "Golden Bough or Gilded Twig?" *Daedalus* 90 (1961), 371–399; Mary Douglas, "Judgments on James Frazer," *Daedalus* 107(4) (1978), 151–164; E. E. Evans-Pritchard, *A History of Anthropological Thought* (London: Faber and Faber, 1981), 132–152; Marc Manganaro, " 'The Tangled Bank' Revisited: Anthropological Authority in Frazer's *The Golden Bough*," *Yale Journal of Criticism* 3 (1989), 107–126; and Marty Roth, "Sir James Frazer's *The Golden Bough*: A Reading Lesson," in Marc Manganaro, ed., *Modernist Anthropology: From Fieldwork to Text* (Princeton: Princeton University Press, 1990), 69–79.

For a rather devastating critique of Frazer's point of departure in *The Golden Bough* with respect to the possibility that Frazer took such poetic license as to basically fabricate most of the bough-plucking and priest-slaying incident at Nemi, see Jonathan Z. Smith, "When the Bough Breaks," in *Map Is Not Territory* (Leiden: E. J. Brill, 1978), 208–239. See also Sabine MacCormack, "Magic and the Human Mind: A Reconsideration of Frazer's *Golden Bough*," *Arethusa* 17 (1984), 151–176, and Pietro Clemente, ed., *I Frutti del Ramo d'oro: James G. Frazer e la eredita dell'antropologia* (Brescia: Grafo, 1984). For an account of Frazer's unfortunate patronizing attitude toward "uncivilized savages," see Bernard McKenna, "Isolation and the Sense of Assumed Superiority in Sir James Frazer's *The Golden Bough*," *Nineteenth-Century Prose* 19 (1992), 49–59.

*   *   *

SYMPATHETIC MAGIC

The Principles of Magic

If we analyse the principles of thought on which magic is based, they will probably be found to resolve themselves into two: first, that like produces like, or that an effect resembles its cause; and, second, that things which have once been in contact with each other continue to act on each other at a distance after the physical contact has been severed. The former principle may be called the Law of Similarity, the latter the Law of Contact or Contagion. From the first of these principles, namely the Law of Similarity, the magician infers that he can produce any effect he desires merely by imitating it: from the second he infers that whatever he does to a material object will affect equally the person with whom the object was once in contact, whether it formed part of his body or not. Charms based on the Law of Similarity may be called Homoeopathic or Imitative Magic.[1] Charms based on the Law of Contact or Contagion may be called Contagious Magic. To denote the first of these branches of magic the term Homoeopathic is perhaps preferable, for the alternative term Imitative or Mimetic suggests, if it does not imply, a conscious agent who imitates, thereby limiting the scope of magic too narrowly. For the same principles which the magician applies in the practice of his art are implicitly believed by him to regulate the operations of inanimate nature; in other words, he tacitly assumes that the Laws of Similarity and Contact are of universal application and are not limited to human actions. In short, magic is a spurious system of natural law as well as a fallacious guide of conduct; it is a false science as well as an abortive art. Regarded as a system of natural law, that is, as a statement of the rules which determine the sequence of events throughout the world, it may be called Theoretical Magic: regarded as a set of precepts which human beings observe in order to compass their ends, it may be called Practical Magic. At the same time it is to be borne in mind that the primitive magician knows magic only on its practical side; he never analyses the mental processes on which his practice is based, never reflects on the abstract principles involved in his actions. With him, as with the vast majority of men, logic is implicit, not explicit: he reasons just as he digests his food in complete ignorance of the intellectual and physiological processes which are essential to the one operation and to the other. In short, to him magic is always an art, never a science; the very idea of science is lacking in his undeveloped mind. It is for the philosophic student to trace the train of thought which underlies the magician's practice; to draw out the few simple threads of which the tangled skein is composed; to disengage the abstract principles from their concrete applications; in short, to discern the spurious science behind the bastard art.

If my analysis of the magician's logic is correct, its two great principles turn out to be merely two different misapplications of the association of ideas.[2] Homoeopathic magic is founded on the association of ideas by similarity: contagious magic is founded on the association of ideas by contiguity. Homoeopathic magic commits the mistake of assuming that things which

---

1. The expression Homoeopathic Magic was first used, so far as I am aware, by Mr. Y. Hirn (*Origins of Art* (London, 1900), p. 282). The expression Mimetic Magic was suggested by a writer in *Folk-lore* (viii.1897, p. 65), whom I believe to be Mr. E. S. Hartland. The expression Imitative Magic was used incidentally by me in the first edition of *The Golden Bough* (vol. ii, p. 268).

2. That magic is based on a mistaken association of ideas was pointed out long ago by Professor E. B. Tylor (*Primitive Culture,* i.116), but he did not analyse the different kinds of association.

resemble each other are the same: contagious magic commits the mistake of assuming that things which have once been in contact with each other are always in contact. But in practice the two branches are often combined; or, to be more exact, while homoeopathic or imitative magic may be practised by itself, contagious magic will generally be found to involve an application of the homoeopathic or imitative principle. Thus generally stated the two things may be a little difficult to grasp, but they will readily become intelligible when they are illustrated by particular examples. Both trains of thought are in fact extremely simple and elementary. It could hardly be otherwise, since they are familiar in the concrete, though certainly not in the abstract, to the crude intelligence not only of the savage, but of ignorant and dull-witted people everywhere. Both branches of magic, the homoeopathic and the contagious, may conveniently be comprehended under the general name of Sympathetic Magic, since both assume that things act on each other at a distance through a secret sympathy, the impulse being transmitted from one to the other by means of what we may conceive as a kind of invisible ether, not unlike that which is postulated by modern science for a precisely similar purpose, namely, to explain how things can physically affect each other through a space which appears to be empty.

It may be convenient to tabulate as follows the branches of magic according to the laws of though which underlie them:—

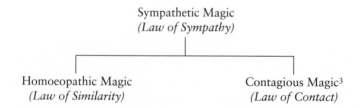

Sympathetic Magic
(Law of Sympathy)

Homoeopathic Magic   Contagious Magic[3]
(Law of Similarity)   *(Law of Contact)*

---

3. It has been ingeniously suggested by Mr. Y. Hirn that magic by similarity may be reduced to a case of magic by contact. The connecting link, on his hypothesis, is the old doctrine of emanations, according to which everything is continually sending out in all directions copies of itself in the shape of thin membranes, which appear to the senses not only as shadows, reflections, and so forth, but also as sounds and names. See Y. Hirn, *Origins of Art* (Londong, 1900), pp. 293 *sqq.* This hypothesis certainly furnishes a point of union for the two apparently distinct sides of sympathetic magic, but whether it is one that would occur to the savage mind may be doubted.

14

The Structure of Russian Fairy Tales

Vladimir Propp

The search for patterns in folklore resulting in Olrik's epic laws, van Gennep's rites of passage, and Frazer's principles of sympathetic magic perhaps reached its peak in 1928 when Russian folklorist Vladimir Iakovlevich Propp (1895–1970) published his pathbreaking monograph *Morfologiia skazki* [The Morphology of the Folktale].

Born in St. Petersburg to a family of German extraction, Propp matriculated at that city's university in 1913 where he specialized in Russian and German philology. Upon his graduation in 1918—he lost some time when he volunteered as a medic at a field hospital in 1915—he taught German to secondary school students, a post he still held when he published his famous *Morphology* in 1928.

It is reported that at Propp's seventieth birthday celebration he indicated that he was largely self-trained in folkloristics. He recalled that he had written *Morphology* "at night, during holidays, at vacation time . . . all by myself, without any advice from anyone, without any guidance" (see B. N. Putilov, "To Vladimir Iakovlevich Propp—100 Years," *Anthropology & Archeology of Eurasia* 35(3) [1996–1997], 84–101).

By 1932 Propp had become a German-language instructor at Leningrad University, attaining a full professorship in the Folklore Division in 1938. At that point he devoted himself completely to folklore rather than to linguistics or language teaching. In 1939 he defended his doctoral dissertation in philological science, "The Genesis of the Fairy Tale," at Leningrad State University (see Dmitrij Zelenin, "The Genesis of the Fairy Tale," *Ethnos 5* [1940], 54–58). Propp's dissertation on the fairy tale used his earlier structural scheme as a point of departure to hypothesize a ritual origin of the scheme. This work was published as *Istoricheskie korni volshebnoi skazki* [Historical roots of magical tale] in 1946. His other major books include *Russkij geroiceskij èpos* [Russian heroic epic poetry] (1955) and the posthumously published *Russkaya skazka* [The Russian folktale] (1984).

Propp also published many important articles, including an extensive comparative study of Oedipus (Aarne-Thompson tale type 931); for a convenient English translation see his "Oedipus in the Light of Folklore," in Lowell Edmunds and Alan Dundes, eds., *Oedipus: A Folklore Casebook* (Madison: University of Wisconsin Press, 1995), 76–121. This study, first published in 1944, is somewhat marred by Propp's rigid adherence to the outmoded nineteenth-century three-stage unilinear evolutionary theory of savagery, barbarism, and civilization. Another interesting article is his "Historical Bases of Some Russian Religious Festivals," in Stephen P. Dunn and Ethel Dunn, eds., *Introduction to Soviet Ethnography*, Vol. 2 (Berkeley: Highgate Road Social Science Research Station, 1974), 367–410.

Propp's innovative achievements in synchronic structural analysis, which secure for him an honored place in the history of international folkloristics, did not always carry over into other theoretical areas. He tended to be an advocate of so-called myth-ritual theory, which argued, for example, that contemporary folklore was derived from earlier primitive ritual. Combining myth-ritual theory with unilinear evolutionary theory, much as Frazer did, Propp believed the origins of fairy tale structure ultimately came from primitive practices and rituals from the distant past. For an introduction to myth-ritual theory, see Robert Ackerman, *The Myth and Ritual School: J. G. Frazer and the Cambridge Ritualists* (New York: Garland, 1991), and Robert A. Segal, ed., *The Myth and Ritual Theory* (Oxford: Blackwells, 1998).

Propp's career was greatly hampered by the political climate existing then in the Soviet Union. His German ancestry was held against him; his *Morphology* and *Historical Roots* were not deemed politically correct in terms of standard Marxist dogma—neither analysis appeared to have anything to do with the political oppression of the folk (people) by the former bourgeoisie. Propp was accused of being unpatriotic because he referenced Western (bourgeois) scholars. A 1948 review of *Historical Roots* likened the work to a London or Berlin telephone directory, a not too snide reference to the fact that Propp cited many non-Russian names in the text and in his footnotes. See Anatoly Liberman's informative lengthy "Introduction" to Vladimir Propp, *Theory and History of Folklore* (Minneapolis: University of Minnesota Press, 1984), ix–lxxxi. The attacks were so pointed that Propp felt obliged to issue a public mea culpa statement in which he pled guilty to the charges of "harmful cosmopolitanism," which he confessed he could not counter (see Liberman, xiv–xv). In a later major work Propp returned to structuralism, but this time he applied the methodology to calendar customs and rituals. This work, *Russkie agrarnye prazdniki* [Russian agrarian holidays], was published in 1963.

In his *Morphology* Propp selected a hundred tales from the celebrated collection by nineteenth-century Russian folklorist A. N. Afanas'ev (1826–1871). But these were not just any folktales; they were what Antti Aarne

(1867–1925) had classified as "Tales of Magic," the first major subset of what he termed "Ordinary Folktales" in his 1910 *Verzeichnis der Märchentypen.* There are many different kinds of folktales—animal tales, formula tales, fables, catch tales, and the like. Propp, however, was concerned with just one kind, what is commonly referred to in English as "fairy tales." (This is an unfortunate misnomer, as fairies rarely appear in "fairy tales." Narratives involving fairies are usually told as true and are set in the real world. Folklorists therefore classify such narratives as legends, not folktales.)

Propp knew very well that he was concerned with fairy tales, or "wonder tales" (Aarne-Thompson tale types 300–749), but he was betrayed by editors and publishers. His original title for the *Morphology* was *Morphology of the Wondertale,* which would have been a much more accurate indication of its content, but his publisher—hoping to attract a wider audience—changed "wondertale" to "folktale" (cf. Liberman, ix). The book attracted little international notice because so few folklorists could read Russian. (Russian folklorist Kirill Chistov maintains that this is not the case but rather reflected general indifference to structuralist approaches in folkloristics. See his "V. Ya. Propp—Legend and Fact," *International Folklore Review* 4 [1986], 8–17.) The work lay relatively dormant for thirty years until it was finally translated into English in 1958, but the English-language edition retained the folktale portion of the title, one supposes to be more faithful to the original Russian wording. In translation the work proved an immediate success, and other translations (into Italian, German, French, and other languages) soon followed.

What exactly was the methodology Propp employed in his *Morphology?* In his response to an unexpectedly negative review of the *Morphology* by French anthropologist Claude Lévi-Strauss, which appeared first in the Italian edition of *Morfologia della Fiaba* in 1966, Propp explained more fully how he came to discover the underlying sequential structure of Russian fairy tales:

Before the revolution, Russian universities cared very little about the literary training of philologists. Folk poetry in particular was completely neglected. To fill that gap, I devoted myself after graduation [1918] to the study of Afanas'ev's famous collection. In a series of wondertales about the persecuted stepdaughter, I noted an interesting fact: in "Morozko" [Frost] (No. 95 in Soviet editions), the stepmother sends her stepdaughter into the woods to Morozko. He tries to freeze her to death, but she speaks to him so sweetly and so humbly that he spares her, gives her a reward, and lets her go. The old woman's daughter, however, fails the test and perishes. In another tale the stepdaughter encounters not Morozko but a *lešij* [a wood goblin], in still another, a bear. But surely it is the same tale! Morozko, the *lešij,* and the bear test the stepdaughter and reward her each in his own way, but the plot does not change. Was it possible that no one should ever have noticed this before? Why did Afanas'ev and others think that they were dealing with different tales? It is obvious that Morozko, the *lešij,* and the bear performed the same action. To Afanas'ev these were different tales because of different characters in them. To me they were identical because the actions of the characters were the same. The idea seemed interesting, and I began to examine other wondertales from the point of view of the actions performed by the characters. As a result of studying the material (and not through abstract reasoning), I devised a very simple method of analyzing wondertales in accordance with the characters' actions—regardless of their concrete form. To designate these actions I adopted the term "functions." My observations of the tale of the persecuted stepdaughter allowed me to get hold of the end of the thread and unravel the entire spool. It turned out that the other plots were also based on the recurrence of functions and that all wondertale plots consisted of identical functions and had identical structure. [See Propp, "The Structural and Historical Study of the Wondertale," in *Theory and History of Folklore,* 67–81.]

What Propp is describing is his discovery that different versions of the same tale—in this instance Aarne-Thompson 480, The Tale of the Kind and the Unkind Girls, often referred to by its title in the Grimm canon, Frau Holle—are just that, namely, different versions of the same tale type. (For one of the classic historic-geographic studies of a folktale, see Warren E. Roberts's comparative study of AT 480, *The Tale of the Kind and the Unkind Girls* [Detroit: Wayne State University Press, 1994], which analyzes more than 900 versions of this well-known tale.) Folklorists before Propp— Aarne, for one—certainly understood that a tale type can manifest itself in a wide variety of versions and variants, but their understanding occurred only at the individual tale type level. Propp's breakthrough was that he realized for the first time that entirely different tale types shared the same basic structure. By analogy, just as versions of a single tale type, such as 480, followed a particular pattern, so did quite distinct different fairy tales follow variations of one and the same basic pattern.

In his *Morphology* Propp identified and discussed a sequence of thirty-one units of action that he termed "functions":

1. One of the members of a family absents himself from home. (absentation)
2. An interdiction is addressed to the hero. (interdiction)
3. The interdiction is violated. (violation)
4. The villain makes an attempt at reconnaissance. (reconnaissance)
5. The villain receives information about his victim. (delivery)
6. The villain attempts to deceive his victim in order to take possession of him or of his belongings. (trickery)
7. The victim submits to deception and thereby unwittingly helps his enemy. (complicity)

8. The villain causes harm or injury to a member of a family. (villainy)
8a. One member of a family either lacks something or desires to have something. (lack)
9. Misfortune or lack is made known; the hero is approached with a request or command; he is allowed to go or he is dispatched. (mediation)
10. The seeker agrees to or decides upon counteraction. (counteraction)
11. The hero leaves home. (departure)
12. The hero is tested, interrogated, attacked, etc., which prepares the way for his receiving either a magical agent or helper. (first function of the donor)
13. The hero reacts to the actions of the future donor. (hero's reaction)
14. The hero acquires the use of a magical agent. (provision or receipt of a magical agent)
15. The hero is transferred, delivered, or led to the whereabouts of an object of search. (spatial transference between two kingdoms, guidance)
16. The hero and the villain join in direct combat. (struggle)
17. The hero is branded. (branding, marking)
18. The villain is defeated. (victory)
19. The initial misfortune or lack is liquidated. (liquidation)
20. The hero returns. (return)
21. The hero is pursued. (pursuit)
22. Rescue of the hero from pursuit. (rescue)
23. The hero, unrecognized, arrives home or in another country. (unrecognized arrival)
24. A false hero presents unfounded claims. (unfounded claims)
25. A difficult task is proposed to the hero. (difficult task)
26. The task is resolved. (solution)
27. The hero is recognized. (recognition)
28. The false hero or villain is exposed. (exposure)
29. The hero is given a new appearance. (transfiguration)
30. The villain is punished. (punishment)
31. The hero is married and ascends the throne. (wedding)

This mere listing of Propp's thirty-one functions scarcely does justice to the brilliance of his analysis. One needs to see the illustrations of each function and to read Propp's interpretations of various series of functions, for example, his distinction between tales that have "seekers" who rescue "victims" and tales in which the victims save themselves. This is significant for feminist theory insofar as heroines of fairy tales in oral versions are frequently victims who are perfectly capable of saving themselves as opposed to written versions (mostly written by males) in which male seekers are required to rescue hapless female victims. The excerpt from Propp's *Morphology* presented here is intended merely to whet the intellectual appetite of the folklore student.

A substantial literature is devoted to Propp's contributions to folkloristics, some of it critical. One possible concern is whether Propp's *Morphology* is applicable to non-Russian fairy tales. His database, after all, was restricted to Russian fairy tales. The answer is that the Russian tales in question are without exception versions of standard Indo-European tale types (as found in the Aarne-Thompson classification system). So although there are differences in versions of international tale types, often clustering according to national or cultural predilections, the basic plot lines of tale types are relatively stable. For this reason Propp's model ought, in theory, to be applicable in some form to other non-Russian versions of the Aarne-Thompson tale types. A few studies have attempted to test the applicability of Propp's schema to different national corpuses of fairy tales. For Chilean tales, see Carlos Foresti, *Analisis morfologico de veinte cuentos de magia de la tradicion oral chilena: Applicacion y discusion del metodo de Vladimir Propp* (Goteborg: 1985). For an Ecuadorian tale, see Laura Hidalgo Alzamora, "Aplicación de la Morfología de Propp al Análisis de un Cuento Folklórico Ecuatoriano," *Folklore Americano* 48 (1989), 135–145. Bible scholars have become just as interested in Propp's *Morphology* as they once were in Olrik's epic laws; see Pamela J. Milne, *Vladimir Propp and the Study of Structure in Hebrew Biblical Narrative* (Sheffield: Almond, 1988).

For more details of Propp's life and career, see, in addition to the essays by Liberman and Putilov, Isidor Levin, "Vladimir Propp: An Evaluation on His Seventieth Birthday," *Journal of the Folklore Institute* 4 (1967), 32–49, and the same author's "Belated Open Letter to Vladimir Jakovlevic Propp," *Linguistica Biblica* 23/24 (1973), 63–68; Levin specifically comments in his "Evaluation" essay that Propp sought "wherever possible to make folkloristics an international discipline." See also Reinhard Breymayer, "Vladimir Jakovlevic Propp (1895–1970)—Leben, Wirken und Bedeutsamkeit," *Linguistica Biblica* 15/16 (1972), 36–66, plus the attached "Bibliographie zum Werk Vladimir Jakovlevic Propps und zur strukturalen Erzählforschung," 67–77; and Irène Sorlin, "Folklore, ethnographie et histoire: Les travaux de V. Ja. Propp et les recherches soviétiques," *Cahiers du Monde russe et soviétique* 29 (1988), 95–138. For discussions of possible precursors to Propp, see Heda Jason, "Precursors of Propp: Formalist Theories of Narrative in Early Russian Ethnopoetics," *PTL* 3 (1977), 471–516, and Irène Sorlin, "Aux origines de l'étude typologique et historique du folklore," *Cahiers du Monde russe et soviétique* 31 (1990), 275–284. In this connection there is some question of the relationship of Propp's work to that of his Russian colleague A. I. Nikiforov (1983–1941), who in 1928 published a very short essay entitled "Towards a Morphological Study of the Folktale." For English translations of this essay, see Felix J. Oinas and Stephen Soudakoff, eds., *The Study of Russian Folklore* (The Hague: Mouton, 1975), 155–161, or "On the Morphological Study of Folklore," *Linguistica Biblica* 27/28 (1973), 25–35, which contains detailed explanatory notes by the translator, Israeli folklorist Heda Jason.

For a small sample of some of the more critical considerations of Propp's *Morphology* by folklorists, see J. P. Guépin, "Propp kan niet en waarom," *Forum der Letteren* 13 (1972), 129–147, and 14 (1973), 30–51; Alsace Yen, "On Vladimir Propp and Albert B. Lord: Their Theoretical Differences," *Journal of American Folklore* 86 (1973), 161–166; E. Meletinsky, S. Nekludov, E. Novi, and D. Segal, "Problems of the Structural Analysis of Fairytales," in P. Maranda, ed., *Soviet Structural Folkloristics* (The Hague: Mouton, 1974), 73–139; Claude Bremond, "Afanasiev and Propp," *Style* 18 (1984), 177–195; V. N. Toporov, "A Few Remarks on Propp's *Morphology of the Folktale*," in Robert Louis Jackson and Stephen Rudy, eds., *Russian Formalism: A Retrospective Glance* (New Haven: Yale Center for International and Area Studies, 1985), 252–271; Satu Apo, "The Variability and Narrative Structures of Wondertales," *Studia Fennica* 33 (1989), 151–160; Lauri Honko, "The Real Propp," *Studia Fennica* 33 (1989), 161–175; and Robert A. Georges, "Some Overlooked Aspects of Propp's *Morphology of the Folktale*: A Characterization and a Critique," in Robert E. Walls and George H. Schoemaker, eds., *The Old Traditional Way of Life: Essays in Honor of Warren E. Roberts* (Bloomington: Trickster Press, 1989), 311–321. Lévi-Strauss's mixed review of Propp's *Morphology*, which first appeared in 1960, is conveniently reprinted in *Theory and History of Folklore*, 167–188. For reviews of the Propp–Lévi-Strauss exchange, see P. W. M. de Meijer, "Eenvoudige Vertelstructuren: Propp en Lévi-Strauss," *Forum der Letteren* 11 (1970), 145–159, and Alan Dundes, "Binary Opposition in Myth: The Propp/Lévi-Strauss Debate in Retrospect," *Western Folklore* 56 (1997), 39–50.

*   *   *

This work is dedicated to the study of *fairy* tales. The existence of fairy tales as a special class is assumed as an essential working hypothesis. By "fairy tales" are meant at present those tales classified by Aarne under numbers 300 to 749. This definition is artificial, but the occasion will subsequently arise to give a more precise determination on the basis of resultant conclusions. We are undertaking a comparison of the themes of these tales. For the sake of comparison we shall separate the component parts of fairy tales by special methods; and then, we shall make a comparison of tales according to their components. The result will be a morphology (i.e., a description of the tale according to its component parts and the relationship of these components to each other and to the whole).

What methods can achieve an accurate description of the tale? Let us compare the following events:

1. A tsar gives an eagle to a hero. The eagle carries the hero away to another kingdom.[1]
2. An old man gives Súčenko a horse. The horse carries Súčenko away to another kingdom.
3. A sorcerer gives Iván a little boat. The boat takes Iván to another kingdom.
4. A princess gives Iván a ring. Young men appearing from out of the ring carry Iván away into another kingdom, and so forth.[2]

Both constants and variables are present in the preceding instances. The names of the dramatis personae change (as well as the attributes of each), but neither their actions nor functions change. From this we can draw the inference that a tale often attributes identical actions to various personages. This makes possible the study of the tale *according to the functions of its dramatis personae.*

We shall have to determine to what extent these functions actually represent recurrent constants of the tale. The formulation of all other questions will depend upon the solution of this primary question: how many functions are known to the tale?

Investigation will reveal that the recurrence of functions is astounding. Thus Bába Jagá, Morózko, the bear, the forest spirit, and the mare's head test and reward the stepdaughter. Going further, it is possible to establish that characters of a tale, however varied they may be, often perform the same actions. The actual means of the realization of functions can vary, and as such, it is a variable. Morózko behaves differently than Bába Jagá. But the function, as such, is a constant. The question of *what* a tale's dramatis personae do is an important one for the study of the tale, but the questions of *who* does it and *how* it is done already fall within the province of accessory study. The functions of characters are those components which could

---

1. *"Car' daet udal'cu orla. Orel unosit udal'ca v inoe carstvo"* (p. 28). Actually, in the tale referred to (old number 104a = new number 171), the hero's future bride, Poljuša, tells her father the tsar that they have a *ptica-kolpalica* (technically a spoonbill, although here it may have meant a white stork), which can carry them to the bright world. For a tale in which the hero flies away on an eagle, see 71a (= new number 128). [L.A.W.] [L.A.W. represents the initials of Louis A. Wagner who edited the second English-language edition of Propp's *Morphology* in 1968—Ed. Note]
2. See Afanás'ev, Nos. 171, 139, 138, 156.

replace Veselóvskij's "motifs," or Bédier's "elements." We are aware of the fact that the repetition of functions by various characters was long ago observed in myths and beliefs by historians of religion, but it was not observed by historians of the tale (cf. Wundt and Negelein[3]). Just as the characteristics and functions of deities are transferred from one to another, and, finally, are even carried over to Christian saints, the functions of certain tale personages are likewise transferred to other personages. Running ahead, one may say that the number of functions is extremely small, whereas the number of personages is extremely large. This explains the two-fold quality of a tale: its amazing multiformity, picturesqueness, and color, and on the other hand, its no less striking uniformity, its repetition.

Thus the functions of the dramatis personae are basic components of the tale, and we must first of all extract them. In order to extract the functions we must define them. Definition must proceed from two points of view. First of all, definition should in no case depend on the personage who carries out the function. Definition of a function will most often be given in the form of a noun expressing an action (interdiction, interrogation, flight, etc.). Secondly, an action cannot be defined apart from its place in the course of narration. The meaning which a given function has in the course of action must be considered. For example, if Iván marries a tsar's daughter, this is something entirely different than the marriage of a father to a widow with two daughters. A second example: if, in one instance, a hero receives money from his father in the form of 100 rubles and subsequently buys a wise cat with this money, whereas in a second case, the hero is rewarded with a sum of money for an accomplished act of bravery (at which point the tale ends), we have before us two morphologically different elements—in spite of the identical action (the transference of money) in both cases. Thus, identical acts can have different meanings, and vice versa. *Function is understood as an act of a character, defined from the point of view of its significance for the course of the action.*

The observations cited may be briefly formulated in the following manner:

1. *Functions of characters serve as stable, constant elements in a tale, independent of how and by whom they are fulfilled. They constitute the fundamental components of a tale.*
2. *The number of functions known to the fairy tale is limited.*

If functions are delineated, a second question arises: in what classification and in what sequence are these functions encountered?

---

3. W. Wundt, "Mythus und Religion," *Völkerpsychologie,* II, Section I; Negelein, *Germanische Mythologie.* Negelein creates an exceptionally apt term, *Depossedierte Gottheiten.*

A word, first, about sequence. The opinion exists that this sequence is accidental. Veselóvskij writes, "The selection and *order* of tasks and encounters (examples of motifs) already presupposes a certain *freedom.*" Šklóvskij stated this idea in even sharper terms: "It is quite impossible to understand why, in the act of adoption, the *accidental* sequence [Šklóvskij's italics] of motifs must be retained. In the testimony of witnesses, it is precisely the sequence of events which is distorted most of all."[4] This reference to the evidence of witnesses is unconvincing. If witnesses distort the sequence of events, their narration is meaningless. The sequence of events has its own laws. The short story too has similar laws, as do organic formations. Theft cannot take place before the door is forced. Insofar as the tale is concerned, it has its own entirely particular and specific laws. The sequence of elements, as we shall see later on, is strictly *uniform.* Freedom within this sequence is restricted by very narrow limits which can be exactly formulated. We thus obtain the third basic thesis of this work, subject to further development and verification:

3. *The sequence of functions is always identical.*

As for groupings, it is necessary to say first of all that by no means do all tales give evidence of all functions. But this in no way changes the law of sequence. The absence of certain functions does not change the order of the rest. We shall dwell on this phenomenon later. For the present we shall deal with groupings in the proper sense of the word. The presentation of the question itself evokes the following assumption: if functions are singled out, then it will be possible to trace those tales which present identical functions. Tales with identical functions can be considered as belonging to one type. On this foundation, an index of types can then be created, based not upon theme features, which are somewhat vague and diffuse, but upon exact structural features. Indeed, this will be possible. If we further compare structural types among themselves, we are led to the following completely unexpected phenomenon: functions cannot be distributed around mutually exclusive axes. This phenomenon, in all its concreteness, will become apparent to us in the succeeding and final chapters of this book. For the time being, it can be interpreted in the following manner: if we designate with the letter A a function encountered everywhere in first position, and similarly designate with the letter B the function which (if it is at all present) *always follows A,* then all functions known to the tale will arrange themselves within

___

4. [Propp is referring to A. N. Veselóvskij, *Poètika* [Poetics], Vol. 2, Fasc. I: *Poètika sjužetov* [The poetics of themes], and V. Šklóvskij, *Theorija prozy* [The theory of prose] (Moscow-Leningrad: 1925), as cited in the notes to Chapter 1 of the *Morphology.*—Ed. Note]

a *single* tale, and none will fall out of order, nor will any one exclude or contradict any other. This is, of course, a completely unexpected result. Naturally, we would have expected that where there is a function A, there cannot be certain functions belonging to other tales. Supposedly we would obtain several axes, but only a single axis is obtained for all fairy tales. They are of the same type, while the combinations spoken of previously are subtypes. At first glance, this conclusion may appear absurd or perhaps even wild, yet it can be verified in a most exact manner. Such a typological unity represents a very complex problem on which it will be necessary to dwell further. This phenomenon will raise a whole series of questions.

In this manner, we arrive at the fourth basic thesis of our work:

4. *All fairy tales are of one type in regard to their structure.*

We shall now set about the task of proving, developing, and elaborating these theses in detail. Here it should be recalled that the study of the tale must be carried on strictly deductively, i.e., proceeding from the material at hand to the consequences (and in effect it is so carried on in this work). But the *presentation* may have a reversed order, since it is easier to follow the development if the general bases are known to the reader beforehand.

Before starting the elaboration, however, it is necessary to decide what material can serve as the subject of this study. First glance would seem to indicate that it is necessary to cover all extant material. In fact, this is not so. Since we are studying tales according to the functions of their dramatis personae, the accumulation of material can be suspended as soon as it becomes apparent that the new tales considered present no new functions. Of course, the investigator must look through an enormous amount of reference material. But there is no need to inject the entire body of this material into the study. We have found that 100 tales constitute more than enough material. Having discovered that no new functions can be found, the morphologist can put a stop to his work, and further study will follow different directions (the formation of indices, the complete systemization, historical study). But just because material can be limited in quantity, that does not mean that it can be selected at one's own discretion. It should be dictated from without. We shall use the collection by Afanás'ev, starting the study of tales with No. 50 (according to his plan, this is the first fairy tale of the collection), and finishing it with No. 151.[5] Such a limitation of material will undoubtedly call forth many objections, but it is theoretically justified. To

---

5. Tales numbered 50 to 151 refer to enumeration according to the older editions of Afanás'ev. In the new system of enumeration, adopted for the fifth and sixth editions and utilized in this translation (cf. the Preface to the Second Edition, and Appendix V), the corresponding numbers are 93 to 170. [L.A.W.]

justify it further, it would be necessary to take into account the degree of repetition of tale phenomena. If repetition is great, then one may take a limited amount of material. If repetition is small, this is impossible. The repetition of fundamental components, as we shall see later, exceeds all expectations. Consequently, it is theoretically possible to limit oneself to a small body of material. Practically, this limitation justifies itself by the fact that the inclusion of a great quantity of material would have excessively increased the size of this work. We are not interested in the quantity of material, but in the quality of its analysis. Our working material consists of 100 tales. The rest is reference material, of great interest to the investigator, but lacking a broader interest.

15

Observations on Folklore

Antonio Gramsci

Most of the contributors in this volume wrote a great deal about folklore. Pitrè and van Gennep, among others, have many, many volumes to their credit. Selecting just one essay from such scholars' output was not an easy task. In the case of Antonio Gramsci (1891–1937), this was not a problem. A political activist rather than a folklorist, Gramsci wrote only a few passages in which he discussed folklore. But these few lines have generated much controversy, perhaps out of proportion to their number. Nevertheless, Gramsci deserves to be considered in any history of international folklorists.

Born in the small town of Ales in the province of Cagliari in Sardinia, Gramsci was one of seven children. When he was just a year old, the family moved to Sòrgono; in 1898 the family moved permanently to Ghilarza. That same year Gramsci's father was arrested for misappropriating public funds, and in 1900 he was sentenced to serve five and a half years in prison. This situation led to extreme poverty for Gramsci's family.

Gramsci suffered poor health all his life, and his physical deformity—he was a hunchback—also proved a liability. Nevertheless, Gramsci did well in school and graduated from the Dettori *liceo* in Cagliari in 1911. He was already very interested in socialism. Depressed economic conditions in Sardinia at that time made it an obvious breeding ground for social and political protest. In 1911 Gramsci was awarded a scholarship offered to disadvantaged students by the University of Turin. In November of that year he traveled to Turin for his qualifying examination, which was his first visit to the mainland of Italy. At the university Gramsci studied with a professor of linguistics, Matteo Bartoli, who was interested in the Sardinian language. As a native speaker Gramsci served as an informant and even asked members of his family for dialect data. During his studies at the university Gramsci joined radical socialist groups, and in December 1915, after graduation, he became a member of the editorial staff of the socialist party organ *Avanti!*

By 1920 Gramsci was involved as a strategist in various strike actions in Turin, and in 1921 he participated in the founding of the Communist Party of Italy and was named to the party's central committee. In 1922, although his health continued to be poor, he visited the Soviet Union, a country he very much admired. One should keep in mind that the Russian Revolution of 1917 in which the tsar was overthrown was initially seen as a beacon of hope for oppressed people in Italy and elsewhere.

When Gramsci returned to Italy he continued to be a leader despite the growing threat of fascism. Gramsci was elected to the Italian parliament, and in May 1925 he delivered his maiden speech there, attacking fascism. The speech was heard by Mussolini. On November 8, 1926, Gramsci was arrested by Mussolini's police as part of a roundup of antifascists and was sent to prison. At his trial in May–June 1928, a fascist Special Tribunal sentenced Gramsci to twenty years, four months, and five days in prison. Although he was transferred from prison to prison he was never released, and he died from a combination of illnesses and a lack of proper medical care at the relatively early age of forty-six.

After being held in prison in the small town of Turi near Bari in the southernmost part of Italy for about two years, Gramsci was finally permitted to read, write letters, and keep a diary. The diary grew to comprise thirty-two notebooks of 2,848 printed pages that contained his jottings on various topics: history, literature, philosophy, politics, and last but not least, folklore! From the outset Gramsci had planned to write something about folklore. In an entry in the first *Notebook,* dated February 8, 1929, he listed sixteen prospective topics; topic number seven was "the concept of folklore." From 1948 to 1951 the Einaudi publishing house in Turin issued Gramsci's *Notebooks* in six volumes. The fifth volume, entitled *Letteratura e vita nazionale,* which appeared in 1950, contained a brief seven-page section entitled "Osservazioni sul folclore." These seven pages changed the direction of Italian folkloristics and eventually influenced folkloristic studies outside of Italy.

The seven pages consisted of a patchwork of four separate entries in Gramsci's notebooks. The first and longest of the four was Gramsci's response to a book review of Giovanni Crocioni's *Problemi fondamentali del Folklore* (Bologna: Zanichelli, 1928). The review was written by Raffaele Ciampini and had appeared in the *Fiera Letteraria* in December 1928. It is sometimes difficult to date Gramsci's passages, but it is reasonable to assume that this one was written sometime in early 1929.

To understand Gramsci's conception of folklore, one must realize that he basically defined "folk" in the traditional European way—that is, as the rural, uneducated peasant. In addition, however, he added the Marxist notion of the folk as the lower stratum of society—oppressed by the bourgeoise, aided and abetted by intellectuals. Defined by Marxist folklore theory, the folk constitute not only the rural "peasant" but also the urban "proletariat." (Maxim Gorki [1868–1936], in an address to the First All-Union Congress of Soviet Writers in 1934, remarked, "One cannot know the true history of the working people unless one is familiar with their oral tradition.") Gramsci also popularized the standard existing left-wing term "subaltern" to refer to the folk. The subaltern in this parlance were victimized by the "hegemony" of the ruling class. On the other hand, Gramsci believed anyone could become an intellectual; he himself was a perfect example of someone from partly peasant origins who through great effort had become transformed into one. When one sees terms such as "subaltern" and "hegemony" in any article on folklore, one can be reasonably certain the writer has been influenced by Gramsci. See Alberto M. Cirese, *Cultura Egemonica e Culture Subalterne* (Palermo: Palumbo Editore, 1971).

What is perhaps most exciting about Gramsci's view of folklore is that he realized that folklore provided a unique source for the study of worldview; as he put it, "It ought to be studied as a 'conception of the world.' " According to strict Marxist theory folklore was an extended "opiate of the masses," a devious means often used by the ruling classes to keep the lower classes subservient, in their customary place. With such reasoning, folklore had to be eliminated to free the oppressed rural peasants and urban proletariat workers from their bondage. Gramsci believed in education. After all, he had benefited from it, rising from an impoverished Sardinian situation to a position of national and even international stature. Thus he contended that teachers needed to study folklore to better understand the worldview of their students and therefore be better able to educate them. For Gramsci, folklore should no longer be considered quaint or trivial subject matter but rather material of the highest value, deserving serious study.

Thus Gramsci's attitude toward folklore appears somewhat ambivalent. He considered it important, worthy of consideration by scholars; but at the same time, to the extent that its influence is baleful, keeping peasants and workers in their oppressed place, it must be eliminated so a more progressive hegemony of the proletariat can replace the older one reflecting the ideology and worldview of the "ruling class."

For some of the folklore scholarship stimulated by Gramsci, see P. Toschi, "Dibattito su Gramsci e il folklore," *Lares* 17 (1951), 153–154; Vittorio Santoli, "Tre osservazioni su Gramsci e il folclore," *Società* 7 (1951), 389–397; Sebastiano Lo Nigro, "Antonio Gramsci e la Letteratura Popolare," *Lares* 23 (1957), 1–14; Pietro Clemente, Maria Luisa Meoni, and Massimo Squillacciotti, eds., *Il Dibattito sul folklore in Italia* (Milan: Edizioni di Cultura Popolare, 1976); Alberto Sobrero, "Folklore e senso comune in Gramsci," *Etnologia Antropologia Culturale* 4 (1976), 70–85; Alberto Maria Cirese, "Gramsci's Observations on Folklore," in Anne Showstack Sassoon, ed., *Approaches to Gramsci* (London: Writers and Readers Publishing Cooperative Society, 1982), 212–247; Moyra Byrne, "Antonio

Gramsci's Contribution to Italian Folklore Studies," *International Folklore Review* 2 (1982), 70–75; and Fabrizio Franceschini, "Fortuna delle note linguistische e demologiche di Gramsci," *Beiträge zur Romanischen Philologie* 27 (1988), 229–238. For a convenient list of all of the allusions to folklore in his letters and notebooks, see Antonio Gramsci, *Arte e folclore,* ed. Giuseppe Prestipino, (Roma: Newton Compton editori, 1976), 251–252.

For a discussion of the fascist approach to folklore in Italy, which was in vogue at the time Gramsci was advocating a Marxist approach, see William E. Simeone, "Fascists and Folklorists in Italy," *Journal of American Folklore* 91 (1978), 543–557. For a striking illustration of how folklore encapsulates worldview, see Sándor Erdész, "The World Conception of Lajos Ámi, Storyteller," *Acta Ethnograhica* 10 (1961), 327–344, reprinted in Alan Dundes, ed., *Sacred Narrative: Readings in the Theory of Myth* (Berkeley: University of California Press, 1984), 315–335.

*   *   *

Folklore. [Giovanni] Crocioni [in *Problemi fondamentali del Folklore,* Bologna, Zanichelli, 1928] criticizes as confused and imprecise the division of folkloristic material provided by Pitrè in his 1897 introduction to the *Bibliografia delle Tradizioni popolari,* and he proposes his own division into four sections: art, literature, science, morality of the people.[1] This division, too, is criticized as imprecise, poorly defined, and too broad. (Raffaele) Ciampini, in the *Fiera Letteraria* of 30 December 1928, asks: "Is it scientific? How, for ex., do superstitions fit into it? And what is the meaning of a morality of the people? How does one study it scientifically? And why, then, not discuss a religion of the people, as well?" It seems to me that until now folklore has been studied (in fact, until now, there has only been the collection of raw material) as a "picturesque" element. It ought to be studied as a "conception of the world" of particular social strata which are untouched by modern currents of thought. This conception of the world is not elaborated and systematized because the people, by definition, cannot do such a

---

1. The bibliographic reference to Crocioni's book, *Problemi fondamentali del Folklore* (Basic Questions in Folklore) is extracted from a review by Raffaele Ciampini, "Folklore," in "I libri della settimana" (Books of the Week) section of *La Fiera Letteraria,* 30 December 1928. Gramsci reconstructs Giovanni Crocioni's views from the review.

The *Bibliografia delle tradizioni popolari d'Italia,* compiled by Giuseppe Pitrè, was first published in 1894 (Turin-Palermo: C. Clausen). Giuseppe Pitrè (1841–1916), a Sicilian doctor, devoted his life to the study of folklore. In 1880 he cofounded the *Archivio delle tradizioni popolari* which he edited until 1906. He also produced the *Biblioteca delle tradizioni popolari Siciliani,* an encyclopedic collection in twenty-five volumes of Sicilian popular songs, legends, tales, word games, proverbs, public spectacles, traditional feasts, etc.

thing; and it is also multifarious, in the sense that it is a mechanical juxtaposition of various conceptions of the world, if it is not, indeed, a museum of fragments of all the conceptions of the world and of life that have followed one another throughout history. Even modern thought and science furnish elements to folklore, in that certain scientific statements and certain opinions, torn from their context, fall into the popular domain and are "arranged" within the mosaic of tradition. (Pascarella's "Scoperta dell'America" shows how notions about Christopher Columbus and other figures, disseminated by elementary school textbooks, are assimilated in bizarre ways.)[2] Folklore can be understood only as a reflection of the conditions of life of the people, although folklore frequently persists even after those conditions have been modified in bizarre combinations.

Certainly, there exists a "religion of the people," especially in Catholic and Orthodox countries (much less so in Protestant countries). The morality of the people is custom and, like superstition, it is closely connected to the real religious beliefs of the people: there are certain imperatives which are much stronger and more tenacious than those of Kantian morals.

Ciampini thinks that Crocioni is quite right in upholding the necessity to teach folklore at the training schools for future teachers, but then he denies the possibility of raising the question of the usefulness of folklore (he means to say, the study of folklore). For him, folklore (that is, the study of folklore) is an end in itself and is only useful insofar as it offers to a people the elements for a deeper knowledge of itself. To study superstitions in order to eradicate them would be, for Ciampini, as if folklore were to kill itself, whereas science is nothing but disinterested knowledge, an end in itself!!! But then why teach folklore in teachers' training schools? To augment the disinterested culture of teachers? The state has its own conception of life and it strives to disseminate it: this is its task and duty. This dissemination does not take place on a *tabula rasa;* it competes and clashes with, for ex., folklore and "must" overcome it. For the teacher, to know folklore means to know what other conceptions are at work in the moral and intellectual formation of the young generations. But folklore studies need a change of attitude besides greater depth: folklore must not be conceived as an oddity,

---

2. In prison, Gramsci had a copy of Cesare Pascarella, *Sonetti,* new ed. (Turin: Tip. Editrice Nazionale, 1926) which contains "La scoperta dell'America" (The Discovery of America) originally published in 1894. The volume is listed by Gramsci among the books sent to his brother Carlo, 11 November 1929.

Cesare Pascarella (1858–1940), a widely read popular poet who wrote in dialect, was influenced and also praised by Carducci. He composed romanticized historical accounts in sonnet form. In "La scoperta dell'America," the adventures of Columbus are narrated from a popular point of view in an effort to endow historical events with a sense of immediacy—hence the folkloristic elements both in the narrative voice as well as in the content of the various descriptions and the reconstruction of events.

a strange, ridiculous or, at best, a picturesque thing; rather, it must be conceived as something very serious and to be taken seriously. Only in this way will its teaching be more effective and better develop the culture of the great popular masses, and the separation between modern culture and popular culture or folklore will disappear. Serious work of this kind would correspond intellectually to what the Reformation was in Protestant countries.

16

Geography and Folk-Tale Oicotypes

Carl Wilhelm von Sydow

Among the founders of folkloristics, perhaps no scholar was more creative and imaginative than Carl Wilhelm von Sydow (1878–1952) of Sweden. Raised in a rural Ryssby parish in Småland province, as a child von Sydow became greatly interested in botany, which later influenced his theoretical formulations in folklore study. He enrolled at Lund University in 1897 where he concentrated on the history of literature and religion. To finance his education, he taught at various folk high schools. As part of his teacher training, he visited a college at Askov in Denmark where he happened to meet the famous Danish folklore collector H. F. Feilberg (1831–1921), who like E. T. Kristensen devoted his long productive life to recording the folklore of Jutland. That meeting changed von Sydow, who had already begun to be intrigued by the folklore of his pupils. Upon his return to Ronneby Folk High School, von Sydow started collecting from his students in earnest. By 1907 he had published *Våra folkminnen—Folksaga, folksägen och folktro* [Our folklore—Folktale, legend, and folk belief].

Also in 1907 von Sydow journeyed to Copenhagen to participate in the fateful meeting with Olrik and Krohn to inaugurate the Folklore Fellows organization. In 1908 he earned a master's degree, and the following year he defended his doctoral thesis, *Två spinnsagor. En Studie i jamförande folksagoforskning* [Two spinning tales: A study in comparative folktale research], essentially a comparative study of the tale commonly known as Rumpelstiltskin, or Aarne-Thompson tale type 500, The Name of the Helper. In that study von Sydow employed the Finnish method that had been developed by Kaarle Krohn, a method he later criticized rather severely.

Von Sydow had hoped to be appointed a lecturer at his alma mater, Lund University, directly following completion of his doctoral dissertation, but that did not happen until 1910 when he became lecturer in Scandinavian

137

and comparative folklore. He had an even longer wait for a professorship, which did not materialize until 1938. In 1914 he established a folklore journal, *Folkminnen och Folktankar.*

In 1927 von Sydow first proposed the concept of "oicotype" (sometimes spelled "oikotype"). The term was borrowed from botany where it referred to a local or regional form of a plant. The word is derived from the Greek root "oikos," meaning house or home, the same root found in such English words as "economy" and "ecology." Von Sydow argued that just as a plant may adapt to different climatic and soil conditions in different areas, so folktales (and by implication other genres of folklore) would take on local characteristics as they moved from one district, region, or country to another. Oicotype is a logical extension of the comparative method. One cannot possibly know how a local variant of a folktale or ballad is unique unless or until one compares that variant with other versions of the same cognate folktale or ballad found elsewhere. If an item of folklore can be shown to have changed to conform with local aesthetics, ideology, values, and the like, then the establishment of an oicotype can be a vital datum for the identification of possible specific features of character or personality. Extending von Sydow's concept, one could even suggest that there might be male and female oicotypes of a particular tale type in a given locale.

For representative discussions of the concept of oicotype, see Elena Bradunas, "If You Kill a Snake, the Sun Will Cry—Folktale Type 425M: A Study in Oicotype and Folk Belief," *Lituanus* 21 (1975), 5–39; Lauri Honko, "The Formation of Oicotypes," in *Folklore on Two Continents: Essays in Honor of Linda Dégh* (Bloomington: Trickster Press, 1980), 280–285; Linda-May Ballard, "The Formation of the Oicotype: A Case Study," *Fabula* 24 (1983), 233–245; Eli Yassif, "From Jewish Oicotype to Israeli Oicotype: The Tale of 'The Man Who Never Swore an Oath,' " *Fabula* 27 (1986), 216–236; and Timothy Cochrane, "The Concept of Ecotypes in American Folklore," *Journal of American Folklore* 24 (1987), 33–55. For a brilliant illustration of the difference between "male" and "female" oicotypes of the same Aarne-Thompson tale type (although the term "oicotype" is not utilized), see anthropologist James M. Taggart's *Enchanted Maidens: Gender Relations in Spanish Folktales of Courtship and Marriage* (Princeton: Princeton University Press, 1990).

Von Sydow was particularly inventive with respect to proposing new terms for folk narrative subgenres. His 1934 article "Kategorien der Prosa—Volksdichtung," his 1937 "Popular Dite Tradition: A Terminological Outline," and his 1938 "Popular Prose Traditions and Their Classification" are in this vein. (All three articles were reprinted in his *Selected Papers on Folklore* [Copenhagen: Rosenkilde and Bagger, 1948].) Most of his suggested terminological innovations were not adopted by the world's folklorists, but several were. These include "dite" for a saying and "memorat(e)" for a personal narrative often, although not always, involving an encounter with a supernatural being. For discussions of these von Sydow terms, see Laurits Bødker, *Folk Literature (Germanic)* (Copenhagen: Rosenkilde and Bagger, 1965), 70, 195–196, and Lauri Honko, "Memorates and the Study of Folk Beliefs," *Journal of the Folklore Institute* 1 (1964), 5–19.

Von Sydow was also very much interested in the transmission of folklore. How exactly did a folktale or a folksong move from one place to another? He was opposed to mechanistic superorganic theories according to which folklore moved by itself without reference to human bearers of tradition. He felt folklore was transmitted from one individual to another. Specifically, he distinguished what he called "active tradition carriers" from "passive tradition carriers." According to von Sydow, the active tradition carriers or bearers were the individuals in a community who actually told the tales or sang the songs. In contrast, the passive tradition carriers or bearers were the audience. They might have heard traditions all their lives but never performed them. Of course, if an active bearer left the community or died, it was possible for a previously passive bearer to become an active bearer to replace him or her. Von Sydow believed folklore moved from one place to another only when one migrating active bearer told a tradition to another active bearer in the new locale.

Von Sydow's distinction appears more applicable to folklore genres that require considerable artistic expertise, such as epics, folktales, and folksongs. It seems less useful for minor genres such as folk speech or gestures where in theory any member of a culture can "perform." The distinction is also useful for prospective folklore collectors who should obviously seek out the active bearers in a community to serve as informants. To be sure, passive bearers might also be interviewed, not so much to elicit texts but rather to learn what texts might possibly mean. A passive bearer might not have told a tale, but he or she, having heard the tale repeatedly might have an opinion as to the tale's meaning(s).

Von Sydow had the reputation of being a contentious personality, and he engaged in heated polemics with various individuals during his career. He was critical of Mannhardt's theories of the last sheaf, claiming they did not stand the test of modern research. For example, calling the last sheaf a "wolf," von Sydow said, was simply a technique used to scare children so they would not trample the corn, and it had nothing whatever to do with demonic belief or vegetation spirits. See "The Mannhardtian Theories About the Last Sheaf and the Fertility Demons from a Modern Critical Point of View," in *Selected Papers on Folklore* (Copenhagen: Rosenkilde and Bagger, 1948), 89–105. Von Sydow's views were confirmed by his student Albert Eskeröd, who wrote a full-fledged study of harvest customs. In his English summary Eskeröd concluded that harvest customs "have nothing at all to do with demons or gods of fertility" (see *Årets Äring: Etnologiska studier i skordens och julens tro och sed* [Stockholm: Nordiska Museet, 1947], 361). Von Sydow was also critical of the Finnish method, claiming that such studies considered only "dry and lifeless extracts" or abstracts rather than the living folktale (see "Finsk metod och modern sagoforskning. Ett svar," *Rig* 26 [1943], 1–23).

But regardless of his tendency to indulge in polemics, von Sydow was un-questionably a dedicated folklorist who made a number of important con-tributions to the lexicon of international folkloristics. For details of his life, see Gösta Berg, "Carl Wilhelm von Sydow (1878–1952)," *Arv* 25–27 (1969–1971), 171–188. For more about Feilberg, see Marius Kristensen, *H. F. Feilberg: Hans Liv og Gaerning* (Copenhagen: Nordisk Forlag, 1923), and Bente Gullveig Alver, "Henning Frederik Feilberg (1831–1921)," *Arv* 25–27 (1969–1971), 225–238. For insights into von Sydow's personality, see Åke Hultkranz, "Trends in Swedish Folklore Research," in Linda Dégh, Henry Glassie, and Felix J. Oinas, eds., *Folklore Today* (Bloomington: Indi-ana University, 1976), 239–249.

*　　*　　*

One of the most serious deficiencies in the study of folk tradition has been that investigators have, to a far too great extent, been content with extracts, instead of seeing their information as part of a natural, living whole. In questions of belief and custom this has led to their concentration overmuch on chance similitude, and neglecting to find out if there was any deeper con-nection. Often enough this chance similitude has been so superficial that it did not even indicate a real analogy. And how much has been considered as belief and ritual, whereas it was only fun and play!

The same fault has been committed in folk-tale research. To be able to survey your material you have, of course, to use extracts; but if you are con-tent with them without bothering about the original, you will not be able to treat your material critically but will get involved in purely schematic meth-ods, which will almost certainly lead you astray. But it is not enough to study folk-tales as tales only. It is also necessary to make oneself familiar with the use of folk-tales, their life in tradition, their transmission and spread. In these respects, great differences prevail between different kinds of folk-tale: Seriously meant fabulates *(Zeugensagen)* and fables have certainly been composed by others than by those who were responsible for the con-struction of the equally simply formed humorous anecdotes. They are used on other occasions, and before a somewhat different audience. They must, therefore, to an extent, obey different laws for their transmission, their spread, *etc.* In exactly the same way the long, fantastic "chimera tales," as I call them, which contain so many episodes, must obey other laws than the short anecdotes, which contain one episode only. Unfortunately the necessity of studying folk-tales in their living context was overlooked from the beginning, and so investigating was built up all the time on faulty theories, formed in the air.

The scientific achievement of Theodor Benfey, in his *Pantschatantra*[1], was of the highest importance, in that he showed how, during the Middle Ages, this old Indian collection of fables was translated from Sanskrit, with Pahlavi, Arabic, and Hebrew as intermediate links, into Latin, and from Latin into later, vulgar tongues. But when he inferred from this that all folk-tales arose in India after Buddha's time and migrated to Europe, he showed how little he knew of the laws and life of tradition. One can conclude nothing about the migration of oral tradition from a literary tradition, which, moreover, hardly contributed to European folk tradition; and the content of European oral folk-tale tradition is generally of quite another kind than that of the literary collections of short stories and fables. This is especially true of our chimera tales, which do not occur at all in Pantschatantra[2], and many of which can be shown to be very much older. Benfey brought the concept of *migration* into folk-tale research. Scholars allowed themselves to be influenced by the word, and constructed theories about migration without basis in reality.

First the Finnish School, Kaarle Krohn and Antti Aarne, systematized folk-tale research, and have produced careful work in a long series of monographs, making many valuable observations. But the most important contribution here, without comparison, consists in the detailed catalogues of the folk-tale treasures of different countries that have been drawn up thanks to Aarne's cataloguing system[3]. By means of these, investigators have got considerably wider facilities in finding the material they may need in studying folk-tales. But as the Finnish School have for the most part been content to study extracts, the life of the tradition has escaped them; and instead they have built on a number of postulates constructed in the air without connection with reality; and so these laboriously produced monographs must be considered as mistaken in their chief results.

In the name of common-sense the Finnish School have rejected Benfey's theory of the origin of all folk-tales in India, and state it as a matter of principle that folk-tales may arise in *any* country. But they consider that certain countries have been the foremost folk-tale nuclei, and that *practically* all folk-tales originate from India. Indeed, it can be said that the Finnish School

---

1. *Pantschatantra: Fünf Bücher indischer Fabeln, Märchen und Erzählungen. Aus dem Sanskrit übersetzt mit Einleitung und Anmerkungen*, von Theodor Benfey I–II. Leipzig. 1859.

2. Apart from Aa 160, which belongs, not to the animal-tale section, but to the chimerates.

3. Aa = Antti Aarne, *The Types of the Folk-Tale*, translated and enlarged by Stith Thompson. Helsinki 1928.

in practice accepts the Benfey theory in its entirety with, however, the reservation, that its validity need not be regarded as absolute.

Benfey's hypothesis of the migration of tales from India had been associated by him with certain important historical events which brought peoples into an intimate contact with one another, resulting in a natural interchange of cultural material. He lays, therefore, great weight on the rise of Buddhism and its preaching missionary monks, on Alexander's conquests, the spread of Islam, and the Crusades. The Finnish School, however, is but little concerned with this, and holds that the wanderings of tales was an automigration, which takes place without any movements of persons, migrations of peoples, or historical events. "It is indeed, as a rule, the tales themselves which spread from mouth to mouth. The storytellers themselves need not go farther than to their neighbours' houses, and this migration can take place at any time," says Kaarle Krohn[4]. This automigration of tales, according to Krohn, takes place either uniformly in every direction like spreading rings on water, or, in a certain direction, like an overflowing river. The Finnish School did not reckon with any kind of frontier, for frontier populations are usually bilingual, and so let the tradition stream through without hindrance. Where the streams of tradition met with no frontiers, then historical events were not required to set them in motion or release them. How consistently and uniformly Krohn holds to the theory of the automigration of tales is clear from the following remarks[5] against Olrik's theory about the myth of the fettered Loki as having originated in Caucasus and through the intermediation of the Goths carried by them from their kingdom on the Black Sea to Scandinavia: "A non-literary connection between Caucasian and Scandinavian traditions presupposes that these traditions exist also in the countries which lie between them." The automigration of tales has not been supported by a single example, and I do not know any real example of automigration for any sort of tradition. But even to those who believe in automigration it should be clear that Scandinavian travellers with the Goths, learning there a number of traditions, could take them with them on their river journeys through Russia and establish them in their own country without giving them on the way to peoples whose language few of them understood. The method of investigations was to collect in extracts as great a number of variants as possible, and to construct the "original form of the tale"—in reality its most complete form—by statistically examining the variations of the different motives; and the country where the variants of the folk-tale were found to be most like the constructed original form was declared to be the homeland of the tale.

Sharp, and in many respects accurate, criticism has been directed against

---

4. *Skandinavisk Mytologi.* Helsingfors 1922, p. 21.
5. *Skand. Mytologi,* p. 21.

the Finnish School by Albert Wesselski, perhaps the foremost scholar of medieval short story literature of our times. But his essential deficiency lies in the fact that he knows nothing about oral tradition, and therefore, quite incorrectly, thinks it has arisen from written literature. And he asserts that the oldest available written form of any folk-tale is the form from which all other variants originate, a conception which is, to put it mildly, grotesque, but which is more or less shared by a number of scholars and literary historians. One may inquire, for example, from what written literature the tales of the Red Indians have been derived, tales which in their technique of composition and force of imagination are quite comparable with European tales. And if the same tale has been written down in different parts of North America, must then the last recorded variants be derived from the first made record? Just as the North American Indians have a tradition of storytelling independent of all written literature, so there exists also in the Old World a story-tradition independent of literature. All that is necessary is to compare on the one side the contents of Pantschatantra and the other novel and fable-collections with, on the other hand, Europe's oral tale-tradition, to see how slight the connection is. Wesselski builds, as much as the Finnish School, on theories constructed in the air without investigation of the real life of the folk-tale in tradition. Whereas the Finnish School only works with extracts, Wesselski has, thanks to his literary studies, a considerably surer grip on the subject, although he has neglected to study the real life, kinds, and distribution of the oral folk-tale, and therefore constantly considers it as degenerate literature. And now I will try to sketch out the main features of the life of folk-tale tradition, and the laws for its spread and variation.

People have far too often imagined that tradition as such is the property of all. Nothing can be further from the truth. It is true of all tradition that in comparison with the whole people its carriers are *very* limited in number. But the proportions are very different for different kinds of tradition. For example the beliefs and customs connected with hunting are something of which the majority have no idea. Only those directly occupied in hunting are real carriers of the proper tradition; and even they have not quite the same methods and ideas, as much of this sort of thing consists of secrets that the initiate will not disclose unnecessarily. If anyone outside the hunter's circle picks up something or other, this will only lead to this outsider's becoming a *passive carrier* of the tradition; it is of no importance for the tradition's continued existence. In the same way, the so-called "wise people" are the real carriers of the peasantry's medical ideas, although, of course, much of this tradition is also found with other people. We may especially remark that old women, without being counted among the wise ones, often have a rich tradition about children's and women's diseases and everything connected with the care of children.

It is the same with folk-tales. The percentage of folk-tale tellers is as small as—perhaps even smaller than—the percentage of "wise ones" in the population of a district. And here too we may distinguish between a larger and a narrower circle. The really active carriers of folk-tale tradition, the *traditors,* are but one or a few in the district, who are called upon when people want to hear folk-tales. Each of them knows but a few tales, but knows them well. They tell them with life and gusto. Sometimes narrators with a bigger repertoire are to be met with, but as far as the chimera tales, which I am especially referring to, are concerned, it is very rare in Teutonic districts for a narrator to know many, and then they are often mingled and arbitrarily altered. As long as a folk-tale traditor remains in his district, anyone else will hardly try to tell *his* tales, for in this they like to observe a kind of literary copyright. Not until he is gone can we reckon on someone else assuming his mantle. Of course, there are many who have heard his tales, but most of them lack the power of remembering a long tale or the capacity to narrate. These can hardly be considered as possessing any folk-tale tradition at all. Others have heard a tale so often that they remember its course fairly well; and by questioning them one would be able to get a fairly good account of the tale; but they do not think of telling it for the entertainment of others, and most of them hardly have the ability to do so. We may call them *passive tradition carriers.* As long as they remain passive they have no part in the handing-down of the folk-tale, but they have some significance. They know the traditor's repertoire and encourage him to tell his tales. So they act as a kind of sounding-board for the tale. It is often due to their presence and insistence that the traditor consents to function; and if he moves from the district and no longer has their insistence, he often ceases to be active.

When the original traditor of a district is gone, perhaps one of these passive hearers summons up courage to try and tell his tales. At first things go perhaps slowly, but if the attempt is repeated several times, he grows more sure of himself. Thus in the main the folk-tale will be told in the same way as before, more especially as the passive tradition-carriers correct deviations: not that this stops the new tale-teller consciously or unconsciously making and keeping to some alteration or other. Some such alterations are pure adiaphora to the audience, and do not touch the real content of the tale. But it might quite as often happen that no one in the district assumes the disappeared traditor's mantle, and then the tale disappears there. If a previously passive tradition-carrier moves to a new place, they may possibly urge him there to become a narrator. One can imagine his new acquaintances urging him to tell something he has heard in his old home as a change from what they already know very well. Then he is subject to less control, and may make bigger alterations on account of lack of memory or personal taste.

The tradition of a whole country is combined from those of the various districts. A certain tale which has belonged to a country from of old is far from being found in every district: it is found only in a *very limited* number of places. It is risky to give a clear idea of the proportions, but I will try. In Denmark and Scania, about 1850, fifteen variants of the tale of King Lindorm[6] were taken down. If we assume that the tale then had double the number of traditors, and thus existed in thirty places, we shall probably be nearest the truth. If, for safety's sake, we increase this number ten times, the result is not more than one in ten thousand of the whole district. There are folk-tales which are spread ten times as much, but hardly more; and if we reckon the number of traditors of one special folk-tale as being at most one *per mille* of a country's population, we are probably, even so, making a high estimate.

A country is often made up of several different cultural districts, with comparatively slight contact with one another. Such districts will then also vary in their folk-tales: partly in that to a certain extent they have different repertories, partly in that tales of the same main type will form special types, *oicotypes*[7] in the different districts.

Starting from what I have already said about carriers of folk-tale tradition, this is not difficult to explain. Within a cultural sphere there is a certain amount of movement in the population. They visit neighbouring districts, and perhaps move to one of them. Sometimes, though rarely, traditors from different districts may meet, compare one another's folk-tale variants, and make alterations by mutual agreement. More often they meet passive tradition-carriers, who may also make observations on this or that episode, this or that motive, and thus work in the same direction. On the other hand, meetings with some traditor from another cultural sphere occur very seldom indeed. This necessarily leads gradually to a common development, so that the tradition of one cultural sphere obtains a uniform stamp when compared with that of another cultural sphere, which, of course, requires a long time.

As a rule a political boundary puts a strong check on moving in and out. Emigrants from a country are but a small part of its whole population. As I have already mentioned, the traditors of a certain tale in a country can hardly amount to one *per mille* of the whole population; but among emigrants they are a still smaller percentage, for, as a rule, only young people

---

6. Aa 433 B.

7. In the science of botany *oicotype* is a term used to denote a hereditary plant-variety adapted to a certain *milieu* (seashore, mountain-land, *etc.*) through natural selection amongst hereditarily dissimilar entities of the same species. When then in the field of traditions a widely spread tradition, such as a tale or a legend [i.e. sagn], forms special types through isolation inside and suitability for certain culture districts, the term oicotype can also be used in the science of ethnology and folklore. One can distinguish between oicotypes of a higher or a lower order: (national, provincial, parochial, *etc.*).

emigrate, and they have not yet acquired any very large number of fixed traditions. For this reason alone then one country can influence another country's folk-tale tradition to but a slight extent. Countries as close as Sweden and Denmark, therefore, which are not even divided by any real linguistic boundary, have in general extremely different traditions, and this is also apparent in the folk-tales. Scania, Halland and Bleking, which were conquered by Sweden from Denmark nearly 300 years ago, and completely incorporated in an incredibly short time, still have typically Danish traditions. The past 300 years which have made closer communication over the boundary possible, have hardly brought with them any alterations in tradition. In contrast to the Finnish School's opinion that national boundaries do not hinder the course of tradition, the circumstances here show that a boundary which is *not* a linguistic boundary, and which has ceased to be a political boundary for nearly 300 years, is still a marked tradition boundary. There are many such tradition boundaries in Europe. As examples of the distinct effect boundaries generally have, we may cite the above-mentioned folk-tale about King Lindorm, which in Scandinavia is only to be found in the old Danish sphere, and is not to be met with in Germany either, a fact which excludes the possibility of its having migrated by itself into Denmark. Another folk-tale, The Princess in the Cave[8], which must have arisen in the early Middle Ages, and which is spread over the whole of Scandinavia and Finland, has not been found in the rest of Europe except in Holstein, which was long under Denmark.

That such a tradition boundary may sometimes be transgressed is plain, but this does not occur by means of a tradition current, flooding over the boundary independently of moving people, but by means of an emigrating traditor. Although many circumstances may cause a traditor who has moved to a new country to cease telling his tales, yet it may be that he goes on telling them, and really succeeds in implanting his tradition there. The folk-tale he thus transmits is of an oicotype strange to the new place, and perhaps it will have to be immediately modified for the new circle of listeners. If there exists a related oicotype in the country, perhaps the two will sooner or later fuse. On the other hand, if it is a folk-tale completely strange to the country, it may agree too little with the temper and other traditions of the people, and so will soon die; but it may adapt itself more and more to prevailing taste, becoming fully acclimatised; but then it develops by degrees into an oicotype separate from that of the country of origin.

An example of a folk-tale thus acclimatised in a new country is the above-mentioned tale of King Lindorm. Its proper disseminative sphere is Italy, the Balkan countries, Turkey and Persia. It does not exist in Western Europe or other Teutonic territory, and must have entered Denmark through, proba-

8. Aa 870.

bly, one single traditor, most likely before the 17th century. It has adapted itself to Danish taste, been influenced by other Danish folk-tales, and made into an independent oicotype.

Quite recently a treatise has been published about that myth of late antiquity, "Great Pan is dead."[9] The author demonstrates that this myth is widespread, but only in North-Western Europe, where it exists, partly in a Celtic oicotype, the only one in the British Isles, partly in a Teutonic oicotype-group. The Celtic oicotype, which is easily recognisable in that the demons appearing in it have cat form, exists sporadically in Scandinavia and Germany too, but constitutes the majority of the French variants. The Teutonic oicotype also exists in French territory, but is in a minority compared with the Celtic one; and the antique myth appears to be clearly a Teutonic oicotype which certainly came to Greece with Teutonic immigrants, of whom there were plenty at that time. But there the myth was so out of place that it could not survive, though it was preserved in writing by Plutarch.

In *Beowulf*, Beowulf's struggle with Grendel and his mother is plainly of Celtic origin, since a similar tale is common in Celtic territory, and agrees perfectly with the rest of Celtic tradition. But nothing similar exists in Teutonic territory, except for an episode in the Icelandic saga about Grettir, an episode which manifestly comes more or less direct from Beowulf itself. In the hero-tale about Sigurd Fafnisbane there are several loans from Celtic folk-tale in the Scandinavian Sigurd tradition, as the Northmen were in constant connection with the Celts through their colonies in Ireland. Thus the episode of how Sigurd roasts the serpent's heart for the sleeping Reginn, fingers it to see if it is done, burns himself, puts his finger in his mouth, and thereby understands bird language, is a manifest loan from the Gaelic *Finn-cycle*. If one compares the episode with related Teutonic and Celtic folk-tales and legends, one cannot avoid the conclusion that it is an obvious Celtic oicotype formation, taken over by the Northern peoples. In the German Niebelungenlied the episode where Sigfrid wins Brynhild for his brother-in-law Gunter is an equally obvious *Russian* folk-tale. German scholars, especially Andreas Heusler, have tried to explain the Russian tale as derived from the German Brynhild episode, for patriotic reasons. But in Teutonic folk tradition there is not a single trace of that kind of motive, and the whole poem seems most unfamiliar to anyone who knows the way of thinking of the Teutonic folk. On the other hand, the Russian folk-tale is popular in Russia, where it has been taken down in quite a number of variants in different parts of that enormous country. It is also in complete correspondence with Russian folk-tale composition, for the "superhumanly strong woman" is a popular motive in several different folk-tale types there,

---

9. Inger M. Boberg, *Sagnet om den store Pans Død*. København 1934 (With summary in German).

and in the whole of Eastern Europe and Near Asia. The Russian folk-tale attracted a German minstrel, who heard it in Russia, and on account of certain associations worked it into the Brynhild poem instead of an earlier motive of perhaps the same content as the Scandinavian Brynhild episode. The great poet of the Niebelungenlied took the motive from the minstrel's more vulgar poem; but it could not remain in the folk-tradition because its whole character was too exotic for the Teutonic conception. This honours the taste of the German people, but it is no shame to the minstrel or the poet of the Niebelungenlied that they used the Russian folk-tale. That *anyone* could believe that the Russian tale originated in Germany results from the fact that the tale was seen in complete isolation, without knowledge of other Russian traditional material; but folk-tales are organically bound up with a great traditional *milieu*, and it is therefore unreasonable to draw wide conclusions from isolated extract material.

The transference of folk-tale tradition may, however, take place on a larger scale. An interesting example of this is Finland. Western Finland was part of Sweden for eight hundred years, but its population was predominantly Finnish. Here Swedish culture was introduced, and here the folk-tales are of purely Swedish type. Eastern Finland, on the other hand, belonged to Russia, and had Russian culture, the Greek-Orthodox Church, and typically Russian folk-tales. The Finnish School noticed this, were astonished that the Russian folk-tales did not migrate further west or the Swedish further east, and thought they ought to explain this by a rule: where two folk-tale currents meet, they check one another. In itself the rule is unreasonable. There has never been any question of folk-tale currents: the two halves of Finland have each been leavened with Russian and Swedish culture respectively on account of immigrating officials, landowners, soldiers, and their servants. It looks as if the original Finnish folk-tales were supplanted in the process, but it may also be that they were of a more particularized kind, and were therefore not noticed by the folk-tale collectors, who collected only folk-tales of international type. After the Russian conquest in 1808 folk-tales of Russian type were found among the Swedish element of the population along the coast; but this is not due to the immigration of East Finns, but to influence from immigrant Russians. This is apparent, among other things, from the fact that the Swedish dialects in Finland have taken over the Russian word *skazka* as a term for a folk-tale.

Here I have touched upon folk-tale transference and the formation of new oicotypes through immigrants. But oicotypification also takes place, of course, if a people is divided up into separate cultural spheres, or further, gives birth to new, separate peoples, so long as they had, before the division, common traditions that afterwards survived. Scholars have forgotten to take this possibility into consideration since the migration theory came into existence, but it is of the very greatest importance. There was a time when all Teutonic peoples spoke the same language and had common traditions, and a number of these still survive in separate oicotypes. The same is true of the Gaels and Kymri. Wherefore in no wise does it follow that every agreement which exists between Gaelic and Kymric tradition can be interpreted as a loan from one people to the other. There was a time when all Indo-Europeans spoke roughly the same language, and also of course, had other traditions in common, these afterwards developing into separate oicotypes. I will give a few examples.

The folk-tale about The Giant Without a Heart[10] is spread among all Indo-European peoples. A giant who has carried away a princess cannot be vanquished because his heart is hidden and strongly guarded. But the hero learns the secret from the princess, and succeeds in getting hold of the heart. When it is destroyed the giant dies. This folk-tale may be divided into two great oicotype groups: the Asiatic, which has it that the giant's life or heart is in, or identical with, a bird or insect in a distant place, guarded by demons or dangerous beasts; and the European, which has it that the heart is in an egg in a bird which is usually enclosed in a whole series of beasts that have to be killed first. Here the migration theory cannot be used, for why should just the boundary between Europe and Asia compel so thorough a remodelling of the tale? The most natural explanation is that the folk-tale was originally a much simpler narrative, based directly on people's belief; but it incited the imagination to extend the account, to make it more thrilling by increasing the difficulties that the hero has to overcome. In so doing, different ways have been followed in Europe and Asia. This puts the origin of the tale back to a couple of thousand years B.C., and this is not in the least unreasonable, as the way of thinking is extremely primitive in it; and the tale seems to have influenced the tale of The Two Brothers, which was written down about 1300 B.C., and with which I shall deal more closely later on in this paper. This tale of The Giant Without a Heart can also give another proof of its age. Among the Slavs and the Celts it developed oicotypes of a kind peculiar to these groups of peoples, but both these oicotypes exhibit such mutual correspondence compared with the Teutonic oicotype that they must have a special connection with one another. A migration over Teutonic territory is not to be thought of: the explanation must lie in the fact that Celts and Slavs dwelt next to one another about 600 B.C., with the result that they then had a whole number of traditions, and among them several folk-tales, in common.

The folk-tale of The Princess on the Glass Mountain[11] (only he who could reach her should have her), spread among all Indo-European peoples, has been oicotypified in this way:—The glass mountain is only in the Teutonic oicotype. It corresponds to a high tower in the Slav oicotype, and to a high palisade in the Indian. Migration from India to Europe is unthinkable, as

---

10. Aa 302.
11. Aa 530.

the Slav oicotype already existed more than a thousand years B.C., when it was imported into Egypt and set down there.

The folk-tale of The Two Brothers, written down in Egypt about 1300 B.C., is of great interest. As folk-tradition it exists exclusively among the *satem*-speaking Indo-Europeans. It is found in two main oicotypes: a Slav, and an Indo-Iranian. I cannot, unfortunately, give here a complete account, but must content myself with a schematic sketch[12]. If we let K signify what is common to both oicotypes, then they have become separate from one another by the Slav adding the motives a, b, c, while the Indo-Iranian has instead added the motives p, q, r. The old Egyptian version has $K + abc + pqr + xyz$. In the whole of its composition the old Egyptian variant is unlike anything that we know of Egyptian folk-tale production, and is typically Indo-European; but in style and content xyz is a purely Egyptian addition, opposed to the rest of the tale both logically and stylistically. The tale cannot have migrated from Indo-Irania to the Slavs, for then the motives pqr would have been found among the Slavs, as they already existed 1300 B.C. in Egypt. And for the same reason the tale cannot have migrated in the opposite direction. It cannot have migrated from Egypt, for then it would be incomprehensible why it should have abandoned just abc + xyz on the way to Persia, and pqr + xyz on the way to the Black Sea countries. Both oicotypes must have developed before 1300 B.C. Two traditors, one from each direction, met and told one another the tale. One introduced the other oicotype's peculiar features into his own version, and in this enlarged form told the tale to an Egyptian scribe, who wrote it down with his own additions. This tale obviously had time to migrate to the rest of Europe, but did not, for folk-tales *do not migrate*. Only three variants have been taken down in Western Europe: one in Småland, Sweden, imported by a Russian prisoner of war in 1808; one in Gothland, taken there by Esthonian servants; and one in Hessen, introduced by an Austrian. But the folk-tale thus imported has been unable to survive anywhere in Western Europe, because it agrees ill with the traditions existing there.

This last example corroborates what I previously asserted: the difficulty of transferring tradition to new surroundings; and in this connection it should be stated that folk-wanderings practically always bring along with them the mass extinction of folk tradition. The abnormal circumstances which existed during the wanderings of the peoples and under the period of transition, present no good occasion for the use of the tradition, and direct attention elsewhere. The Teutonic folk-migrations surely put an end to

---

12. v.Sydow, »Den fornegyptiska sagan om de två bröderna«. *Vetenskaps-Societetens i Lund Årsbok* 1930 pp. 51–89. [See also Susan Tower Hollis, *The Ancient Egyptian "Tale of Two Brothers": The Oldest Fairy Tale in the World* (Norman: University of Oklahoma Press, 1990).—Ed. Note]

masses of Teutonic traditions, not least folk-tales. Interest turned instead to the great events of the day, and a fruit of this was the Teutonic heroic epic. On account of the uncertain conditions which prevailed for centuries, and settlements often of but a short period, even in Tacitus' time the continental Teutons must have been far poorer in tradition than the Scandinavians who remained at home. On the conquest of new countries the tradition of the indigenous population got the upper hand of that of the conquerors. So in Switzerland tradition is Celtic although the language is German. Iceland was uninhabited when the Northmen came there, but the settlers had not much use for folk-tale tradition then: the family-saga achieved predominant interest at the cost of the folk-tradition proper. The folk-tradition now existent in Iceland is extremely unlike that of Scandinavia, although there are a number of traditions taken from Norway that have developed into peculiar oicotypes. In Sweden, Norrland was the district most recently colonized, to a large extent so recently that many good traditions are still available there which are associated with the first Swedish colonization. But apart from this, folk-traditions there are much scantier and poorer than they are in those parts of Sweden which have been inhabited from an earlier period, in spite of the fact that the traditions of the North have been less interfered with by modern culture. Among the richest and most outstanding folk-traditions in Europe is that of the Gaels in Ireland and Scotland; and it is one of the most important objects of European folk-tale research to pay as much attention to it as possible. Its rich vitality is to be attributed partly to the fact that the people have had their present dwelling-places so long, partly that there used to be professional narrators, there being nothing analogous to them in Teutonic territory. Ireland has probably preserved both Celtic and pre-Celtic traditions too.

I have been thinking chiefly of the long chimera folk-tales, but on the whole the same things are true of the shorter forms of narrative, although they have far more traditors, and so are transmitted more readily. The law of oicotypification is also true of them, and may also be more or less applied to other kinds of tradition, such as belief and custom. But I should perhaps stress that oicotypification takes time, and if folk-tales are found that have not been oicotypified, it is usually due to the fact that they are recent, and have perhaps been spread in a literary way.

But I must return to what I asserted in the beginning: we must build our research on the life and laws of the tradition, not on dry and lifeless extracts. The flesh which research puts on such dry lifeless bones is, and remains, dead, without connection with a living reality, and therefore without value[13].

---

13. This paper was read on Aug. 1. 1934, at the International Congress of Anthropological and Ethnological Sciences, held in London. Reprinted from *Béaloideas* VII (1932), pp. 346–355.

17

Irish Tales and Story-Tellers

Séamus Ó Duilearga

If one surveys the overall history of the development of international folkloristics, there may be some surprise at where the most activity has occurred. The smaller countries are often the ones in which interest in folklore has been the greatest. The most extensive collecting efforts have taken place in countries such as Denmark, Estonia, Finland, Hungary, Ireland, and Latvia. The reason for this might be that smaller countries have often feared for the loss of their identity, and inasmuch as identity is very much tied to folklore, nationalistic and patriotic scholars felt the necessity of preserving as much of their heritage—their precious folklore—as possible.

Nowhere is this factor more evident than in Ireland. For centuries the Irish have been concerned about the ever increasing influence of England and English culture. Irish writers had to decide, for example, whether to write in Gaelic (which thereby precluded any appreciable audience in the English-speaking world) or in English, which was and is regarded as a "foreign" tongue.

In any event, the collecting of folklore in Ireland has been extraordinary. In the nineteenth century it was carried out by individual collectors, but in the twentieth century a remarkable national effort has been organized. Much of the credit for this unique national enterprise belongs to Séamus Ó Duilearga (1899–1980), whose name in English is James Delargy.

Delargy was born in the seaside resort of Cushendall in County Antrim on the northeast coast of Northern Ireland. His father died when Delargy was only two, and a few years later he and his mother and brother moved to what has been called the most beautiful of the nine glens of Antrim: Glenariffe. It was there that Delargy heard his first folktale from the village's part-time barber. In an interview in 1974 when Delargy was seventy-five, he still remembered the incident that inspired him to become a folklorist:

*   *   *

153

He was a very knowledgeable man. He could build a boat and shoe a horse, and dance a jig, and had many other accomplishments. He was a friendly man and had a way with children, and my mother sent for him when she made the great decision to have my red hair cut for the first time. He came with a smile on his face, and a big pair of scissors in his hand, and he frightened the life out of me, for I knew that something terrible and irredeemable was going to happen, and that I was drawing away from my mother's apron-strings and about to take my first steps forward into a strange world. So I cried, and howled, and poor Jimmy stood there with the scissors in his hand, and looked at my poor mother who felt half-resentful herself and was on the brink of tears. I forget now which of them solved the difficulty, and stopped me from howling my lungs out. Anyhow the upshot of it all was that if I stayed quiet and let him cut my hair he would tell me a story. That's how I heard my first folk-tale.

What might have been a nightmare became a longed-for ritual, for every time Jimmy came to cut my hair he brought with him a new story. It might be a tale about the fairies in Tiveragh, the fort on the hill above the village where the 'wee folk' lived, and rode around the country on the yellow benweed which made the finest horses that ever you could see, much finer than the shaggy 'shilty' ponies which we children saw the farmers driving in flocks off the hills of Glenariffe and Garron to the fair at Cushendall. Or it might have been the story of the _grógach_ a wee hairy fairy who used to help the farmers in old times to thresh their corn but had a great dislike for anyone who offered to reward him.

When I look back on the road that I have travelled and count the milestones, and think of some of the strange things that have happened to the little red-haired boy who lived long ago—and long ago it is—in the Glens, I think that these tales told by the long dead part-time barber gave a twist to the road that lay ahead. If that be so, soft may the sod lie on Jimmy's head, and God give him peace, for those tales have indeed brought me into pleasant paths and friendly company, not only in the Glens of Antrim but through most of Ireland and many another land besides.

*   *   *

(This extract from the 1974 interview appears in T. K. Whitaker, "James Hamilton Delargy, 1899–1980," _Folk Life_ 20 [1981–1982]:101–106.)

In 1907 the Delargy family moved from the north to settle in the south. James eventually attended Castleknock College near Dublin where he became fascinated with the Irish language. During holidays with his aunt in Cushendall, Delargy sought the last speakers of Irish, and he recorded his first tale in Antrim Irish in 1920. By 1923 he had earned an M.A. in Celtic studies and was fortunate enough to be an assistant to Douglas Hyde, then professor of modern Irish at University College, Dublin. Also in 1923 Delargy met one of his principal informants in County Kerry, a seventy-year-old farmer-fisherman named Seán Ó Conaill, who spoke no English, only Irish.

Delargy was in the right place at the right time, for in 1926 the An Cumann le Béaloideas Éireann [the Folklore of Ireland Society] was founded. He was appointed editor of the society's journal, *Béaloideas,* the first issue of which appeared in 1927. In that issue editor Delargy spelled out his goals: "The aim of our Society is a humble one—to collect what still remains of the folklore of our country. . . . We are certain that the nonsensical rubbish which passes for Irish folklore, both in Ireland and outside, is not representative of the folklore of our Irish people." Delargy edited the journal for forty-six years, from 1927 to 1973!

In that same year (1927), Delargy attended a lecture by Norwegian folklorist Reidar Christiansen (1886–1971), at which Christiansen introduced Delargy to a Swedish folklorist who had come to Ireland to learn Irish—Carl Wilhelm von Sydow. In 1928 Delargy journeyed to Sweden to learn more about the study of folklore. By this means Delargy, who had not been formally trained in folkloristics, was put in touch with major international folklorists.

In 1930 the Irish government established the Institiúd Béaloideas Éireann [the Irish Folklore Institute], followed by the creation of the Coimisiún Béaloideas Éireann [the Irish Folklore Commission] in 1935. According to Delargy, it was largely appeals von Sydow made directly to President de Valera of Ireland that led to the Irish government's decision to set up the Irish Folklore Commission. This was an extraordinary event, as it marked one of the few times in history that a government financed folklore research with sufficient funds to permit the hiring of full-time folklore collectors, eventually nine in number.

Delargy was the honorary director of the commission, and he had the good sense to employ, among others, Sean O'Sullivan (1903–1996), who was recruited as archivist in 1935, and Kevin O'Danaher. No academic program in folkloristics existed in Ireland at that time, so Delargy sent O'Sullivan to the Dialect and Folklore Archive at the University of Uppsala in Sweden for three months' training. Upon his return, O'Sullivan began to catalog thousands of pages of folklore material collected from all over Ireland, especially the Irish-speaking areas. The Irish Folklore Commission holdings grew to more than 2 million pages, which does not include 25,000 photographs and other pictorial representations of folk tradition. See Séamus Ó Duilearga, "The Irish Folklore Commission and Its Work," in *Travaux du Ier Congrès International de Folklore* (Tours: Arrault, 1938), 37–41; Francis Shaw, "The Irish Folklore Commission," *Studies: An Irish Quarterly Review of Letters, Philosophy & Science* 33 (1944), 30–36; and especially Bo Almqvist, "The Irish Folklore Commission: Achievement and Legacy," _Béaloideas_ 45–47 (1977–1979), 6–26. For a short but sparkling overview of the history of Irish folktale collecting activity, see Henry Glassie, _Irish Folktales_ (New York: Pantheon Books, 1985), 11–26. It is easy to demonstrate the effect of the extensive Irish collecting effort on world folklore scholarship. In folklorist Stith Thompson's 1961 second revision of Aarne's tale type index, he made a special point of including figures indicating the numbers of texts available (including archive holdings) of individual tale types. For example, if one checks the figures for Aarne-Thompson tale type 300, The Dragon-Slayer, one sees 61 Estonian, 88 Lithuanian, 37 Swedish, 38 Norwegian, 30 French, and 33 Hungarian texts— not inconsiderable numbers of texts. However, 168 Finnish texts and 527 Irish texts are also listed, a testament to the truly extraordinary collecting activity in Finland and especially Ireland. Actually, the Irish tale type index, published two years after the last revision of the Aarne-Thompson index, gives the number of Irish versions of The Dragon-Slayer as 652. See Seán Ó Súilleabháin and Reidar Th. Christiansen, _The Types of the Irish Folktale_, FF Communications No. 188 (Helsinki: Academia Scientiarum Fennica, 1963). With these statistics in mind, one can easily understand why professional folklorists are so appalled when amateurs restrict their analysis of folktales to just a single version—as often as not the Grimm version, which it turns out is a synthetic, conflated, composite text never originally told in that form by any German nineteenth-century informant.

With his increasing familiarity with Irish folklore, O'Sullivan was able to publish _A Handbook of Irish Folklore_, first in Irish in 1937 and later in English in 1942. Although intended as a guide for collectors, the work also served as a de facto definition of Irish folklore and folk life (peasant ethnography). O'Sullivan went on to write many other important books; for example, he teamed up with Reidar Christiansen to compile the Irish tale type index, _The Types of the Irish Folktale_. O'Danaher was productive as well, specializing in vernacular architecture and other forms of material culture. See his valuable _A Bibliography of Irish Ethnology and Folk Tradition_ (Dublin: Mercier, 1976), and his "Supplement to a Bibliography of Irish Ethnology and Folklore," _Béaloideas_ 48–49 (1980–1981), 206–227.

In 1934 University College, Dublin, had established a lectureship in Irish folklore, and Delargy was appointed to fill it. By 1946 the lectureship had become a professorship of Irish folklore. But Delargy had little time for teaching; he felt his primary responsibility was to direct the activities of the Irish Folklore Commission and to carry out fieldwork himself. Because he was the professor of folklore but did not teach and did not allow O'Sullivan or O'Danaher to do so in his place, the academic side of folkloristics in Ireland did not develop as it should have. Consequently, when Delargy retired there was no qualified Irish applicant for the chair—by that time

O'Sullivan and O'Danaher were too old—and as a result Delargy was succeeded as professor of Irish folklore by Swedish folklorist Bo Almqvist. In
1971 the Irish Folklore Commission was transformed into the Department
of Irish Folklore at University College, Dublin, granting a doctorate in that
subject.

Delargy's only book was the result of seven years of interviews with Seán
Ó Conaill in Kerry. This substantial 492-page collection of folklore from a
single informant was published in 1948 in Irish, with only a summary in
English. Delargy was no theoretician, and his publication record is relatively
modest (see Thomas Wall, "Publications of Professor Séamus Ó Duilearga,"
in his festschrift *Hereditas* [Dublin: An Cumann le Béaloideas Éireann,
1975], 425–431). Why, then, is he included in a volume with the likes of
Grimm, Mannhardt, van Gennep, and other major figures in folkloristics?
The answer lies in one pivotal essay.

On November 28, 1945, Delargy gave the Sir John Rhys Lecture, which
was published in the *Proceedings of the British Academy* 31 (1945), 177–
221. This essay, entitled "The Gaelic Story-Teller, with Some Notes on
Gaelic Folk-Tales," summarized Delargy's fieldwork experience and was
full of exquisite nostalgic vignettes of some of his key informants. Delargy
later presented other, abridged versions of this classic essay. One was "Irish
Tales and Storytellers" for the festschrift for Friedrich von der Leyen in
1963, and another reprise, "Once upon a Time," was published in the festschrift for Iorweth C. Peate, *Studies in Folk Life,* in 1969. Few accounts of
fieldwork offer such vivid, if somewhat romanticized, portraits of storytellers. This essay succeeds admirably in conveying the mood and substance of
the rapport that sometimes comes about from the interaction between collector and informant. And above all, it shows how much folklorists and folk
both value folklore.

For a famous storyteller's eloquent account of her life story, see Peig Sayers (1873–1958), *The Autobiography of Peig Sayers of the Great Blasket
Island,* written in Gaelic in 1935 and published in English translation in
1974 by Syracuse University Press, as well as her sequel, *An Old Woman's
Reflections,* first published in 1939 (and reprinted by London: Oxford University Press, in 1962). For one of the finest examples of folklore fieldwork
in Ireland or, for that matter, anywhere in the world, see Henry Glassie's
remarkable tour de force, *Passing the Time in Ballymenone: Culture and
History of an Ulster Community* (Philadelphia: University of Pennsylvania
Press, 1982). For Delargy's succinct overview of the importance of folklore,
see his "The Study of Irish Folklore," *The Dublin Magazine* 17(3) (1942),
19–26.

*   *   *

The oral traditions of the people of Ireland and Western Scotland form a natural unit—a *kulturgebiet* and a *sprachgebiet* quite distinct in Europe—a community of tradition, language and manners. Along these western coasts of Ireland and Scotland is still spoken a Celtic language in which is preserved the oldest written vernacular literature in Europe north and west of the Alps; in the words of Kuno Meyer, "The earliest voice from the dawn of West European civilization".[1] From the farmers and crofter-fishermen who speak Gaelic as their mother tongue, and who today are the sole custodians of the oldest *unwritten* literature and tradition of the West we have recorded in recent years, and are still recording, an immense body of oral tradition.

These traditions are the State Papers of the unknown Irish dead. Annals and parchments tell us something of the life and times of the ruling classes, both Gaelic and Anglo-Irish; the conservative memory of the Gaelic storyteller is the muniment chest of the long unwritten story of the common people of Ireland.

The predominant feature of medieval Irish literature and of modern oral tradition in Gaelic is the prose narrative, the aristocratic sagas of the eighth century and the democratic wonder-tales and *seanchas* (*sagen*) of the surviving Gaelic speaking story-tellers of today. In no other European country—not even in Iceland—is there such a remarkable continuity of tradition linking the living oral literature of the Gaelic West from the Hebrides to Kerry with that of the manuscript tradition in an unbroken chain of over 1,200 years.

The manuscripts preserved in the archive of the Irish Folklore Commission[2] contain one of the largest collections of *märchen* in Europe, over 35,000; our collectors have been instructed to concentrate on the *sagen* of which we have already gathered about 100,000, but this represents only a fraction of the *sagen-schatz* still available orally in almost every part of the country.

The only real authorities on Irish tradition are the story-tellers themselves. They belong to a different world from their commentators, and even the best-equipped collector, no matter how much he knows of the material he is recording, feels at times like a child in an infant school under the tutelage of a benevolent but omniscient master. One must cultivate an academic humility and a feeling of respect and reverence when working with these exponents of ancient lore. One never knows what the fireside *seanchas* may reveal—and a chance phrase or rustic aphorism, flashing suddenly across the familiar commonplace, may lift the curtain of the centuries and give a glimpse of "old unhappy far-off things and battles long ago". For the illiter-

---

1. Kuno Meyer: Selections from Ancient Irish Poetry, London, 1913, vii.
2. Established by the Government of Ireland in 1935 with its headquarters in University College, Dublin.

ate but intelligent minds of men and women whom I have known were fed not by the ephemeral scribblings of the literate but by voices from an immemorial past.

The[3] art of story-telling has been cultivated in Ireland by successive generations of both aristocratic and plebeian story-tellers from immemorial antiquity, and must have attained a very high degree of perfection in medieval times to judge from the detritus of the epic literature of the Ms. tradition which has come down to us from the eighth century. But the written saga is but a pale ghost of the tale that once was told, and the personality and polished artistry of the medieval story-teller can only be guessed at by the student of the written word who has not had the privilege of hearing the living voice of the modern reciter of Irish wonder-tales, the democratic descendant of the aristocratic story-teller of a thousand years ago. The literature of the ancient and medieval world drew the breath of life from the story-teller and the singer. The tale and the song remain but how little do we know of those from whose lips they passed to the written page! While marginalia and colophons occasionally include the names of some of the scribes of the mss., the tablets of memory have preserved no clue to the identity of the authors of the oral literature of the fireside.

The repertoire of many Irish story-tellers reminds me of the omnibus collections of medieval Irish vellum mss. These old tradition-bearers, like the old manuscripts, are libraries in themselves. Questioning them, we can turn over page after page in their capacious memories, and listen to what we would have told, heroic tale or place-name legend, a religious tale which might have come from a saint's life, a *fabliau,* a collection of aphorisms, genealogies of local families and so on. For here we have the spoken word where the manuscript has the written. Of my friends, the story-tellers of Ireland, it may be said that they have no counterpart in western Christendom.

Here is a picture of a Kerry story-teller, now dead, from whom we have obtained a great many tales. He was an old man of eighty-five when our collector met him. His first remark was to regret, as most of the old people do, that this work of collection had not been started sooner. Had he come, the old man said, even five years before, he would have been able to tell him a tale for every day in the year.

Our collector in his diary describes the old story-teller seated at the fireside:

"His piercing eyes are on my face, his limbs are trembling, as, immersed in his story, and forgetful of all else, he puts his very soul into the telling. Obviously much affected by his narrative, he uses a great deal of gesticulation, and by the movement of his body, hands, and head, tries to convey

---

3. Extracts from the writer's The Gaelic Story-Teller, London 1946. (Proceedings of the British Academy Vol. xxxi.) Out of print.

hate and anger, fear and humour, like an actor in a play. He raises his voice at certain passages, at other times it becomes almost a whisper. He speaks fairly fast, but his enunciation is at all times clear. I have never met anyone who told his tales with more artistry and effect than this very fine old story-teller. He says that his story-telling has been spoiled by being forced, through love of the tales, to tell them in English to young people who did not know Irish. In that way, through lack of practice, and an appreciative Irish-speaking audience, he had lost command over his vast store of tales, and in the end had forgotten almost all of them. He does not like to tell his tales on the recording machine, as it hampers the movements he considers essential to heighten the effect of the story. Once he became so exhausted that he gave up in the middle of a tale, but I coaxed him to continue."

The art of the folk-tale is in its telling. It was never meant to be written nor to be read. It draws the breath of life from the lips of men and from the applause of the appreciative fireside audience. Although there are still many Irish people who can tell the long and intricate *märchen*, it is but rarely now that they are told. The days of the folk-tale are numbered even in Ireland.

The ancient literatures of the continental and insular Celts were preserved orally, memory and mnenonics taking the place of parchment. When the pen takes the place of memory literature suffers much more than a sea-change. The shadow of the spoken word may linger, but the voice and the *mise en scène* of tradition are gone, the audience must be imagined, for the listener has given place to the reader, the narrator to the writer. Oral tradi-tional narrative is like the stone axe of neolithic man, at first rough hewn, later chipped and hammered into a more agreeable symmetry of line, and finally smoothed and refined and polished, a primitive *objet d'art*. So it must have been with the oral fabric, and the polish and patina of long practised skill produced at length the finished literary product of narrative prose.

A story consists of three parts: the tale itself, the reciter, and the audience. The tales were meant to be told by gifted narrators to a critical adult audi-ence who knew the tale themselves—in other words the active tradition-bearers told the tales to an audience of potential, passive tradition-bearers, from which one perhaps might in turn become an active tradition-bearer by telling the tale himself to other people. One must never forget the existence of the audience when studying folk-tradition—these invisible literary critics are there all the time. The story-teller reacted to their presence, to their at-tentive interest and their occasional plaudits and conventional phrases of approval.

No two Irish story-tellers will tell the same hero-tale or *märchen* in pre-cisely the same way. Many story-tellers, masters of their craft, give full scope to their imagination and to their delight in narrative, impressing upon their tale their predilections, their shrewd philosophical observations, and their own strong character and individuality.

The faces of the audience are ever before the story-teller, for he looks at them and to them seeking for their silent and at times their openly expressed approval. Not so the singer—often he sings, his face half hidden by a hand, his head turned aside from his neighbours; at times he seeks the hand of a friend, and thus encouraged, sings his songs of many verses, somewhat like the singers of Finland, chanting the *runot* of the Kalevala.

At the end of a tale in one of my notebooks from Co. Clare I wrote: "30 December 1929. This is the worst told tale I have ever heard" and to one familiar with the story the omissions, hesitations and inconsistencies were exasperating. The audience was quite disgusted. Now and then I would catch the eye of Johnny Carey, a good story-teller, who was sitting beside the fire smoking, and he would shake his head sadly. To him it was sacrilege to mishandle a story so. The unfortunate reciter, who was really doing his best, used to cough at times—he had a cold, but it suited him to cloak his deficiencies with a loud cough now and then, and the resting place in the narration thus created allowed him time to think. Very often, story-tellers cough when they are not sure what they are going to say! Finally, old Carey could stand the strain no longer, being outraged beyond endurance, and he shouted at the story-teller telling him what he had omitted and admonishing him! Carey and the other listeners had known the reciter's father, who was the best story-teller in the district; the son remembered the tales, but could not tell them properly.

The illiterate literary critic can be as merciless in his judgement as his sophisticated colleague writing in a room full of books, and we can be assured that medieval as well as modern oral narrative had to pass through the purgatorial fire of many centuries before reaching the high standard required of it by the cynical critics of the Gaelic-speaking world.

The old-time Gaelic story-teller was a conscious literary artist, proud of his art, jealous of his rivals, eager to pass on the tradition as it had come to him, intolerant of change, conservative as to form and order and plot; but the style and the language are stamped with his own personality, and as he had an eye for the symmetry of the spoken word, he felt at liberty—true artist that he was—to elaborate inside the traditional framework of the narrative the events of the story, and to clothe the commonplaces of fiction with the rich garment of poetic prose. The same subtle speech which had impressed the Romans when they first met the Celts, an epigrammatic speech full of rapid thrust and parry, interspersed with "duels in quatrains", is still the speech of the older generation of Gaelic speakers, and one of the features of Gaelic oral tradition which links the folk-tale of today to the aristocratic manuscript literature of the eighth century.

The professional *scéalaige* of early and medieval Ireland, whose capacious

memory retained the mnemonic vertebrae of as many as 150–350 intricate
sagas, is the aristocratic ancestor of the non-professional country story-tellers
whom I have known who could recite the same number of tales. The technique must have been common to both, although the style of the elaboration
of the frame-work was different. But the narrative was meant to be recited—to be told—and I do not believe that many of the tales preserved to
us in the written literature of medieval Ireland were ever told as they are
written. Nobody would have listened to them. No! They were elaborated by
the individual story-teller inside the rigid frame-work. The narrative *style*
may have changed from one age to another, but one feature of the style of the
eighth century literary tales is a commonplace in the oral tales of today—the
marked predilection for dialogue as an embellishment of the narrative. The
tale may be told in the past tense—and, apparently to relieve tedium—for
narrative in *oratio obliqua* can be tiresome—the story-teller may suddenly
switch over to the historic present or to the easy conversational style.

It should be noted that there were no professional story-tellers in Ireland
in modern times, nor does it appear from the evidence available that story-
telling was peculiar to any class of the rural community.

Stories were told as a rule at night around the winter fire from the end of
harvest until the middle of March, "*O Shamhain go Bealtaine*". It would
seem that a prohibition existed on the telling of heroic tales during the day-
time. "Whistling at night or *fianaíocht* by day" were considered unlucky,
according to the proverb. The recital of Gaelic "hero-tales" was almost
without exception restricted to men. "A woman *fianaí* or a crowing hen!"
the proverb runs. There are exceptions to this rule, but still the evidence is
unmistakable that the telling by women of Finn-tales was frowned upon by
the men.

All the story-tellers whom I and my colleagues have known are country
people, of the small farmer-fisherman type, or farm labourers. I have never
got a story from anyone else. The custodians of the oral archive of memory
have been a gifted élite of the illiterate poor of the centuries, a tiny fraction
of the population, be it noted, for it is not given to all to be a story-teller or
a singer. What the necessary conditions are to belong to this chosen—or,
rather, self-chosen—few are not so easy to determine: First of all, a good
memory; secondly, the blessed gift of intelligent illiteracy which is the main-
stay of memory, and, above all, a rude but nevertheless genuine artistic feeling, added to a desire to save something of value which might so easily be
lost. A story-teller must also have something of the actor in him, for he is
the sole interpreter on the stage by the footlights of the turf-fire of the events
of the tale, the delineator of the character of the various actors who pass to
and fro across the stage of the narrative.

The grown-up audience of the story-teller were like children in their preference for certain beloved tales and never seemed to tire of listening to the
same stories. Should the reciter make any mistake, as, for instance, omit

some detail in the narrative, the courtesy of his listeners would prevent them from interruption but not from correction at the end of the tale. I have seen that happen very often, and I have often noticed how the story-teller's wife, or some other woman relative, would gently remind the reciter of an incident omitted. From long experience these women were familiar with the tales, although they would never presume to tell them. The tales were told usually by men to men, but the women and children could listen to them, provided they kept quiet—it would appear, however, that they were not encouraged! One old woman remembered how as a child she was sent off to bed before the story-telling began, but so eager was she to hear the tales that she crept to the edge of the loft where she slept, and out of the darkness peeped down into the kitchen where the audience was engrossed in the narrative, and listened to the story-teller until she fell asleep.

One of our most valued informants told me of how he had learnt his stories long ago:

"The other boys thought I was too young to go with them to the house where Diarmaid (a wandering beggar-man) was staying, but I used to slip in unobserved and hide under the kitchen table where I could listen to the tales, undisturbed. There is not a word the story-teller said that I could not repeat next morning."

But for the boy under the kitchen-table it is certain that some of the old man's tales would have been lost, as he alone of all that listening company has survived to tell them.

The following anecdote furnishes another example of the subterfuges practised by story-tellers to add to their store of tales:

A certain wandering beggar-man was inordinately proud of a long folk-tale called *Fáilte Uí Chealla*, 'O'Kelly's Welcome'; to what type this tale belonged has not transpired. He used to tell this story in the houses at which he put up on his rounds, but he was afraid that a man named Lynch in Valentia Island, who was well known as a gifted story-teller, might learn the tale and thus be a rival.

One night the 'traveller' got lodgings in the house of a farmer called Ó Conaill in Gleann, on the mainland, some few miles from Valentia. On his arrival, Ó Conaill immediately sent word to his friend, Lynch, who hurried off to Gleann, entered the house secretly, and concealed himself in a loft directly over the fireplace. On the fall of night, when the story-telling was about to begin, the beggar-man looked carefully at the assembled company, eager to hear him tell his jealously guarded tale.

'Is Lynch here?' he asked his host.

'Oh, sure he's in Valentia and probably asleep by this time!' said the farmer.

On this assurance being given, the tramp began his tale. When at length he came to the end there was a triumphant shout from the concealed story-teller, who jumped down off the loft into the midst of the startled audience. 'I have the tale now in spite of you!' cried Lynch to the poor beggar-man. Lynch began to tell the tale then to prove his words, and the dawn was breaking before he finished.

To tell a story is to hear a story, and so it has fallen to me often to tell a story in order to awaken interest, or, better still, to tell it so badly that some-one in the audience would politely insist on telling it himself! Once a start is made, the stream of narrative so long blocked up by disuse and neglect flows freely again, and, indeed, with the cooperation of others in the audi-ence it may freshen to a torrent. In the old days conservative rural protocol required—as the proverb ran—"from the man of the house the first story",—*ar fhear an tí an chéad sgéal*—the guest to tell stories after that until dawn! One can always adroitly manage it so that the man of the house be induced to tell more, and others present to help him by giving their quota to the night's entertainment. There were unities to be observed—time, place and occasion. The time—at night; the place—around the fire; the occa-sion—when an audience of grown-up people was present who wished to hear a tale, and this happened very often at a wake, when, in the presence of the dead, the night was passed seemly in tale and gossip. Over and over again in making inquiries, I have been told that such a tale was heard at a wake; that people used to go miles to a wake in the hope of hearing a fa-mous story-teller. There were other occasions, of course, also, particularly at the winter *veillée* or *céilidhe*, (there are many Irish names for the custom) where people gathered to pass away the time, singing, story-telling, gos-siping.

These fireside literary circles are still to be met with in outlying corners where the radio has not yet disturbed the traditional peace of these old Gaelic gatherings. But they will soon, like much else besides, be a memory: the young people of the Irish countryside are, as elsewhere, *novarum rerum cupidi*.

In writing the following note on an Ulster *céilidhe* I have had access to the valuable data on stories and story-telling compiled in the little commu-nity of Gaelic-speaking fisherman in Teilionn, S. W. Donegal, by Seán O Heochaidh, a full-time collector of the Irish Folklore Commission in that area since 1935.

Sixty to eighty years ago but few people in Teilionn were literate, but in their isolated lives story-telling and singing had reached an advanced stage of perfection. The unlettered literary and musical critics of Teilionn, as of many other Gaelic communities besides, required of the story-teller and the singer an artistic standard of which the book-learned modern can have no conception. Keen rivalry existed between villages in both story-telling and singing, and contestants from neighbouring districts would meet in houses selected for the purpose, where their merits were adjudged both by popular acclaim, and by the higher criticism of the older people of the community.

In every townland in the district there was at least one house to which, as a rule, the same literary clientèle would resort during the nights of winter, usually from mid-September to 17 March; but the story-telling did not really start until *Oidhche Shamhna* (31 October). O Heochaidh points out that the old story-tellers seemed to be loath to tell folktales in their own homes, and preferred to go to a *toigh áirneáil*[4] than to tell their tales in the presence of their own families. In the congenial atmosphere of the house of story-telling, undisturbed by the noise and prattle of children, their sensitive artistry was appreciated by the grown-up audience, mainly men, for whom these tales were intended. In return for the hospitality of the occupiers, the guests attended to their simple wants, bringing turf from the stack, water from the well, and helping in various ways to put the house in order. The stage was soon set for the story-teller, a blazing turf fire provided the light, a stool or chair of the household's slender store was assigned to him in the place of honour beside the fire, and here he awaited the arrival of the visitors; some of these were old men like himself who had been preparing, perhaps for hours before, for the night's entertainment. The lanes and bridle-tracks were none too good in old times, and infirm old people, crippled with rheumatism, found it hard to make their way along the rough pathways to the *toigh áirneáil.* When the house was full to the door, the man of the house would fill his pipe with tobacco, and give it to the most respected guest. The person thus favoured smoked it for a while, then handed it back to its owner; after that it went around the company from one to another. By the time the last man had had his smoke, all the current topics of interest had been discussed, and the story-telling could now begin.

The shanachies of Teilionn belonged to three classes: (1) those who could tell the long folk-tales (*märchen*); (2) those who specialised in *seanchas*[5] only, and (3) the singers, and those who, while they could not sing themselves, knew the words of a large number of songs. These three distinct groups of tradition are rarely found in one person. In the *céilidhe*-house each of these three types of tradition-bearer was expected to contribute to the night's entertainment, but the teller of Finn- and hero-tales was held in highest esteem, and his tales were more popular than the shorter and more realistic stories.

Story-telling was a feature also after "stations" or religious services conducted in private houses; at wakes (usually of old people); at christenings; at quiltings (*cuiltéireacht*) attended only by women, gossip and *seanchas* were the rule, although songs were occasionally sung there also. Fishermen

---

4. The nearest Irish counterpart of the German *spinnstube.*
5. *Sagen,* and social-historical material.

mending their nets have been known to send for a story-teller to help while
away the time. Quarry-workers in Valentia Island, Co. Kerry, found relief
from their labours in listening to stories, having taken the precaution of
posting guards to warn them of the foreman's arrival! At patterns at holy
wells, as, for example, at Daigh Brighde, near Liscannor, Co. Clare, tales
and songs furnished relief during the long hours of the night-vigil. Fishermen, engaged in salmon-fishing off the rocky coast of Sliabh Liag, in S. W.
Donegal, used to say their night prayers while waiting for the haul, and
these were followed usually by story-telling. It is on record that so attentive
were the fishermen on one occasion to the folk-tale being told that the look-
out abandoned his post to listen, and the boat had a narrow escape from
being rammed by a passing steamer. The tale was never finished, to the regret of the old man who, many years afterwards, recalled the incident.

The traditional phrase with which most of the longer *märchen* end is in-
dicative of the attitude towards his traditions of the old type of Irish *sean-
chaí: Sin é mo sgéal-sa! Má tá bréag ann bíodh! Ní mise a chúm ná a cheap
é.* (That is my story! If there be a lie in it, be it so! It is not I who made or
invented it). The tale must be passed on as it has been received, unaltered,
not in regard to language, but in form and plot.

The story-teller's realization of his responsibility as guardian of inherited
tradition is well exemplified by the following anecdote:

An old Teilionn (Donegal) story-teller named Dónal Eoin Mac Briarty
was dying. A friend went to see him. The dying man had his face turned to
the wall, and had apparently said good-bye to this world; but on hearing
the voice of his old friend, he turned around slowly in the bed, and, fixing
his eyes upon his visitor, he said: "Is that, you, Hughie Hegarty?" "Yes",
said Hughie. "Give me your hand", said the old story-teller. "You are welcome. Sit down there until I tell you the last story I shall tell in this world".

He began the story then, and took over an hour to tell it. It was a tale his
friend had never heard before. As he came towards the end, he faltered, but
continued, although with difficulty, until the last word was said. He then
pressed his friend's hand, turned his face to the wall, and said not another
word until God closed his eyes.

The first story-teller I ever met in the south was a certain Seán O Conaill,
a farmer-fisherman of the tiny mountain-hamlet of Cillrialaig, in the southwest corner of Co. Kerry. Seen from the sea one has the impression that this
cluster of six houses hangs between sea and sky, clinging to the precipitous
slopes of the mountain, 300 feet above the sea. It is a lonely, wind-swept
place where man has formed here and there out of the rocks and boulders
and rough mountain land a crazy quilt of tiny fields to grow his oats and
rye, hay, and potatoes. Past the houses the rocky road winds like a ribbon
along the side of the hill to reach here at journey's end the last of all inhab-

ited places on the edge of the known world. Here, forty years ago, I met the man in whose tales and traditions I found the inspiration to collect or have collected, in so far as in me lay, the unwritten oral literature and tradition of the people of Ireland. He was then seventy years of age. He had a local reputation as a story-teller in a parish where there were many story-tellers. He had never left the district nor had he been to school, and he could neither speak nor understand English. But he was one of the best-read men in the unwritten literature of the people whom I have ever known, his mind a storehouse of tradition of all kinds, pithy anecdotes, and intricate hero-tales, proverbs and rimes and riddles, and other features of the rich orally-preserved lore common to all Ireland three hundred years ago. He was a conscious literary artist who took a deep pleasure in telling his tales; his language was clear and vigorous, and had in it the stuff of literature.

It was my custom to visit him three nights a week during my holiday visits to the locality. His house was a two-roomed thatched cottage, one room a kitchen where all the indoor work was done, the other a bedroom. Over the bedroom was a loft which contained also a bed, fishing gear, a spinning-wheel and the various lumber of an old farm-house.

On the kitchen hearth was a turf fire, and on either side of the fire was a little stone seat from which one could look up the chimney and see the stars. To the right of the fire was a well-scoured table, and in the corner a bag of salt for salting fish. On this bag I used to sit, pulling in the table beside me, and there at various times I wrote down from the dictation of my friend nearly 200 pieces of prose narrative. Before we began to work, I used to help Seán and his old wife to tidy up the house: I swept the floor, strewed clean sand on it, brought in an armful of turf, and lit the oil-lamp. Part of my task was to chase the hens which hopped in over the half-door. From the doorway one gazed right down into the sea, and the distant roar of the waves crept into the kitchen and was the ever-present background of the folk-tale.

While I wrote from Seán's dictation, the neighbours would drop in, one by one, or in small groups, and they would listen in patience until the last word of the tale was written. Then the old story-teller would take a burning ember from the fire, light his pipe, lean back in his chair, and listen to the congratulations of the listeners, who, although they had probably often heard the tale before, found pleasure in hearing it again.

One of the finest tales which I wrote from him he had heard fifty years before in a village a few miles away. It was late, he told me, when he left his neighbour's fireside; the night was very dark, and the familiar pathway across the hills seemed rougher than usual. Seán was repeating the tale he had learnt as he made his way homewards, and so intent was he on his task that he stumbled and fell into a mountain-stream that ran across his path.

"But," he said to me, "I didn't mind. I had my story!"

In Seán O Conaill's youth, story-tellers were a common-place in the district, but as he grew older the old tales were not so much heard as formerly.
Finally, there came a time when it was but rarely that he had an opportunity
himself of practising his art in public. So, lest he should lose command over
the tales he loved, he used to repeat them aloud when he thought no one
was near, using the gesticulations and the emphasis, and all the other tricks
of narration, as if he were once again the centre of a fireside story-telling.
His son told me that he had seen his father telling his tales to an unrespon-
sive stone-wall, while herding the grazing cattle. And on another occasion,
on returning from market, as he walked slowly up the hills behind his old
grey mare, he could be heard declaiming his tales to the back of the cart! In
this way he kept a firm grip on stories which he had not told to an audience
for over twenty years; and when I began to visit him I found that he could
repeat these tales to me without hesitation.

When, at last, my work was done, and the last tale was written, my old
friend turned to me and said: "I suppose you will bring out a book of these
stories some day. I've told you now all the tales I can remember, and I'm
glad that they have been written. I hope they'll shorten the night for those
who read them or hear them being read, and let them not forget me in their
prayers, nor the old people from whom I myself learned them."

I recall to mind, as I write, a story-teller from the wild coast of Clare
whose tales I wrote down over thirty years ago in his little house looking
out across the sea to the stony fields of the Aran Islands. Stephen Helery had
an amazing fluency in Irish, and a really first-class collection of folk-tales.
His language had the flavour of an older time, it was full of wit and exuber-
ant fancy, where even the commonplace attained an unwonted dignity. The
tales poured forth in a spate of idiomatic Irish which up till then no pen had
recorded, while Stephen's only companion, a half-wild cat of uncertain
breed, stared at its master across the fire-place, and a hen and chickens
picked at invisible food on the earthen floor. Like the baseless fabric of a
vision all that Irish story-telling world of Clare which I knew has gone, all
that remains being the dead words on a manuscript page of the wealth of
living story and song with which Stephen and my other story-teller friends
had enthralled the listening company by their hospitable firesides.

Perhaps the memory I cherish most of all is the last message of an old
Galway story-teller from whom we had recorded 158 tales. One of these
ran to 34,000 words. He died before we could get the rest—and we had
drawn up a list of 150 more. Well, poor Éamonn Burke died, and that was
the end of the tales, for they went with him, and no one in the district knew
them, or could tell them as the old man could, with a wealth of imagery, of
thrust and parry, and with all the other traditional graces associated with
the lost art of medieval story-telling. A short time before death he told a

friend of mine to send me this message: "When I am dead, bury me in the old graveyard of Muigh-inis, beside the sea, where I can hear the waves on the beach, and the cry of the sea-birds, and let you and Liam Costelloe come to my grave and raise the three keens of sorrow over me".

When I take my notebook out of my pocket to begin a night's questioning or recording I never know what I may hear from my story-teller friends. Usually, I get a medieval miscellany of tales and proverbs and extempore quatrains, with a few riddles or prayers or charms thrown in; it is routine work for the most part, and sometimes I get tired, or the story-teller reaches for his pipe, and we have a welcome pause. And it often happens that a chance phrase will flash across this beloved labour, to be remembered afterwards down the years when the story-teller is dead, and even the scene of our midnight gathering has vanished like the passing of a cloud. I recall the remark of a poor old man telling me an ancient tale of the *Cailleach Bhéarra,* the Old Woman of Beare, who had lived to a great age, and when very old had a sudden desire to go to the top of a hill close to where she had lived all her long life. The old story-teller wished to make clear what time of day it was when she set out on her travels, and he used a phrase which I have never forgotten: "She went out 'when the dew was thinking of falling'."

The old man who used that wonderful phrase is dead and gone this many a year. His grave has no memorial, but the phrase I have quoted will, I hope, be more lasting than bronze to keep alive his memory.

When I decide to make arrangements to open up a new district for the collectors of the Irish Folklore Commission, I make my first acquaintance with the area by seeing as much of it as possible on foot, wandering with a fishing rod along the trout-streams or walking for the length of a day through hills or across the boglands which for me have a singular fascination. And in this pleasant way I meet farmers or herds, water-bailiffs and game-keepers, children returning from school, the postman on his rounds, or the local shopkeeper or teacher. From them I learn that so-and-so is a good story-teller or singer, that such an old woman has a large collection of ancient prayers and charms and is an expert in the lore of medicinal herbs. Or it may be that I meet the story-tellers themselves down by the river. I remember old Seán O Sé coming along to help me land a salmon from the stream at the bottom of his land, and then we sat down on a grassy knoll, our faces to the sun and our backs to the wind, and smoked and chatted; and that was how I met one of the best Kerry story-tellers I have ever known.

In one of these tramps across the hills of West Cork, I heard word of a story-teller who was one of the last of his kind in the district, and so I arranged with some friends of mine who knew him to pay the old man a visit. I transcribe the following from my diary, written at the time (1935):

"We took a road leading into a barren waste of hills and bogland, and at last came to a lonely house where the mountain road stopped, as if it had made up its mind that it served no purpose to go further. On all sides stretched a wilderness, and in the far distance lay the sea. We made our way as best we could to the house of old O Murachú, the blind story-teller. It was getting dark, but there was still a glimmer of light in which we picked our steps through the stones and heather; there was no path, not even a semblance of one. At length my friend pointed forward, and I saw a wreath of smoke, and a moment afterwards we were in sight of a tiny house where the old man lived alone.

"My friend went forward to explain our errand, and I heard the whisper of a Gaelic conversation. Clearly, the old man required to be assured that the stranger from the city was really interested in old stories and knew Irish. A few moments later, I joined my friend and we entered the house. O Murachú was a tall, well-built handsome man. He had been blind since childhood, and had lived quite alone in this backward spot for many years, his sole companion a huge and very intelligent sheep-dog. Well, of course, following Irish and oriental custom, we first talked of many things which had no bearing on the purpose of my visit—the weather, the price of cattle, the wet harvest, politics, but eventually we came down to business. Yes, he knew a few tales—but he hadn't told them for years—the "young people nowadays did not want to hear them any more"—he was out of practice. But there are many things in an old man's head if there be someone to question him. First of all, I had to show the old man that I knew many tales myself, and, finally, I told one tale (which I guessed he knew) wrongly so that he would interrupt me! This little trick always works with a real story-teller. So the old man told me that the version I had was wrong, but that *he* knew the right way to tell it, and then he began. I knew the tale by heart, but it was a real pleasure to hear it told by a master as the light of a flickering turf-fire flitted over his blind face, and the hills themselves seemed to listen, so profound was the stillness in which this age-old tale was told. His Irish was a delight to listen to, for this corner of Ireland was once a land of poetry, where verse came as easily as prose to the lips of southern peasants.

"As the night wore on, under careful questioning the list of tales grew—it ran to 26 numbers when I rose to go. But, of course, we must have something to eat or drink—how sorry he hadn't known we were coming—at least we would have a cup of milk. The milk was in a pail hung on a nail under the rafters. I had noticed a big cat with a hungry look in its eyes sitting in the chimney-corner—so the blind man had to keep the milk out of its way! As I drank the milk I wondered how we would find our way to the road. The night was very dark, and there were dangerous cliffs in the hills over which we might easily stumble. The old man groped for his stick, called on his dog, and said he would show us the way. And so he did, setting off at a great pace, we in his wake, and so at length we reached the high road, said farewell to the blind man, and continued our journey along the mountain road to our distant lodging."

The following description of a western story-teller I have taken from my notes for 1932.

"One evening in the Spring of 1932 a friend dropped me from his car at the entrance to the little lane that led to the house of the story-teller. The lane was passable by day-light; without a guide one was liable to a broken leg at night on the boulders which lay scattered there since the receding ice had forgotten them aeons ago.

As I came in sight of the house, which was a few yards only from the sea-shore, an old man dressed in the white homespun of the Connemara peasant, hobbled out on a stout stick from the door of his cabin and made his way slowly towards me. He addressed me in Irish in a deep rich voice, and enquired suspiciously my errand. I told him that the district-justice had sent me to him to hear some of his stories. He bade me enter, still suspicious but courteous. We sat on either side of the fire, and at first there was an awkward silence. But just then, the door being open, in rushed a young pig and scuttled under the table. I chased the unwelcome stranger into a pile of fishing-net in the corner, and the old man and I caught it and threw it out the door. The ice was broken, the tempo of the conversation became warmer, and in a short time I was seated at the table, sharing the old man's frugal meal. After the meal, we sat beside the fire and smoked, and then the secret was out. The old fellow thought that I might be a policeman. The district was well-known as a centre of the illegal *poitín* manufacture, and all strangers were suspect. It was not long until some of the potent but forbidden drink was produced, and I was given a small glass of it. He was now in very good humour, and agreed at once to tell a tale—although he pointed out that *märchen* should not be told during the day but only at night—this is universal in my experience with the real story-teller.

I shall never forget, as long as I live, the tale I now heard. It was AaTh 313, and although I have often heard it I never met anyone who told it so well. O Briain was the finest story-teller I have ever met—or ever shall meet. He would have been regarded as a good story-teller 500 years ago. A few months afterwards, I brought a dictaphone to the house, and now when I wish to recapture the magic of that amazing version I listen again to the tale and hear the voice of the dead story-teller. On that occasion thirty years ago I wrote the following in my diary!

"At 4 p. m. to Séan O Briain where I recorded AaTh 313, the finest story

I ever heard, and also wrote from dictation 21 large quarto pages of the hero-tale, Sir Slanders. It was somewhat difficult to write as there were five of the old man's grandchildren playing on the floor of the tiny house, and these ran in and out chasing hens and chickens, dogs and geese which persisted in coming in through the open door. The house is situated within a few yards of the sea, and in a high tide, the water seeps in under the door and comes up the floor "but", said the old fellow, "it never yet put out the fire, thanks be to God!" The old man had his eye on the grazing cattle which he could see through the little window beside him, and now and again he would stumble to the door, giving orders in unmistakable language to the children to keep out the cattle from the patch of cultivated ground among the boulders which he called the "garden". At about 10 p. m. a local man called who asked me if I would like to see *poitín* being made. I was delighted and agreed. He and I made our way across a moor, walking for an hour until we reached a lake far away in the hills. My guide leaned up against a rock, and, putting his fingers to his lips, whistled shrilly. A boat now appeared, the oars flashing in the moonlight, and we were rowed across to an island. The island contained four or five men who were grouped around a huge cauldron under which was roaring a large turf fire. It was a strange sight, the blazing fire, the men in various attitudes leaning against the rocks, dark shapes with the firelight playing on their faces. From where I sat I could dip my hand into the lake water which lapped the rocks; overhead a full moon rode through the scudding clouds. And so I remained in this friendly company, listening to their stories and their chat until it was time to say goodbye and set off for home."

The active interest of the countryside in my work was encouraging and very helpful. People would come to tell me of story-tellers in their own neighbourhood, or bring them to my lodging; others, listening to a tale, would tell me that they had heard another way of telling it, and this they would give me, or even if not the complete tale one or more motifs from a forgotten version. Others would remind story-tellers of tales which they had heard them tell years before, and thus bring back to mind tales which otherwise would have gone the way of so many others. In this way the number of tales and traditions at my disposal grew to an alarming degree, but I succeeded in getting most of them; it was a game played against a single opponent—Death—sometimes he won, sometimes I did.

"When I was a boy growing up", said an old man to me, "I was very fond of hearing the old stories, and that's the way I learned them. When I would be working in the field, it is often that I would be thinking about them, and telling them to myself, so that I could keep them in my mind, for I wished to be able to tell them, and I had a real affection for the old people from whom I heard them."

My mind goes back to an experience of my own of June 1952. I had gone to see an old friend of mine, of 95, who was ill and confined to bed. Many a happy day I had spent with him, and many a tale, long and short, I had recorded from him. I had a few words with his wife in the kitchen, and then a voice from the next room, weak but insistent, bade me come in. When I entered the room, I saw at once that the old man was not long for this world. We talked about the old days twenty three years before when I had first come to stay with him, and the nights of story-telling and the old story-tellers now dead who had told their tales as he had told his, and were so proud that they had been written down at last and were safe. After a while I said, "Johnny, I suppose you find it hard to sleep at night?" "I do, indeed", he said, "and sometimes I'm lonely, and when I have said my prayers, I tell the old stories to myself, and it helps to pass the night for me!" He was the last of them all, no one was left to tell a tale, and it was a lonely place now, and he was lonely too, but he found consolation in his prayers and in the exotic company of the heroes of his long Irish wonder-tales. When I rose to go, he and I knew it was the last time we should meet, and the tears rolled slowly down his wrinkled face; he took my hand, and in the old manner kissed it, and I turned away suddenly, and the tears blinded me.

"Denn es muß von Herzen gehen was auf Herzen wirken soll".

The use of the recording-machine has contributed more than anything else to the success of our work. Once the story-teller has heard his own voice repeated from the record he has just made there is no stopping him. I remember a fine old man in Clare, Tomás O Hiomhair, who was so pleased with the sound of his own voice and with the flattering attention paid to his folk-tales that he insisted upon filling nine dozen records I had taken with me. On an average each record contains 1,100 words. He never stopped or fumbled for a phrase but dictated at an even pace until my store of records was exhausted. Then he pushed the machine aside, lit his pipe with an ember from the fire beside him, and turned to the neighbours who had come night after night to listen to him: "Well, men", said he, "ye can talk now if ye have anything to say!"

Poor old Tomás, the night he died he told three tales to a friend who was visiting him, and asked him to tell them to me the next time I visited the neighbourhood. The tales died with him for the good man to whom Tomás had entrusted them was no story-teller, nor had he a good memory. He had been to school and had read too much!

Apart from the tales which lived a sedentary life on the lips and in the memories of a settled rural population, there were the tales which wandered around together with their owners, the Irish *wander-leute,* the people of the roads. The most important of these was the *bacach* or beggar-man, who with bag on back, stick in hand, perhaps a dog at heel, wandered up and

down the country usually following the same itinerary. Many of these un-
fortunates in the past were dispossessed tenants, who had been thrown out
on the roadside at the whim of the landlord; others were broken-down
school-masters who, through drink or other causes, had lost their employ-
ment and taken to the roads of Ireland. Sixty years ago, before the days of
old-age pensions the roads of Ireland were full of these restless wanderers,
who found shelter at night in a rich farmer's barn, or in the houses of the
poor claimed the bed of straw on the kitchen floor beside the fire, traditionally known as *leaba an duine bhoicht,* the poor man's bed, and wherever
they went, they were assured of a meal shared with their hosts, poor themselves, but ever ready with a bite for the stranger. Many of these beggar-
men were story-tellers, and some of them master-craftsmen in the art of narrative.

Then there were wandering pipers and fiddlers, very often blind men who
had taken to music for a livelihood, and wandered about the country, sometimes guided by a child, or by a dog. These were welcome guests, eagerly
sought for by the country people, and wherever they stayed at night, their
lodging was paid for by music and by song. Side by side with them, we may
place the ballad-singers who frequented towns, or gatherings of the people
such as the patterns, pilgrimages to holy wells, fairs and markets. They were
the political pamphleteers of the people, rather like the bards of an earlier
time or the peasant-poets of the 18th century.

Itinerant dancing-masters there were too, much sought after a century
ago, or even within living memory. And in an older time, before the introduction of compulsory primary education (1831) there were the poor scholars who loom large in the folk-memory and to whom is often accredited the
introduction of many tales recorded by our collectors in recent years.

A strange, motley crowd these people of the roads, but of importance to
the student of Irish folk-tales, for they undoubtedly helped in the spread of
folk-tales, and folk-songs. It is too soon to determine how great this influence was from these wandering people, but we must always bear them in
mind as possible traditors.

A story-teller in the West of Ireland told me how he learned to read English. He had a smattering of the language from an irregular attendance at
school, and when he grew up, as he was a strong and hardy fellow, he went
to England like many another to make his fortune. He worked in the ship-
yards on the Tyne. One day he picked up in the street a wet and ragged
novelette. He brought it to his lodging, spelled his way through it, and many
years after he retold the English tale to a friend of mine in Irish. Like many
story-tellers a good tale, no matter what its origin, appealed to him. Once
the tale was mastered by him, and this usually at the first hearing, he could
recast it in the traditional mould of his native stock of tales, embellishing it

with the runs and phraseology of the older type in a manner apt to deceive the unwary.

Some years ago this story-teller was given a selection of the Grimm tales as an experiment to see what would happen, and his retelling of these German *kunst-märchen* appeared to me when I heard them to surpass the originals!

That there were men like him at an earlier time is best exemplified in a note at the end of a 17th century romantic tale: "Be it known, readers of this story that I, Brian O Corcráin, got the bones of this tale from a gentleman who said that he had heard it told in French, and, as I was interested in it, I have recounted it as follows, and to embellish it I have added these little verses; and the story was never in Irish before."

A Danish colleague of mine once said to me. "One should realize that the bearer of tradition is both a reciter and a poet". To be a real story-teller, to have a pride in one's art, one must have the instinct of a poet in one's choice of language, and in the style of one's oral narrative. We speak of a *writer*, that is, in the English etymological sense, a maker, a craftsman—and the Scottish language uses *makar* in the sense of poet. Literature is not only written, it can also be spoken, and it was spoken first before recording the composition in a more permanent form was ever contemplated. At any rate, I have known story-tellers whose art entitled them to be regarded as worthy colleagues of men of formal letters. One did not meet them often, it is true, just as one does not often encounter in the flesh or through the proxy of the printed word outstanding literary men among the host of those who write. The old man of whom I have written above was a literary man in a real sense, with a fine feeling for a telling phrase, one who toyed with it on his tongue like a connoisseur of vintage wines.

Yes, they had their standards, these old people. These standards were applied only to the more intricate forms of narrative, the long hero-tale, in particular, with its wealth of incident, its large number of characters. Above all, it was required of the narrator to include at certain places in the narrative the long passages of high-flown and half-obscure rhetoric, which were so appreciated by the audience, because they did not understand them.

Great powers of memory and of artistry are required of the story-teller who seeks to relate this intricate type of narrative, and tales of this kind do not pass readily over linguistic frontiers. The mortality in tales must always have been great as they try to slip into a new country. I have myself seen what happens when a tale is bandied back and forth between Irish and English, and I have taken down the same tale in English as well as in Irish from different narrators in the same locality just to observe what process—if any—was at work. Certain types of peculiarly Irish tales succumbed immediately, being stifled when translated into a different linguistic milieu, just as an orchid will wither if planted out of doors from a hot house. The Irish hero-tale lives and dies a monoglot—it belongs entirely to the old Irish world and can never speak any language but Irish. Some *märchen* of the international type passed readily enough from English to Irish; the change, however, from Irish to English is not so easily effected, nor is the result so pleasing, but some *märchen* pass the linguistic frontier. What their fate will be in the new language is already determined, but the factor is due to change of taste more than anything else. Survivals there will be, of course, in a later generation, but the day of the folktale as a living pulsating literary genre has gone with the grown-up audience for whom it was intended.

Irish folk-lore contains the most important single body of oral literature in the West of Europe, and its significance for the student of early and medieval Western European culture cannot be overstressed. To this vast repository, from ages long before recorded history until the present, the tenacious tradition of many generations of my people has contributed—and therein preserved—memories of long vanished civilizations and cultures, and the echoes of many voices from the limbo of the past. And the unlettered Irish story-tellers of the centuries have in these traditions a fitting epitaph.

18

Symbolism in Dreams

Sigmund Freud

The name Sigmund Freud, the founder of psychoanalysis, is widely known, but his connection to the field of folkloristics is not. Born to Jewish parents in Moravia in 1856, at age four Freud moved to Vienna, where he lived until 1938. When Germany annexed Austria he reluctantly left for sanctuary in London, where he died in 1939. There are dozens of biographies of Freud, but Ernest Jones's somewhat partisan three-volume *The Life and Work of Sigmund Freud* (1953–1955) remains probably the best and most definitive primary source.

Discussions of psychoanalysis are virtually infinite in number. Psychoanalytic theory has been applied to all subjects covered in both the humanities and the social sciences. One has only to consult Alexander Grinstein's fourteen-volume *Index of Psychoanalytic Writings* (New York: International Universities Press, 1956–1975) or the nearly 20,000 entries in Norman Kiell's two-volume *Psychoanalysis, Psychology, and Literature* (Metuchen, N.J.: Scarecrow Press, 1982), plus his *Supplement* volume in 1990 with more than 7,000 additional references, to get some idea of the enormity of the literature spawned by psychoanalytic theory. These works include substantial listings of psychoanalytic studies of folklore.

Freud had a lifelong interest in folklore. He collected Jewish jokes as a hobby, which inspired one of his most important and enduring works, *Wit and Humor in the Unconscious,* published in 1905. In this pioneering study Freud showed how many of the rhetorical devices he had discovered in dreams (e.g., condensation, displacement, projection, and similar devices), reported in *The Interpretation of Dreams* (1900), were also found in jokes.

In 1909 David Ernst Oppenheim (1881–1943), a classicist teaching at the Akademisches Gymnasium in Vienna, sent Freud a paper in which he utilized psychoanalytic concepts in discussing classical mythology. Freud acknowledged receipt of the paper in a letter to Oppenheim dated October 28,

1909, in which he wrote, "I have long been haunted by the idea that our studies on the content of the neuroses might be destined to solve the riddle of the formation of myths and that the nucleus of mythology is nothing other than what we speak of as 'the nuclear complex of the neuroses'." This led to a collaboration between Freud and Oppenheim on a research project in which folktales containing dreams were assembled. Most were found in the periodical *Anthropophyteia* (1904–1913), a journal founded by folklorist Friedrich Krauss (1859–1938) to serve as an outlet for the publication of obscene folklore. The journal was modeled after an earlier similar French journal *Kryptadia* (1883–1911). (For details about the life of folklorist Krauss, see Raymond L. Burt, *Friedrich Salomo Krauss (1859–1938)* [Vienna: Verlag der Österreichischen Akademie der Wissenschaften, 1990].)

It turned out that the symbolism of the dreams contained in the folktales was interpreted by the tales themselves and, more important, that the folk interpretation of the symbols corresponded to so-called Freudian symbolism. This meant that Freudian symbolism was hardly invented by Freud but rather that he simply articulated symbolic equations already known in some sense by the folk.

Unfortunately, Freud and Oppenheim evidently had a falling out before their joint work could be presented. By October 1911 Oppenheim had resigned from the Vienna Psychoanalytic Society to join the ranks of Alfred Adler (1870–1937), one of the many dissidents who became disaffected enough to form his own branch of psychology, Individual Psychology. After Oppenheim's death in the Theresienstadt concentration camp during World War II, his widow took the manuscript to Australia. In 1956 Oppenheim's daughter sold the manuscript to the Freud Archives, and it was finally published in both German and English translation in 1958 under the title *Dreams in Folklore* (New York: International Universities Press, 1958). One of its conclusions was that "we have been able to establish the fact that folklore interprets dream symbols in the same way as psychoanalysis." It is a pity that this paper did not appear in print until forty-seven years after it was written in 1911.

Freud's active interest in folklore continued even though his joint project with Oppenheim fell temporarily by the wayside. In 1910 Krauss, anxious to defend his journal *Anthropophyteia* from charges that it contained pornographic and obscene matter, requested a letter of support from Freud. Freud's letter was published in *Anthropophyteia* in that same year. In fact, Freud's name appeared on the editorial masthead of the journal from 1910 to 1912. The fact that Freud's name appeared on such an important folklore journal is a strong indication of his involvement with folklore research. In 1913 Freud accepted Krauss's invitation to write a special introduction to the German translation of John G. Bourke's *Scatalogic Rites of All Nations,* first published in 1891. Also in 1913 Freud wrote two papers directly concerned with folklore, "The Occurrence in Dreams of Material from Fairy-Tales" and "The Theme of the Three Caskets." As a therapist Freud was mainly concerned with using folklore to help his patients, but at the same time he was intrigued by the idea that the treatment of patients might provide valuable clues for the interpretation of folklore. He concluded the first section of "The Occurrence in Dreams of Material from Fairy-Tales" with this statement: "If we carefully observe from clear instances the way in which dreamers use fairy tales and the point at which they bring them in, we may perhaps also succeed in picking up hints which will help in interpreting remaining obscurities in the fairy tales themselves."

Freud's fascination with folklore is also attested to by the fact that he labeled one of his most important discoveries—namely, that boys wished to kill their fathers and marry their mothers—by referring to an ancient tale from classical Greek tradition. He called this wish the Oedipus complex. As with Freudian symbolism, Freud was suggesting that the folk had already articulated much of what he was describing in psychological terms.

During the years 1915 to 1917, Freud gave a series of twenty-eight lectures at the University of Vienna. The first fifteen of these lectures were delivered in winter 1915–1916, with the remainder given the following winter. The lectures were published in three installments, the first in July 1916 and last two in May 1917. The initial English translation of the book, *A General Introduction to Psychoanalysis*, appeared in 1920. Lectures five through fifteen treated the subject of dreams; the tenth lecture was entitled "Symbolism in Dreams." That is the essay presented here.

What is noteworthy is not just the impressive array of symbolic equations Freud manages to discuss but his claim that the source of these equations is folklore. In the essay, Freud calls *Anthropophyteia* "indispensable" and offers an explanation for what Olrik termed "the law of three," as well as the possible symbolic import of "pulling off a branch," which may illuminate the unconscious motivation for Frazer's choosing his key passage in *The Golden Bough*. Freud was familiar with Frazer's magnum opus, which along with Frazer's four-volume *Totemism and Exogamy* (1910) was one of the principal sources for his controversial *Totem and Taboo*, published in 1913. Freud sent a copy of *Totem and Taboo* to Frazer who failed to acknowledge receipt of it. (For a detailed discussion of the sources Freud used in this work, see Edwin R. Wallace, *Freud and Anthropology: A History and Reappraisal* [New York: International Universities Press, 1983].)

Freud has a multitude of both critics and defenders; it would require a book-length treatise to list them all. Representative works include Adolf Grunbaum, *The Foundations of Psychoanalysis: A Philosophical Critique* (Berkeley: University of California Press, 1984); E. Fuller Torrey, *Freudian Fraud: The Malignant Effect of Freud's Theory on American Thought and Culture* (New York: HarperCollins, 1992); Paul Robinson, *Freud and His*

Critics (Berkeley: University of California Press, 1993); and Seymour Fisher and Roger P. Greenberg, *The Scientific Credibility of Freud's Theories and Therapy* (New York: Columbia University Press, 1985). Freud was a prolific writer; see *Sigmund Freud's Writings: A Comprehensive Bibliography* (New York: International Universities Press, 1977), compiled by Alexander Grinstein. For an unusual Freudian study of Freud, see folklorist Elliott Oring's *The Jokes of Sigmund Freud* (Philadelphia: University of Pennsylvania Press, 1984) in which the Jewish jokes Freud analyzed in his *Wit and Humor in the Unconscious* (1905) are in turn analyzed by Oring to reveal Freud's ambivalence about his Jewish identity.

One common criticism is relevant to the excerpt presented here, and that is the accusation that Freudian symbolism is arbitrary, fixed, and universal. In *The Interpretation of Dreams* Freud was very clear about his views. He noted specifically that he held "that the same dream-content may conceal a different meaning in the case of different persons, or in different connections" and that dream symbols "often possess many and varied meanings, so that, as in Chinese script, only the context can furnish the correct meaning" (see *The Basic Writings of Sigmund Freud* [1938], 194, 371). Symbolic systems are undoubtedly culturally relative. Critics of Freud typically cite the quote "sometimes a cigar is only a cigar," meaning that objects should be understood in literal rather than symbolic terms, and they even attribute the aphorism to Freud himself. In reality, although he smoked cigars Freud never made the statement, and it is somewhat ironic, if not downright meanspirited, for anyone to use such a false pseudo-attribution to make light of Freud's approach to symbols. In any case, if Freud is correct that "Freudian symbols" come from folklore, then critics should be critical of folklore, not of Freud!

The issue in the present context is not whether Freud was a successful therapist (many of his patients seem never to have been completely cured), whether with the male bias typical of his time he misunderstood women's psychology, or whether he mistakenly believed in the phylogenetic origin of individual fantasies. The issue is simply, did Freud make an important contribution to the development of international folkloristics? Not all folklorists would agree that he did, but some (myself included) definitely would say he did. For further discussion of Freud's impact on folkloristics, see Elliott Oring's entry on Freud in the *Enzyklopädie des Märchens* (1985), 266–275. For a small sample of the voluminous literature in which Freudian insights are applied to folklore, see Paulo de Carvalho-Neto, *Folklore and Psychoanalysis* (Coral Gables: University of Miami Press, 1972); Bruno Bettelheim, *The Uses of Enchantment: The Meaning and Importance of Fairy Tales* (New York: Vintage Books, 1977); Dan Ben-Amos, "Bettelheim among the Folklorists," *Psychoanalytic Review* 81 (1994), 509–535; and Alan Dundes, "The Psychoanalytic Study of Folklore," *Annals of Scholar-*

ship 3(3) (1985), 1–42, *From Game to War and Other Psychoanalytic Essays on Folklore* (Lexington: University Press of Kentucky, 1997), and *Two Tales of Crow and Sparrow: A Freudian Folkloristic Essay on Caste and Untouchability* (Lanham: Rowman and Littlefield, 1997). For access to the voluminous scholarship devoted to the study of symbolism, see Manfred Lurker, *Bibliographie zur Symbolkunde* (Baden-Baden: Verlag Heitz, 1968), which contains more than 11,000 entries.

*   *   *

We have found out that the distortion in dreams which hinders our understanding of them is due to the activities of a censorship, directed against the unacceptable, unconscious wish-impulses. But of course we have not asserted that the censorship is the only factor responsible for the distortion, and as a matter of fact a further study of dreams leads to the discovery that there are yet other causes contributing to this effect; that is as much as to say, if the censorship were eliminated we should nevertheless be unable to understand dreams, nor would the manifest dream be identical with the latent dream-thoughts.

This other cause of the obscurity of dreams, this additional contribution to distortion, is revealed by our becoming aware of a gap in our technique. I have already admitted to you that there are occasions when persons being analysed really have no associations to single elements in their dreams. To be sure, this does not happen as often as they declare that it does; in very many instances the association may yet be elicited by perseverance; but still there remains a certain number of cases where association fails altogether or, if something is finally extorted, it is not what we need. If this happens during psychoanalytic treatment it has a certain significance which does not concern us here; but it also occurs in the course of interpretation of dreams in normal people, or when we are interpreting our own. When we are convinced in such circumstances that no amount of pressing is of any use, we finally discover that this unwelcome contingency regularly presents itself where special dream-elements are in question; and we begin to recognize the operation of some new principle, whereas at first we thought we had only come across an exceptional case in which our technique had failed.

In this way it comes about that we try to interpret these "silent" elements, and attempt to translate them by drawing upon our own resources. It cannot fail to strike us that we arrive at a satisfactory meaning in every instance in which we venture on this substitution, whereas the dream remains meaningless and disconnected as long as we do not resolve to use this method. The accumulation of many exactly similar instances then affords us the required certainty, our experiment having been tried at first with considerable diffidence.

I am presenting all this somewhat in outline, but that is surely allowable for purposes of instruction, nor is it falsified by so doing, but merely made simpler.

We arrive in this way at constant translations for a series of dream-elements, just as in popular books on dreams we find such translations for everything that occurs in dreams. You will not have forgotten that when we employ the method of free association such constant substitutions for dream-elements never make their appearance.

Now you will at once say that this mode of interpretation seems to you far more uncertain and open to criticism than even the former method of free association. But there is still something more to be said: when we have collected from actual experience a sufficient number of such constant translations, we eventually realize that we could actually have filled in these portions of the interpretation from our own knowledge, and that they really could have been understood without using the dreamer's associations. How it is that we are bound to know their meaning is a matter which will be dealt with in the second half of our discussion.

We call a constant relation of this kind between a dream-element and its translation a *symbolic* one, and the dream-element itself a *symbol* of the unconscious dream-thought. You will remember that some time ago, when we were examining the different relations which may exist between dream-elements and the thoughts proper underlying them, I distinguished three relations: substitution of the part for the whole, allusion, and imagery. I told you then that there was a fourth possible relation, but I did not tell you what it was. This fourth relation is the symbolic, which I am now introducing; there are connected with it certain very interesting points for discussion, to which we will turn attention before setting forth our special observations on this subject. Symbolism is perhaps the most remarkable part of our theory of dreams.

First of all: since the relation between a symbol and the idea symbolized is an invariable one, the latter being as it were a translation of the former, symbolism does in some measure realize the ideal of both ancient and popular dream-interpretation, one from which we have moved very far in our technique. Symbols make it possible for us in certain circumstances to interpret a dream without questioning the dreamer, who indeed in any case can tell us nothing about the symbols. If the symbols commonly appearing in dreams are known, and also the personality of the dreamer, the conditions under which he lives, and the impressions in his mind after which his dream occurred, we are often in a position to interpret it straightaway; to translate it at sight, as it were. Such a feat flatters the vanity of the interpreter and impresses the dreamer; it is in pleasing contrast to the laborious method of questioning the latter. But do not let this lead you away: it is no part of our task to perform tricks nor is that method of interpretation which is based on a knowledge of symbolism one which can replace, or even compare with, that of free association. It is complementary to this latter, and the results it yields are only useful when applied in connection with the latter. As regards our knowledge of the dreamer's mental situation, moreover, you must reflect that you have not only to interpret dreams of people whom you know well; that, as a rule, you know nothing of the events of the previous day which stimulated the dream; and that the associations of the person analysed are the very source from which we obtain our knowledge of what we call the mental situation.

Further, it is especially remarkable, particularly with reference to certain considerations upon which we shall touch later, that the most strenuous opposition has manifested itself again here, over this question of the existence of a symbolic relation between the dream and the unconscious. Even persons of judgement and standing, who in other respects have gone a long way with psychoanalysis, have renounced their adherence at this point. This behaviour is the more remarkable when we remember two things: first, that symbolism is not peculiar to dreams, nor exclusively characteristic of them; and, in the second place, that the use of symbolism in dreams was not one of the discoveries of psychoanalysis, although this science has certainly not been wanting in surprising discoveries. If we must ascribe priority in this field to anyone in modern times, the discoverer must be recognized in the philosopher K. A. Scherner (1861); psychoanalysis has confirmed his discovery, although modifying it in certain important respects.

Now you will wish to hear something about the nature of dream-symbolism and will want some examples. I will gladly tell you what I know, but I confess that our knowledge is less full than we could wish.

The symbolic relation is essentially that of a comparison, but not any kind of comparison. We must suspect that this comparison is subject to particular conditions, although we cannot say what these conditions are. Not everything with which an object or an occurrence can be compared appears in dreams as symbolic of it, and, on the other hand, dreams do not employ symbolism for anything and everything, but only for particular elements of latent dream-thoughts; there are thus limitations in both directions. We must admit also that we cannot at present assign quite definite limits to our conception of a symbol; for it tends to merge into substitution, representation, etc., and even approaches closely to allusion. In one set of symbols the underlying comparison may be easily apparent, but there are others in which we have to look about for the common factor, the *tertium comparationis* contained in the supposed comparison. Further reflection may then reveal it to us, or on the other hand it may remain definitely hidden from us. Again, if the symbol is really a comparison, it is remarkable that this comparison is not exposed by the process of free association, and also that the dreamer knows nothing about it, but makes use of it unawares; nay, more, that he is actually unwilling to recognize it when it is brought to his notice. So you see that the symbolic relation is a comparison of a quite peculiar kind, the nature of which is as yet not fully clear to us. Perhaps some indication will be found later which will throw some light upon this unknown quantity.

The number of things which are represented symbolically in dreams is not great. The human body as a whole, parents, children, brothers and sisters, birth, death, nakedness—and one thing more. The only typical, that is to say, regularly occurring, representation of the human form as a whole is that of a *house,* as was recognized by Scherner, who even wanted to attribute to this symbol an overwhelming significance which is not really due to it. People have dreams of climbing down the front of a house, with feelings sometimes of pleasure and sometimes of dread. When the walls are quite smooth, the house means a man; when there are ledges and balconies which can be caught hold of, a woman. Parents appear in dreams as *emperor* and *empress, king* and *queen* or other exalted personages; in this respect the dream attitude is highly dutiful. Children and brothers and sisters are less tenderly treated, being symbolized by *little animals* or *vermin.* Birth is almost invariably represented by some reference to *water*: either we are falling into water or clambering out of it, saving someone from it or being saved by them, i.e. the relation between mother and child is symbolized. For dying we have setting out upon a *journey* or *travelling* by train, while the state of death is indicated by various obscure and, as it were, timid allusions; *clothes* and *uniforms* stand for nakedness. You see that here the dividing line between the symbolic and the allusive kinds of representation tends to disappear.

In comparison with the poverty of this enumeration, it cannot fail to strike us that objects and matters belonging to another range of ideas are represented by a remarkably rich symbolism. I am speaking of what pertains to the sexual life—the genitals, sexual processes and intercourse. An overwhelming majority of symbols in dreams are sexual symbols. A curious disproportion arises thus, for the matters dealt with are few in number, whereas the symbols for them are extraordinarily numerous, so that each of these few things can be expressed by many symbols practically equivalent. When they are interpreted, therefore, the result of this peculiarity gives universal offense, for, in contrast to the multifarious forms of its representation in dreams, the interpretation of the symbols is very monotonous. This is displeasing to everyone who comes to know of it: but how can we help it?

As this is the first time in the course of these lectures that I have touched upon the sexual life, I owe you some explanation of the manner in which I propose to treat this subject. Psychoanalysis sees no occasion for concealments or indirect allusions, and does not think it necessary to be ashamed of concerning itself with material so important; it is of the opinion that it is right and proper to call everything by its true name, hoping in this way the more easily to avoid disturbing suggestions. The fact that I am speaking to a mixed audience can make no difference in this. No science can be treated *in usum delphini*, or in a manner adapted to school-girls; the women present, by appearing in this lecture-room, have tacitly expressed their desire to be regarded on the same footing as the men.

The male genital organ is symbolically represented in dreams in many different ways, with most of which the common idea underlying the comparison is easily apparent. In the first place, the sacred number *three* is symbolic of the whole male genitalia. Its more conspicuous and, to both sexes, more interesting part, the penis, is symbolized primarily by objects which resemble it in form, being long and upstanding, such as *sticks, umbrellas, poles, trees* and the like; also by objects which, like the thing symbolized, have the property of penetrating, and consequently of injuring, the body,—that is to say, pointed weapons of all sorts: *knives, daggers, lances, sabres*; fire-arms are similarly used: *guns, pistols and revolvers*, these last being a very appropriate symbol on account of their shape. In the anxiety-dreams of young girls, pursuit by a man armed with a knife or rifle plays a great part. This is perhaps the most frequently occurring dream-symbol: you can now easily translate it for yourselves. The substitution of the male organ by objects from which water flows is again easily comprehensible: *taps, water-cans*, or *springs*; and by other objects which are capable of elongation, such as *pulley lamps, pencils which slide in and out of a sheath*, and so on. *Pencils, penholders, nail-files, hammers* and other *implements* are undoubtedly male sexual symbols, based on an idea of the male organ which is equally easily perceived.

The peculiar property of this member of being able to raise itself upright in defiance of the law of gravity, part of the phenomenon of erection, leads to symbolic representation by means of *balloons, aeroplanes*, and, just recently, *Zeppelins*. But dreams have another, much more impressive, way of symbolizing erection; they make the organ of sex into the essential part of the whole person, so that the *dreamer himself flies*. Do not be upset by hearing that dreams of flying, which we all know and which are often so beautiful, must be interpreted as dreams of general sexual excitement, dreams of erection. One psychoanalytic investigator, P. Federn, has established the truth of this interpretation beyond doubt; but, besides this, Mourly Vold, a man highly praised for his sober judgement, who carried out the experiments with artificial postures of the arms and legs, and whose theories were really widely removed from those of psychoanalysis (indeed he may have known nothing about it), was led by his own investigations to the same conclusion. Nor must you think to object to this on the ground that women can also have dreams of flying; you should rather remind yourselves that the purpose of dreams is wish-fulfillment, and that the wish to be a man is frequently met with in women, whether they are conscious of it or not. Further, no one familiar with anatomy will be misled by supposing that it is impossible for a woman to realize this wish by sensations similar to those of a man, for the woman's sexual organs include a small one which resembles the penis, and this little organ, the clitoris, does actually play during childhood and in the years before sexual intercourse the same part as the large male organ.

Male sexual symbols less easy to understand are certain *reptiles and fishes*: above all, the famous symbol of the *serpent*. Why *hats and cloaks* are used in the same way is certainly difficult to divine, but their symbolic meaning is quite unquestionable. Finally, it may be asked whether the representation of the male organ by some other member, such as the *hand* or the *foot*, may be termed symbolic. I think the context in which this is wont to occur, and the female counterparts with which we meet, force this conclusion upon us.

The female genitalia are symbolically represented by all such objects as share with them the property of enclosing a space or are capable of acting as receptacles: such as *pits, hollows and caves*, and also *jars and bottles*, and *boxes* of all sorts and sizes, *chests, coffers, pockets*, and so forth. *Ships* too come into this category. Many symbols refer rather to the uterus than to the other genital organs: thus *cupboards, stoves* and, above all, *rooms*. Room symbolism here links up with that of houses, whilst *doors and gates* represent the genital opening. Moreover, material of different kinds is a symbol of woman,—*wood, paper*, and objects made of these, such as *tables* and *books*. From the animal world, *snails and mussels* at any rate must be cited as unmistakable female symbols; of the parts of the body, the *mouth* as a representation of the genital opening, and, amongst buildings, *churches and chapels* are symbols of a woman. You see that all these symbols are not equally easy to understand.

The breasts must be included amongst the organs of sex; these, as well as the larger hemispheres of the female body, are represented by *apples, peaches and fruit* in general. The pubic hair in both sexes is indicated in dreams by *woods and thickets*. The complicated topography of the female sexual organs accounts for their often being represented by a *landscape* with rocks, woods and water, whilst the imposing mechanism of the male sexual apparatus lends it to symbolization by all kinds of complicated and indescribable *machinery*.

Yet another noteworthy symbol of the female genital organ is a *jewel case*, whilst "jewel" and "treasure" are used also in dreams to represent the beloved person,[1] and *sweetmeats* frequently stand for sexual pleasures. Gratification derived from a person's own genitals is indicated by any kind of *play*, including playing the piano. The symbolic representation of onanism

---

1. [Cf. sweetheart, sweetest.—Tr.]

by *sliding or gliding* and also by *pulling off a branch* is very typical. A particularly remarkable dream-symbol is the *falling out* or *extraction of teeth;* the primary significance of this is certainly castration as a punishment for onanism. Special representations of sexual intercourse are less frequent in dreams than we should expect after all this, but we may mention in this connection rhythmical activities such as *dancing, riding* and *climbing,* and also *experiencing some violence,* e.g., being run over. To these may be added certain manual occupations, and of course being threatened with weapons.

You must not imagine that these symbols are either employed or translated quite simply: on all sides we meet with what we do not expect. For instance, it seems hardly credible that there is often no sharp discrimination of the different sexes in these symbolic representations. Many symbols stand for sexual organs in general, whether male or female: for instance, a *little child,* or a *little* son or daughter. At another time a symbol which is generally a male one may be used to denote the female sexual organ, or vice versa. This is incomprehensible until we have acquired some knowledge of the development of conceptions about sexuality amongst human beings. In many cases this ambiguity of the symbols may be apparent rather than real; and moreover, the most striking amongst them, such as weapons, pockets and chests, are never used bisexually in this way.

I will now give a brief account, beginning with the symbols themselves instead of with the objects symbolized, to show you from what spheres the sexual symbols have for the most part been derived, and I will add a few remarks relating particularly to those in which the attribute in common with the thing symbolized is hard to detect. An instance of an obscure symbol of this kind is the *hat,* or perhaps head-coverings in general; this usually has a masculine significance, though occasionally a feminine one. In the same way a *cloak* betokens a man, though perhaps sometimes without special reference to the organs of sex. It is open to you to ask why this should be so. A *tie,* being an object which hangs down and is not worn by women, is clearly a male symbol, whilst *underlinen* and *linen* in general stands for the female. *Clothes and uniforms,* as we have heard, represent nakedness or the human form; *shoes and slippers* symbolize the female genital organs. *Tables and wood* we have mentioned as being puzzling, but nevertheless certain, female symbols; the *act of mounting* ladders, steep places or stairs is indubitably symbolic of sexual intercourse. On closer reflection we shall notice that the rhythmic character of this climbing is the point in common between the two, and perhaps also the accompanying increase in excitation—the shortening of the breath as the climber ascends.

We have already recognized that *landscapes* represent the female sexual organs; mountains and rocks are symbols of the male organ; *gardens,* a frequently occurring symbol of the female genitalia. *Fruit* stands for the breasts, not for a child. *Wild animals* denote human beings whose senses are excited, and, hence, evil impulses or passions. *Blossoms and flowers* represent the female sexual organs, more particularly, in virginity. In this connection you will recollect that the blossoms are really the sexual organs of plants.

We already know how rooms are used symbolically. This representation may be extended, so that *windows and doors* (entrances and exits from rooms) come to mean the openings of the body; the fact of rooms being *open or closed* also accords with this symbolism: the *key*, which opens them, is certainly a male symbol.

This is some material for a study of dream-symbolism. It is not complete, and could be both extended and made deeper. However, I think it will seem to you more than enough; perhaps you may dislike it. You will ask: "Do I then really live in the midst of sexual symbols? Are all the objects round me, all the clothes I wear, all the things I handle, always sexual symbols and nothing else?" There really is good reason for surprised questions, and the first of these would be: How do we profess to arrive at the meaning of these dream-symbols, about which the dreamer himself can give us little or no information.

My answer is that we derive our knowledge from widely different sources: from fairy tales and myths, jokes and witticisms, from folklore, i.e. from what we know of the manners and customs, sayings and songs, of different peoples, and from poetic and colloquial usage of language. Everywhere in these various fields the same symbolism occurs, and in many of them we can understand it without being taught anything about it. If we consider these various sources individually, we shall find so many parallels to dream-symbolism that we are bound to be convinced of the correctness of our interpretations.

The human body is, we said, according to Scherner frequently symbolized in dreams by a house; by an extension of this symbolism, windows, doors and gates stand for the entrances to cavities in the body, and the façades may either be smooth or may have balconies and ledges to hold on to. The same symbolism is met with in colloquialisms; for instance, we speak of "a thatch of hair," or a "tile hat," or say of someone that he is not right "in the upper storey."[2] In anatomy, too, we speak of the openings of the body as its "portals."[3]

We may at first find it surprising that parents appear in our dreams as kings and emperors and their consorts, but we have a parallel to this in fairy

---

2. [In German, an old acquaintance is often addressed as "old house" (*altes Haus*); the expression "giving him one on the roof" (*einem eins aufs Dach geben*) corresponds to "hitting him over the head."]

3. [The *portal* vein carries nourishment from the bowels to the body *via* the liver. The *pylorus* (from πύλη = gate) is the entrance to the small intestine. In German, the apertures of the body are called *Leibespforten* (gates of the body).—Tr.]

tales. Does it not begin to dawn upon us that the many fairy tales which begin with the words "Once upon a time there were a king and queen" simply mean: "Once upon a time there were a father and mother"? In family life the children are sometimes spoken of jestingly as princes, and the eldest son as the crown prince. The king himself is called the father of his people.[4] Again, in some parts, little children are often playfully spoken of as little animals, e.g. in Cornwall, as "little toad," or in Germany as "little worm," and, in sympathizing with a child, Germans say "poor little worm."

Now let us return to the house symbolism. When in our dreams we make use of the projections of houses as supports, does that not suggest a well-known, popular German saying, with reference to a woman with a markedly developed bust: "She has something for one to hold on to" (*Die hat etwas zum Anhalten*), whilst another colloquialism in the same connection is: "She has plenty of wood in front of her house" (*Die hat viel Holz vor dem Hause*), as though our interpretation were to be borne out by this when we say that wood is a female maternal symbol.

There is still something to be said on the subject of wood. It is not easy to see why wood should have come to represent a woman or mother, but here a comparison of different languages may be useful to us. The German word *Holz* (wood) is said to be derived from the same root as the Greek υλη, which means stuff, raw material. This would be an instance of a process which is by no means rare, in that a general name for material has come finally to be applied to a particular material only. Now, in the Atlantic Ocean, there is an island named Madeira, and this name was given to it by the Portuguese when they discovered it, because at that time it was covered with dense forests; for in Portuguese the word for wood is *madeira*. But you cannot fail to notice that this *madeira* is merely a modified form of the Latin *materia*, which again signifies material in general. Now *materia* is derived from *mater* = mother, and the material out of which anything is made may be conceived of as giving birth to it. So, in the symbolic use of wood to represent woman or mother, we have a survival of this old idea.

Birth is regularly expressed by some connection with water: we are plunging into or emerging from water, that is to say, we give birth or are being born. Now let us not forget that this symbol has a twofold reference to the actual facts of evolution. Not only are all land mammals, from which the human race itself has sprung, descended from creatures inhabiting the water—this is the more remote of the two considerations—but also every single mammal, every human being, has passed the first phase of existence in water—that is to say, as an embryo in the amniotic fluid of the mother's womb—and thus, at birth, emerged from water. I do not maintain that the dreamer knows this; on the other hand, I contend that there is no need for him to know it. He probably knows something else from having been told it

---

4. [Cf. the Russian expression, "Little father."—TR.]

as a child, but even this, I will maintain, has contributed nothing to symbol-formation. The child is told in the nursery that the stork brings the babies, but then where does it get them? Out of a pond or a well—again, out of the water. One of my patients who had been told this as a child (a little count, as he was then) afterwards disappeared for a whole afternoon, and was at last found lying at the edge of the castle lake, with his little face bent over the clear water, eagerly gazing to see whether he could catch sight of the babies at the bottom of the water.

In the myths of the births of heroes, a comparative study of which has been made by O. Rank—the earliest is that of King Sargon of Akkad, about 2800 B.C.—exposure in water and rescue from it play a major part. Rank perceived that this symbolizes birth in a manner analogous to that employed in dreams. When anyone in his dream rescues somebody from the water, he makes that person into his mother, or at any rate *a* mother; and in mythology, whoever rescues a child from water confesses herself to be its real mother. There is a well-known joke in which an intelligent Jewish boy, when asked who was the mother of Moses, answers immediately: "The Princess." He is told: "No, she only took him out of the water." "That's what *she* said," he replies, showing that he had hit upon the right interpretation of the myth.

Going away on a journey stands in dreams for dying; similarly, it is the custom in the nursery, when a child asks questions as to the whereabouts of someone who has died and whom he misses, to tell him that that person has "gone away." Here again, I deprecate the idea that the dream-symbol has its origin in this evasive reply to the child. The poet uses the same symbol when he speaks of the other side as "the undiscovered country from whose bourne *no traveller* returns." Again, in everyday speech it is quite usual to speak of the "last journey," and everyone who is acquainted with ancient rites knows how seriously the idea of a journey into the land of the dead was taken, for instance, in ancient Egyptian belief. In many cases the "Book of the Dead" survives, which was given to the mummy, like a Baedeker, to take with him on the last journey. Since burial-grounds have been placed at a distance from the houses of the living, the last journey of the dead has indeed become a reality.

Nor does sexual symbolism belong only to dreams. You will all know the expression "a baggage" as applied contemptuously to a woman, but perhaps people do not know that they are using a genital symbol. In the New Testament we read: "The woman is the weaker *vessel*." The sacred writings of the Jews, the style of which so closely approaches that of poetry, are full of expressions symbolic of sex, which have not always been correctly interpreted and the exegesis of which, e.g. in the Song of Solomon, has led to many misunderstandings.⁵ In later Hebrew literature the woman is very frequently represented by a house, the door standing for the genital opening;

---

5. [Cf. "I am a wall and my breasts like towers: then was I in his eyes as one that found favour." Cant. viii. 10.—Tr.]

thus a man complains, when he finds a woman no longer a virgin, that "he has found the door open." The symbol "table" for a woman also occurs in this literature; the woman says of her husband "I spread the table for him, but he overturned it." Lame children are said to owe their infirmity to the fact that the man "overturned the table." I quote here from a treatise by L. Levy in Brünn: *Sexual Symbolism in the Bible and the Talmud.*

That ships in dreams signify women is a belief in which we are supported by the etymologists, who assert that "ship" (*Schiff*) was originally the name of an earthen vessel and is the same word as *Schaff* (a tub or wooden vessel). That an oven stands for a woman or the mother's womb is an interpretation confirmed by the Greek story of Periander of Corinth and his wife Melissa. According to the version of Herodotus, the tyrant adjured the shade of his wife, whom he had loved passionately but had murdered out of jealousy, to tell him something about herself, whereupon the dead woman identified herself by reminding him that he, Periander, "had put his bread into a cold oven," thus expressing in a disguised form a circumstance of which everyone else was ignorant. In the *Anthropophyteia,* edited by F. S. Krauss, a work which is an indispensable textbook on everything concerning the sexual life of different peoples, we read that in a certain part of Germany people say of a woman who is delivered of a child that "her oven has fallen to pieces." The kindling of fire and everything connected with this is permeated through and through with sexual symbolism, the flame always standing for the male organ, and the fireplace or the hearth for the womb of the woman.

If you have chanced to wonder at the frequency with which landscapes are used in dreams to symbolize the female sexual organs, you may learn from mythologists how large a part has been played in the ideas and cults of ancient times by "Mother Earth" and how the whole conception of agriculture was determined by this symbolism. The fact that in dreams a room represents a woman you may be inclined to trace to the German colloquialism by which *Frauenzimmer* (*lit.* "woman's room") is used for *Frau,* that is to say, the human person is represented by the place assigned for her occupation. Similarly we speak of the Porte, meaning thereby the Sultan and his government, and the name of the ancient Egyptian ruler, Pharaoh, merely means "great court." (In the ancient Orient the courts between the double gates of the city were places of assembly, like the market-place in classical times.) But I think this derivation is too superficial, and it strikes me as more probable that the room came to symbolize woman on account of its property of enclosing within it the human being. We have already met with the house in this sense; from mythology and poetry we may take towns, citadels, castles and fortresses to be further symbols for women. It would be easy to decide the point by reference to the dreams of people who neither speak nor understand German. Of late years I have mainly treated foreign patients, and I think I recollect that in their dreams rooms stand in the same way for women, even though there is no word analogous to our *Frauenzim-*

mer in their language. There are other indications that symbolism may transcend the boundaries of language, a fact already maintained by the old dream-investigator, Schubert, in 1862. Nevertheless, none of my patients were wholly ignorant of German, so that I must leave this question to be decided by those analysts who can collect instances in other countries from persons who speak only one language.[6]

Amongst the symbols for the male sexual organ, there is scarcely one which does not appear in jests, or in vulgar or poetic phrases, especially in the old classical poets. Here, however, we meet not only with such symbols as occur in dreams but also with new ones, e.g. the *implements* employed in various kinds of work, first and foremost, the *plough*. Moreover, when we come to male symbols, we trench on very extensive and much-contested ground, which, in order not to waste time, we will avoid. I should just like to devote a few remarks to the one symbol which stands, as it were, by itself; I refer to the number *three*. Whether this number does not in all probability owe its sacred character to its symbolic significance is a question which we must leave undecided, but it seems certain that many tripartite natural objects, e.g. the clover-leaf, are used in coats-of-arms and as emblems on account of their symbolism. The so-called "French" lily with its three parts and, again, the "trisceles," that curious coat-of-arms of two such widely separated islands as Sicily and the Isle of Man (a figure consisting of three bent legs projecting from a central point), are supposed to be merely disguised forms of the male sexual organ, images of which were believed in ancient times to be the most powerful means of warding off evil influences (*apotropaea*); connected with this is the fact that the lucky "charms" of our own time may all be easily recognized as genital or sexual symbols. Let us consider a collection of such charms in the form of tiny silver pendants: a four-leaved clover, a pig, a mushroom, a horseshoe, a ladder and a chimney-sweep. The four-leaved clover has taken the place of that with three leaves, which was really more appropriate for the purposes of symbolism; the pig is an ancient symbol of fruitfulness; the mushroom undoubtedly symbolizes the penis, there are mushrooms which derive their name from their unmistakable resemblance to that organ (*Phallus impudicus*); the horseshoe reproduces the contour of the female genital opening; while the chimney-sweep with his ladder belongs to this company because his occupation is one which is vulgarly compared with sexual intercourse. (Cf. *Anthropophyteia.*) We have learnt to recognize his ladder in dreams as a sexual symbol: expressions in language show what a completely sexual significance the word *steigen,* to mount, has, as in the phrases: *Den Frauen nachsteigen* (to run after women) and *ein alter Steiger* (an old roué). So, in French, where the word for "step" is *la marche,* we find the quite analogous expression for an old rake: *un vieux marcheur.* Probably the fact that with many of the larger

---

6. [This is certainly so with English patients.—Tr.]

animals sexual intercourse necessitates a mounting or "climbing upon" the female has something to do with this association of ideas.

Pulling off a branch to symbolize onanism is not only in agreement with vulgar descriptions of that act, but also has far-reaching parallels in mythology. But especially remarkable is the representation of onanism, or rather of castration as the punishment for onanism, by the falling-out or extraction of teeth; for we find in folk-lore a counterpart to this which could only be known to very few dreamers. I think that there can be no doubt that circumcision, a practice common to so many peoples, is an equivalent and replacement of castration. And recently we have learnt that certain aboriginal tribes in Australia practice circumcision as a rite to mark the attaining of puberty (at the celebration of the boy's coming of age), whilst other tribes living quite near have substituted for this practice that of knocking out a tooth.

I will end my account with these examples. They are only examples; we know more about this subject and you can imagine how much richer and more interesting a collection of this sort might be made, not by dilettanti like ourselves, but by real experts in mythology, anthropology, philology, and folk-lore. We are forced to certain conclusions, which cannot be exhaustive, but nevertheless will give us plenty to think about.

In the first place, we are confronted with the fact that the dreamer has at his command a symbolic mode of expression of which he knows nothing, and does not even recognize, in his waking life. This is as amazing as if you made the discovery that your housemaid understood Sanscrit, though you know that she was born in a Bohemian village and had never learnt that language. It is not easy to bring this fact into line with our views on psychology. We can only say that the dreamer's knowledge of symbolism is unconscious and belongs to his unconscious mental life, but even this assumption does not help us much. Up till now we have only had to assume the existence of unconscious tendencies which are temporarily or permanently unknown to us; but now the question is a bigger one and we have actually to believe in unconscious knowledge, thought-relations, and comparisons between different objects, in virtue of which one idea can constantly be substituted for another. These comparisons are not instituted afresh every time, but are ready to hand, perfect for all time; this we infer from their identity in different persons, even probably in spite of linguistic differences.

Whence is our knowledge of this symbolism derived? The usages of speech cover only a small part of it, whilst the manifold parallels in other fields are for the most part unknown to the dreamer; we ourselves had to collate them laboriously in the first instance.

In the second place, these symbolic relations are not peculiar to the dreamer or to the dream-work by which they are expressed; for we have discovered that the same symbolism is employed in myths and fairy tales, in popular sayings and songs, in colloquial speech and poetic phantasy. The province of symbolism is extraordinarily wide: dream-symbolism is only a small part of it; it would not even be expedient to attack the whole problem from the side of dreams. Many of the symbols commonly occurring elsewhere either do not appear in dreams at all or appear very seldom; on the other hand, many of the dream-symbols are not met with in every other department, but, as you have seen, only here and there. We get the impression that here we have to do with an ancient but obsolete mode of expression, of which different fragments have survived in different fields, one here only, another there only, a third in various spheres perhaps in slightly different forms. At this point I am reminded of the phantasy of a very interesting insane patient, who had imagined a "primordial language" (*Grundsprache*) of which all these symbols were survivals.

In the third place, it must strike you that the symbolism occurring in the other fields I have named is by no means confined to sexual themes, whereas in dreams the symbols are almost exclusively used to represent sexual objects and relations. This again is hard to account for. Are we to suppose that symbols originally of sexual significance were later employed differently and that perhaps the decline from symbolic to other modes of representation is connected with this? It is obviously impossible to answer these questions by dealing only with dream-symbolism; all we can do is to hold fast to the supposition that there is a specially close relation between true symbols and sexuality.

An important clue in this connection has recently been given to us in the view expressed by a philologist (H. Sperber, of Upsala, who works independently of psychoanalysis), that sexual needs have had the largest share in the origin and development of language. He says that the first sounds uttered were a means of communication, and of summoning the sexual partner, and that in the later development the elements of speech were used as an accompaniment to the different kinds of work carried on by primitive man. This work was performed by associated efforts, to the sound of rhythmically repeated utterances, the effect of which was to transfer a sexual interest to the work. Primitive man thus made his work agreeable, so to speak, by treating it as the equivalent of and substitute for sexual activities. The word uttered during the communal work had therefore two meanings, the one referring to the sexual act, the other to the labour which had come to be equivalent to it. In time the word was dissociated from its sexual significance and its application confined to the work. Generations later the same thing happened to a new word with a sexual signification, which was then applied to a new form of work. In this way a number of root-words arose which were all of sexual origin but had all lost their sexual meaning. If the statement here outlined be correct, a possibility at least of understanding dream-symbolism opens out before us. We should comprehend why it is that in dreams, which retain something of these primitive conditions, there is such an extraordinarily large number of sexual symbols; and why weapons and tools in general stand for the male, and materials and things worked on for the female. The symbolic relations would then be the survival of the old identity in words; things which once had the same name as the genitalia could now appear in dreams as symbolizing them.

Further, our parallels to dream-symbolism may assist you to appreciate what it is in psychoanalysis which makes it a subject of general interest, in a way that was not possible to either psychology or psychiatry; psychoanalytic work is so closely intertwined with so many other branches of science, the investigation of which gives promise of the most valuable conclusions: with mythology, philology, folk-lore, folk psychology and the study of religion. You will not be surprised to hear that a publication has sprung from psychoanalytic soil, of which the exclusive object is to foster these relations. I refer to *Imago*, first published in 1912 and edited by Hanns Sachs and Otto Rank. In its relation to all these other subjects, psychoanalysis has in the first instance given rather than received. True, analysis reaps the advantage of receiving confirmation of its own results, seemingly so strange, again in other fields; but on the whole it is psychoanalysis which supplies the technical methods and the points of view, the application of which is to prove fruitful in these other provinces. The mental life of the human individual yields, under psychoanalytic investigation, explanations which solve many a riddle in the life of the masses of mankind or at any rate can show these problems in their true light.

I have still given you no idea of the circumstances in which we may arrive at the deepest insight into that hypothetical "primordial language," or of the province in which it is for the most part retained. As long as you do not know this you cannot appreciate the true significance of the whole subject. I refer to the province of neurosis; the material is found in the symptoms and other modes of expression of nervous patients, for the explanation and treatment of which psychoanalysis was indeed devised.

My fourth point of view takes us back to the place from which we started and leads into the track we have already marked out. We said that even if there were no dream-censorship we should still find it difficult to interpret dreams, for we should then be confronted with the task of translating the symbolic language of dreams into the language of waking life. SYMBOLISM, then, is a second and independent factor in dream-distortion, existing side by side with the censorship. But the conclusion is obvious that it suits the censorship to make use of symbolism, in that both serve the same purpose: that of making the dream strange and incomprehensible.

Whether a further study of the dream will not introduce us to yet another contributing factor in the distortion, we shall soon see. But I must not leave the subject of dream-symbolism without once more touching on the puzzling fact that it has succeeded in rousing such strenuous opposition amongst educated persons, although the prevalence of symbolism in myth, religion, art and language is beyond all doubt. Is it not probable that, here again, the reason is to be found in its relation to sexuality?

19

Wedding Ceremonies in European Folklore

Géza Róheim

Freud's writings had little, if any, immediate direct impact on the development of international folkloristics. Giuseppe Cocchiara (1904–1965), in *The History of Folklore in Europe* (Philadelphia: ISHI, 1981), first published in Italian in 1952, does not mention Freud's name. Nor is there any reference to Freud in other histories of folkloristics, such as Inger M. Boberg's *Folkemindeforskningens Historie* (Copenhagen: Einar Munksgaards Forlag, 1953). Nor does his name appear in the standard history of Austrian folkloristics, Leopold Schlmidt's *Geschichte der Österreichischen Volkskunde* (Vienna: Österreichischer Bundesverlag, 1951). A number of Freud's early followers, however, inspired by him, did write psychoanalytic studies of folklore. Among them were Otto Rank (1884–1939), whose *The Myth of the Birth of the Hero* was first published in 1909 with the English translation reprinted in *In Quest of the Hero* (Princeton: Princeton University Press, 1990), 3–86, and his biographer Ernest Jones (1879–1958), whose 1912 essay "The Symbolic Significance of Salt in Folklore and Superstition" and 1928 paper "Psycho-Analysis and Folklore" (read at the Jubilee Congress of the English Folk-Lore Society) were both reprinted in *Essays in Applied Psycho-Analysis*, Vol. 2, *Essays in Folklore, Anthropology, and Religion* (London: Hogarth Press, 1951), 22–109, and 1–21.

Another offshoot of Freud's interest in folklore is reflected in the writings of C. G. Jung (1875–1961) and his disciples. Jung (like Adler and Rank), however, left the Freudian fold to found an alternative psychology. The Jungian approach to folklore specifically disavows psychoanalytic theory. Instead, Jungians refer to their brand of psychology as "analytical psychology" and never as psychoanalysis. Jungian psychology tends to be somewhat mystical, assuming as it does the existence of ultimately unknowable pan-human "archetypes" that emerge from a "collective unconscious" to become manifest in myths and fairy tales. Nevertheless, there are almost as many Jungian analyses of folklore as there are psychoanalytic ones. Perhaps the best entrée to such analyses lies in the numerous books of Marie-Louise von Franz (1915–1998), including *An Introduction to the Interpretation of Fairytales* (Dallas: Spring Publications, 1970).

One problem in both psychoanalytic and Jungian studies of folklore is that most psychoanalysts and Jungian analysts had little or no knowledge of the discipline of folkloristics. Their database inevitably proved remarkably limited, consisting essentially of the Grimm tales, classical mythology, and the Bible. But since folklorists evinced little interest in applying any form of psychology to their subject matter, the vast collections of folklore available were not looked at from this perspective.

Perhaps the most notable exception to this generalization is Géza Róheim (1891–1953) of Hungary. Born in Budapest to a relatively wealthy merchant family, Róheim became interested in folklore as a teenager. At age seventeen, while still a gymnasium (high school) student, he presented a formal paper, "The Mythology of the Moon," to the Hungarian Ethnological Society. In 1911 he published his first article in Hungarian, "Dragons and Dragon Killers." At that point Róheim was essentially committed to solar mythological theory, having not yet discovered Freud in nearby Vienna.

At that time there were no chairs in folklore or anthropology in Budapest, so Róheim went to Leipzig and Berlin in Germany for graduate work. It was evidently there that he learned about Freud. In recounting the intellectual influences that shaped him, Róheim referred to Frazer's *The Golden Bough,* "with its bold reasoning theories and dynamism: all true ethnologists felt its influence." "And at last came Freud, the *Traumdeutung,* the *Totem und Tabu,* the real keys to the mystery. Dead material comes to life, passive knowledge becomes active. And there is nothing else. Freud and psychoanalysis mean more than any other influence" (see Kincsö Verebélyi, "On the 85th Anniversary of Géza Róheim: The Hungarian Forerunner of Psychoanalytic Anthropology," *Acta Ethnographica* 26 [1977], 208–218).

In 1918 Róheim attended the Congress of the International Psychoanalytical Association in Budapest where he met Freud for the first time. In 1928 Róheim the folklorist went into the field to test Freudian concepts in a non-Western setting. Freud liked the idea and prevailed on one of his patients and benefactors, Princess Marie Bonaparte, to fund Róheim's research—the same Marie Bonaparte who paid the ransom to the Nazi Gestapo in Vienna to permit Freud to leave Austria in 1939. By this means, in 1929 Róheim traveled to Australia where he carried out fieldwork, as well as to Normanby Island where he spent nine months. On his way back to Hungary in 1930, he stopped in the United States to carry out an additional two months' fieldwork with Native Americans at Yuma in the Southwest.

Róheim's training was unparalleled. Beginning as a comparative folklorist, well-versed in European folkloristics, he underwent a didactic analysis with Sandor Ferenczi (1873–1937), one of Freud's most astute students, during 1915 and 1916. He then went to Australia and elsewhere to test Freudian concepts in the field. A Ph.D. rather than an M.D., Róheim was much more scholarly than most of his psychoanalyst colleagues. He was widely read in folklore and ethnography, as the footnotes to his many books and articles attest.

In fall 1938 political events in Hungary and in Europe forced Róheim to leave his beloved homeland, much as Bartók did two years later. After a year as a teaching associate and analyst at the Worcester State Hospital in Massachusetts, Róheim moved to New York City where he entered private practice as a lay analyst. All of his adult life, however, Róheim continued to carry out research on folklore. Perhaps his major work was *The Gates of the Dream,* published in 1953, the year of his death. In this tour de force he displays his enormous erudition, citing mythological material from all over the world. His central thesis, that myth is derived from dreams, is open to debate; it is just as likely that dreams are derived in part from the myths told in the dreamer's society, but Róheim's analyses of individual items of folklore are often brilliant.

One year after his death, his remarkable study of European wedding customs appeared in the Indian psychoanalytic journal *Samiksa.* As Róheim explains in his introduction, the essay was originally written in Hungarian in 1924, but because of its length it was not included in his 1925 book on Hungarian folklore. The essay is vintage Róheim; it shows a magisterial control of European folklore scholarship, and the comparative data are presented in typical Frazerian fashion, although clearly informed by Freudian insights. Unfortunately, Róheim's writing style is somewhat choppy and disjointed—he himself likened the style to that of patients' free associations—and his analytic commentary tends to be a bit cryptic. Still, it is one thing for Freud to contend that dream symbols come from folklore; it is quite another to demonstrate the symbolic nature of folklore itself, which is what Róheim tries to do.

For a generous sampling of seventeen of Róheim's other folklore studies, see his *Fire in the Dragon and Other Psychoanalytic Essays on Folklore* (Princeton: Princeton University Press, 1992). Among his posthumously published books concerned with folklore are *Hungarian and Vogul Mythology* (Locust Valley: J. J. Augustin, 1954) and *Magic and Schizophrenia* (New York: International Universities Press, 1955). Róheim was interested in many types of folklore including myth, folktale, and folk belief. For the latter, see his "Hungarian Calendar Customs," *Journal of the Royal Anthropological Institute* 56 (1926), 361–384, and Éva Pócs, "Géza Róheim and the Study of Hungarian Folk Beliefs," *Acta Etnographica Hungarica* 38

(1993), 31–41. For a list of 163 of his publications, see "Bibliography of Géza Róheim's Writings" in his festschrift volume, George B. Wilbur and Warner Muensterberger, eds., *Psychoanalysis and Culture: Essays in Honor of Géza Róheim* (New York: International Universities Press, 1951), 455–462.

✳   ✳   ✳

INTRODUCTION

In 1925 I published a book on Hungarian folklore (Magyar Nephit es Nepszokasok, Hungarian Folk-Beliefs and Customs, Atheneum, 1925). The aim of this book was (a) ethnological, i.e., to clarify the relationship of Hungarian folklore to that of other nations who were in contact with the Hungarians, (b) psycho-analytical, i.e., a psychological explanation of these beliefs and customs. The chapter on wedding ceremonies exceeded the limits the publisher set for the book and could not be included. The Hungarian manuscript has been with me ever since 1924. I decided now to omit ethnological considerations, i.e., the specific Hungarian point of view, and to reduce the number of data used for substantiating conclusions. I then rewrote the paper in abridged form in English. The relative preponderance of Hungarian data is explained by the origin of the paper.

1. THE BEST MAN

The elaborate character of the marriage ritual is a characteristic trait of European folklore. We find a number of people officiating as representing either the groom or the bride. For brevity's sake, we denominate those on the groom's side as the 'best man' though, as we shall see, this office is frequently split up into various representatives.

At Agard (mixed Hungarian-Slovak, county Nograd) we have the master of ceremonies (*nasznagy*) who really represents the groom's father, the 'inviter' (*hivogato*) and the best man (*voefely*) who takes care of the food and the drinks at the wedding.

The bed is made. The best man, accompanied by the inviter, goes into the bridal chamber. The best man has three lighted candles in his right hand. He dances with several girls and so does the inviter. Finally the best man dances with the bride. He manages to whisk her out of the room. The young men are in ambush and they beat her with their hats till she makes her escape and ascends on a rope ladder to the garret. The best man follows her and pulls the ladder up. Here he takes the wreath of the bride and also deprives her of the *parta* (circular ornate headdress worn only by virgins). He now sticks the parta and the wreath on a pitchfork. The parta is really his now, but the bride usually buys it back.[1]

The meaning or latent content of this custom is perfectly obvious. It is ceremonial defloration, carried out not by the groom but by the best man. The three candles symbolize the male genital, the garland and the *parta* the female.

At Nagy Bako the master of ceremonies (nasz nagy) holds the three candles. He raises the candles high and asks those present to testify that there is "no fault" in the bride (i.e., that she is a virgin).[2] The meaning of the wreath made of rosemary is quite conscious in Slavonia. The bride tears it into pieces herself and puts the pieces into the groom's topboots. She says she is giving him her maidenhead.[3]

In some parts of Gocsej 'inviter' and the 'best man' are the same person. Invitations took place on horseback. Croatians and Vends keep the two offices separate. The inviter is called *pozovec* (caller). On account of his clowning Hungarians call him *vicsori* (grinner) or dog chaser, etc. His stick or club is covered with a porcupine-skin and he drags a cock along. The cock is tied to his leg by a string.[4] The rooster is called "cock of the bride."[5]

The custom of the wreath and the symbolism of defloration is attested as far back as the time of King Bela IV.

The son of Bela IV married Kunigunda, daughter of Otto, margrave of Brandenburg. The wedding was celebrated with great pomp on October 25 of the year 1264. Prince Bela put a garland of gold on the head of his bride. The garland was immediately taken off by one of the barons on the point of his sword, "iuxta ritum suæ gentis." In sources dating around 1683 emphasis is placed on the garland as symbol of virginity and on the 'naked' sword that effects the defloration.[6]

In the Upper Palatinate, in Baden and Voigtland, the 'Hochzeitsbitter' (inviter) carries a stick, in old times a sword, decorated with the rosemary gar-

---

1. Reso Endel, S.: *Magyarorszagi nepszokasok* (Folk customs in Hungary) Budapest, 1867, pp. 3, 5. Cf illustration XLIV. in A Magyarsag Nep rajza (Hungarian Ethnography) Vol. 1, 1941.
2. Wagner, A.: Nepszokasok Nagy Bakonak Videken (Folk customs at Nagy Bako) *Ethnographia*, VI, pp. 316, 317.
3. Garay, A.: Szlavoniai regi magyar faluk (Old Hungarian Villages in Slavonia), *Neprajzi Ertesito*, 1911, pp. 233–236.
4. Gonczi, F.: *Gocsei*. Budapest, 1914, pp. 332, 334.
5. Kotze, I.: Nepelet es nepszokasok Baranya megyeben (Folk Life and Customs in Baranya) *Ethnographia*, I, pp. 456, 460.
6. Baroti, L.: Osregi magyar lakodalmi szokas (Ancient Hungarian Wedding Custom) *Ethnographia*, XXXIII, p. 93, quotes Cosm. Prag. Cont. Der ungarische oder dazianische Simplicissimus, 1683, XX, Apor, Metamorphoses Transsilvaniae.

land.[7] In Bavaria he is called "Henneklemmer" (hen thief) because while inviting the people he is supposed to steal a hen[8] (i.e., the bride). In some parts of Germany he must be a man that can crack jokes.[9]

We have an elaborate description of his function in Slovak wedding customs. The best man has a crooked stick, he uses this to hook the bride and drag her up into the attic. Here she is deprived of her wreath and decorated with the *parta*, (cf. above). The first of the 'best men' follows her into the bridal chamber holding twelve candles in his right hand. Having lit the candles he conducts the bride into the room. He distributes the candles giving one to each of the 'official persons' at the ceremony and keeping two himself. Then they all dance in a circle and sing wedding songs. The bride runs back into the bridal chamber, the others after her.

The best man takes her garland off her head and sticks it to the point of his sword. He says, "Judith won a great victory over Holofernes when she cut his head off. My victory is of the same order but I did not achieve it by trickery, purely by my valour I obtained the crown of glory. But I got something else beside glory and this I share with you."

He takes meat and cake from the point of his sword and deposits them on the table before the master of ceremonies but he is careful to keep the garland on his sword lest someone should steal it.

Sometimes the bride's girl friends get the wreath, but in some places she keeps it because with it she keeps the love of the groom.

The best man says: "I have endured much but the victory is mine. The prize (the bride) I now recommend to you."

He has the first dance with the bride. Then she dances with the groom and with all the men. This is the 'bride's dance.' The initiative is hers. The dancers pay for the dance and they have the right to order her around. They tell her to bring wine, to sweep the room, to hop on one foot, etc.

The best man says: "Dear young woman! May I take the wreath off your head?"

She replies: "No, I would rather you cut my head off."

He continues: "I take the wreath off without damage to the maidenhead."

Then he sticks it on a fork or sword and says: "I have fought with a virgin. You may think this is only a joke but I can assure you, it is not so easy. Love has its arrows and these arrows are capable of inflicting wounds. It was difficult indeed."

---

7. Schonwerth, F.: *Aus der Oberpfalz*. 1859, I, p. 63. Meyer, E. H.: *Badisches Volksleben im XX. ten Jahrhundert*. Strassburg, 1900, p. 269. Kohler, J. A. E.: *Volksbrauch, Aberglaube etc. im Voigtlande*. Leipzig, 1867, p. 233. Reichhardt, R.: *Geburt, Hochzeit und Tod*, 1919, p. 47.

8. Buschan, A.: *Die Sitten der Volker*, IV. Das deutsche Volk, 1922, p. 151. (Hutchinson, H. N.: *Marriage Customs in Many Lands*. London, 1897, 260.)

9. Sartori, P.: *Sitte und Brauch*, 1910, I, p. 63.

Then he relates how she defended her virginity and how he could only conquer with the aid of his sword.[10]

Roumanian customs offer variations of the same theme. At Arad, after undoing the wife's hairdress they celebrate the bride's dance. All those who are present dance with the bride but they have to pay for the dance. Finally when the groom sees that she is tired, he puts money in the dish and takes her away. The best man says: "The young kid wishes to storm a fortress, but his strength is insufficient. He asks those present to contribute according to their ability to give more power to his mace."

Then they give all sorts of presents, crockery, linen, money, etc.[11]

In Serbia the *caus* appears in an ornate costume. He carries a bottle of wine. Everybody has to drink from it and give him a silver piece. A fox's tail hangs from his hat. He carries a mace and uses it to hit every one within reach. Another important person is called 'kum'. It is usually the godfather who is asked to help in the name of "God and St. John." Then there is the 'djeve', usually the bridegroom's brother who accepts the custody of the bride from her brother.[12] The Montegrinian *dever* points a rifle at the bride. Then he makes her step on a knife and throws a few coins on her head.[13] In Serbia and in the neighbouring areas the clowning of the 'inviter' is very important.[14]

Krauss regards the curious costume as a satire directed against the way the gentlefolk dress.[15] This is quite improbable; it is simply clowning.

These data reveal that the 'best man' or 'inviter' is a duplicate of the groom. His main function is the '*symbolic defloration*'. In this respect he represents the 'taboo of virginity'[16]. The point is not merely that someone else should deflect the bride's hostility, but obviously castration anxiety. When the 'best man' compares his victory to that of Judith against Holofernes he is talking about his 'head', not her maidenhead.

The swords and maces as penis symbols sound quite heroic, one is reminded of the Nibelungen with Siegfried as Gunther's 'best man', the only hero who can deflorate the dreaded Brunnhild.

---

10. Sztancsek, I.: "Tot lakodalmiszokasok" (Slovak wedding customs) *Ethnographia.* 1903, pp. 61, 63.

11. Moldovan, G.: *Alsofeher varmegye roman nepe* (Roumanians in the County Alsofeher) Nagybecskerel, 1895, p. 281. Idem, *A magyarorszagi romanol* (Roumanians in Hungary) Budapest, 1913, p. 179.

12. Reinsberg-Duringsfeld,: *Das Hochzeitsbuch.* p. 18 F 1 65.

13. Piprek: *Slawische Brautwerbungs-und Hochzeitsgebranche.* 1914, pp. 124, 125.

14. Juga, V.: *A magyaronszagi szerbek* (Serbians in Hungary). 1913 p. 129. Bekefy, R.: *Kethely es Kornyekenek Neprajza* (Ethnography of Kethely and neighbourhood), 1884, p. 55.

15. Krauss, F. S.: *Sitte und Brauch der Sudslaven.* 1885, p. 383.

16. Freud, S.: *Gesammelte Schriften.* 1924, V, pp. 212–251.

Folk-custom deals with the theme on a symbolic and humoristic level, the epic makes it heroic, in Somali custom, it is brutal, sadistic.

"A Midgan (pariah caste) woman comes with a sharp knife and scrapes off the skin, then she joins the labia, binds the legs and pours resin on the wound." The clitoris and labia are cut off, thorns are used as needles and hair from a horse's tail as thread, the husband cuts the flesh with a knife and then opens the hymen with his penis[17].

And finally in Central Australia:

When a girl arrives at a marriageable age the man to whom she has been allotted speaks to his cross-cousins and to other men of the same marriage group. They cut the girl's hymen open with a stone-knife, and then they have intercourse with her, first the *ipmanna* (grandparent or grandchild generation), then the *ankalla* (cross-cousins; as a marriage this would be half-right), then the other potential husbands and finally she is handed over to her real husband.[18]

The best man, the 'inviter', the 'master of ceremonies' are all duplicates, repetitions of the groom or the groom's father. The cook in these country weddings, always a female, represents the bride (or her mother). She has to be compensated for her wounded hand, but the wound comes later and it is not the hand either.

2. THE BARRIER

Wedding rites are essentially rites of transition. The girl is now a woman, a mother imago for the younger people and the same is valid for the boy; he is now a father. Officially it is also the beginning of sexlife—the whole transition idea is therefore concentrated in the bridal bed.

For the people of Eger the bridal bed is the most important piece of furniture.

The bed is in a corner of the '*best room*', ornate with carvings and painted in red, blue and white. It must have six pillows and one coverlet stuffed with the best feathers. The bride has worked on all this herself, the feathers are those of her geese, the linen woven of flax, they grew in her own garden. All her free time was devoted to this work. The bed represents her past life as a girl. They never use it except if the wife is about to die, then they open it for her so that she can dream herself back into her youth[19]. The bed has to be

17. Roheim, G.: Psycho-analysis of Primitive Cultural Types, *Int. J. of Psa*, XIII, 1932, p. 199

18. Spencer, B. and Gillen, F. J.: *The Arunta*. London, 1927, pp. 472, 473.

19. Benkoczy. E.: Az egervideki nep (The people of Eger) *Ethnographia*, 1909, p. 236.

transported to her new home. This is a significant phase in the whole transition ritual.

For the people of Braunschweig the essential thing in the wedding is handing over the dowry to the groom. This takes place on the cart called 'Kastewagen' (cart with chests). The chests are piled upon the cart and the best quality linen called 'Brautgewebe' is in the chests. Salt and bread are essential, these are the first things carried into the new house. Beds, chests, furniture are all piled up on the wagon. Most important of all is the bride's spindle decorated with little figures representing boys and girls to make sure that they will have many children. The bride is seated on the wagon beside the spindle. The coachman's fee consists in linen that is sufficient for a shirt and he wears this like a belt around his waist. At the groom's house she throws a coin away "to get rid of bad luck"[20]. At Schonbrunn and in Silesia, the cradle, a broom and salt are essential. They hide a coin among the feathers of the coverlet, then they will always have money.[21]

The Slovak wedding, like the Hungarian, focuses around the bed itself. After supper the groom's relatives try to take possession of the bed and the chests. But the cook sits on one of the chests. Every piece has to be bought by the groom and his friends. Finally they have everything, they put it on a wagon and drive home with a *detour*.

The women of the groom's family try to make the bed, but now it is the best man and his friends, who steal everything and run away, the women run after them and buy everything back with pennies[22]. According to another report the bride cannot be present when all this happens because she could not stand all the obscene remarks that go with this transaction. The best men ask, what about the bed-linen? The women's chorus sings an appropriate song.[23] This is repeated several times. The men say all right, if we can't have the bed we can do without the bride. The mother of the bride starts praising the bed, how expensive it was, how beautiful it was, etc. Finally they conclude the bargain. They stick a big cake into the bag among the ribbons and one of the best men now grabs the whole thing and puts it on the wagon[24]. At Szeged the engagement money (*Jegypenz*) is payed for the bed by the best man. Pots are thrown at the wheels, rifles crack while they drive to the groom's house with the bed. All the noise is made to frighten the witches who might otherwise become dangerous. The best man says:

---

20. Andree, R.: *Braunschweiger Volkskunde*. 1901, pp. 301, 302.

21. Kohler: *Voegtland*, p. 235. Drechsler, P., *Sitte, Brauch und Volksglaube in Schlesien*, Leipzig, I, 1903, pp. 241, 242.

22. Piprek: *Brautwerbung*, p. 103. Stancsek, Slovak wedding customs, *Ethnographia*, 1903, pp. 54, 65.

23. Cf. E. M. Loeb: Courtship and Love Song, *Anthropos*, XLV, 1950, 821–851.

24. Sztancsek, l. c., 61–66.

> God grant us a good evening
> I have fulfilled my first task
> Look what a nice bed I have bought.[25]

In Northern Hungary, the bride's bed is the symbol of marriage. It must be in the groom's house before the ceremony in the church. Transporting the bed is the most festive part of the ceremony.[26]

The way from the bride's house to the groom's is barred usually by ropes made of straw.

At Kis Kun Halas the cortege arrives at the bride's house. The gate is open but they can't enter because the noise and the shooting has made the horses shy and they shy even more when they see a straw man with feathers on his head, a necklace of *paprika* (bell-peppers) and a sword in his hand. Wound around him is a straw rope that bars the entrance. After turning back several times one of the men thinks it is enough and jumps off the carriage to cut through the straw rope. But this is not so easy because a wire is hidden in the straw[27]. At Gocsej the young lads of the village take the nails out of the wheels, tie the horses' reins into magic knots. They barricade the gates of both houses with ropes, the narrow streets with poles. They tear bridges down or remove the boards. Others burn wolves' toe nails or horses' toe nails under the bridge, the horses will not be able to pass because of the smell.

They refuse to let them go into the bride's house before paying "gate money[28]."

At Hadhaz lads used to ride in advance of the carriage and cut the straw rope through with their sabres. Sometimes the sabres broke because a chain was hidden in the straw[29]. In Tyrol the way is barred by poles and other obstacles. Free passage can be obtained by payment in wine. 'Klause-machen' is the word for a more elaborate form of the same custom. They make a gate of green boughs barred by a chain with straw in the middle. Masked figures bargain with the groom before they permit him to cut through the obstacle.[30]

At Eichsfeld the lads barricade the entrance of the village if the bride comes from another village and then they have ropes in each street[31]. In Ba-

25. Kovacs, J.: *Szeged es nepe* (Szeged and its people) 1901, p. 286.

26. Pinter, S.: A palocz szuletese hazassaga es halalozasa, (Birth, marriage and death of the Paloc) *Ethnographia,* II, pp. 102, 103.

27. Thury, J.: Kis Kun Halas neprajza (Ethnography of Kis Kun Halas) *Ethnographia,* I, pp. 385, 387.

28. Gonczi, F. *Gocsej.* 1914, pp. 341, 342.

29. Trencseny, L.: Lakodalmi szokasok Hajdu Hadbazon (Wedding Customs at Hajdu Hadhaz) *Ethnographia,* V. 1894, p. 257.

30. Reinsberg-Duringsfeld, Hochzeitsbuch, 18 F I. V. Hutchinson, l. c. 255.

31. Kuck und Sohnrey: *Feste und Spiele des deutschen Landvolks.* 1911, p. 236.

varia the Catholic church collects the passage money. The master of ceremonies has a sword and when the guests steal the bride he brings her back[32]. In Alsace when they permit the bride to pass through one of these straw obstacles she is handed a glass of wine. She drinks and smashes it. If it breaks into bits the marriage will be a happy one. The others who hold the rope, get money from the groom[33].

In the Rhine province the chain is wound round with straw, but at one place, unknown to the groom, there is only straw. The groom must first answer three riddles and then they allow him to feel for this place with his sword till he finds the spot, cuts it through and enters[34]. According to Czech custom the drwzba does the bargaining and the groom pays. The drwzba compares the groom to the mythical Bratislav who obtained his bride by breaking through an iron chain. The carriages then gallop through but the groom's carriage must be first in the race[35]. According to Roumanian custom three riders gallop in advance to announce that the groom is coming. The gate is barred by a chain and the host opens it only after a long dispute[36].

The custom is very widespread[37]. Van Gennep has made a comprehensive study. In the Hautes Alpes there is violent resistance if the girl comes from another village but if the youngsters catch the hen that is carried by the bridal cortege they eat it and further resistance ceases. At La Grave the barrier of ribbons and flowers is erected when they come out of church. At Agnielle the groom has to cut through the ribbons. At Serrois the important thing was for the bride to jump over the obstacle so that her shoes would show[38]. Sometimes it is a real barricade made of logs, sometimes an *arc de triomphe* of boughs and flowers[39].

"In old times the inhabitants of houses where the cortege passed would erect *"la barriere de la mariée."* The road to the church is closed by a ribbon, there is a table with food and drinks. The young people, friends of the bride and groom, erect these barriers. The right of way had to be purchased with candy or money[40]. There is another obstacle beside the material one of the barrier. The groom has to solve riddles.

At Kethely (Hungary) the flag is an important feature. The women make

32. Bronner, F. J.: *Van deutscher Sitte und Art.* 1908, pp. 290–293.
33. Samter, E.: *Geburt, Hochzeit und Tod.* 1911, p. 163.
34. Wrede: *Rheinische Volkskunde.* 1919, pp. 127, 128.
35. Reinsberg-Duringsfeld, l. c., p. 197.
36. Madovan, G.: *A magyarorszagi romanok* (Roumanians in Hungary), 1913, pp. 167, 173.
37. For India, Th. Zachariæ, Zum altindischen Hochzeitsritual, *Wiener Zeitschrit für die Kunde des Morgenlandes,* XVII.
38. Gennep, A. V.: *Le Folklore des Hautes Alpes.* Paris, 1946, pp. 131–144.
39. Idem, *Le Folklore de l' Auvergne et du Velay.* Paris, 1942, p. 53.
40. Idem, *Le Folklore du Dauphine.* 1932, p. 132.

it with a red apple on the top and decorate it with flowers. They call it 'truth.'[41] While the women are preparing the flag the best man has to answer riddles.[42]

For instance:

Why doesn't the cock wear pants?

Answer:

Because while he is taking his pants off the hen would run away.

The chest is now ready and the best man and the '*vidor*' (Humorist) are ready to take it. But the bride's girl friends, cooks, elder women sit on the chest and won't let them have it till they answer some of these riddles.

Who was born, gave birth and never died? Lot's wife. What is most valuable in the chest? The pinafores, etc.

At Gocsej there is a whole legion of questions.

Which foot did they use when they first stepped over the threshold? The one that was behind. Several riddles refer to animals in the ark or to Jonah in the whale. The bulk of the riddles is obscene; Gonczi mentions this but refrains from publishing them[43].

At Kis Kanizsa the riddles must be answered before the groom and his friends can enter the room.

What was first, the beard or the man?

The beard, because God created animals first and the goat has a beard[44]. The people of Somogy county have a long list of mostly Biblical riddles[45].

Water is the lock (Red Sea), wood the key (staff of Moses), the hare crossed (the Jews), the hunter was drowned (the Egyptians). What is there on a new house that no one made? A crack.

At Csantaver (County Bacs) the questions are these:

When did God have a tail? When he took the shape of a dove and descended on Christ.

Which is the smallest fish in the Tisza?

The fish whose tail is nearest to its head. (Two more refer again to Noah's ark and Jonah in the whale.)[46]

Gyorffy comments on the fact that one of the functions of the best man or the inviter was to tell obscene stories.[47] At Beny they shout when they

41. At Kalotaszeg a pseudo-passport shown by the groom's friends is called 'truth'. Janko, J.: *Kalotaszeg magyar nepe* (Hungarians of Kalotaszeg). p. 152.

42. Bekefy, R.: *Kethely konyekenek neprajza* (Ethnography of Kethely and neighbourhood). 1884, p. 57.

43. Gonczi, F.: *Gocsej*. 1914, pp. 312–314.

44. Banekovics, J.: Kiskanizsai lakodalom (Wedding at Kiskanizsa) *Ethnographia*, VII, p. 190.

45. Peterdi, L.: Eljegyzesi e lakodalmi szokasok (Customs of betrothal and weddings) *Ethnographia*, XI, p. 401.

46. *Bacsmegye Monographia* (Monography of County Bacs). p. 335.

47. I. Gyorffy,: *Nagykunsagi Kronika* (Chronicle of the Nagykunsag). 1922, p. 153.

receive the bridal bed. Our horse has hay, our bride is beautiful! May the groom's penis be so thick that the bride can close her hand round it.[48]

At Szeged the riddles are of a well known type with two sets of answers. The riddle is seemingly obscene, but the polite answer is the real one.[49] For instance it is hairy outside, wet inside. Young men delight "in it." The answer is not vulva but wine bottle (*kulacs*), in Hungary covered on the outside with a foal's hide.

> The second riddle is this:
> Go home, go to bed,
> Do like every evening
> Stick the two hairy ones together
> Leave the balls in between

Now everybody would assume that it is coitus. But the answer is, go to bed, close your eyes (hairy ones), leave the eyeballs in between.

> The third question is this:
> Which is the last hole in the plough?

First they are baffled by the question, then they return with the correct answer; the cauldron's opening, because when they put the plough into the cauldron it will never be a plough any more (it is now scrap iron). The 'virgin garland' is the reward for knowing all the answers.[50]

The last riddle is significant, the plough evidently means the penis, the cauldron the vulva.

In Neuern the contest of wits is between the bride's mother and the groom. She demands all sorts of impossible things. A gigantic tree that comes from heaven, a bridge of silver, etc. He brings with seeming exertion a straw (the tree) and some silver coins (the bridge).[51] The coins are spread out on the table, the bride walks over them but only if she is a virgin.[52]

Bolte published the *Kurtze Anleitung, Wie man auf einer Landhochzeit bei der loblichen Bauernschaft bitten soll, 1690.* The groom is asking for the wreath that represents her virginity and she always creates new obstacles. We quote some of her questions and his answers.

---

48. Novak, L. J.: Adatok Beny kozseg neprajzahoz (Contributions to the Ethnography of Beny) *Neprajzi Ertesito,* 1913, p. 41.

49. Cf. Taylor, A.: *English Riddles from Oral Tradition.* Los Angeles, 1951, p. 687.

50. Kovacs, J.: *Szeged es Nepe.* 1901, pp. 288, 283.

51. John, A.: *Sitte, Brauch etc. in deutschen Westboehmen.* 1905, p. 151.

52. *Ibid.,* p. 156.

Question

> What is whiter than snow
> What is blacker than a raven
> What is deeper than the grave
> What is prouder than a lad?

Answer

> The sun is whiter than snow
> Its feathers are darker than a raven
> The well is deeper than the grave
> The horse prouder than the lad.

The girl says her body is covered with armour of gold, the lad says, he will jump so high that he gets the wreath, etc.

Then the girl says: "In my father's garden there is a white rosebush. On the bush a white dove. If you can ride round the bush three times without frightening the dove, the wreath is yours."[53]

We notice that we are still discussing the same theme as in the first chapter.

All the procrastination about the bride's bed, the resistance and the violence, all amount to the coy behaviour of a virgin who has to be coaxed or forced into giving in. In fact the hymen is even projected into space, the straw rope cut through by the groom with his sword. His club has to be fortified for he is an invading army and she a fortress. Defloration is the riddle, the task that may be represented as very easy or very difficult. Jonah in the whale, animals in Noah's ark—the penis or the embryo in the woman. Wolfgang Schultz is right[54] in assuming that the original meaning of the riddle is always sex, the rest is symbolism, camouflage. Every bridegroom is an Oedipus confronted by the Riddle of the Sphinx or the Riddle of Jokaste—it amounts to the same thing.

3. THE THRESHOLD

At Beny a boy is lying on the threshold. The bride should step over him, then she will be smart in all things. They give her a broom so that her house should always be kept clean. She tastes honey and sugar, her married life will be sweet. She looks into the chimney; this is to ensure her children having black eyes.[55]

---

53. Bolte, I.: Kranzwerbung, ein Gesellschaftsspiel des 17. Jahrhunderts, *Zeitschrift des Vereins für Volkskunde*, VII, pp. 382–392.

54. Schultz, W.: *Ratsel des hellenischen kulturkreise*. Berlin, II, 1912, p. 96.

55. Novak, I. L.: Adatok Beny kozseg neprajzahoz (Contributions to the Ethnography of Beny) *Neprajszi Ertesito*, 1913, p. 41.

At Nagy Bako she is received by the mother-in-law with a loaf of bread and a glass of wine. After having tasted these she steps over the threshold. A trough of water may be there, she has to kick and upset it.[56] At Gocsej if she steps on the threshold, the farmer will soon die! If she can jump three rungs of the ladder—for three years she will not conceive. She tastes the soup; she will be a good cook. She dips the bucket into the well and pours the water back, then she won't talk too much. The groom lifts her three times; delivery will be easy.[57] At Cserhat the houses have two thresholds. She jumps over the lower one several times, then she won't have too many children.[58]

At Kethely the performance with the broom comes later. After the dance she has to start sweeping, the others continue to dance and when she has swept one spot they throw sand there, so she has to sweep it again. "What kind of a wife are you going to be if you can't even clean the room," they say.[59] In Nyitra there is a boy on the threshold, she steps over him, then she will have male children.[60] At Cserhat she is seated on a chair that is covered with a fur coat; her sons will have curly hair.[61]

In Slavonia the new couple is led into the room. A sickle and a borer are on a chair but covered. She is seated, then she will be diligent with the sickle at harvest. Then there is the borer, that is for the groom but they don't say for what activity.[62]

At Ljubova (Bosnia) the bride approaches a barrel of water that is placed before the threshold. She pulls the tap out with her teeth, the water pours out. Then she places a silver coin on the barrel. Before the threshold she bows three times, she puts money on it and touches the doorpost with her right hand.[63]

At Meduna, she bows, kisses the threshold and puts a coin on it. Then she kisses her mother-in-law and receives a few coins from her mouth.[64] At Foca, the Mohammedan bride is expected by her mother-in-law on the threshold. The mother-in-law holds a child and the child pours water on the

---

56. Wagner, A.: Nepszokasok Nagy Bakonak videken (Folk Customs at Nagy Bako) *Ethnographia*, VI, p. 315.
57. Gonczi, *op. cit.*, p. 340.
58. Istvan Kiskeri Balogh Cserhati neprajzi adatok (Ethnographica of Cserhat) *Ethnographia IX*. 131]
59. Bekefy, *op cit.*, p. 76.
60. Am Urquell. V, p. 190.
61. Balogh, Cserhat. *Ethnographia*, IX, p. 135.
62. Garay, I.: Szlavoniai magyar faluk (Hungarian villages in Slavonia) *Neprajzi Ertesito*, 1911, p. 234.
63. Lilek, Vermahlungsgebrauche in Bosnien und der Herzogevina, *Wissenschafliche Mitteilungen aus Bosnien*, VII, p. 303.
64. *Ibid.*, p. 303.

threshold. The bride goes in under her husband's extended arm, kisses the threshold, then the fireplace and then her mother-in-law's hand and knees.[65]

According to the Croats of Murakoz water is poured out in order to facilitate delivery.[66] In Serbia kicking at a jar of milk and upsetting it serves the same purpose.[67]

A Roumanian bride is not allowed to touch the threshold, she jumps over it, or they carry her over. Then she anoints the threshold with butter and honey.[68] Slovaks put a sack of meal on the ground; she jumps at it and delivery will be as easy as meal pouring out of the sack. Her in-laws are standing on the threshold. At the kitchen door she overturns a glass of water. She steps on an egg; delivery will be easy, three times she crawls through a hoop—result as above.[69] At Szabadka the Serbian best man gallops along on horseback and throws a boy into the bride's lap. She enters the house on a carpet.[70]

At Vakuf she first kisses the threshold, then the fireplace and then they put the boy in her lap[71]. In Mostar she has a sack of corn on her lap. She starts to stir the fire and then they give her the boy. She turns him round three times; her children will be male[72].

At Krasso-Szoreny, the Bulgarian and the Roumanian peasants put a little boy into the bride's lap. She kisses the child and touches its penis, then her children will be male[73].

In Russia (Gouv. Kaluga) we find the following variation. The boy seated on the bride's lap is about 10 years old. He has a stick in his hand and with this he pretends to cut her pigtail. He desists when the best man gives him cokopeks[74]. In some places the groom sits on the bride's lap[75]. The Tshuvash have the Russian custom in the following form. A boy who is a relative of the groom gets into the carriage and lifts the bride's right leg three times[76].

Another group of customs connects the threshold with food, drink, seeds and various symbols of fertility.

---

65. Lilek, *l. c.*, pp. 315, 316, 319.
66. Gonczi, A murakozi nep lakodalmi szohasai (Wedding Customs at Murakoi) *Ethnographia*, I, p. 320.
67. Piprek, *l. c.*, p. 128.
68. Flachs, Rumanische Hochzeits-und Totengebrauche. 1899, p. 37.
69. Sztancsek, op. cit., *Ethnographia*, 1904, pp. 57–61.
70. Ivanyi, I.: A szabadkai buney vacok. *Ethnographia* II, p. 197. Juga, V.: A *magyaronszagi szerbek* (Serbians in Hungary). 1913, p. 155.
71. Lilek, *Vermahlung*, pp. 312, 316. The flowing water, the thresholds occur in various sequences. Piprek, *Brautwerbung*, pp. 129, 130, 100. Lilek, *l. c.*, p. 303.
72. Krauss, F. S.: *Sitte und Brauch*. P. 430, cf. pp. 428, 431, 447.
73. Czirbusz, G.: A *krassovan bolgurok* (Bulgarians in Krasso). 1913, p. 165.
74. Piprek, *Brautwerbung*, p. 18.
75. *Ibid.*, p. 12.
76. Meszaros, G.: A *csuvas osvallas emlekei* (Tshuvash Heathen Religion). Budapest, 1909, p. 460.

Germans in Western Hungary throw small balls of sugar on the bride. The number of balls she keeps on her lap indicates the number of boys she will have[77]. In Silesia peas and barley are thrown on the bride to make her happy[78]. Each seed or pea that sticks to her clothes means a child[79]. In Brandenburg wheat or rye in the bride's hair symbolize fertility[80]. Ruthenian women throw seeds or wheat and hops on the young couple when they are dancing or wheat and flowers of hops when they are having supper[81]. If a grain of wheat gets jammed in between the bride's toes, the child will be crippled. Russians throw seeds of wheat on groom and bride in order to make their union fertile. The groom's mother is present with her coat turned inside out. She brings the hops and wheat. Three times she circles round the cortege, finally the 'druzko' (best man) gets hold of her and throws her on his coat that is spread out somewhere. Then she starts strewing the seeds[82].

Another version: The bride's mother appears with her lambskin coat turned inside out (the woolly side is now visible). In her apron she has oats, nuts, sunflower seeds and coins that she has been collecting ever since her son's birth. She throws all these on the groom's followers[83]. The latent meaning becomes clearer in the following version. In Ukrajna the bride's mother kisses her son-in-law and hands him a vessel of water with oats in it. The groom pours the water on his stick[84]. Among Mohammedans in Bosnia it is the 'kum' (best man) who throws coins and almond seeds on the bride[85].

So far the main traits are these: (a) the threshold, (b) the boy, (c) the woolly coat, (d) seeds, coins, water, (e) the bride's mother-in-law, (f) we should note stepping over certain objects.

In Brandenburg it is a torch placed on the threshold, in Hessen a knife, in East Prussia a broom, in Waldeck a broom or axe[86]. Among English Gypsies this is the whole marriage ceremony; jumping over a broom[87]. At Trencseny,

---

77. Nitsch, M.: *A dunantulinimetsegrol* (Germans in West Hungary). 1913, p. 80.

78. Drechsler, P.: *Sitte, Brauche.* I, pp. 267, 268.

79. Wuttke, A.: *Der deutsche Volksaberglaube.* 1900, p. 374.

80. Andree, R.: *Braunschweiger Volkskunde*, p. 307.

81. Nemes, M.: A talabor volgyi ruthen nep lakodalmi szokasai (Wedding customs of Ruthenians at Talabor) *Ethnographia*, VI, p. 433. Szabo, *A magyarorszagi ruthenek* (Ruthenians in Hungary). 1913, p. 155.

82. Piprek, *Brautwerbung*, p. 16.

83. Piprek, *Brautwerbung*, pp. 36, 37.

84. Reinsberg-Duringsfeld, *Hochzeitsbuch*, p. 36.

85. Piprek, *l. c.*, p. 133.

86. Wuttke, *op. cit.*, pp. 371, 373.

87. Thompson, T. W.: Ceremonial Customs of British Gypsies, *Folk-lore*, 1913, XXIV, p. 336.

she sits on a mortar and the moment she rises another girl will sit on it. This means that the second girl is to find a husband within a year. In some villages there must be feathers on the mortar. She blows at the mortar, this will make delivery easy[88]. It is evident that most of these rites are either 'cousins' or 'grandchildren' of the ceremony as it was performed in Rome.

Two boys of good family preceded the *cortege* of the bride. One carried a lighted torch, the other a vessel with pure spring water. A spindle and three coins to be sacrificed to the Lares formed part of the bride's outfit. There was a lot of *fescennini versus* (obscene talk) going on. Nuts were strewn everywhere, in honour of *concubinus,* the personification of unbridled lust. At the threshold of the groom's house the bride anointed the doorposts with oil and wound wool around them. The bride stepped over the threshold. In the room her husband expected her with fire and water taken from the fireplace. In the room she sits on wool and then on a stone phallos in homage to the phallic god Mutunus Tutunus.

Preller quotes:

Tutunus, cuius immanibus pudendis horrentique fascino vestras ineqitare matronas et auspicabile ducitis et optatis (Arnobius IV, 7).

Tutinus in cuius sinu pudendo nubentes praesident ut illarum pudicitiam prior deus delibases videatur (Arnobius IV, 11 et Lactantins I, 20, 36).

Priapus nimis masculus super cuius immanissimum et turpissimum fascimum sedere nova nupta iubebatur more honestissimo et religiosissimo matronarum (Augustinus VI, 9).

In other words, the Roman bride was actually deprived of her virginity by the stone phallos of the god[89].

The boy in her lap, the woolly coat she sits on, the mortar she sits on, the knife, broom etc., she steps over are all phallic symbols. I have discussed the significance of 'stepping over.' "Thus in all these instances stepping over manifestly signifies intercourse"[90]. In any case when jumping over a wife or stepping over her legs is mentioned it is regarded by the Baganda as equivalent to or instead of having sexual intercourse with her[91].

Door and threshold as entrance to the female body are symbols of such universal significance[92] that we can do without further proofs. But the question arises; the threshold is female, but *whose vulva* is it? Since it is the bride who is going to have intercourse it must be her vulva. Is she then going into her own vulva?

---

88. Sztancsek, I.: Tot lakodalmi szokasok (Slovak marriage customs) *Ethnographia,* 1903. pp. 436, 437. Pechany, *A magyarorszagi totok* (Slovaks in Hungary). 1913, p. 110. Piprek, *op. cit.,* pp. 29, 107, 110.
89. Preller, L.: *Romische Mythologie.* Berlin, 1858, pp. 583–586.
90. Roheim, G.: The Significance of Stepping Over, *Int. J. of Psa.* III, 1922, p. 325.
91. Roscoe, I.: *The Baganda,* 1911, pp. 357, 395.
92. Cf. for instance Trumbull, H. C.: *The Threshold Covenant.* Edinburgh, 1896.

The confusion in symbolism might be simply due to the sociological fact of *patrilineal* marriage. However I would be inclined to borrow from dream symbolism and say that going *into* her *own vulva is having intercourse*[93]. However, this is not all. We notice that in these rites fireplace, oven or chimney have a very important function.

In Serbia the young woman walks round her mother-in-law three times and three times round the oven and she bows respectfully toward the oven[94]. At Ljubovo she bows three times, then deposits a coin on the threshold and does the same at the oven[95]. At Medua the mother-in-law expects her daughter-in-law at the fireplace. She takes a few pennies from her mother-in-law's mouth[96]. In Styria she places a few pennies on the threshold. Then she kisses her mother-in-law, and goes to the fireplace to give a present "for the fireplace and for the mother-in-law"[97]. The Esthonian bride was led around in the house. Rooms, stables, garden-well and fireplace, wherever she went she would throw some ribbons or coins.

According to Kreutzwald the coins ar given as an expiation to the "fire and water mother" (i.e. spirits).[98]

Considering all this we see a close parallelism, a kind of combination of the fireplace and the mother-in-law. We notice how many of these rites aim at creating good will between mother-in-law and daughter-in-law, an obvious reaction formation to the well-known antagonism. But underlying this there is another meaning. The young woman is coming into the house of the older woman, coitus is also a regression into her own mother.[99] The ritual attempts to fuse the younger and the older woman from the man's point of view, the wife and the mother.

4. THE WRONG BRIDE

At Cserhat the bride suddenly disappears. The groom looks for her but they have dressed her as a man or an old woman so as to make her unrecognizable[100]. Among the Palocz of Northern Hungary they bring a stranger, then a girl dressed as an old woman, and when all these are rejected, the real one[101]. At the Nyarad they have several old women they insist that one

---

93. Cf. Roheim, *The Gates of the Dream.* 1953. The Basic Dream.
94. Krauss, F. S.: *Sitte und Brauch,* p. 436. Piprek, *Brautwerbung,* p. 130.
95. Lilek, op. cit., *Wissenschaftliche Mitteilungen aus Bosnien,* VII, p. 303.
96. *Ibid.,* p. 305.
97. *Ibid.,* p. 316.
98. Schroeder, L. v., *Die Hochzeitsbrauche der Esten.* Berlin, 1888, p. 131.
99. Cf. Roheim, *op. cit.*
100. Balogh, I. K.: Cserhati neprajzi adalekok (Ethnographica of the Cserhat) *Ethnographia,* IX, p. 133.
101. Istvanffy, S.: Matraalji palocz lakodalom (Palocz wedding at the Matra) *Ethnographia,* V, p. 45.

of them is the real bride and are sorry that she looks different. At last they bring the real one in all her finery[102].

In the Alfold (Lowlands) while the groom is haggling about the price of the bridal bed, an apparition called 'the Spinning Woman', a man dressed as an old woman, presents itself in the yard and starts a furious 'spinning' or rather pretends to do so. She is a widow and will take good care of any man who marries her[103]. In Esztergom County they bring a dirty Gypsy woman. Sometimes the lad says 'yes', he is so embarrassed—then of course there is great fun[104]. In Baranya they first bring an old woman, then one who is dressed as if she were pregnant and at last the real one[105]. In Szabolcs the groom's people say they are merchants who want to buy wheat. One girl is dressed up to look very old, one very young. Both are rejected till the right one comes. She is 'pure wheat' and accepted[106]. At Harta we have an old wrinkled hag who can hardly walk[107]. In Hont they dress someone to look like a very old hag. At Tokaj they bring an old woman, then a young girl and then the real bride[108]. The Germans in Czechoslovakia called the old or masked person 'die alte Braut' and the groom must give her a present to buy his freedom. She says, she is pregnant and that the groom is the father of her child. A doll figures as the child. Sometimes there are two or three masked persons[109]. The old woman with the spindle is called Spille Gritte in Silesia[110]. This is the same as Holle, the mother imago[111]. At Vogelsberg the old woman is got up like a scarecrow. He says he does not know this ghost and his friends shout, "Take the old witch back"[112]. In Bavaria they first offer 'the wild woman' (a demon). The 'wrong bride' is supposed to take bad luck out of the house[113].

The Croatians in Western Hungary had a whole group of 'wrong brides.' The oldest and ugliest came first, then younger and prettier ones progres-

102. Gal, K.: Lakodalmi szokasok (Wedding Customs) *Ethnographia*, VI, p. 401.
103. Reso-Ensel, S.: *Magyarorszagi nepszokasok* (Folk Customs of Hungary). Pesten: 1867, pp. 39, 40.
104. Novak, J.: op. cit., Neprajzi Ertesito. 1913, p. 44.
105. Berze Nagy: *Baranyai Magyar Nephagyomanyok*. III, pecs, 1940, p. 129.
106. Monograph of County Szabl Budapest, n. d., p. 163.
107. Simonyi, J.: Kalocsa kornyeke (Kalocsa and neighbourhood) *Fold rajze Kozlemenyek*, X, p. 317.
108. Hontvar megye Monographija. 97, Kiss, in *Ethnographia*, II, p. 246.
109. John, A.: *Sitte, Brauch und Volksglaube im deutschen Westboehmen*, 1905, pp. 127, 138, 152, 157.
110. Drechsler, *Sitte, Brauch und Volksglaube in Schlesien*, 1903, I, pp. 245, 256.
111. Kuhnau, R.: *Schlesische Sagen*, 1911, II, p. 53.
112. Hepding, H.: Die falsche Braut, *Hessische Blatter für Volkskunde*, V, p. 162, *l. c.* p. 151.
113. Buschan, G.: *Sitten der Volker*. IV, 1922, p. 154.

sively, finally the real one[114]. The bride's grandmother is the old hag in Bretagne[115]. In Moravia 'the old woman' or comic person cries and wails and reminds the groom that he promised to marry her. He pays her off[116].

In these comic scenes we find the real but unconscious nucleus of the whole ritual. The past girl friend is the old woman, the mother, and this is the main transition in the transition rite; from mother to wife.

5. THE WEDDING MEAL

The peasant is often underfed but a peasant wedding is a colossal affair. It may go on for three days (in old times even more) with a hundred guests. The farmer has been making colossal efforts to get all the food for the crowd and although the guests co-operate too, families are capable of getting into financial ruin just for this occasion[117].

The meal used to be something like this in Hungary around 1760:

1. Soup with noodles;
2. Boiled beef with horseradish;
3. Stuffed cabbage, sausages;
4. Suckling with sweet sauces;
5. Shank of beef, with a sour sauce;
6. Blood pudding;
7. Chicken fricassee;

and only after this would they start the roast (beef, lamb, pork, hare, turkey, goose) and finish with all sorts of cakes.[118]

The menu varies according to the economic status of the family or the whole village. However, our sources emphasize (for Hungary) that two courses were indispensable, beef, broth and millet.[119]

The best man brings in each course. He does so with verses that by this time have been printed in popular leaflets but were originally handed down orally. We shall give samples of these verses.

---

114. Szegedy, Nyugatmagyarorszagi horvat lakodalmi szokasok (Croatian Wedding Customs in Western Hungary) *Ethnographia*, XXXII, p. 62.
115. Reinsberg-Duringsfeld, *l. c.*, p. 246.
116. Piprek, *op. cit.*, p. 89.
117. Books on folklore hardly ever mention the setting in which the ritual is carried out. My remarks are valid for Hungary, but I assume it must be about the same in other countries in Europe.
118. Reso Ensel, *Magyarorszagi nepszokasok.* 1867, p. 33.
119. *Ibid.*, p. 28.

> I just arrived from the Garden of Eden
> And I ate from the fruit of that beautiful Garden
> I was a gardener there for a long time
> And grew nice cabbage in plenty
> I know the major part of Great Hungary
> But I would not find anything like this cabbage
> This is the coat of arms of our noble country
> Even our king takes care of this.[120]

Most of the sayings follow the pattern of *absurdity*.

"I went into a garden, I climbed a cucumber tree there, I wanted to gather pears and apples but the gardener got hold of a radish and threw the carrot at me. The axe hit my back and I ran away. I saw a tree, on it a cave with little starlings in it. I wanted to get one of them but I could not put my hand in, so I crawled in myself. Now how to get out? I remembered an old axe made of my grandfather's overcoat, so I ran and fetched it and with it I cut myself out of the cave. People shouted, "Best man loosen your belt." So I did that. All the little starlings flew away. I had no wings so I could not fly after them, So I flew nevertheless till I got to the kitchen, I caught their tail and here they are," (meaning[121] the food).

At Kethely the best man says:

"Do not despise my invitation for this magnificent wedding for one drumstick of a turkey one glass of wine and a little music. Yesterday I went shooting with the bride and the groom. It was very difficult but we managed to shoot two sparrows. They gave two tons of meat and five of feathers. This may perhaps be enough."[122]

At Gocsej:

"My dear friends, bring all your knives and weapons. I have brought seven crows. The coachman was a fly, the butler a mosquito, the wheels were made of carrots, the axis was a reed, the pole was made of straw. However you can't rely on all this because there are many pigs here and they like carrots. So I took the whole thing to the mill and put 12 measures of wheat into a nutshell. Then I made the sacks pull the cart and I put the oxen on the cart. But by the time I got to the mill lo and behold! the mill had gone to pick strawberries. By the time I got back a great tree sprouted from a whip. I thought I would climb it and get some birds, flesh. But by the time I climbed up my hand would not fit into the cave. So I pushed my head in and I got stuck. Now I thought of my grandfather's axe made of the cloth of his

---

120. Cabbage means sauerkraut. Nyary, *Ertesito,* 1906, p. 230. Thury, *Ethnographia,* I, p. 395.
121. Reso Ensel, *op. cit.,* p. 292.
122. Bekefy, *Kethely,* p. 56.

great coat. However, I had bad luck, I cut my neck with it. Forthwith I dropped into a pond full of fish. My buttocks made the fish jump out of the lake; three carloads of them. This will be all right for Friday, I thought, but a naked gypsy lad ran away with them. He put the whole lot in his lap,"[123] (etc.).

A similar saying from the same area:

"When I started inviting guests I met a louse on my way. I just put it in my pocket. At home I killed it. The meat will be enough for all the guests. The hide I used for the bride's top-boots. Friday goes, Saturday comes, I am telling you sad news. The bride complained: All she got was a small one. But the groom smiled: His hand slipped into her trouser's pocket. The bridesmaid looks at him with one eye. She hopes God will grant her wish."[124]

It is easy to guess what the 'best man' is talking about.

In Bacs County:

> An old hedge hog we shall have potted
> And a sick flea on the spit
> In jelly we have nine storks
> Moreover some fat sparrows.[125]

Considering these (and some others not quoted here), the total of 'motives' found in these sayings will be as follows:

1. Starlings (flying, tail feathers torn out);
2. Grandfather's axe of cloth. He cuts himself out of a hole or chops his own head off;
3. Animal that is both small and huge;
4. Oxen on the wagon, sacks drawing it;
5. The mill has gone to pick strawberries;
6. A tree grows from a whip;
7. Greetings in a foreign language;
8. Fish knocked out of pond.

All these motives have their parallel in a type of folktale called 'lying stories.'

In Kriza (Vadrozsak II, 131) we find parallels to the following traits: 4, 5, 6, 2, 1, 8.

In Horger (Hetfalusi casango Mesek Nepk., Gy. 369) 4, 5, 6, 1, 2, 7, 8.

In Berze (Hevesmegyei Nepmesek Nepk., Gy. IX, 550) 4, 5, 6, 1, 7, 8.

---

123. Gonczi, *Gocsej*, pp. 333, 334, 345.

124. Sebok, S.: Bessenyoi parasztlakodalom (Peasant Wedding at Bessenyo) *Ethnographia*, 1905, XVI, p. 154.

125. *Bacsmegye Monographia* (Monography of Bacs County). N.D.

The stories in question are called (i) My father's wedding; (ii) My father's christening; (iii) How I went up to heaven. These 'lying stories' are not just lies ad. lib. but lies of a certain type.

My Father's Wedding

"Suddenly I noticed that my father wants to get married to my mother. So he told me to go to the mill and have wheat ground. (Then he describes how he does everything the opposite way it should be).

I stuck the whip's handle into the ground and went to look for the mill. The green pig was not on the nail so I knew the mill had gone to pick strawberries. The oxen couldn't wait for years so I ran after the mill with a stick and just as I was going to beat it, I hear the noise, it is grinding my wheat. As I came down into the valley I just dipped my nose into cow's shit, not too deep, I saw a white horse, it got so frightened that it ran straight out of this world and never came back.

Then I saw that my whip had taken root and grown into a huge tree with lots of starlings in it. I climbed up but my hand would not fit in the hole, so I stuck my head in and got many starlings. The miller grave me a basket of grain. I twisted it into a rope but a worm bit the rope off before I reached bottom.

Then he flies up lifted by the starlings, women look at him in amazement, he drops his pants and falls into the middle of a river (fish, gypsy boy as above).

I saw a horse, put the saddle on the brown horse and rode away on a yellow one, I took my skull off to break the ice and drank some water. I pulled myself out of there by my hair and as I was galloping along two men said: Where's your head? I grabbed my buttocks but it wasn't there so I went back, found my head and it had made itself a new man, limbs, body, etc. Finally he gets back to his father who had given him up for dead.

"I had brought my father's soul. We put the sacks of flour on the cart and had the wedding. I danced the bride's dance with my mother, everybody else left and we stayed together. I was born a year later and I am my father's legal offspring."[126]

Another story of the same kind:

When my mother was born the midwife told me to go and fetch my godmother. But as she was dead, I had to get her. I did not know how to get back. Saint Joseph said: Here is some grain, twist it into a rope. It was too short but when I folded it double it was all right. However, half way between Heaven and Earth a mouse gnawed the rope. I crashed into the earth up to my waist. I cut one leg off with my pocket-knife; then I ran home, got

---

126. Kriza, J., *Vadrozsak* (Briar Roses). Budapest, 1911, III, pp. 131–137.

a shovel and dug the other leg out. By the time I got home my mother had been baptized.[127] Another type; starlings fly skyward with the hero. Women see him and say 'Avaunt Satan.' He misunderstands them and thinks he is to loosen his pants. He acts accordingly and flops down among them.[128]

'Father's wedding' is the old Oedipal theme in a comic garb (also mother's baptism) while the flying stories sound like dreams. There are frequent references to castration (tail torn out, head or leg chopped off).

In the Upper Lausitz we have the following story: "A flea flew from the roof. The noise was terrific nothing broke. . . . You (meaning the groom and the bride) have to cross a big hill and *this won't be as easy as when the cock mounts the hen*. It is just a year now since the giant married Margaret and they have produced 16 lads, 18 girls, 19 boys and 13 daughters."[129] The connection of the 'absurd' with the anxiety connected with defloration could not be put with greater clarity.

The tiny thing that becomes huge is the phallos. We find parallels in the gigantic axe of the Kalavala Runo (XX) again as part of the wedding meal.[130]

There is a lot of horseplay and also serious observances going on in connection with the meal.

Children catch sparrows in traps, bathe them and strew paprika on their feathers. They let them loose among the guests.[131]

In Borsod they bring three covered dishes. One of them contains roast chicken, the second a live cat, the third ashes, bones, etc. The master of ceremonies has to guess which of the three dishes contains the chicken. If he guesses right he and his friends will eat it.[132] The Slovaks have the custom in a less distorted form. The covered dish is placed before the young couple. They are told to lift the cover, a live mouse or cat jumps out[133]—the child.[134]

The custom of eating out of one plate is very frequent.

At Aranyosszek, the young couple eat out of the same plate and each eats only one morsel. This means that as long as they live, they will have enough

---

127. Bano, I., *Baranyai nepmesek* (Folk Tales of Baranya). Budapest, 1941, II, p. 238.

128. *Ibid.*, II, pp. 147, 192.

129. Bolte, Eine Predigtparodie, *Zeitschrift des Vereins für Volkskunde*, XII, p. 224. Muller, Predigtparodien aus der Oberlausitz, *Zeitschrift des Vereins für Volkskunde*, XIX, pp. 175, 176.

130. Cf. Krohn, K., *Kalevalan runojen historia*, 1903, p. 622.

131. Gonczi, *op. cit.*, p. 346.

132. Istvanffy, G., A Borsod megyei paloczok (Palocz people in Borsod) *Ethnographia*, XXII, 1911, p. 226.

133. Sztancsek, I., *op. cit.*, *Ethnographia*, 1904, pp. 52, 53.

134. Cf. Hutchinson, *Marriage Customs*, p. 240. Schulenburg, W. V., *Wendisches Volksthum*. 1882, p. 27.

food.[135] The one plate means that they shall always be united.[136] They drink off each other's cup in order to live always in harmony.[137]

In Silesia a special 'Brautsuppe' is prepared only for the young couple.[138] In Russia they drink of the same glass and share a chicken.[139] Germans had the same custom it was called 'Liebeshuhn' or 'Brauthuhn.'[140]

Food is used as a symbol for expressing what everybody is thinking.

In many places the bride (or both bride and groom) are supposed to be reluctant to eat. Yugoslavs say, "She refuses to eat like a peasant bride."[141] Or "She wants to be coaxed like a peasant bride."[142] In Nyitra they don't eat, their plates are reversed.[143]

The custom of abstaining from coitus for the first three nights is very ancient.[144] But finally (or immediately) she is starting sex life—therefore she is supposed to eat the pig's tail that is hidden in the stuffed cabbage.[145] In the Schwarzwald they bring the pig's tail in with due ceremony in a separate dish. The bride is supposed to get hold of it and throw it at the 'best man.'[146] In Voigtland it is the whole hind part of the pig with the tail: the tail is decorated with a bunch of flowers.[147]

The two significant elements of the meal are the wedding cake and the tree or bough.

At the Balaton they called it 'tree of life.' A common but strong weed was covered with dough and then baked. They hung grapes, nuts, etc. on the branches and placed the whole on the table.[148]

White Russians combine the Korovay (round wedding cake) with a branch. The whole thing is full of little figures. The bride on her knees, opening her skirt. Opposite stands the groom, a *carrot* in his right hand. Other figures represent birds, animals, all in pairs or actually copulating. The boar is on the sow, the stallion on the mare, the cock on the hen, etc.[149]

---

135. Janko J., *Torda, Aranyosszek Toroczko magyar nepe*, 1893, p. 210.

136. Kalman, G., Lakodalmi szokasok a Nyarad mellett (Wedding Customs of the Nyarad) *Ethnographia*, VI, p. 104.

137. Gonczi, *l. c.*, pp. 346, 347.

138. Drechsler, *l. c.*, I. p. 267.

139. Schroeder, L. v., *op. cit.*, pp. 82–84.

140. Weinhold, K., *Deutsche Frauen.* 1897, I, p. 387.

141. Hoblik, M., Lakodalmi szokasok Veroce varmegye felso vide (Wedding Customs in Veroce County) *Tudomany Tar*, IV, 1839, p. 239.

142. Piger, R., Geburt, Hochzeit und Tod, *Zeitschrift des Vereins für Volkskunde*, VI, p. 261.

143. Reso Ensel, *op. cit.*, p. 204. Sztancsek, *op. cit.*, *Ethnographia*, 1904, p. 52.

144. Schroeder, *op. cit.*, pp. 192–199.

145. Janko, *Torda*. p. 211.

146. Reichhardt, *Geburt, Hochzeit und Tod.* p. 100.

147. Kohler, A. E., *Volksbrauch etc. aus dem Voigtlande.* Leipzig, 1867, p. 237.

148. Janko, *A balaton melteki lakopsag neprajza* (Ethnography of the inhabitants of the shore of the Balaton). 1902, p. 390.

149. Piprek, *Brautwerbung*, p. 59.

Ruthenians have a pine tree decorated with feathers and flowers, this is 'the symbol of the wedding.'[150] A parallel to the tree is the red flag erected at the groom's place if the bride has proved her virginity in the bridal night.[151] The *pornul nuptii*[152] (apple tree of the wedding) is a conspicuous feature, they hang nuts and cakes on it. This is the *fruit of the tree,* they can take it off only when the priest permits. It is evident that we have here an allegory and that they are thinking of the tree in the Garden of Eden. On receiving the priest's permission bride and groom share an apple.[153] We have another Roumanian version of the same custom when they put up "the apple tree of the wedding" a year after the wedding. They will have a tree in heaven in the shade of which they can rest. In the mountains it is custom-ary for a girl who has had an illegitimate child to be wedded to a poplar or a willow.[154] Hungarians call the tree 'tree of life.' Since there are candles on it lit by the bride,[155] it is somewhat like a Christmas tree.

The phallic meaning of the tree is parallel to the female meaning of the cake. If the cake is baked by a pregnant woman the marriage will be fertile (Yugoslav).[156] A Russian bride bakes two round cakes, symbolizing the union of the couple.[157]

In many cases we have a combined object representing both the male and the female symbol. At Beny they bring something called the 'May of the Bride.' It is a circular wooden structure covered with dough with apples, flasks of wine and flags. Bride and groom are also there, figures made of dough. Hungarians call it 'a menyasszony maja' which for those who do not know the derivation means 'the bride's liver' but it is really derived from the German *Brautmai*. Next morning each guest gets a little piece of the dough. The wood is also called 'parto fa.'[158]

The bride may be represented by a kerchief hanging on the tree. The *ker-chief tree* is a young sapling with kerchief and some pretzels on top.[159]

While the bride is in church they put the tree up with jugs, plates, etc., on top. On a barrel they put up a bough of pine tree with all sorts of things hanging from the top. In old times the 'bridal kerchief' would be stuck out

---

150. Kaindl, R. F., Ruthenische Hochzeitsgebrauche in der Bukovina, *Zeitschrift des Vereins für Volkskunde*, XI, p. 163. Idem, *Die Huzulen*. Wien, 1894, p. 20.
151. *Ibid.,* p. 166.
152. Moldovan, *A magyar orszagi romanok* (Roumanians in Hungary). 1913, pp. 159, 162.
153. Idem, *Alsofrher.* p. 283.
154. *Ibid.,* p. 180.
155. *Magyarsag Neprajza* (Ethnography of the Hungarians), IV, p. 170.
156. Piprek, *l. c.,* p. 127.
157. *Ibid.,* p. 3.
158. Novak, *op. cit., Ertesito,* 1913, p. 44. The "wood of seeing damage," cf. infra.
159. Reso Ensel, *op. cit.,* p. 139.

of the roof hanging on a pole. One of the guests had to shoot it off or climb up and get it.[160] The same custom obtained in Udvarhely but here the tree was called 'engagement tree' (jegyfa).[161] The best man breaks a round cake into bits, everybody scrambles for it. This is one of the many symbolic sharings of the bride. The round cake is called 'stomach' in Felasberg— obviously representing the bride's body.[162] She throws the cake in the direction of the latest newly sown field.[163] (New field—new woman.) In Baden the tree is called 'Maien' or 'Christbaum' or 'Adam and Evabaum.'[164] In Saterland the tree as a motive of art is sewn into the bed cloth with a cock sitting on the top of the tree, a form of symbolism that is easily understood, as Mannhardt says.[165]

6. THE REACTION OF THE VILLAGE

As long as the wedding lasts the bridegroom is regarded as a sultan,[166] in Syria bride and groom were queen and king[167], among the Malays 'king for a day.'[168] Tatars in Asia Minor bow to the groom, they are his subjects.[169] The Ruthenian bridegroom keeps a cap decorated with a wreath on his head during the meal, he is now a prince and she a princess.[170] The Roumanian 'inviter' appears as the 'ambassador' of the 'king' and the 'queen.'[171] According to the Hungarians at Tornyospalca the groom keeps his hat on, it is his crown.[172] Bride and groom are adults now, 'kings' and the whole village is going to approve of their having intercourse. What more natural than that they should be punished? At Tetetlen uninvited lads from another village come in masks, and greet the young couple with the following 'good wishes.'

---

160. Janko, *Kalotaszeg*, pp. 148, 152, 143.
161. As related by Mr. Laszlo, Hungarian Ethnographical Museum (in 1924).
162. Richter, M., Lakodalmi szokasoka nyitra megyei nemet falvakbaz (Wedding Customs of German villages at Nyitra) *Ethnographia*, XV, pp. 427, 428.
163. Frischauf, E., Ein niederosterreichischer Hochzeitsbrauch. *Zeitschrift für Volkskunde*, IV, p. 215.
164. Meyer, E. H., *Badilsches Volksleben*. 1900, pp. 250, 311.
165. Mannhardt, W., *Wald-und Feldkulte*. I, 1905, p. 46.
166. Westermarck, E., *Marriage Ceremonies in Morocco*. London, 1914, p. 97, cf. pp. 102, 113, 274.
167. Wetzstein, Die Syrische Dreschtafel, *Zeitschrift für Ethnologie*. VI, p. 288.
168. Skeat, W., *Malay Magic*. 1900, p. 388.
169. Garnett, L. M. I., *The Women of Turkey*. 1897, p. 351.
170. Kaindl, R. F., Hochzeitsgebrauche, *Zeitschrift des Vereins für Volkskunde*. XI, p. 284. Idem, *Huzulen*, p. 16. Piprek, *l. c.*, pp. 26, 62.
171. Moldovan, *Magyaraorzagi romanok*, pp. 163, 167, 168.
172. Kiss, A., Tornyospalcai babonak (Superstitions at Torayospalca) *Ethnographia*, II, p. 250.

Poison should grow on your prick
And may it wither like bark
We hope lice will chew the edges of your arse
And vermin will make their home in it
Corns, bloody shit and constipation
May they all visit you at the same time
And as many blue flies as there are in Debrecen
May they all sting your arse at the same time.[173]

In Northern Hungary, the masked lads come in the morning. One of them is 'the prisoner', he is chained and they make him dance through the village. Sometimes it is several lads wrapped in straw with the pots on their head.[174]

At the Cserta the 'motive' is displaced, the master of ceremonies and prominent guests are brought to the wedding in chains.[175]

One of the games the maskers play is that they persuade an unsuspecting lad that he should be the bull and he should roar. They tie a rope round him and drag him to the master of ceremonies. He decides that the bull must be slaughtered. They bring an axe and they start pulling the lad up onto the roof. Somebody cuts the belt that holds his pants and he falls off in the nude. The young girls are terribly embarrassed.[176] Next day the masks come again. This end phase of the marriage is called *tyukvero* (beating the hen) or *karlato* (seeing the damage).

The lads of Kiskun Halas go round the place after the wedding in masks, and grab what they can. They are supposed to be especially after poultry and that is why they call it 'hen beater', i.e., to steal hens.[177]

However, there are special ceremonies connected with the cock that gives this name a deeper significance.

At Miskol, cutting the cock's neck was an intrinsic part of the ceremony. They catch a cock, tie its wings, tie a ribbon round its beak and lead it through the village. The cock is accompanied by masked persons and a gypsy. The procession halts at the church door, more gypsies appear, there is music and verses. They go back to the groom's house. The cock is accused, a court is to bring the verdict. The accusation is, he cohabits with his mother and daughters and has many wives. Considering the fact that if he is not punished, others might follow his example, the sentence is death. They pull

---

173. Liszt, N., Tetelteni keresztelesi es lakodalmi szokasok (Baptism and wedding customs in Tetetlen) *Ethnographia*, 1908, p. 241.

174. Istvanffy, G., A borsodmegyei palocok (Paloe people of Boryod county) *Ethnographia*, 1911, p. 226.

175. Gonczi, *Gocsej*, p. 352.

176. Mrs. Redey Hoffmann, *Ethnographia*, XXXVII, p. 25.

177. Thury, Kis Kun Halas, *Ethnographia*, I, p. 405.

the cord, one of them, 'the Turk', cuts the neck with his sword, they tell the groom to remember what happened and to act accordingly.[178] At Felsobanya they have been fattening a cock for this occasion. They tie the cock to a pole and blindfold the groom. He is supposed to kill the cock. He has a pole in his hand and while the band is playing he slashes about at random. Finally he manages to hit it, and it is eaten by the guests.[179] At Banokszentgyorgy, the 'inviter' goes about with a live cock he pulls by the leg.[180] In Baranya we have the same custom. The cock has been tended since it came out of the egg by the bride and they call it 'bride's cock.' This is to make the transition easier from her parents' house to her own.[181] At Gocsej, they bring a cock's head and neck with the cock's comb chewing the meal. The cock has a feather stuck in its head. They offer it to the bride, she grabs it and throws it out to the children.[182] At Kolesd the rice is brought in with the following verses.

From morning to now I chased the cock
Up to the haystack of uncle N. N.
I nearly lost my top boots
But now he won't run around any more.
He is not going to say, ho Kati was it good?
I chased him through barns and stables
His fucking soul! I got him when he mounted her
I pulled him off, his tail came off
Since then the poor cock is short
I just got him by the neck and stuck him into the dish of rice.[183]

It is quite clear who the cock is—they mean the groom. At Kethely we have the reverse of the Gocsej ceremony. The hen's neck is offered to the groom. He takes it into his mouth and starts crowing.[184]

In some versions the criminal is a human being. He is covered with rags and straw, blindfolded and he has a pot on his head. "This is a great criminal, a murderer, he must be executed"—they say. The 'executioner' is a man dressed as a woman. He (or she) swings his axe (a leaf), the pot is off, the 'criminal' falls. He is dead, they start a dirge.

178. Reso Ensel, *Magyarorszagi nepszokasok* (Folk Customs in Hungary). 1867, pp. 71, 72.
179. *Ibid.,* p. 131.
180. Gonczi, *op. cit.,* pp. 334, 341.
181. Kotse, I., Nepelet es nepszokasok Baranyaban (Folk Life and Customs in Baranya) *Ethnographia,* I, p. 456.
182. Gonczi, *l. c.,* p. 345.
183. Koritsanszky, O.: Lakodalmi Tokasok Kolesden (Wedding Customs in Kolesd) *Ethnographia,* XV, p. 311.
184. Bekefy, *Kethely,* p. 68.

At the same time we have another 'hangman' and another 'executioner'. This time the criminal is the young husband or wife. At the end of the wedding they choose one of the men as 'criminal'. He is tied hand and foot with ropes of straw. Another man dressed in a ragged woman's garment is his 'wife.' On both sides men march with all sorts of tools. They arrive at the market place. The 'criminal' kneels. A pot full of ashes is put on his head. The executioner swings his toy-sword, the pot is off, the criminal dead. At an inn they celebrate his wake.[185] At Borsod the groom is the criminal. The village lads tie him hand and foot and pretend to hang him. The bride ransoms him with cake and brandy.[186] At Gocsej he is tied to a ladder, at Hete's 'hung'. One of the best men holds the bride by a kerchief round her waist. The bride ransoms the groom and then they 'hang' her and the groom ransoms the bride. It was customary for the groom to run away and sit on the roof with the wine and throw the pretzels to the children.[187] At Somogy the wedding ends by hanging them both. First the bride. They ask her "Who is he to you." If she is embarrassed she delays the answer till finally she says "My husband!" Then they let her go. He is quicker to answer "My wife!"

At Kalotzeg the same 'confession' is connected with the well. They tie the groom to a ladder and let him down into the well. They all start a lively discussion; who takes care of this one. Finally the bride has to shout out. "This is my husband, please don't throw him into the well!"[188]

Among the White Russians the *'vercerniki'* go from house to house with a white cock. They make the cock dance. They kill the hens of all those who had been invited at the wedding.[189] We must not forget that these customs are closely connected with the bridal night. In Westfalen (Germany) the lads would force their entrance into the bridal chamber and make the cock they had brought with them crow.[190] Observances with the hen go parallel. The Roumanians tear the hen into little bits, everybody eats a little piece, including the groom.[191] The only person who does not taste it is the bride—since she is the hen. The Russians have a shower for the bride before the wedding. The girls catch a hen and dress it. This is the 'ceremonial hen,' the symbol of the bride's fertility.[192] Among the Little Russians, she hides a black hen

185. Istvanffy, G., Matraalji paloc lakodalom (Paloc wedding at the Matra) *Ethnographia*, V, p. 47.

186. Idem, *Ethnographia,* 1911, p. 225.

187. Gonczi, *op. cit.,* p. 353.

188. Peterdi, Eljegyzesi eslakodalmi szokasok (Betrothal and wedding customs) *Ethnographia*, XI, p. 103.

189. Piprek, *op. cit.,* p. 69.

190. Weinhold, K., *Die deutschen Frauen,* 1897, I, pp. 387–388.

191. Moldovan, Romanok, p. 175.

192. Piprek, *l. c.,* p. 10.

under the oven and says, "Is the hole deep under the oven?" Then her mother-in-law will die within a year.[193] Among the Yugoslavs the 'inviter' carries a live cock. Everybody knows that it means the groom.[194]

The Slovaks get a strong cock. It pulls a toy carriage with the wedding cake on the carriage. In Gomor they stick a pole into the earth and tie the cock to the pole. The *'judge'* pronounces the sentence of death and the 'executioner' chops its head off. Sometimes the 'executioner' is blindfolded or the groom is the blindfolded executioner,[195] and that is how he has to cut the cock's neck off.[196] The Czech best man cuts a live cock's neck at supper on the table.[197] At Beraun, they say, "We shall chop his head off and seal this bond with his blood." They dance round the bird and the best man must chop its head off with the third stroke of his sword, whereupon the others attack it with brooms, sticks, etc. If he can't manage with the third stroke *he must flee* and the others make fun of him.[198] In Bosnia it is the groom who cuts the cock's neck on the threshold, before the bride steps over the threshold.[199]

In Austria (Budweis) a cock is killed at the first wedding during the carnival period. On the wedding day, they put a red cap and a pair of pants on the cock. He is accused of various crimes and sentenced to death. The 'executioner' chops its head off, and the accuser gets the head.

At Koniginhof the cock's head is chopped off once every five years. One girl is chosen as "bride of the cock." She is blindfolded and if she is a virgin *she will manage to cut the cock's head off at the first stroke.* They roast the cock and the 'bride' eats the first piece.

At Walkenstein the ceremonial cock is called Haushahn. Its wings are clipped and the young bride is supposed to chase it around in the room till it collapses.[200]

In the two last cases castration comes from the female, or rather the groom's castration anxiety is activated by the bride's 'virginal' behaviour.

In some cases this type of ritual alternates with that of masked persons who pretend to shave the groom with a knife of wood. Germans in Southern Hungary regard it as a preliminary to marriage. The groom must be shaved, this is his initiation into manhood. They bring a brick of terrific size and

193. *Ibid.*, p. 41.
194. Krauss, F. S., *Sitte und Brauch*, pp. 445, 446.
195. Sztancsek, *op. cit.*, *Ethnographia*, 1904, pp. 211–214.
196. Kurz, S., Lajos komaromi nepi szokasok (Folk Customs of Lajos Komarom) *Ethnographia*, VII, p. 104.
197. Piprek, *op. cit.*, p. 93.
198. Piprek, *l. c.*, pp. 97, 98, 99.
199. Lilek, *Vermahlung*, p. 322.
200. Vernaleken, T., *Mythen und Brauche des Volkes in Oesterreich*. Wien, 1859, pp. 303–306.

shave his face. For soap they use ashes and mud. Then they lift him to the top of the room and knock his head against the ceiling. They declare he has a toothache and play at pulling his tooth with a bridle.[201] The widespread custom of going to the well is the equivalent of initiation for the bride. A Roumanian mother-in-law puts a bridle on her and drives her to the well as if she were a horse.[202]

SUMMARY

These customs and many others we omitted show the striking homogeneity of European folklore. At present the tendency would be to regard the whole complex as to medieval diffusion.[203] I still think, however, that we are justified in attributing some of these customs to the period of Indo-European unity.

In India we find the 'inviter,'[204] the pseudo-bride,[205] the barrier,[206] strewing seeds,[207] stepping over the threshold,[208] stepping on the foot[209] (omitted from this paper), sitting on the hide of an animal,[210] the fire and water sacrifice[211] (omitted). It is true that we can also find a few parallel traits in China. These are the sacrifice to the water, cock and hen, the bride's feet not touching the earth, and she not eating.[212] However that may be, the fact remains that primitive tribes have elaborate initiation rites with very little ritual emphasis on marriage while in Europe we find only survivals of the puberty ritual with a very complicated ceremonial as a preliminary to marriage. In a tribe like the Pitjentara the turning point in life is the relation of the growing generation to the elders. But in a European village the main *transition* is for the *bride* from virginity to womanhood, i.e., defloration. The rites of the straw barrier and of the threshold are really rites of defloration—

201. Czirbusz, G., *Adel magyararorszagi nemetek* (Germans in Southern Hungary). 1913, p. 184.
202. Flachs, *op. cit.*, p. 37.
203. Liungman, W., Traditionswanderungen Euphrat-Rhein, *F.F. Communications* No. 119, Helsinki, 1938.
204. Hillebrandt, A., *Ritual-Litteratur: Grundriss der Indo-Arischen Philologie.* 1901, p. 64.
205. Crooke, W., *Popular Religion of Northern India.* 1896, II, p. 8.
206. Zachariae, Zum Altindischen Hochzeitsritual, *Wiener Zeitschrift für die Kunde des Morgenlandes.* XVII.
207. Atharva Veda XIV, 2, p. 114.
208. Crooke, Lifting the Bride, *Folk-Lore*, XIII, 1902.
209. Hillebrandt, *l. c.*, p. 66. Schroeder, *Hochzeitsbrauche*, p. 79.
210. Hillebrandt, *l. c.*, p. 68.
211. Schroeder, *l. c.*, pp. 137–140.
212. Stenz, G. M., *Beitrage zur Volkskunde Sud-Schantungs.* 1907, pp. 83–89.

complicated by other factors. The bride's 'virginal' behaviour activates the castration anxiety of the male of which we have seen many instances in our customs. This same 'taboo of virginity' is also responsible for duplicate-formation for all the 'best men', 'inviters', etc. who represent the groom. The symbolism of cock and hen and the rejected wrong bride show quite clearly that underlying these 'sociological' factors the nucleus of the problem is the Oedipus complex. Several rites symbolize sharing the bride by the groom's friends. I would not regard this as a 'survival' of group marriage but simply as the obvious psychological attitude of those who are participating in a wedding ceremony.

Both among primitives and in the rites we have discussed the tendency to punish the main actor of the drama is quite evident. But among primitives the punishing is done by the fathers, the elder men. Circumcision, tooth-avulsion, scarification, they all mean: How dare you grow up!—as said by the fathers. But in our wedding rites it is the lads who are co-eval with the groom or younger who do the punishing. What they are doing is different.[213] The lad is now a house-owner, he has a wife, he is a 'king' i.e., a father. The young people are abreacting their Oedipal revolt in humorous, permissible form, against the new 'father'-to-be.

---

213. In form only.

20

Strategy in Counting Out: An Ethnographic Folklore Field Study

Kenneth S. Goldstein

As the discipline of international folkloristics developed, it became increasingly obvious that the "lore" could no longer be considered separately from the "folk" who created and transmitted it. Relying solely on folklore texts taken out of context led to possible errors in interpretation. Instead, folklorists came to understand that folklore had to be analyzed as it was *performed*. Observation of the performance of folklore could allow the trained folklorist to discern elements not always known or admitted by the performers.

An excellent illustration of the potential risks involved in studying folklore texts alone is provided by a novel essay by American folklorist Kenneth Goldstein (1927–1995). A dedicated fieldworker, Goldstein published his doctoral dissertation, at the University of Pennsylvania, *A Guide for Fieldworkers in Folklore,* in 1964. His doctorate was awarded in folklore in 1963, the first such degree at the University of Pennsylvania. This degree came ten years later than the first doctorate in folklore at Indiana University, earned by Warren Roberts (1924–1999) in 1953 for his comparative study of Aarne-Thompson tale type 480.

Goldstein did not become an academic folklorist until relatively late in life. Born in Brooklyn, New York, in 1927, he enrolled in the City College of New York after completing his military service, graduating in 1949 with a B.A. in business administration. This was followed by an M.B.A. in 1951. But his avocational love of English folksong was his passion. He combined business with pleasure by producing more than 500 commercial folksong records during the 1950s and early 1960s. Also during the period 1951–1957 he spent summers in the field in New York, Massachusetts, and North Carolina, perfecting his fieldwork techniques.

Tiring of his status as a self-trained amateur, Goldstein decided to go back to school to earn an advanced degree in anthropology. He was accepted at the University of Pennsylvania, but first he attended the Folklore Institute at Indiana University in summer 1958. With the help of a Fulbright fellowship, Goldstein spent 1959–1960 collecting folklore in Scotland. When the University of Pennsylvania established its doctoral program in folklore in 1962, Goldstein immediately switched from anthropology to folklore, where he remained ever after.

In his research Goldstein never lost his original interest in the field experience. He was one of the few folklorists who tried to bring theoretical issues to bear on the conduct of fieldwork and vice versa. The essay included here on "counting-out rhymes" exemplifies this intellectual penchant. First, most folklorists consider such rhymes a very minor genre, perhaps not even worthy of serious scholarly attention. Second, it had been customarily assumed that this pregame activity was strictly a traditional mechanical way of selecting in a fair and just way who would be "it" in a given game. Prior to Goldstein's study, folklorists had classified counting-out as a game of chance. Even some children who performed counting-out rhymes claimed this was the case. By actually observing performances of counting-out, however, Goldstein discovered that at least in American contexts counting-out was frequently not at all a matter of chance.

For an appreciation of Goldstein, see his colleague Dan Ben-Amos's obituary, "Kenneth S. Goldstein (1927–1995)," *Journal of American Folklore* 109 (1996), 320–323; see also W. F. H. Nicolaisen, "Kenneth S. Goldstein, 1927–1995," *Folklore* 107 (1996), 92. For Goldstein's account of how he shifted from being a statistician to working in the recording industry and eventually becoming a folklorist, see Peter Narváez's 1979 interview, "Producing Blues Recordings," *Journal of American Folklore* 109 (1996), 451–457. See also Neil V. Rosenberg, "Kenneth S. Goldstein, Producer of Folk Revival and Country Recordings," *Journal of American Folklore* 109 (1996), 457–461. For Goldstein's reflective assessment of nearly forty years of fieldwork, see his "Notes toward a European-American Folk Aesthetic: Lessons Learned from Singers and Storytellers I Have Known," *Journal of American Folklore* 104 (1991), 164–178.

For some of the counting-out rhyme scholarship inspired in part by Goldstein's article, see Andy Arleo, "With a Dirty, Dirty Dishrag on Your Mother's Big Fat Toe: The Coda in the Counting-Out Rhyme," *Western Folklore* 39 (1980), 211–222; Carola Ekrem, *Räkneramsor bland finlandssvenska barn* [Counting-out rhymes among Finnish-Swedish children] (Helsingfors: Svenska litteratursällskapet i Finland, 1990); and Elliott Oring, "On the Tradition and Mathematics of Counting-out," *Western Folklore* 56 (1997), 139–152. See also Michael H. Kelly and David C. Rubin, "Natural Rhythmic Patterns in English Verse: Evidence from Child Counting-out Rhymes,"

Journal of Memory & Language 27 (1988), 718–740; and David C. Rubin, *Memory in Oral Traditions: The Cognitive Psychology of Epic, Ballads, and Counting-out Rhymes* (New York: Oxford University Press, 1995), 227–256.

For a valuable compendium of English-language counting-out rhymes, see Roger D. Abrahams and Lois Rankin, eds., *Counting-Out Rhymes: A Dictionary* (Austin: University of Texas Press, 1980). For a partial bibliography of Goldstein's publications, see Stephen Winick, "A Selected List of the Works of an Unconventional Scholar: Kenneth S. Goldstein," in Roger D. Abrahams, ed., *Fields of Folklore: Essays in Honor of Kenneth S. Goldstein* (Bloomington: Trickster Press, 1995), 330–336. For a sample of the growing interest in "performance" in folkloristics, see Dan Ben-Amos and Kenneth S. Goldstein, eds., *Folklore: Performance and Communication* (The Hague: Mouton, 1975); Richard Bauman, *Verbal Art as Performance* (Rowley: Newbury House, 1978); Elizabeth C. Fine, *The Folklore Text: From Performance to Print* (Bloomington: Indiana University Press, 1984); and Richard Bauman, ed., *Folklore, Cultural Performances and Popular Entertainments* (New York: Oxford University Press, 1992).

*　　*　　*

Though considerable attention has been paid to game activities by travellers, historians, antiquarians, and numerous others for almost two centuries, much of the scholarship of such pastimes, until well into the twentieth century, consisted of little more than gathering and publishing descriptions and the related texts.[1] A few scholars attempted interpretation and analysis,[2] but the majority were content to present their texts and descriptions in regional and national collections with occasional comparative references to analogous items among other peoples.[3]

---

1. See, for example, Joseph Strutt, *The Sports and Pastimes of the People of England*, London, 1801, and numerous later editions; the many editions of John Brand's *Observations on Popular Antiquities*, Newcastle, 1777, London, 1810, itself based on Henry Bourne's *Antiquitates Vulgares*, Newcastle, 1725, and later revised and edited by Henry Ellis, London, 1813, two volumes, culminating in a completely new edition in dictionary form by W. Carew Hazlitt under the title *Faiths and Folklore*, London, 1905, two volumes.

2. A prime example is William W. Newell in his *Games and Songs of American Children*, New York, 1883, new edition 1903. Many of Newell's speculations and theories, especially those concerning games as "survivals" of earlier times and places, were popular with other collector-scholars for many years before being challenged and discarded.

3. For example, James O. Halliwell, *The Nursery Rhymes of England*, London, 1841, with later editions; Robert Chambers, *Popular Rhymes of Scotland*, Edinburgh, 1925, though the important edition for our purpose is the third edition of 1842 and its later reprintings; Alice Bertha Gomme, *The Traditional Games of En-*

It is no wonder, then, that so little attention of any serious nature was paid to this folklore genre until after World War II. When this new interest finally manifested itself, it was more through the work of social and behavioral scientists than of folklorists that this previously "minor" genre was raised to the status of an area of prime interest and importance. The work of Huizinga and Caillois in defining the nature of play,[4] the social-psychological insights into children's play activities of Piaget and Erikson,[5] and, more recently, the work of Roberts, Arth, Bush, and Sutton-Smith in relating games to other aspects of culture[6] have written new chapters in game scholarship. Among folklorists the recent work of Robert Georges with his interest in the relevance of behavioral models for the analyses of traditional play activities, of Alan Dundes and his interest in the structural analysis of games, and of Roger D. Abrahams and his application of rhetorical models to the performance of folklore, show promise of removing game scholarship from the arid and sterile domain of description and comparativist annotation along historical and geographical lines.[7]

Folklorists, moreover, have the means to make a still larger contribution to the study of games by the application in their field work of the concept which has come to be known as the "ethnography of speaking folklore," or the study of folklore "texts in their contexts" for the purpose of determining the rules which govern any specific folklore event.[8] Since much of the recent research and scholarship on games involves correlations of game types to

---

gland, Scotland and Ireland, London, 1894, 1898, two volumes; G. F. Northall, *English Folk Rhymes,* London, 1892; continental works of the same order were Eugène Rolland, *Rimes et jeux de l'enfance,* Paris, 1883, and F. M. Böhme, *Deutsches Kinderlied und Kinderspiel,* Leipzig, 1897.

4. J. Huizinga, *Homo Ludens: A Study of the Play Element in Culture,* English translation, London, 1949, New York, 1950; Roger Caillois, *Man, Play, and Games,* Glencoe, Ill., 1961.

5. Jean Piaget, *The Moral Judgement of the Child,* New York, 1965, and *Play, Dreams and Imitation in Childhood,* London, 1951; Erik H. Erikson, *Childhood and Society,* 2nd revised and enlarged edition, New York, 1963.

6. John M. Roberts, Malcolm J. Arth, and Robert R. Bush, "Games in Culture," *American Anthropologist* 61 (1959), 597–605; Brian Sutton-Smith, "Cross Cultural Study of Children's Games," *American Philosophical Society Yearbook,* 1961, 426–429; John M. Roberts and Brian Sutton-Smith, "Child Training and Game Involvement," *Ethnology* I (1962), 166–185, and "Cross Cultural Correlates of Games of Chance," *Behavior Science Notes* 3 (1966), 131–144.

7. Robert A. Georges, "The Relevance of Models for Analyses of Traditional Play Activities," *Southern Folklore Quarterly* 33 (1969), 1–23; Alan Dundes, "On Game Morphology: A Study of the Structure of Non-Verbal Folklore," *New York Folklore Quarterly* XX (1964), 276–288; Roger D. Abrahams' work on rhetorical models in folklore is a continuing project. [See "Introductory Remarks to a Rhetorical Theory of Folklore," *Journal of American Folklore* 81 (1968), 143–158. Ed. Note]

8. Alan Dundes and E. Ojo Arewa, "Proverbs and the Ethnography of Speaking Folklore," *American Anthropologist* 66 (1964), No. 6, part 2, 70–85.

other aspects of culture (e.g., social systems, religion, child training, etc.),[9] the classification of games can be crucial to the findings. And the accurate classification of games by types calls for better understanding of play events and the rules which govern those events. Folklorists whose field research is directed at developing ethnographies of games may find the work rewarding not only to their own better understanding of the mechanics by which folklore is expressed, performed, transmitted, circulated, and used, but to the development of closer interdisciplinary ties between folklore and the behavioral sciences.

The prospect of doing such ethnographic studies of games is especially intriguing because of all the genres of folklore the games genre is one of the few for which rules of performance are consciously recognized by the participants and are sometimes overtly expressed. The opportunity thus presents itself to study the manner in which the stated rules relate to the actual rules which operate in playing the games. Any attempt at doing an ethnography of a game could serve not only as a model for the collecting of data concerning game events, but also as a base for evaluating the reliability of earlier descriptions of games and thus of effecting criticism of research in any way involving game classification based on such descriptions.

This paper is an attempt at an ethnographic study of the game activity known as "counting-out." The game was selected because all previous studies of this game type had consisted of descriptions of the manner in which certain rhymes were used, of their poetics, music, rhyme, and rhythm patterns, or attempts at devising a classification system for its many texts.[10] Nowhere, however, was there any description of the rules actually at work in "counting-out."

My field work was carried out in a six block area in the East Mount Airy section of northwest Philadelphia between January 1966 and June 1967. The area, a racially integrated middle class neighborhood, contains young white collar workers, professionals, and businessmen, mainly homeowners with larger than average size families. Their children use the mostly tree-shaded, exclusively residential streets as their playgrounds.

My informants consisted of 67 children between the ages of four and fourteen, who comprise eight separate, independent, and essentially non-overlapping play groups. As might be expected these groups were peer-ori-

---

9. See note 6.

10. For some of the more important works on "counting-out" see Henry C. Bolton, *The Counting-Out Rhymes of Children*, London, 1888; Emil Bodmer, *Empros oder Anzählreime der französischen Schweiz*, Halle, 1923; Jean Baucomont, Frank Guibat, Tante Lucile, Roger Pinon, and Philippe Soupault, *Les Comptines de langue française*, Paris, 1961, containing an extensive international bibliography on "counting-out." I am grateful to Roger Pinon for making the latter two works available to me.

ented according to age. The eight groups consisted of four pairs of age groups, the first containing larger pre-school and kindergarten children whose ages ranged from four to seven, the second pair of school children from six through eight, the third of children from eight through twelve, and the fourth from eleven through fourteen. The first two pairs, containing the youngest children, had both boys and girls, though one group in each age category was predominantly male and the other mainly female. The members of each of the oldest groups were exclusively male or female. The groups were selected from among the many to be found in the neighborhood because of their age and sex composition after an initial survey indicated these were the major factors contributing to their own sense of group identity and awareness.

Collecting methods employed in obtaining data for this paper consisted of observations made both in natural and induced natural[11] contexts, followed first by non-directed and then by directed interviewing, the latter including hypothetical situation questioning.[12] Interview data was then checked by additional observations, reinterviewing of the same informants over time, and interviewing informants from one group on information obtained from other groups.

GENERAL DATA

"Counting-out" is used for selecting personnel for two other kinds of game activities: for games for which an "it" figure must be chosen, and for games for which sides must be chosen. "Counting-out" is introduced to younger children in the first age group (four through seven years) by older members of the group who report learning it from siblings and from contacts with members of the second age group (six through eight years) on the street and in school play. The rhymes are learned first (as early as two years of age) and the activity later (at four or five). It is less frequently used by both sexes in the final age group (eleven through fourteen), with other selection methods employed in its place (e.g., coin tossing, bat holding, drawing lots, and spinning bottles). Girls employ "counting-out" more frequently for choosing sides than for determining who shall be "it," with boys revers-

---

11. For a description of the induced natural context technique, see Kenneth S. Goldstein, *A Guide for Field Workers in Folklore*, Hatboro, Penna., 1964, 87–90, and "The Induced Natural Context: An Ethnographic Folklore Field Technique," *Essays on the Verbal and Visual Arts: Proceedings of the 1966 Annual Spring Meeting of the American Ethnological Society*, Seattle, 1967, 1–6.

12. The hypothetical situation is described in Melville J. Herskovits, "The Hypothetical Situation: A Technique of Field Research," *Southwestern Journal of Anthropology* 6 (1950), 32–40.

ing this pattern. Though size of the play group employing "counting-out" may theoretically vary from two to quite large numbers, in actual play conditions it was never used when the group numbered more than ten. At such times (and such cases were only among boys), selection was made by "odds or even" coin tossing or finger matching, though there were no "rules" against the use of "counting-out" in such instances.

STEPS INVOLVED IN "COUNTING-OUT"

1. One member of a group suggests playing a specific "it" game or one for which sides must be chosen.
2. A number of others verbally agree (sometimes a majority of the group, at other times only one or two with the others silently acquiescing).
3. The method of selection is determined by the first suggestion made.
4. If "counting-out" is suggested the counter is appointed by one of the following methods:

   a. The person who suggests the game announces himself as counter.
   b. A recognized leader of the group assumes the role without asking or being asked.
   c. A suggestion is made by one member of the group that some other member should do the counting, with the others agreeing verbally or silently.

5. The other members of the group gather in a circle around the counter or are lined up by him in a specific order.
6. The counter begins, sometimes with himself and at other times with the nearest person on his left. The direction of counting is clockwise.
7. Counting continues until the counter indicates who is "it," or until sides have been chosen.

The steps outlined above follow in the order given. After the counter has been selected (step 4), the alternative forms of succeeding steps are left completely to his choice.

REASONS FOR USING "COUNTING-OUT" AS THE METHOD OF SELECTION

When queried as to why "counting-out" rather than some other method was employed in the task of choosing "it" or in determining the composition of sides, the answers given were as follows:

equal chance............. 90%   (Typical answers: "Everybody has the
                                  same chance." "It's more democratic.")
removal of friction ... 18%   (Typical answers: "We don't fight about
                                  it." "Less trouble.")
supernatural decision   8%   (Typical answers: "Fate decides." "God
                                  does the choosing.")
        (The percentages add to more than 100 because some
              children gave more than one answer.)

The answers given would appear to clearly indicate that the great majority
of the children queried considered "counting-out" to be a game of chance.
It should be noted that this is also the opinion of those scholars who have
tried their hand at classifying games; Roger Caillois and Brian Sutton-Smith,
among others, refer to "counting-out" as a game of chance.[13] It is, however,
precisely on this matter that my field work resulted in my finding that for a
large number of the children involved "counting-out" is far from being a
game of chance. It is, rather, a game of strategy in which the rhymes and
movements of the players are manipulated to limit or remove chance as a
factor in selection.

THE STRATEGY OF COUNTING-OUT

What we find here is that children—like their parents—do *not* in fact do
or believe what they *say* they do or believe. As stated earlier, more than for
any other folklore genre, rules are an essential part of games at an overt and
sometimes verbalized level. But the rules which are verbalized by informants
and which are then presented by collectors in their papers and books for
our analysis and study are an idealized set of rules—they are the rules by
which people *should* play rather than the ones by which they *do* play. The
field results presented in the remainder of this paper indicate that for games
we may have to know *two* sets of rules: the ideal ones *and* those by which
the ideal rules are applied, misapplied, or subverted.

Only a few of the children were at first willing to admit that "counting-
out" rhymes, player movements, or both were manipulated by certain of
their peers. By using the hypothetical situation interview technique, I was
able to discover how, by whom, and when manipulative strategies were applied, and through later observations and reinterviews I confirmed earlier
collected data as well as adding several strategy devices to my list. The fol-

---

13. Roger Caillois, *Man, Play, and Games,* Glencoe, Ill., 1961, 36; Brian Sutton-
Smith, *The Games of New Zealand Children,* Berkeley and Los Angeles, 1959,
89–90.

lowing is a description of the strategies employed by the children in the groups I studied:

Extension of Rhyme

If the counter finds that the rhyme ends on a child whom he does *not* wish to be "it," he may add one or more phrases or lines to the rhyme until it ends on the one whom he wishes to be "it." In the example given below, when the "Eenie, meenie, meinie, mo" rhyme was used in a group of six children, the final word ended on player 4. The counter wanted someone else to be "it" and extended the rhyme so it ended on player 5. He could simply extend it still further to have it end on 6, or carry it out to end on anyone in the group including himself.

Position of Players

1	2	3	4	5	6
Eenie	meenie	meinie	mo,	Catch	a feller
by the	toe;	If he	hollers	let him	go,
Eenie	meenie	meinie	mo. #	(My	mother
says	that	you	are	it.) #	(But
I	say	that	you	are	out.) #

(John J., age 10)

Controlling selection of "it" by extending the rhyme is the most common "counting-out" strategy, with better than fifty percent of both boys and girls in the two oldest age groups employing it.

Specific Rhyme Repertory

In order to insure the selection of himself when he wishes to be "it," the counter may employ one of a special set of rhymes, the specific rhyme to be used depending upon the number of players involved. Each of the rhymes has a different number of stresses, and the counter knows which of the rhymes to apply in any specific group numbering up to eight players so that the final stress will end on himself. In the example given below, the informant had a fixed repertory of four rhymes, including ones of seven stresses, eight stresses, nine stresses, and sixteen stresses. If there are three players in the group she may employ either the seven or sixteen stress rhyme; for four players she would use the nine stress rhyme; for five players the sixteen stress rhyme; for six players the seven stress rhyme; for seven players the eight stress rhyme; and for eight players the nine stress rhyme. Conversely, if the counter wanted to be sure she was *not* "it," she would select a rhyme—again according to the number of players—in which the final stress would fall on someone other than herself.

> *Seven* stresses: Andy / Mandy / Sugar / Candy / /
> Out / Goes / He. #
> Counter is "it" when there are 3 or 6 players; not "it" when there are 4, 5, 7, or 8 players.

> *Eight* stresses: Inka / Bink / A Bottle / Of Ink / /
> I / Say / You / Stink. #
> Counter is "it" when there are 7 players; not "it" when there are 3, 4, 5, 6, or 8 players.

> *Nine* stresses: Apples / Oranges / /
> Cherries / Pears / And A Plum / /
> I / Think / You're / Dumb. #
> Counter is "it" when there are 4 or 8 players; not "it" when there are 3, 5, 6, or 7 players.

> *Sixteen* stresses: Eena / Meena / Mina / Mo / /
> Catch / A Tiger / By The / Toe / /
> If He / Hollers / Let Him / Go / /
> Eena / Meena / Mina / Mo. #
> Counter is "it" when there are 3 or 5 players; not "it" when there are 4, 6, 7, or 8 players.

(Sarah M., age 11)

Use of specific rhyme repertory to control "counting-out" was employed by three children, all girls in the eight through twelve age group. Each of the girls employed a different set of rhymes, and each was aware that the others employed a similar strategy.

Skipping Regular Counts

To ensure against his being "it," the counter will skip over himself on the second and successive times around. In the example given below, in which five players were involved, the counter simply passed by himself each of the last three times. Normally the rhyme would have ended on the counter, but by omitting himself he arranged for it to fall on someone else.

Back / Side / Front / Side / /
1   2   3   4
Looking / For A / Little / Ride; / /
5   2   3   4
In / And Out / And Up / And Down / /
5 2   3   4
Goes In / Red / And Comes Out / Brown. #
5   2   3   4

(Jerry B, age 9)

(The numbers below the text indicate the positions of the players on whom each of the words falls.)

The children employing this strategy have no idea whether any particular rhyme will end on them and, when they don't wish to be "it," will use this strategy with any "counting-out" rhymes they perform. Skipping regular counts is the second most popular form of strategically manipulating "counting-out;" one-third of all informants have done it at one time or another. It should be noted that while other strategies were considered "clever," this one was frowned upon as being "dishonest" and "against the rules!"

Stopping or Continuing

The first person "counted-out" may be designated "it" or the counter may continue by repeating the rhyme until all but one player has been "counted-out" and that player is "it." In the case of the "one potato, two potato" rhyme, the "potatoes" are the fists which the players extend for counting. The fist which the counter points to on the word "more" is withdrawn. The counter repeats the rhyme until both fists of one player have been withdrawn and that person may be designated "it" or, if the counter wishes someone else to be "it," he may continue repeating the rhyme until there is one player left who has not been "counted-out" and that player is "it." If, for example, there were five players, the first to be counted out would be number three; if the counter continued the rhyme he himself would be the last remaining person counted. The informants who used this strategy (with the one exception of the case cited in 5, below) did so without knowing on which players the first or last "out" would fall. They were merely shifting the chance factor from first to last but not to any specific player. The choice of stopping or continuing was employed by twenty children, evenly distributed between sexes in the six through eight and eight through twelve age groups.

Changing Positions

The counter, using the "One Potato, Two Potato" rhyme mentioned above, had memorized the "first out" position for any number of players from two through ten. After each player was counted-out, he would start the rhyme again from his own position after first moving to a new position either himself or the next payer he wanted to count-out, according to the memorized list of "first out" positions for the specific number of players remaining. In the example given below, involving ten players, the counter wanted a specific player to be counted-out first. He therefore placed that player in the second position. The next player whom he wished to count-out was originally in the fourth position; he therefore shifted his own position so that player would be in the eighth position and would be counted-out next.

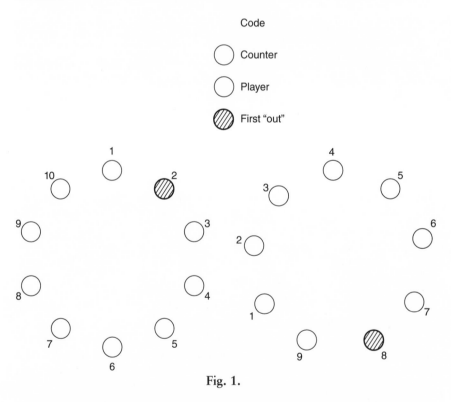

Fig. 1.

In addition to employing this strategy for choosing sides, the informant also employed a variation of it together with the "stopping or continuing" strategy for selecting "it." By memorizing both the "first out" and the "last remaining" position for any number of players through ten, he could always place himself relative to any other player so as to be able to completely control the selection according to his whim.

In the table given below, for use with the "One Potato, Two Potato" rhyme, the positions of the players are those in relation to the counter who is in position number 1. The first column indicates the number of players. The second column refers to the position of the first player to be counted "out" and the third column refers to the position of the "last remaining" position for any number of players through ten.

Number of Players	Position of Player	
	First Out	Last Remaining
10	2	1
9	8	3
8	8	4
7	7	4
6	6	3
5	3	1
4	3	2
3	1	3
2	1	2

(Samuel G., age 9)

The "changing position" strategy was used by one extremely precocious nine year old boy who was considered somewhat of a mathematical genius at school. One member of his play group, who was aware that some kind of manipulation was going on without knowing exactly what it was, would frequently thwart the change of position of the counter by changing his own position in the remaining group. Eventually, the precocious boy who had worked out the strategy began to count out the other youngster first so he would be free to make his further manipulations without interference.

Respite by Calling-Out

When a child wished to remove himself from the possibility of becoming "it" or to thwart any of the strategies indicated above, he could do so by calling out "safe" (in one group), "free" (in another group), or "in-or-out" (in a third group). This could be done only after counting began, and only one child in any instance of "counting-out" would be permitted to do so. What is surprising is that despite the fact that all eight groups had respite or truce terms for other game activities only three had specific terms for removing oneself from a "counting-out" situation.

From the data given in this paper it is readily apparent that at least for some children "counting-out" is a game of strategy rather than of chance. If games serve as mechanisms through which children are prepared for adult roles in life, as some social psychologists maintain, then identifying a game as one of chance when it, in fact, is one of strategy may complicate any attempt at relating the end result of a socialization process with prior childhood activities. Similarly, if one sees in the play activities of children a mirror of the real adult world and its values, concepts, tendencies, and ways of thought, then incorrect classification of a society's games may result in a wholly reversed or otherwise inappropriate or false picture of that world.

If we are to fully utilize the great store of information imparted to us in the cross cultural game studies of Roberts, Arth, Bush, and Sutton-Smith[14] in which game types have been correlated with other facets of culture and from which various generalizations have been made as to the involvements of individuals and groups in games, the cultural and social functions of games, and the cultural evolution of games, then a clear and precise classification and identification of games must be made before such correlations may be entirely trusted.

Though carefully selected, my sample was a small one and may be viewed by some as inadequate for making any generalization other than that some children in Northwest Philadelphia play "counting-out" as a game of strategy.[15] If, however, the reclassification of *one* game results from an intensive ethnographic study of the manner in which it is played, then it should certainly prove profitable to reexamine other games employing the same methods.

---

14. See note 6.

15. After the presentation of this paper at the American Folklore Society Meeting in Toronto, November, 1967, several members of the audience informed me they knew of similar and, in some cases, other strategies employed in "counting-out" in other parts of the United States, Canada, Europe, and Africa. To my knowledge none of these has been reported in print.

Suggestions for Further Reading in the History of Folkloristics

No comprehensive history of international folkloristics offers worldwide coverage of the discipline. One is therefore forced to rely on histories of folkloristics limited to nations, to groups within nations, or to individual folklore genres, each of which has its own history of scholarship. Listing historical surveys of folkloristics in every country of the world, covering every folk group in those countries, would be a gigantic task, even assuming one had the polyglot expertise to do so. The following list is intended to be a selected bibliography of sources for anyone with a serious interest in the history of folkloristics. With a few exceptions the list is limited to national surveys of folkloristics, and it is by no means exhaustive. It should, however, give some indication of how widespread the interest in folkloristics is as well as some idea of how long folklorists have been engaged in recording and analyzing folklore.

Acosta Saignes, Miguel. 1967. "Materiales para la historia del folklore en Venezuela," *Archivos Venezolanos de Folklore* 8:5–27.

Azadovski, Mark. 1933. "The Science of Folklore in the USSR," *KOKS* 4:39–60.

Azadovskii, Mark. 1958. *Istoriia russkoi folk'kloristiki*. 2 vols. Moscow: Uchpedgiz.

Balys, Jonas. 1935. "A Short Review of the Collection of Lithuanian Folk-Lore," *Tautosakos Darbai* 1:1–26.

Bascom, William. 1964. "Folklore Research in Africa," *Journal of American Folklore* 77:12–31.

Basgöz, Ilhan. 1972. "Folklore Studies and Nationalism in Turkey," *Journal of the Folklore Institute* 9:162–176.

Ben-Amos, Dan. 1963. "Folklore in Israel," *Schweizerisches Archiv für Volkskunde* 59:14–24.

Ben-Amos, Dan. 1991. "Jewish Folklore Studies," *Modern Judaism* 11:17–66.

Bendix, Regina. 1997. *In Search of Authenticity: The Formation of Folklore Studies*. Madison: University of Wisconsin Press.

Bienkowska, Danuta. 1973. "History of Polish Folklore Research: 1945–70," *Journal of the Folklore Institute* 10:197–211.

Birlea, Ovidiu. 1974. *Istoria folcloristicii românesti*. Bucharest: Editura enciclopedica româna.

Boberg, Inger M. 1953. *Folkemindeforskningens Historie i Mellem- og Nordeuropa.* Copenhagen: Einar Munksgaards Forlag.

Bönisch-Brednich, Brigitte. 1994. *Volkskundliche Forschung in Schlesien: Eine Wissenschaftsgeschichte.* Marburg: N. G. Elwert Verlag.

Boratav, Pertev Naili. 1952. "Les Travaux de Folklore Turc (1908–1951)," *Anadolu* 1:71–85.

Brückner, Wolfgang, and Klaus Beitl. 1983. *Volkskunde als akademische Disziplin. Studien zur Institutionenausbildung.* Wien: Der Österreichischen Akademie der Wissenschaften.

Brúeyre, Loys. 1896. "Littérature Orale et Traditionnelle: Éléments de Folk Lore," *Revue des Études Historiques* 62:10–35.

Brunvand, Jan H. 1972. "The Study of Romanian Folklore," *Journal of the Folklore Institute* 9:133–161.

Bunkse, Edmunds V. 1979. "Latvian Folkloristics," *Journal of American Folklore* 92:196–214.

Cadilla de Martinez, Maria. 1942. "El Folklore," *Anuario de la Sociedad Folklorica de Mexico* 3:43–66.

Carmichael, Charles Henry Edward. 1893. "The Study of Folk-Lore," *Transactions of the Royal Society of Literature,* 2d Series 15:84–130.

Carnoy, Henry. 1902. *Dictionnaire international des folkloristes contemporains.* Paris: G. Colombier.

Carrizo, Juan A. 1953. *Historia del folklore argentino.* Buenos Aires: Instituto Nacional de Tradición.

Carvalho-Neto, Paulo de. 1969. *History of Ibero-American Folklore.* Oosterhout: Anthropological Publications.

Carvalho-Neto, Paulo de. 1974. "História do folclore Chileno: 1900–1920 (A Teoria e o Método)," in *In Memoriam António Jorge Dias.* Lisboa: Instituto de alta cultura, pp. 97–114.

Chistov, K. V. 1963. "Folklore Studies and the Present Day," *Soviet Anthropology and Archeology* 1(4):37–48.

Chitimia, I. C. 1968. *Folclorişti şi Folcloristică Românească.* Bucharest: Editora Academiei Republicii Socialiste România.

Christiansen, Reidar Thoralf. 1927. "Die volkskundliche Sammelarbeit und ihre wissenschaftlilche Verwertung in Norwegen," in John Meier, ed., *Nordische Volkskundeforschung.* Leipzig: Friedrich Brandstetter, pp. 19–32.

Christiansen, Reidar Thoralf. 1937. "Norwegian Folklore Research through 25 Years," *Folk* 1:80–92.

Cirese, Alberto M. 1975. "Folklore in Italy: A Historical and Systematic Profile and Bibliography," *Journal of the Folklore Institute* 11:7–79.

Clemente, Pietro. 1982–1983. "Folklore Studies and Ethno-Anthropological Research in Italy: 1960–1980," *Ethnologia Europaea* 13:37–52.

Cocchiara, Giuseppe. 1933. "La Scienza delle Tradizioni Popolari e l'Italia," *Convivium* 5:700–718.

Cocchiara, Giuseppe. 1952. *Storia del folklore in Europa.* Torino: Boringhieri. English translation: *The History of Folklore in Europe.* Philadelphia: ISHI, 1971.

Cocchiara, Giuseppe. 1981. *Storia del folklore in Italia.* Palermo: Sellerio.

Corso, Raffaele. 1939. "Lo Stato attuale degli studi delle tradizioni popolari in Italia," *Folk-Liv* 147–159.

Dannemann, Manuel. 1960. "Los estudios folklóricos en nuestros ciento cincuenta años de vida independiente," *Anales de la Universidad de Chile* 118(4), No. 120:203–217.

Dannemann, Manuel. 1976. "La disciplina del folklore en Chile," *Archivos del Folklore Chileno* 10:23–74.

Dawkins, R. M. 1930. "The Recent Study of Folklore in Greece," in *Papers and Transactions of the Jubilee Congress of the Folk-Lore Society*. London: William Glaisher, pp. 121–137.

Dégh, Linda. 1949. "History of Hungarian Folklore," *Folia Ethnographia* 1:72–98.

Dekker, A. J. 1989–1990. "Die Geschichte und Stellung der Volkskunde in der Niederlanden," *Rheinisches Jahrbuch für Volkskunde* 28:89–105.

Deva, Indra. 1972. "Folklore Studies: A Trend Report," in *A Survey of Research in Sociology and Social Anthropology*, Vol. 3. Bombay: Popular Prakashan, pp. 197–239.

Dias, Jorge. 1956. "The Quintessence of the Problem: Nomenclature and Subject Matter of Folklore," in *Actes du Congrès International d'Ethnologie Regionale*. Arnhem: Rijksmuseum voor volkskunde, pp. 1–14.

Dinekov, Peter. 1981. "The Development of Bulgarian Folklore Studies," *International Folklore Review* 1:43–47.

Dömötör, Tekla. 1972. "Folklore Research in Hungary since 1950," *Arv* 28:5–20.

Dorson, Richard M. 1961. "Folklore Research in Japan," *Journal of American Folklore* 74:401–412.

Dorson, Richard M. 1968. *The British Folklorists: A History*. Chicago: University of Chicago Press.

Eder, Matthias. 1959. "Japanese Folklore Science Today," *Folklore Studies* 18:289–319.

Eminov, Sandra. 1975. "Folklore and Nationalism in Modern China," *Journal of the Folklore Institute* 12:257–277.

Erixon, Sigurd. 1967. "Folk-Life Research in Our Time, from a Swedish Point of View," *Gwerin* 3:275–291.

Finnegan, Ruth. 1976. *Oral Literature in Africa*. Oxford: Oxford University Press.

Fowke, Edith. 1988. *Canadian Folklore*. Toronto: Oxford University Press.

Freudenthal, Herbert. 1955. *Die Wissenschaftstheorie der deutschen Volkskunde*. Hannover: Niedersächsischer Heimatbund.

Gaidoz, Henri. 1907. "De l'Étude des Traditions Populaires ou Folk-Lore en France et à l'Etranger," *Explorations pyreneennes: bulletin trimestriel de la Société Ramond* 1:174–193.

Geramb, Victor von. 1953. "Der Volksbegriff in Geistesgeschichte und in der Volkskunde," *Zeitschrift für Volkskunde* 50:7–34.

Gittée, Auguste. 1886. "Les études folkloristes en France," *Revue de Belgique* 53:117–131.

Gittée, Auguste. 1886. "Le folklore et son utilité générale," *Revue de Belgique* 54:225–257.

Gougaud, L. 1920. "Les Études de folk-lore en France et à l'Etranger," *Les Lettres* 10:427–440.

Grambo, Ronald. 1977. "Folkloristic Research in Norway 1945–1976," *Norveg* 20:221–286.

Grambo, Ronald. 1983. "Folkloristic Research in Norway 1977–1982," *Norveg* 26:107–155.

Guichot y Sierra, Alejandro. 1922. *Noticia Histórica del Folklore.* Sevilla: Hijos de Guillermo Alvarez.

Gusev, V. Y. 1961. "Folklore Research in the USSR," *Soviet Review* 2:51–58.

Handoo, Jawaharlal. 1987. "South Indian Folklore Studies: Growth and Development," *Journal of Folklore Research* 24:135–156.

Hauffen, Adolf. 1910. "Geschichte der deutschen Volkskunde," *Zeitschrift für Volkskunde* 20:1–17, 129–141, 290–306.

Hautala, Jouko. 1968. *Finnish Folklore Research 1828–1918.* Helsinki: Societas Scientiarum Fennica.

Herzfeld, Michael. 1982. *Ours Once More: Folklore, Ideology, and the Making of Modern Greece.* Austin: University of Texas Press.

Hines, Donald M. 1972. "The Development of Folklife Research in the United Kingdom," *Pennsylvania Folklife* 21:8–20.

Hoffmann-Krayer, E. 1908. "Wege und Ziele schweizerischer Volkskunde," *Schweizerisches Archiv für Volkskunde* 12:241–260.

Honko, Lauri. 1979. "A Hundred Years of Finnish Folklore Research: A Reappraisal," *Folklore* 90:141–152.

Honko, Lauri. 1985. "Zielsetzung und Methoden der finnischen Erzählforschung," *Fabula* 26:318–335.

Howell, Dana Prescott. 1992. *The Development of Soviet Folkloristics.* New York: Garland.

Hung, Chang-tai, 1985. *Going to the People: Chinese Intellectuals and Folk Literature 1918–1937.* Cambridge: Council on East Asian Studies, Harvard University.

Hustvedt, Sigurd Bernhard. 1930. *Ballad Books and Ballad Men.* Cambridge: Harvard University Press.

Islam, Mazharul. 1970. *A History of Folktale Collections in India and Pakistan.* Dacca: Bengali Academy.

Jacobeit, Wolfgang. 1965. *Bäuerliche Arbeit und Wirtschaft: Ein Beitrag zur Wissenschaftsgeschichte der deutschen Volkskunde.* Berlin: Akademie-Verlag.

Kallas, Oskar Th. 1923. "Estonian Folklore," *Folklore* 34:101–116.

Karlinger, Felix. 1962. "Volksforschung in Italien," *Hessische Blätter für Volkskunde* 53:182–191.

Koppe, Friedrich. 1930. *Volk als Begriff und Idee.* Berlin: Kranich Verlag.

Krappe, Alexander Haggerty. 1928. "The Study of European Folklore since 1914," *Romanic Review* 19:35–40.

Krohn, Kaarle. 1892. "Histoire du traditionisme en Esthonie," *Journal de la Société Finno-Ougrienne* 10:101–110.

Krohn, Kaarle. 1927. "Geschichte und Bedeutung volkskundlicher Arbeit in Finnland," in John Meier, ed., *Nordische Volkskundeforschung.* Leipzig: Friedrich Brandstetter, pp. 7–18.

Kunio, Yanagida. 1944. "Die japanische Volkskunde. Ihre Vorgeschichte, Entwicklung und gegenwärtige Lage," *Folklore Studies* 3:1–76.

Kyriakidis, Stilpon. 1931. "Le folklore en Grèce de 1919 à 1930," *Byzantion* 2:737–770.

Kyriakidou-Nestoros, Alke. 1972. "The Theory of Folklore in Greece: *Laographia* in Its Contemporary Perspective," *East European Quarterly* 28:487–504.

Legros, Elisée. 1962. *Sur les noms et les tendances du folklore.* Liège: Editions du Musée Wallon.

Levy, Paul. 1911. "Geschichte des Begriffes Volkslied," *Acta Germanica* 7(3):290–492.

Levy, Paul. 1913. "Zur Unsicherheit im Begriffe Volkslied," *Germanisch-Romanische Monatsschrift* 5:659–667.

Levy, Paul. 1932. "La notion 'Volkslied,' " *Revue Germanique* 23:1–12.

Lindgren, E. J. 1939. "The Collection and Analysis of Folk-Lore," in Frederic Bartlett, M. Ginsberg, E. J. Lindgren, and R. H. Thouless, eds., *The Study of Society: Methods and Problems.* London: Routledge and Kegan Paul, pp. 328–378.

Loorits, Oskar. 1936. "Estonian Folklore of Today," *Acta Ethnologica* 1:34–52.

Lutz, Gerhard. 1958. *Volkskunde: Ein Handbuch zur Geschichte ihrer Probleme.* Berlin: Erich Schmidt Verlag.

Machado y Alvarez, Antonio. 1885. "Breves indicationes acerca del significado yu alcance del término 'Folk-Lore'." *Revista de España* 102:195–207.

Machalski, Franciszek. 1970. "Notes on the Folklore of Iran," *Folia Orientalia* 12:141–154.

Manuel, E. Arsenio. 1967. "On the Study of Philippine Folklore," in Antonio G. Manuud, ed., *Brown Heritage: Essays on Philippine Cultural Tradition and Literature.* Quezon City: Ateneo de Manila University Press, pp. 253–286.

Marót, Karl. 1938. "Zur Entwicklungsgeschichte der Volkskunde in Ungarn," *Ungarische Jahrbücher* 18:123–152.

Meertens, P. J. 1949. "Nederlandse Volkskundestudie voor 1888," *Volkskunde* 50:22–33.

Meertens, P. J. 1952. "Volkskunde in Zwitserland," *Volkskunde* 53:178–184.

Meisen, Karl. 1958. "Die Volkskunde in Deutschland im 19. und 20. Jahrhundert," *Volkskunde* 17:112–124.

Merino de Zela, E. Mildred. 1987. "Los Estudios de Folklore en Sudamérica," *Folklore Americano* 43:99–126.

Meyer, Richard M. 1895. "Die Anfänge der deutschen Volkskunde," *Zeitschrift für Kulturgeschichte* 2:135–165.

Moedano N., Gabriel. 1963. "El folklore como disciplina anthropológica; su desarrollo en México," *Tlatoani* 17:23–55.

Mogk, Eugen. 1914. "Die Geschichtliche und Territoriale Entwicklung der Deutschen Volkskunde," *Archiv für Kulturgeschichte* 12:231–270.

Molina, Anatilde Idoyaga. 1982. "El lugar del folklore en las ciencias del hombre," *Scripta Ethnologica, Supplementa* 1:1–52.

Möller, Helmut. 1964. "Aus den Anfangen der Volkskunde als Wissenschaft," *Zeitschrift für Volkskunde* 60:218–241.

Nania, Salvatore. 1955. "A Glimpse at the History of Folklore in Italy," *Midwest Folklore* 5:153–158.

Naoe, Hiroji. 1949. "Post-War Folklore Research Work in Japan," *Folklore Studies* 8:277–284.

Noy, Dov. 1980. "Eighty Years of Jewish Folkloristics: Achievements and Tasks," in Frank Talmage, ed., *Studies in Jewish Folklore*. Cambridge: Association for Jewish Studies, pp. 1–11.

Oinas, Felix. 1961. "Folklore Activities in Russia," *Journal of American Folklore* 74:76–84.

Oinas, Felix. 1966. "The Study of Folklore in Yugoslavia," *Journal of the Folklore Institute* 3:398–418.

Olrik, Axel. 1912. "The 'Folklore Fellows': Their Organisation and Objects," *Folklore* 23:111–114.

Oriol, Jacques, Leonce Viaud, and Michel Aubourg. 1952. *Le Mouvement Folklorique en Haiti*. Port-au-Prince: Imprimerie de l'Etat.

Ortutay, Gyula. 1955. "The Science of Folklore between the Two World Wars and during the Period Subsequent to the Liberation," *Acta Ethnographica* 4:5–89.

Özturkmen, Arzu. 1992. "Individuals and Institutions in the Early History of Turkish Folklore, 1840–1950," *Journal of Folklore Research* 29:177–192.

Pande, Trilochan. 1963. "The Concept of Folklore in India and Pakistan," *Schweizerisches Archiv für Volkskunde* 59:25–30.

Paredes, Américo. 1969. "Concepts about Folklore in Latin America and the United States," *Journal of the Folklore Institute* 6:20–38.

Paris, Gaston. 1878. "De l'étude de la poésie populaire en France," *Mélusine* 1:1–6.

Pulikowski, Julian von. 1933. *Geschichte des Begriffes Volkslied in musikalischen Schrifttum; ein Stuck deutscher Geistesgeschichte*. Heidelberg: Carl Winter.

Rabaçal, Alfredo João. 1968. *Os Conceitos de Folclore e Etnografia em Portugal e no Brasil*. Barcelos: Museu de Cerâmica Popular Portugesa.

Ramírez, Tulio López. 1945. "Estudio y Perspectivas de Nuestro Folklore," *Acta Venezolana* 1:199–220.

Ramos, Artur. 1943. "Definição e limites do folk-lore," *Revista Brasileira* 3:137–151.

Reuschel, Karl. 1907. "Volkskunde und volkskundliche Vereine," *Deutsche Geschichtsblätter* 9(3):63–83.

Robe, Stanley L. 1967. "Contemporary Trends in Folklore Research," *Latin American Research Review* 2(2):26–54.

Romero, Jesús C. 1938–1940. "Observaciones acerca del término Folklore," *Anuario de la Sociedad Folklorica de Mexico* 1:17–40.

Romero, Jesús C. 1947. "El Folklore en México," *Boletin de la Sociedad Mexicana de Geografia y Estadistica* 63:657–798.

Roukens, Winand. 1963. *Europese Volkskunde in een Verenigde Wereld*. Roermond: J. J. Romen.

Rousseau, Felix. 1921. *Le folklore et les folkloristes wallons*. Bruxelles: Van Oest.

Roy, Sarat Chandra. 1932. "The Study of Folk-Lore and Tradition in India," *Journal of the Bihar and Orissa Research Society* 18:353–381.

Sainéan, Lazare. 1902. "L'état actuel des études de folk-lore," *Revue de Synthese Historique* 4:147–174.

Saintyves, P. 1932. "Les Origines de la méthode comparative et la naissance du folklore. Des Superstitions aux survivances," *Revue de l'Histoire des Religions* 105:44–70.

Salminen, Vaino, and Gunnar Landtman. 1930. "The Folklore of Finland and How It Was Collected," *Folklore* 41:359–369.

Sayce, R. U. 1947. "Some Recent Trends in Swedish Folk Studies," *Folklore* 53–54:378–389.

Scheub, Harold. 1985. "A Review of African Oral Traditions and Literature," *African Studies Review* 28(2–3):1–71.

Schier, Bruno. 1973. "Funfzig Jahre ostdeutsch-westslawischer Volksforschung: Mein kleiner Beitrag zu dieser grossen Forschungsaufgabe," *Jahrbuch für Ostdeutsche Volkskunde* 16:406–422.

Schmidt, Leopold. 1951. *Geschichte der österreichischen Volkskunde.* Wien: Bundesverlag.

Schulze, Fritz Willy. 1949. *Folklore. Zur Ableitung der Vorgeschichte Einer Wissenschaftsbezeichnung.* Halle: Max Niemeyer Verlag.

Schulze, Robert. 1959. *Die Anfänge der Volksglaubensforschung.* Bad Harzburg: H. O. Rosdorff.

Sébillot, Paul. 1913. "Notes pour servir à l'histoire du folk-lore en France." *Revue des Traditions Populaires* 28:49–62, 171–182.

Sen Gupta, Sankar. 1965. *Folklorists of Bengal.* Calcutta: Indian Publications.

Sen Gupta, Sankar. 1967. *A Survey of Folklore Study in Bengal.* Calcutta: Indian Publications.

Siddiqui, Ashraf, and A. S. M. Zahurul Haque. 1964. "Folklore Research in East Pakistan," *Asian Folklore Studies* 23:1–14.

Simeone, William E. 1961. "Italian Folklore Scholars," *Journal of American Folklore* 74:344–353.

Simpson, Georgiana R. 1921. *Herder's Conception of "Das Volk."* Chicago: University of Chicago.

Sydow, Carl Wilhelm von. 1927. "Volkskundliche Arbeit in Schweden," in John Meier, ed., *Nordische Volkskundeforschung.* Leipzig: Fredrich Brandstetter, pp. 33–40.

Thomas, Juliette. 1975. "The Development of Folklore Studies in Wales, 1700–1900," *Keystone Folklore* 20(4):33–52.

Toschi, Paolo. 1937. "Letteratura Popolare," in *Un Cinquantennio de Studi Sulla Letteratura Italiana (1886–1936),* Vol. 2. Firenze: G. C. Sansoni, pp. 29–62.

Tronchon, Henri. 1930. "Quelques notes sur le premier mouvement folkloriste en France: Voix Françaises, voix étrangères," in *Mélanges d'histoire littéraire générale et comparée offerts à Fernand Baldensperger,* Vol. 2. Paris: Librairie ancienne honoré champion, pp. 296–311.

Tuohy, Sue. 1991. "Cultural Metaphors and Reasoning: Folklore Scholarship and Ideology in Contemporary China," *Asian Folklore Studies* 50:189–220.

Upadhyaya, Hari S. 1965. "A Survey of Hindi Folklore," *Southern Folklore Quarterly* 29:239–250.

Upadhyaya, Hari S. 1968. "History of Folktale Scholarship in India from 1873 to 1962," *Journal of the Ohio Folklore Society* 3:227–242.

Upadhyaya, K. D. 1954. "A General Survey of Folklore Activities in India," *Midwest Folklore* 4:201–212.

Van Gennep, Arnold. 1932. "Le Folklore en France depuis la Guerre," *La Grande Revue* 36:543–565.

Van Gennep, Arnold. 1939. "Le Folklore en France," *Revue de Paris* 46(13):195–216.

Van Heurck, Emile H. 1914. *L'Oeuvre des Folkloristes anversois.* Anvers: Buschmann.

Vance, Lee J. 1893. "Folk-Lore Study in America," *Popular Science Monthly* 43:586–598.

Vega, Carlos. 1945. "La Ciencia del Folklore en la Argentina," *Anales del Asociacion Folklorica Argentina* 1:27–33.

Vidossi, Giuseppe. 1939. "Zur Geschichte der Italienischen Volkskunde," *Zeitschrift für Volkskunde* 48:7–17.

Viski, Karl. 1946–1952. "Forschungsbericht über die Entwicklung der ungarischen Volkskunde seit 1919," *Sudost-Forschungen* 11:211–272.

Voskuil, J. J. 1984. "Geschiedenis van de volkskunde in Nederland: Portret van een discipline," *Volkskundig Bulletin* 10:50–63.

Vrabie, Gheorghe. 1968. *Folcloristica Română: Evolutie, Curente, Metode.* Bucharest: Editura pentru Literatura.

Wei-pang, Chao. 1942. "Modern Chinese Folklore Investigation," *Folklore Studies* 1:55–76, 79–88.

Wilson, William A. 1976. *Folklore and Nationalism in Modern Finland.* Bloomington: Indiana University Press.

Wiora, Walter. 1971. "Reflections on the Problem: How Old Is the Concept Folksong?" *Yearbook of the International Folk Music Council* 3:23–33.

Yen, Chun-chiang. 1967. "Folklore Research in Communist China," *Asian Folklore Studies* 26(2):1–62.

Zumwalt, Rosemary Lévy. 1988. *American Folklore Scholarship: Dialogue of Dissent.* Bloomington: Indiana University Press.

Index

Aarne, Antti, 84, 120–21, 141, 156
Abrahams, Roger D., 234
Academie Celtique, 17
active bearer, 139, 144
Afanas'ev, A. N., 120
analytical psychology, 197
Anthropophyteia, 178, 179, 191, 192

Barons, Krišjānis, 63–64
Barry, Phillips, 60
Bartók, Béla, article by, 63–72
Béaloideas, 10, 155
Beckwith, Martha Warren, 27
Benedict, Ruth, 109
Benfey, Theodor, 43, 141, 142
Bolte, Johannes, 27, 84, 209
Brentano, Clemens, 4, 5
Bureus, Johannes, 18

cartographic method, 28
Christiansen, Reidar, 155, 156
Clodd, Edward, 49, 112–13
closing, law of, 88
concentration on a leading character,
    law of, 95–96
contagious magic, principle of, 114–15,
    116–18
contrast, law of, 91–92
counting out, 231–44
Crane, T. F., 84

Danaher, Kevin, 50, 156–57
defloration, 203

dite, 28, 138
Dorson, Richard M., 47
Dragon-Slayer, 156
Duilearga, Seamus Ó, article by, 153–76
Dulaure, Jacques-Antoine, 17
Dyer, T. F. Thiselton, 49, 51–52

epic laws, 83–97
evil eye, 112–13

'fairy tales, structure of, 119–30
fakelore, 47
Feilberg, H. F., 137
ᵃ female symbols, 186–87
Finnish Literary Society, 37
Finnish method, 39–40, 41, 42–45,
    140, 141, 142, 143
folk, definition of, vii
folk life, viii
Folklore Fellows, 83, 84
folklore as a source of Freudian sym-
    bols, 188, 193
Frazer, James George, 15, article by,
    109–18, 179
Freud, Sigmund, 114; article by, 177–
    95, 197–99
* functions, structural units of fairy tales,
    122–23, 127

Gaidoz, Henri, 15, 17
Georges, Robert, 234
Geyer, Stefi, 67, 68
Glassie, Henry, 156, 157

253

Golden Bough, 15, 111, 112, 114
Goldstein, Kenneth S., article by, 231–44
Gomme, George Laurence, 10, 62
Gramsci, Antonio, article by, 131–36
Grimm, Hermann, 25–26
Grimm, Jacob, article by, 1–7, 9, 11, 12, 17, 19, 29
Grimm, Wilhelm, 1–4, 25
Grundtvig, Svend, 5

Hansel and Gretel, 5
Handwörterbuch des deutschen Aberglaubens, 28
Hardy, Thomas, 112–13
Herder, J. G., 2, 64
Hoffmann-Krayer, Eduard, 60
homeopathic magic, principle of, 114–15, 116–18
Hurt, Jakob, 55
Hyde, Douglas, 48–49, 154–55

initial and final position, law of, 93, 96
Irish Folklore Commission, 155, 158, 169

James, William, 109
Jones, Ernest, 177, 197
Jung, C. G., 197–98

Kalevala, 37–38, 41, 42
Kind and Unkind Girls, The tale of the, 121–22, 231
Kinder- und Hausmärchen, 1, 2, 27
Köhler, Reinhold, article by, 25–29, 33, 61
Kolberg, Oskar, 55
Krauss, Friedrich, 178, 191, 203
Krohn, Julius, 38–39, 42
Krohn, Kaarle, article by, 37–45, 83, 84, 137, 141, 142

laws of folklore, 44–45. *See also* epic laws
Leland, Charles G., 10
Lévi-Strauss, Claude, 121
Lönnrot, Elias, 37, 41

Lord, Albert, 66
lore, definition of, vii

Mannhardt, Wilhelm, article by, 15–24, 110, 139
Marin, Francisco Rodriguez, 63
Marxist folklore theory, 132–33
memorate, 138–39
Merton, Ambrose, 9, 12. *See* William Thoms
Moe, Moltke, 85
monogenesis, 40
Müller, Max, article by, 31–35
multiple existence, viii
myth-ritual theory, 120

Needham, Rodney, 99
Notes and Queries, 9

Oedipus complex, 179, 230
oicotype, concept of, 138, 145, 146–50
Olrik, Axel, article by, 83–97, 137, 142, 179
opening, law of, 88
Oppenheim, David Ernst, 177–78
Oring, Elliott, 180
O'Sullivan, Sean, 155, 156–57

Paris, Gaston, 26
Parry, Milman, 65–66
passive bearer, 139, 143–44
patterning, law of, 94, 96
phallic symbols, 185–86
Pitrè, Giuseppe, 16, 32, 33; article by, 55–62, 134
Polívka, Georg, 27, 84
polygenesis, 40, 43
Propp, Vladimir, article by, 119–30

Rank, Otto, 190, 195, 197
repetition, law of, 89, 96
riddles, 208–10
rites of passage, 102–3, 106
Róheim, Géza, 101; article by, 197–230
Rumpelstiltskin, 137

seanchas, 158, 165
Sébillot, Paul, 60, 61
single-strandedness, law of, 94
Sokolov, Boris and Yuri, article by,
   73–82
solar mythology, 31, 198
subaltern, 133
superorganic theories, 139
Sydow, Carl Wilhelm von, 16, 83; article
   by, 137–51
sympathetic magic, principles of, 114–
   15, 116–18

tableaux scenes, law of, 94, 96
Thompson, Stith, 84, 156
Thoms, William, article by, 9–14
three: law of, 89–91, 96; symbolism of,
   185
threshold rituals, 210–15
traditor. See active bearer

twins, law of, 92–93, 96
two to a scene, law of, 91, 96

unilinear evolutionary theory, 110, 120
unity of plot, law of, 95–96

Volksgeist, 2
Volkskunde, viii, 9, 10
Van Gennep, Arnold, article by, 99–108,
   207

wedding customs, 197–230
Wesselski, Albert, 143
Wolf, Johann-Wilhelm, 18

Yanagita, Kunio, 56
Yeats, W. B., article by, 47–53

*Zeitschrift für deutsche Mythologie und
   Sittenkunde,* 18

About the Editor

Alan Dundes is known as one of the world's leading authorities on folklore. In more than thirty books he has unveiled the meanings in the oral traditions of many cultures. He lives in Berkeley, where he is professor of anthropology and folklore at the University of California.